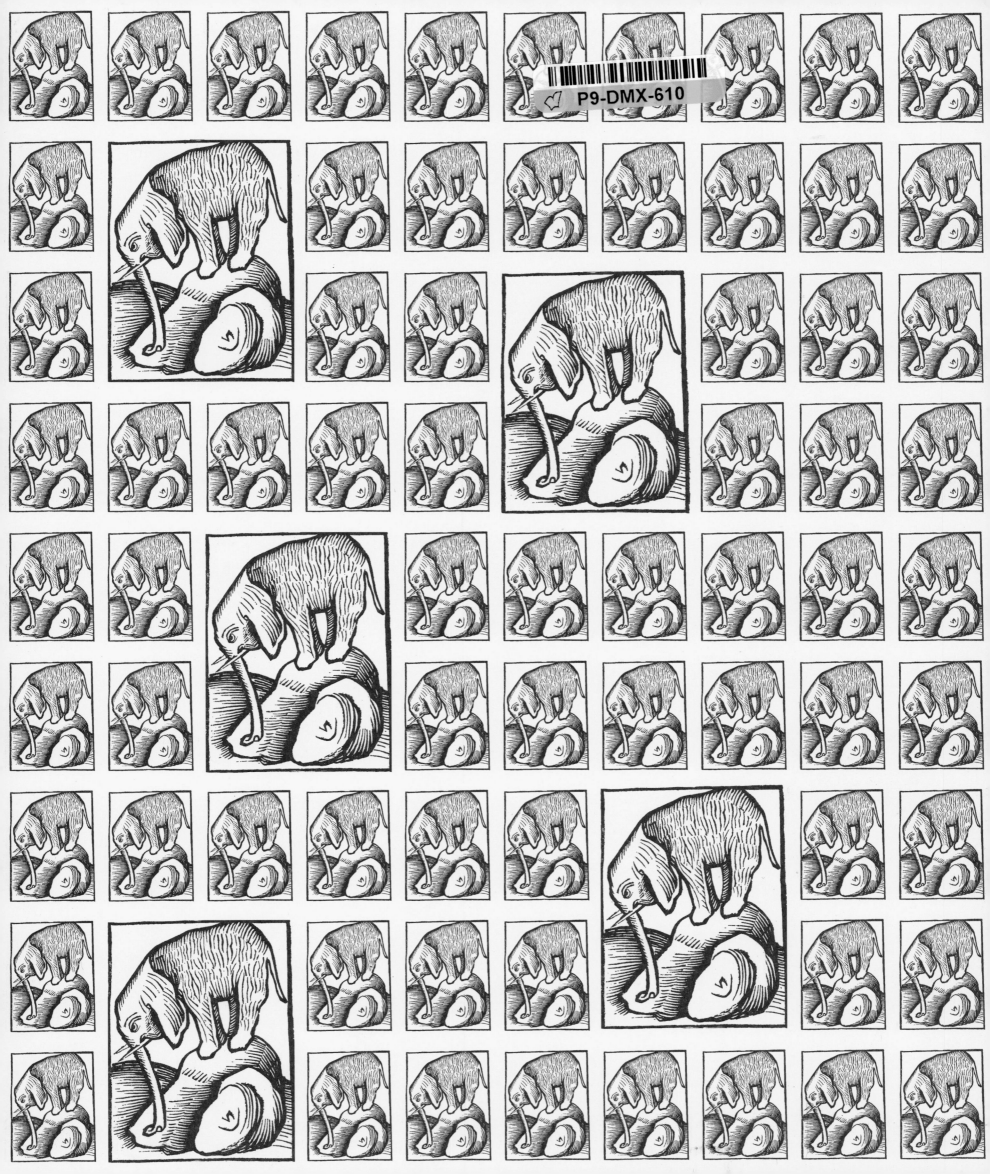

# Elephants

# Elephants
## A Cultural and Natural History

Karl Gröning
Text: Martin Saller

KÖNEMANN

# Contents

# Contents

# Foreword

The elephant, the largest and most magnificent of the land animals, is on the list of threatened species. This alarming fact serves as a reminder of the state of our planet and is a warning too loud to ignore. These gray giants, whose ancestry can be traced back fifty million years, have a special status amongst the large animal species. Their anatomy still poses questions for science to answer. They possess the strength of Titans, yet they are by nature gentle creatures, who do not misuse their power, and carefully avoid harming other living things. Ever since the appearance of those recent arrivals, human beings, on the evolutionary scene, elephants have been their companions along the way. The mountainous flesh of the mammoths fed the first hunters during the last Ice Age. With the emergence of the great civilizations in the Far East and the Mediterranean region, the good-natured pachyderm was tamed, and entered the service of humankind; faithful, intelligent and ready to learn. The elephant became the mount on which royalty would ride; the strength of its muscles accomplished the work of heavy machinery.

Humanity has misused the peace-loving giants as living 'battle-tanks' in the wars of the nations. Countless atrocities have been committed against them out of greed for the ivory of their tusks. Even so, the admiration for these primeval giants has endured. The Roman writer Pliny, who gave us a portrayal of his times, expressed the effusive opinion that "elephants are receptive to love and renown" and that they "possess the virtues of honesty, consideration and justice to a higher degree than the majority of men."

The elephant's gigantic stature, near-human qualities of character, and singular harmony of animal instincts have caused it to become a symbolic figure in myths and religions, and a herald of kingly greatness, preserved in innumerable images.

In India, people raised the elephant to the position of an auspicious animal in the service of the gods. In the figure of Ganesh, the round-bellied Hindu god of wisdom and success, the trunk and head of the elephant are actually linked to the body of the god. Festively decorated in temple service, the elephant itself becomes a work of art.

In early northern Europe, before an elephant had ever been seen in the flesh, extravagant tales of this creature preceded it, finding visible expression in extraordinary pictures of the imagination.

Later, elephant sculptures became symbolic figures in Christianity too. In the Middle Ages, the figure of the elephant came to represent prudence and constancy, restrained strength and temperance.

In our sober consumer society, the amiable elephant lends its appealing image to the poet and the artist, to political claims and humorous caricature, for picture book illustrations, for advertising graphics …

This book, then, will follow the trail of the elephant through the many thousand years of human cultural and artistic history.

# Primeval wanderer

Like a being from the beginning of time, the towering female elephant strides into the dawning day with her calf. Her outstretched trunk wards off the danger which lurks everywhere since

the expulsion from the biblical Garden of Eden – from a world of ecological balance, where harmony reigned amongst the creatures of the earth. The sight has an air almost of unreality amid the din of our mechanized world! The elephant is a miracle of nature. Its ancestry can be traced back an unimaginable fifty million years, and affords profound insights into the appearance and disappearance of creatures since the beginning of time. "The idea of the elephant is imperishable," remarked Arthur Schopenhauer (1788–1860) in admiration. The gray giant is a master survivor; it has been able to exploit every one of the earth's vegetation and climate zones. It now finds itself driven back into cramped corners of our degraded planet, under threat everywhere. Must this gentle primeval wanderer cede its place in the world, on account of the absolute claims laid by that latecomer, *Homo sapiens*, to all the space and resources?

Over millions of years, nature in its extravagance experimented with over 300 proboscidean species, which populated the earth in early times, along with other prehistoric animal societies. The process of constant change in environmental conditions and life forms has left only the elephants we know today.

# The elephant in the Garden of Eden

According to the biblical story of Creation, which gathers together billions of years of development into a single week, the appearance of the land animals came only after the seas and air were filled with life, commanded by God on the fifth day:

"And God said, Let the waters bring forth abundantly the moving creature that hath life, and fowl that may fly above the earth in the open firmament of heaven. And God created great whales, and every living creature that moveth, which the waters brought forth abundantly, after their kind, and every winged fowl ..."

The seas, the waters, are the source from which all life sprang. So the chronology of the Creation story in the book of Genesis is in complete accord with the discoveries of science. Not until the sixth day did God say:

"Let the earth bring forth the living creature after his kind ... And it was so ... and God saw that it was good ..."

In the poetic portrayal of the Divine creation command, the giant of the seas, the whale, is mentioned by name. The giant of the land, the elephant, does not have the honor of special mention. It is included in the vast variety of species which are to populate the earth. True, the elephant was not destined to play a specific role in the events of the Bible, as was the whale. Later, the whale was to swallow the prophet Jonah, and spew him up, so that he could fulfill his divinely-commanded task of proclaiming the destruction of Nineveh to the inhabitants of the city, whereupon they immediately repented and were saved.

With its dignity and distinction, the elephant had no need of special singling out. Its stature and character alone made it one of the most glorious creatures in the Garden of Eden. When Eve reached out to pluck the forbidden fruit, the consequence was the expulsion of the first human couple from those pleasant realms, where all creatures lived in harmony. The elephant, at least, was able to preserve for his kind something of the peace-loving nature of paradise and carry it with him into the sinful world and the fierce battle for survival.

Painters and sculptors of the Middle Ages and the Renaissance, exuberantly recreating in their imaginations the world of paradise in the Garden of Eden, immortalized the gentle giant again and again in paint and in stone, in the midst of heavenly scenery.

Raphael and studio of Raphael,
*The Creation of the Animals*
(Detail),
c. 1518/19,
fresco.
Vatican Loggias, Rome

Jan Breughel the Elder,
*The Earthly Paradise* (Detail),
c. 1600,
oil on copper.
46cm x 67cm
Musée du Louvre, Paris

*Adam naming the Animals,*
Brussels, 16th century,
tapestry.
Galleria dell' Accademia, Florence

The Bible tells us that in the garden which God planted, "eastward in Eden," He brought all the animals He had made to the man, to see what he would call them "and whatsoever Adam called every living creature, that was the name thereof. And Adam gave names to all cattle, and to the fowl of the air, and to every beast of the field ..." (Genesis 2:19). Accordingly, God was giving charge over all creatures to the first man, Adam. Even the giant among the animals had to share in bearing this burden.

# The origin of life

135 million years ago

65 million years ago

Present day

The face of the earth is a changing one. The positions of the continents as we know them developed over millions of years. Individual plates, for example Australia, Antarctica, and South America, drifted off from the two land masses Laurasia and Gondwanaland. The continental region of Afroarabia was also once part of the southern flank of Eurasia.

Modern methods of geological dating use the rate of decay of radioactive substances, which is predictable, to calculate an approximate age. According to this, our earth is estimated to be about five billion years old.

About three billion years ago, a solid crust formed over the fluid, glowing ball. The scientific theory is that as continents and oceans formed, life came into being by 'chemical evolution.' In a seething atmosphere of hydrogen, methane and other gases, the effect of ultra-violet rays from the sun, processes of radioactive decay, and the discharge of primeval thunderstorms led to the formation of carbon chemical-phycompounds: the building-blocks of all organic life.

Laboratory experiments have confirmed that these chemical-physical processes are possible. How these building-blocks, these molecular chains, came together to create living organisms is a question that science ascribes to the play of chance over vast periods of time. Theology, following in the wake of scientific discoveries as it does, has a biblical account of creation whose images lend themselves to endless interpretation. This gives it a freedom to follow scientific research, and also to state that at the beginning of everything stands the creative activity of God.

All life on earth developed from primitive early forms. Specialization in order to adapt to particular environments led to the development of major groupings in the animal and plant kingdoms. In an evolutionary process spanning many millions of years, these diversified into hundreds of thousands of genera and species. The science of paleontology has traced the major lines of development by studying petrified fossils and the physical structures of animals living today. Chance finds of objects from the endless span of geology has not provided a complete chain of events, and scientific hypothesis will remain indispensable in bridging the gaps when we research into prehistory. From fossil finds, which can be placed in order of age according to the geological strata in which they are found, we can divide the history of evolution broadly into three phases.

In the Paleozoic era, which lasted from about 545–250 million years ago, a very varied fauna of fish-like vertebrates developed in the seas.

The Mesozoic era, between 250 and 65 million years ago, includes the Triassic, Jurassic and Cretaceous geological periods. This was the era of the reptiles, crawling creatures inhabiting land and water, whose family tree culminated in the evolution of the enormous dinosaurs. The first mammals and birds also began to evolve.

During the Cenozoic era, which covers the Tertiary and Quaternary periods (65 million to 10,000 years ago), we find the development of today's life-forms. The first early proboscideans appeared about fifty million years ago, during the Tertiary, the time of the explosive development and spread of mammals.

*Phiomia*, which appeared about thirty-five million years ago, was an evolutionary intermediate. This creature stood only about 4 feet 6 inches high.
Painting: Prof. Zdenek Burian

# The Moeritherium

On the continent of Africa, at the El Faiyum oasis, about 60 miles southwest of Cairo, an important insight into the family history of the elephant in prehistoric times was gained. Researchers also made interesting discoveries about the early history of various other species.

The depression, with an area of 690 square miles, has sunk to a depth of 160ft below sea level, so giving access to the overlying rock strata from the Tertiary period. This was the time when much of the appearance of the world as we know it was formed, when plants and animals began to assume something like the forms we know today.

The lush, fertile land of the oasis still contains a lake, which today is only 19 miles by 6 miles, and is linked to the Nile by a canal. At the time of the Pharaohs, the lake filled most of the depression. In ancient Egypt, this reservoir of water was used to regulate water levels in the river valley when the Nile was low. Lake Moeris as it was once called (modern name: Lake Qarun) features in the accounts of Herodotus, the much-traveled father of Greek history, back in the fifth century BC.

In 1871, in the rock walls of the line of fracture around the depression, the German explorer Georg Schweinfurth discovered many fossils in the various strata. Reports of this brought the British scientist, Charles Andrews, to the oasis in 1901, where he exposed the remains of a large number of prehistoric animals in the course of digging over a three-year period. During this work, he found the bones of a remarkable animal, unlike any other known creature, which raised many puzzling questions. It was named 'Moeritherium' (Greek therion = animal), after the ancient name of the lake.

The creature was about the size of a pig. Its eyes and ears were high up on its head – so above the waterline for a swimming animal – and the bone structure indicated a robust, stocky body. The obvious comparison was with that of a pygmy hippopotamus. But careful study of the remains led to the sensational conclusion that this was an early type of proboscidean, an ancient relative of the elephant, which wallowed in swampy areas about 50 million years ago.

At that time, the area of the present-day Faiyum oasis was still the coastal zone of the Tethys, an extension of the Indian Ocean, which separated Eurasia and Africa. In the early Tertiary, the Tethys Ocean was considerably narrowed by tectonic processes. The young folded mountains of Eurasia were formed as a result of this. Our modern Mediterranean Sea is a remnant of the Tethys, which once separated continents.

The structure of the skull demonstrates that *Moeritherium* did not yet have a trunk, though it did have a rudimentary one, much like a tapir's snout. Assigning it to the order Proboscidea (Latin proboscis = trunk) made it possible to assess the teeth, which is particularly informative when tracing ancestry. As well as molars and canine teeth, the upper jaw had three incisors on each side, the middle one of which was enlarged like a boar's tusk. The tusks of the elephant, too, are massively enlarged incisor teeth and not canines, which is what they are in other species of mammal which have developed tusks. *Moeritherium* also had two incisors on each side in the lower jaw, with the outer one enlarged in a tusk-like way.

*Moeritherium* was initially placed in the direct line of ancestry of the elephant. However, it is only a relation from the distant past; along with the other proboscideans it would have had an unknown common ancestor which still lived as an amphibian. *Moeritherium* was a side-branch which disappeared in the Oligocene epoch.

At the beginning of the 20th century, French researchers also discovered the remains of a *Moeritherium* in West Africa, even smaller than its cousin at El Faiyum. Its fossilized bones lay in even older strata. Further finds prove that *Moeritherium*, or intermediate evolutionary forms resembling it (known as Moeritherioidea) populated wide areas of the Dark Continent.

The pig-sized forebear of the proboscidean order lived 50 million years ago in swampy regions. Painting: Z. Burian

Here, perhaps, was the cradle of the elephant: the oldest elephant species, *Moeritherium*, was found at the El Faiyum oasis located near the Nile.

# The sea cow – the elephant's nearest kin

Bush hyrax, Masai Mara, Kenya. 'The elephant's little brothers' is the name some African peoples give these entertaining animals, which have many anatomical similarities with the elephant.

In the geological strata containing the bones of *Moeritherium*, remains were found of other relatives of the elephant which still exist today. These were skeletons belonging to the order of sea cows, the legendary 'sirens of the sea,' which seem at first sight to have no obvious connection with the biggest land animal.

It is easier to imagine that such animals as the rhinoceros or hippopotamus might be related to the elephant, than the long, round sea cow. However, certain typical features of the skeleton and body structure prove sea cows to be close relatives of today's Asian and African elephants; slightly more distant relatives of the elephant are the hyraxes, animals which resemble marmots.

The orders of the proboscideans, the sea cows and the hyraxes have two mammary glands on their chest, the structure of the heart is similar, and there are parallels above all in the arrangement of the teeth. As in the elephant, the molars of the sea cow work their way forwards until they gradually break off to be replaced by those from behind.

Manatees belong to a genus of round-tailed sea cows, which live on the eastern coasts of South America and the Amazon and Orinoco Basins; another species inhabits the shallow coastal strips of West Africa. A second type of sea cow, with a forked tail shape, has just one species. These are the dugongs, which live in the shallow coastal waters of the Indian Ocean. Two incisors have become tusks, reminiscent of the elephant.

These two types, which feed peaceably on aquatic plants in the shallow waters of warm seas, still retain the rudimentary bony remnants of their ancestors' hind legs. The sea cows are evidently descended from land mammals which returned to the sea. The bony construction of their forelimbs, now transformed into flippers, also provides clues about how their land-living ancestors were built. They were primitive amphibian ungulates, animals which already shared with the various sea cows, the proboscideans and the hyraxes (or at least, had begun to) the highly specialized development of the last digits of the limb (the tips of the toes) into small hooves or claws.

It is no surprise that the elephants' closest relative lives in the sea; in female elephants, as in sea cows, the vaginal opening is located down on the lower belly, which is a feature typical of the marine mammals.

Like elephants, hyraxes (about the size of a rabbit) walk on the soles of their feet; they have clawed toes, four on the forepaws and three on the rear. The flexible, calloused pads on their soles, separated by deep clefts, act as suction cups and enable the hyrax to tackle even vertical rock faces, or to move sure-footedly along tree branches. Hyraxes look like small rodents, but their teeth are arranged quite differently. In the upper jaw are two small tusks, which are formed (like those of the elephant) from incisors.

The home of the hyrax is Africa, though these entertaining herbivores are also found in the Near East. There are three types: the rock hyrax, bush hyrax and tree hyrax.

The sea cows are the archetype of the legendary mermaids and the sirens which once tried to entice Odysseus with their charms and their song. These animals can lift themselves upright for a short while, one-third of their bodies rising out of the water. From a distance and with a little imagination, it might be possible to take the females, with their clearly-developed teats reminiscent of women's breasts, for half-human creatures.
Drawing: Gisela Pferdemenges

The sea cow, closest relative of the elephant, which lives in shallow, warm coastal waters. There are various genera. The massive dugongs, the forked-tailed sea cows, inhabit the coasts of the Indian Ocean and Australia. They can reach a length of 9ft and a weight of 370lb.

Manatees (belonging to the genus of sea cows with rounded tails) live on the coast of Central America and in the waters of the Amazon and Orinoco Basins. There is also a West African species. Sea cows still have, in their skeletal structure, the rudimentary bony remnants of the hind legs of their ancestors, land mammals which returned to the sea.

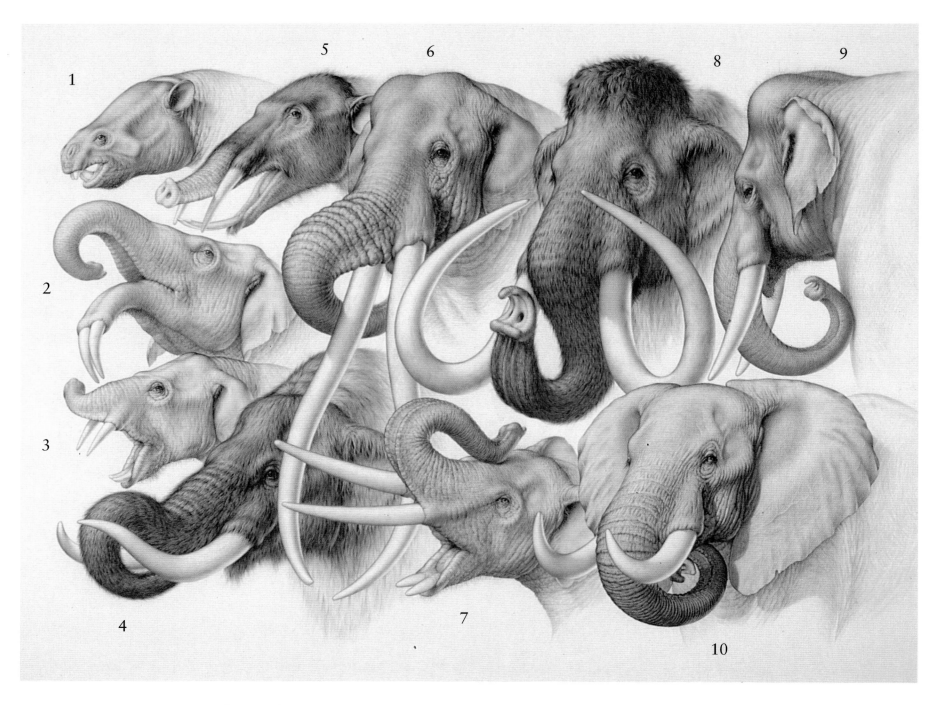

# Proboscideans conquer the continents

The illustration shows the heads of some of the prototypes of species that appeared in the highly-branching evolutionary tree of the proboscideans (order Proboscidea).
Drawing: Karel Havlicek

1) *Moeritherium*, earliest relative of the elephant
2) Deinothere
3) Paleomastodon
4) Mastodon
5) Gomphothere
6) *Stegodon*
7) *Primelephas*
8) Mammoth
9) Asian elephant
10) African elephant

The process which produced the order of animals we call proboscideans was not a direct line. From their primitive, amphibian ancestor, by way of the elephant-like Elephantoidea through to the elephants (Elephantidae), nature extravagantly experimented with over 300 species of proboscidean, keeping only those best able to survive.

In this evolutionary process, massive bodies and columnar legs, tusks and extended, grasping trunks developed quickly and at an early stage. Growing to giant size, the proboscideans spread from their African origins across the continents, with the exception of Australia, which was less accessible, and so developed its own peculiar fauna.

Growing numbers forced a constant search for new feeding grounds and habitats. The animals moved into the steamy rain forests of tropical regions, dry plains with baking sun, and the temperate zones, which have snow in winter. They reached the inhospitable northern latitudes of Eurasia, and when the Bering land bridge appeared they spread into America too.

These massive pachyderms demonstrated extraordinary adaptability to a range of climates and conditions. Adaptation and selection equipped their bodies with the best means to survive in each.

For some 20 million years, elephants of many species populated the earth. Their heyday did not end until during the last ice age.

Paleontologists, working in co-operation with geologists, have analyzed vast numbers of fossil finds and recently arrived at a fairly complete understanding of the history of the largest land mammal, going back millions of years; final certainties inevitably lie buried in earth history.

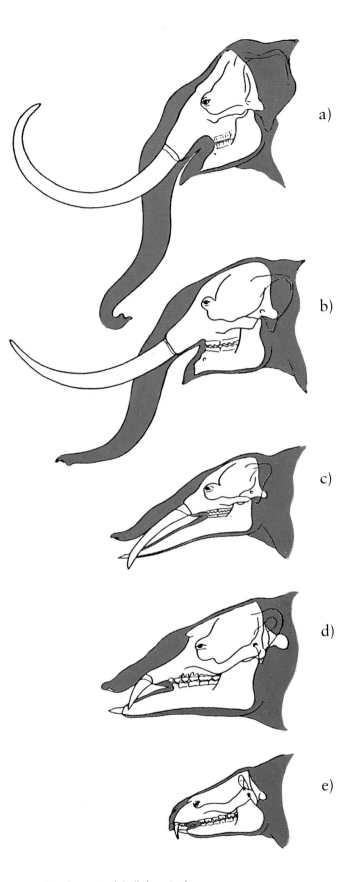

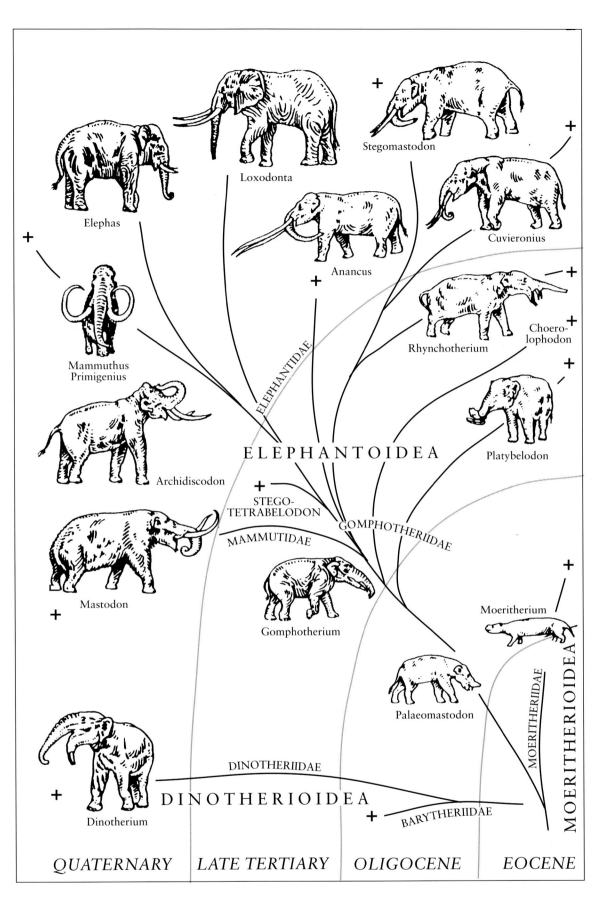

Development of skull shape in the
course of evolution, from above:
a) *Elephas columbi*
b) Mastodon or *Mammut
   americanum*
c) *Tetrabelodon angustidens*
d) Paleomastodon
e) *Moeritherium*

Simplified evolutionary tree of
the true elephants (family
Elephantidae). Black lines
indicate relationships; broken
lines mark divisions of time.
Extinct family lines are marked
with a cross.

# Evolutionary tree of the elephant

The deinothere, with its typical downward-pointing tusks in the lower jaw. This giant is a relative of the elephant and not a direct ancestor as previously thought. Painting: Z. Burian

The elephant's evolutionary tree has many branches. Four main groups can be distinguished amid all the variety of the species:

The gomphotheres, the Mammutidae, the stegodonts and the Elephantidae, which is the youngest group produced by evolution. Alongside these, a separate family developed: the deinotheres.

## The deinotheres

The deinotheres developed in Africa, and evidence for their existence goes back 25 million years. They formed an early side-branch in the development of the elephant-like Elephantoidea. The deinothere is, in fact, a relative of the elephant and not a direct ancestor, as one might have been led to believe.

The deinotheres, unlike other proboscideans, had no tusks in the upper jaw. The tusks in their extended lower jaw pointed downwards and were curved backwards, a shape suitable for digging out aquatic plants.

Deinotheres spread from Africa across Europe and south-east Asia, but they did not reach as far as America. They died out about a million years ago.

## The gomphotheres

In the Miocene epoch, the many varieties of gomphotheres were the most widespread of the proboscideans. They are considered to be descendants of an evolutionary intermediate, *Phiomia*, which appeared 35 million years ago. *Phiomia* had two downward-curving tusks in the upper jaw of its elongated skull and two straight tusks in the lower jaw. Its descendants, the gomphotheres, included – in some lines of development – creatures up to 10ft high at the shoulder. The upper jaw of these animals had two long, slightly downward-curving tusks, while the lower included shorter tusks. Skeletons of animals belonging to this line have been found in Africa, Eurasia and America.

In another line of development, the tusks of the lower jaw reduced in size, finally disappearing completely, whilst those of the upper jaw lengthened considerably. In a few evolutionary varieties, upper jaw and tusks reached such proportions that their length (with head) almost equalled that of the body. *Anancus* is the most typical example of this.

*Phiomia*, an evolutionary intermediate. These early proboscideans, with tusks in the upper and lower jaw of an elongated head, are considered to be ancestors of the gomphotheres, a widely-distributed group of many varied forms, existing on into historic times. Painting: Z. Burian

## The Mammutidae

For various reasons of scientific classification, paleontologists have renamed the 'Mastodontidae;' this family is now called 'Mammutidae.' This can cause some confusion for the non-specialist. The Mammutidae of this new classification should be distinguished from the well-known ice-age 'mammoth,' which has the scientific name *Mammuthus primigenius*.

Remains of the first Mammutidae, descended from the paleomastodon, were found in 25 million-year-old Oligocene strata in Africa and Eurasia. Around seven million years ago, this family of proboscideans also colonized North America, where numerous fossil remains were found. When the Central American land bridge was formed, a few million years ago, the animals advanced into South America.

The Mammutidae were about the size of today's elephants, but more solidly built, with a hairy body. Individual varieties also attained giant size. Situated in the upper jaw were two massive, slightly downward-curving tusks; the two small, straight tusks in the lower jaw disappeared completely in the course of evolution.

There were also branches of development comprising animals equipped for life in cold regions. A good example is *Mammut americanum*, a member of the family Mammutidae.

*Mammut americanum* became adapted to life in cold regions in the course of evolution. In his reconstruction, the painter Robert Larson places this creature in a Central American setting.

## The stegodonts

The stegodonts were widely distributed in Asia, where they first appeared in the Oligocene. In body structure and shape of head they resembled the Mammutidae, but there is a distinction in the teeth. The family falls into two groups, *Stegodon*, whose name means 'roofed-tooth' from the gable-like ridges of their molars, and *Stegolophodon*.

During the Pleistocene glacial periods (650,000-10,000), which led to massive lowering of sea levels, they were able to advance as far as Japan, Taiwan, and the island groups of the Philippines and Indonesia. There, in the phases of isolation after sea levels rose again, pygmy forms also developed.

Stegodonts established themselves in Asian habitats. They advanced as far as Japan and, when land access was possible, colonized Indonesian island areas. The painter Maurice Wilson has set the reconstruction of his subjects, the Asian *Stegodon ganesa,* in an idyllic family group.

# The Elephantidae

The evolutionary development that produced the Elephantidae, the mammoth, and the present-day types of elephant, which are the Asian elephant (*Elephas maximus*) and the African elephant (*Loxodonta*), began about 16 million years ago, roughly in the middle of the Miocene series.

The ancestor of this line, *Primelephas*, had only small lower tusks, and even these eventually disappeared. The tusks in the upper jaw became stronger and increased in length.

The most important evolutionary step was the change in the chewing teeth. The grinding surfaces of the molars formed into transverse ridges of dentine covered with hard enamel; the dips in between contained tooth cement, a softer material.

As a result, these parts wore down at different rates, and the tooth was not worn smooth. The chewing surfaces remained rough, able to cope with tougher food items like plains grass and tree branches, enabling the animals to exploit more barren habitats.

Fossil finds show that the first representatives of the genus *Mammuthus* lived in Africa about three million years ago. They did not yet inhabit cold regions, but lived in bush steppe and forests. They were similar in build to modern Asian elephants, but larger, measuring over 13ft at the shoulder, and they had longer, weightier tusks.

It was not until 120,000 years ago that the giants spread to inhabit cold regions too, by way of a line of evolutionary changes. The woolly mammoth (*Mammuthus primigenius*) colonized Eurasia and North America, into the subpolar tundra. A thick, shaggy coat protected the animal from the cold and snow. It was smaller than its predecessor, the steppe mammoth (*Mammuthus trogontherii*).

The period which saw the development of the mammoth also saw that of the genus *Elephas*, in Africa, the line which leads to the Asian elephant, *Elephas maximus*. Elephas spread throughout the southern part of Eurasia, a particularly successful species being *Elephas antiquus*, known as the forest elephant.

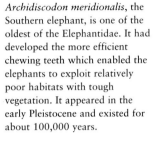

*Archidiscodon meridionalis*, the Southern elephant, is one of the oldest of the Elephantidae. It had developed the more efficient chewing teeth which enabled the elephants to exploit relatively poor habitats with tough vegetation. It appeared in the early Pleistocene and existed for about 100,000 years.

Palaeoloxodon meridionalis, the forest elephant, was considerably larger than the woolly mammoth, with quite long legs and massive tusks, slightly bent at the tips. During the long interglacial periods, it inhabited wooded grassland and forests in Central Europe. As the climate cooled it retreated southwards. In Central Europe it was then replaced by *Mammuthus trogontherii* and later, as the northern ice sheet advanced, by the mammoth (*Mammuthus primigenius*). The last representatives of the forest elephant died out in Spain early in the Würm glacial period. Painting: Z. Burian

During the time about 500,000–70,000 ago, in the warmer interglacial periods, this animal began to inhabit the whole of southern Eurasia, which was still extensively forested, and even reached Britain. As the last glacial period began and the ice sheet advanced again, the forest elephant disappeared from the European continent.

*Loxodonta africana*, the most recent distinct elephant species, appeared about one and a half million years ago. Major differences can be seen between it and the Asian elephant. As well as the enormous savannah elephant, there is a smaller forest (or round-eared) elephant (*Loxodonta africana cyclotis*), which lived in the rain forests. At one time African elephants inhabited the whole of the African continent. There were still African elephants, probably forest elephants, living in North Africa in the mountain regions of today's Maghreb 2,000 years ago. Now they are found only south of the Sahara.

# The story of the Flood

As the last ice age died away, some 10,000 years ago, the melting of the great ice sheet produced a rise in sea level – accompanied by tectonic upheavals and climatic shocks – and brought about dramatic changes of environment on earth. These had a profound effect on the evolutionary process in fauna and flora; in the animal world there is evidence of mysterious deaths. Echoes of the prehistoric catastrophes are found in historical times, in the Flood stories of a number of peoples. One of the oldest of these stories is the Gilgamesh Epic, back to which it is possible to trace the biblical story of the Flood.

*Noah's Ark* (Detail), stained glass window. 12th–13th century, Chartres Cathedral, France

How did whole branches of the family of the elephants disappear? The biblical Flood interprets the environmental catastrophes of the evolution process.

# The elephant in Noah's Ark

The Old Testament story of the Flood is known across the world. The book of Genesis tells of the angry God of such human emotions, who causes the great flood to come upon sinful humanity, consuming everything on earth.

Filled with anger at the wickedness of humankind, we read, God regretted having created them. And so He said:

"... I will destroy man whom I have created from the face of the earth; both man, and beast, and the creeping thing, and the fowls of the air ..."

But Noah, the only just man amongst them all, and his family found mercy before God. In order that they should survive, God commanded Noah to build an ark, we are told, to prepare for the time of the great flood:

"Make thee an ark of gopher wood; rooms shalt thou make in the ark, and thou shalt pitch it within and without with pitch ... And behold, I, even I do

Above and opposite:
The biblical story of the Flood is a great film topic. Two scenes from John Huston's film 'The Bible,' 1965. On the screen, Noah plays his flute as he leads the animals two by two into the safety of the ark. The elephants, borrowed from a circus, gave particular visual impact to the scene.

bring a flood of waters upon the earth, to destroy all flesh, wherein is the breath of life ..."

Noah did as commanded. Then, when the time approached, "were all the fountains of the great deep broken up, and the windows of heaven were opened" and the Lord said to Noah:

"Come thou and all thy house into the ark; for thee I have seen righteous before me in this generation. Of every clean beast thou shalt take to thee by sevens, the male and his female; and of the beasts that are not clean by two, the male and his female. Of fowls also of the air by sevens, the male and the female; to keep seed alive upon the face of all the earth. For yet seven days, and I will cause it to rain upon the earth forty days and forty nights; and every living substance that I have made I will destroy from off the face of the earth. And Noah did according to all that the Lord commanded him ... and the waters prevailed upon the earth an hundred and fifty days."

Thus it came about that our elephant too survived in that ark which Noah built, which finally landed on Mount Ararat.

An old Jewish legend tells of the exciting incidents inside the ark, as it was tossed on the floodwaters: The dung collecting in the ark was causing it to list to one side. In despair, Noah asked the Lord what to do, and the Lord told him to move the elephant to the other side of the ark. But

now that the balance of the pile of dung had shifted, scores of rats and mice ran out of it, and began to gnaw holes in the wooden sides. Noah turned to the Lord again for help, and was told to strike the lion on the nose. The lion sneezed out two cats, which controlled the rats and mice. These were the first cats on earth ...

The story of the Flood, which has appeared again and again in human cultural history, has found expression in various literary and pictorial forms. We are reminded of the elemental forces of nature, which repeatedly put our human powers firmly in their place.

In Christian art, the symbolic march of the animals into the safety of the ark is a frequent motif; a special focus falling on the archetype of the elephant. The magnificent mosaic in the Basilica of San Marco in Venice deserves particular mention. Michelangelo depicted the subject in a fresco of the Sistine Chapel.

Finally, in our business-oriented times, the renowned biblical story of the Flood has been commercialized through the medium of film.

Above:
Vaulted mosaic in the vestibule of
San Marco, Venice, 13th century.
After the great rains, Noah sends
out the dove to look for dry land.

# The great Flood in the Gilgamesh Epic

The oldest surviving version of the story of the Flood comes from southern Mesopotamia, where the Sumerians, who were the inventors of cuneiform writing, created an early great culture from the end of the fourth millennium BC. Around 1700 BC, the Babylonians took over the legend, which found expression in the Gilgamesh Epic, preserved for us in fragmentary form on cuneiform clay tablets. The elephant finds only a short, unflattering mention in the Babylonian version of the legend: "... an elephant which tears off his carpet."

In the Sumerian-Babylonian Flood story, which was probably known to the Jews from the time of their Babylonian exile, we also find the roots of the Old Testament account; the earliest parts of this may date from around 1,000 BC.

According to the Gilgamesh Epic, the gods were angry at humanity whom they had created; man having been – as in the Bible – shaped from clay by miraculous divine power. The gods punished them with a great flood, which was to destroy them. However, the god of fresh water and of wisdom, Ea, pitied humanity, and decided to save one just man at least: Utnapishtim and his family. Following Ea's instructions, Utnapishtim built an ark and called into it "all manner of the seed of life" and "the wild beasts of the field."

When the waters consumed humanity, the gods watched in horror and regretted their decision, "and wailed and wept." Utnapishtim and his family survived the flood, in the ark. Set down on Mount

Nasir, he sent out birds to gather information; when a raven eventually found dry land and did not return from its journey, Utnapishtim climbed out of the ark and then made a sacrifice "and the gods smelled the pleasing odor."

Left: Elephants and other animals go two by two into the ark. From the illuminated manuscript 'Histoire universelle en français de la création du monde jusqu'à César.' This early encyclopedic document was written in around AD 1210, by a monk in Lille, in northern France.

# The mysterious mass extinctions

The Ice Age features in the biblical narrative in these words: "And in the second month, on the seven and twentieth day of the month, was the earth dried. And God spake unto Noah, saying, Go forth of the ark, thou, and thy wife, and thy sons, and thy sons' wives with thee ... And Noah builded an altar unto the Lord; and took of every clean beast, and of every clean fowl, and offered burnt offerings on the altar. And the Lord smelled a sweet savor; and the Lord said in his heart, I will not again curse the ground any more for man's sake; for the imagination of man's heart is evil from his youth; neither will I again smite any more every thing living, as I have done. While the earth remaineth, seedtime and harvest, and cold and heat, and summer and winter, and day and night shall not cease." (Genesis chapter 8)

The stories in which the Bible recounts the history of the earth pass over millions of years, from the origin of life to the Divine judgment of the Flood. The task falls to modern science to interpret the ancient story of the Flood, which is echoed by discoveries of mass extinctions in the animal world.

Around a million years ago, some eleven species of giant proboscidean inhabited the continents. Then, within a comparatively short space of time, two-thirds of these disappeared. Only three species survived: the mammoth, which also became extinct 3,000–4,000 years ago, the Asian and the African elephant.

In Europe, where mammoths continued to be hunted by Stone Age Man, there were no proboscideans left by 5,000 years ago, in the Bronze Age. The elephants' range of distribution across the globe decreased by two-thirds, and they remained only in southern Asia and Africa.

How did this happen? Science still does not have a clear explanation for the widespread extinction. Natural disasters were certainly an important cause.

The Tertiary period, which lasted about seventy million years from the end of the Cretaceous to the Pleistocene, seems to have been, geologically, a fairly stable period in earth history, as we see from the condition of the rock strata. This explains the continuous evolutionary development of large mammals during this time.

Then, however, vast tracts of the earth were shaken by major natural events: by volcanic eruptions and by movements of the earth's crust, uplifting mountains and bringing about profound changes of climate. Clouds of volcanic dust in the stratosphere reduced the quantity of the sun's rays that could penetrate and bring heat and light, perhaps causing sudden onsets of fatal cold.

About one million years ago a long series of glacial (ice age) periods began. During these glacial periods, enormous masses of water froze to solid ice, thereby diminishing the cycle of evaporation and rainfall. As a consequence, sea levels decreased dramatically while areas of dry land increased sharply.

In Europe the ice covered Scandinavia, northern Germany as far as the Elbe, great swathes of Britain, and a belt in northwest Russia. The Siberian tundra remained free of ice, however, which explains how the mammoth survived there for so long a period.

During the warm interglacial periods, the great ice sheet melted, sea levels rose dramatically, and huge masses of water flooded broad coastal regions and inland depressions. There must have been particularly devastating and widespread floods in the Mediterranean area, which was a rainy region in the last ice age.

The story of the Flood

The landscape of the Lake of Zurich during the Ice Age (Quaternary).
Color print. Painting: Ernst Heyn

The mass extinctions of the giant proboscideans began in the northerly regions of the earth with the overwhelming tectonic upheavals and climatic changes; their physical size and enormous food requirements made them especially susceptible to environmental changes. Various major factors may have contributed: cold, isolation of entire races of animals in newly inhospitable regions as a result of mountain uplift, devastating floods and sudden violent natural disasters. The destructive power of these events is indicated by finds of piles of elephant bones in the north of America. A further possibility is that disease caused or at least hastened the extinction of species.

A pygmy elephant in a prehistoric island setting, in an illustration based on comparative studies of skeleton finds and living animals. Island isolation, scarcity of food in long periods of drought, and inbreeding may have led to the pygmy forms, which also existed in many other island animals, such as deer.
Painting: Z. Burian

## Pygmy elephants populate Mediterranean islands

During the climatic and tectonic upheavals which changed the shape of the continents in the most recent period of earth history, a side-branch of the proboscideans developed: pygmy elephants, only about the size of a Shetland pony. Fossil evidence for the mysterious process of evolution which reversed the change toward giant forms and led to these pygmy forms has been found in many parts of the world. A large number of remains were found in particular on Mediterranean islands such as Sicily, Malta, Crete, Cyprus, and Tilos. On Malta, the bones of a mini-elephant only 3ft tall at the shoulder were excavated, the size of a roe deer.

The pygmy forms probably emerged when areas were turned into islands by the rising sea level, or by movements of the earth, isolating them in a restricted, island habitat. They would have had to adapt to a restricted food supply, and become subject to the uncertain effects of inbreeding.

The animals isolated must mainly have been remnants of the successful *Palaeoloxodon antiquus*, the prehistoric forest elephant. These disappeared from the European continent, along with other species of proboscidean and large mammal, around 70,000 years ago, as the ice of the last glacial period advanced.

Excavations on the island of Tilos in the early 1970s brought particularly interesting discoveries about the development of pygmy elephants. In the deposits of a cave which now lies 400ft above sea level, along with the remains of other long-extinct animals, were found numerous bones of two forms of pygmy elephant, from individuals of different ages, and small tusks. Amongst them were embryonic tusks only $1^1/_2$ in) long and $^1/_2$ in thick, a most unusual find.

The upper, more recent layers of cave deposit contained the remains of a very small pygmy form, the species *Palaeoloxodon falconeri*, with a shoulder height of about 4ft. Radiocarbon dating produced an age of approximately 4,500 years for the remains.

In the deeper, older layers of sinter deposits were found remains of a considerably larger pygmy form of elephant, scientifically dated as having lived around 45,000 years ago. This very small pygmy form discovered would appear to be, according to the most recent theories, the end result of a process of adaptation by the elephant to ever-poorer environmental conditions.

On today's Mediterranean holiday islands, pygmy elephants lived in prehistoric times. The last mini-elephants died out completely about 4,500 years ago.

☐ Occurrence of pygmy elephants

SICILY
MALTA
CRETE
TILOS
CYPRUS
*Mediterranean Sea*

0    500 km

One of those who discovered and studied the Malta fossils was the British surgeon Andrew Leith Adams. In his 'Notes of a Naturalist in the Nile Valley and Malta,' he attempted to illustrate the appearance of the prehistoric island creatures, all now extinct. This shows:
1) *Palaeoloxodon mnaidrensis*, shoulder height 6ft
2) The pygmy elephant *Palaeoloxodon melitensis*, shoulder height 4ft 6in
3) *Palaeoloxodon falconeri*, the smallest pygmy elephant, shoulder height 3ft
4) Hippopotamus
5) Giant dormouse
6) Swans
7) Large freshwater turtle

Casts of pygmy elephant skeletons from remains found with many other fossils in the Spinagallo Cave near Syracuse, Sicily. These are the skeletons of full-grown animals, a bull and a cow. Senckenberg-Museum, Frankfurt

The last of the very small pygmy elephants died out about 4,000 years ago. Their decline may have been caused by a deterioration in the climate; a dry period in the Mediterranean region. Disease may also account for their death, or extermination by humans, who left evidence of their presence in the more recent layers at the Tilos site: stone implements and coarse pottery fragments dated to the Bronze Age.

Pygmy forms of proboscidean species also developed in other island regions of the world which had some time previously been connected to the mainland, and later isolated by the rising sea in interglacial periods. For example, pygmy elephant remains were found on the Indonesian island of Celebes, amongst other places.

On the island of Santa Rosa, off the Californian coast, a completely preserved skeleton of a pygmy mammoth was found in a crumbling coastal dune. The animal had a shoulder height of only about $5\frac{1}{2}$ ft. During a period of low sea levels in the last ice age, Santa Rosa had been connected to the mainland – which explains the find.

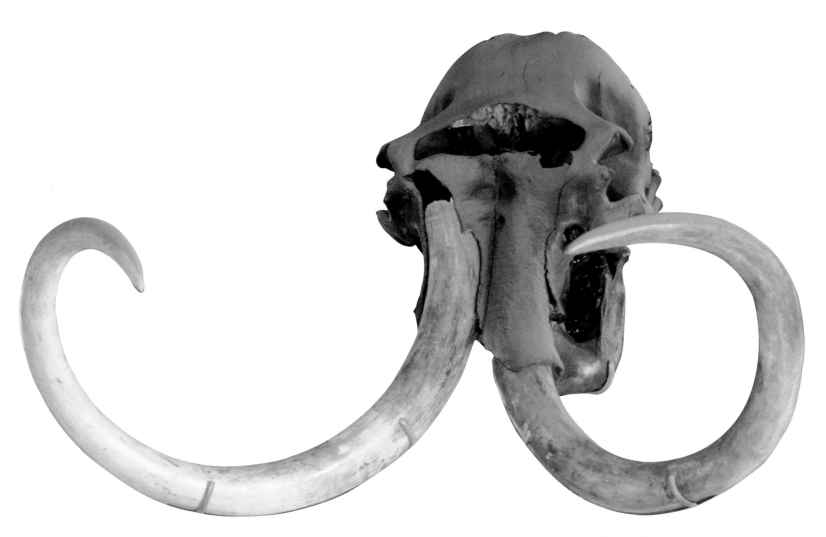

## Polyphemus, the Bible and the true nature of fossils

Mammoth skull
Musée Nationale d'Histoire
Naturelle, Paris

Many finds of fossilized
mammoth remains were made in
medieval western Europe, where
elephants were only a distant tale.
The discoverers were unable to
identify the enormous bones with
any known animal, so fantastic
stories of giants, monsters, and
legendary beasts sprang up. In a
climate of belief governed by piety
and a literal interpretation of the
Bible, there was no concept of
geological timescales, even
amongst scholars.

Even in early historic times, people knew of the buried, preserved or fossilized remains of the proboscideans, but it went far beyond their imagination to see these as evidence of life in previous ages; they had no concept at all of the lengths of time involved.

Chance finds were encounters with the unknown. The size of an elephant skull or bone exceeded all they knew, and their thoughts went to magic, ghosts and gods. This gave rise amongst the ancient cultures to legends of giants, dragons and fabulous creatures, stories which still survive today.

In the world of ancient Greek legend, Homer's 'Odyssey' is based on traditional tales, and tells of the Trojan War and the guileful Odysseus's homeward journey. The terrible Cyclops in the 'Odyssey,' Polyphemus, his one eye set in his forehead, calls to mind a curious feature of the elephant skull. The large nasal opening at the base of the trunk could be interpreted as an eye socket, with a little imagination. It is possible that fossilized skulls with this strange opening inspired the poet's imagination back in the 8th century BC, when the heroic legend originated, and led him to think of one-eyed giants.

At the beginning of modern times, stories of giants and fabulous creatures went hand-in-hand with finds of proboscidean remains. The massive bones and tusks were wondered at and preserved in cabinets of curiosities by feudal overlords. Bones

were nailed to doorways and city gates, to bring luck or ward off evil spirits. Superstition and religious simplicity abounded during this period.

The age of the world, the origin of human beings and animals, were questions no-one asked in that climate of Christian belief; the Bible held the answers in the Creation Story.

The theologian James Ussher, created archbishop in 1625 by King James I of England, even calculated the precise date of creation as 4004 BC. He reached this archiepiscopal conclusion (in his 'Annals of the Old and New Testaments' and 'History of the World from the beginnings to Vespasian') as the result of simple addition. It gained general acceptance.

The discovery of prehistoric human stone tools together with mammoth bones at Gray's Inn, London, led people to interpret the mammoth as an elephant, sent to Britain on one of the Roman emperor Claudius's campaigns; this preserves the biblical time-scale. The stone tools also found there were conveniently ignored…

In Switzerland, in 1577, giant bones were found. Assuming them to be human, people at first wanted to give them a Christian burial, but this was abandoned when a doctor of medicine, Felix Platter, declared them to belong to a 20ft tall giant. A Christian burial would definitely be wrong for such a creature as that…

They were mammoth bones, as was established 200 years later by the German zoologist, Friedrich

Belief in the existence of the fabulous beast, the unicorn, continued in Christian Europe far into the 19th century, and the tusk of the narwhal – and many a fossilized mammoth tusk – were ascribed to it. According to legend, the unicorn's wildness is tamed when it lays its head in the lap of a virgin. In late medieval representations, this becomes a symbol of Marian purity. Powdered horn from a unicorn was said to give protection from animal bites and poisoning, and above all, to be an aphrodisiac. So narwhal teeth, which were thought to be horn from the unicorn's forehead, were kept in princely treasurehouses, in costly containers, and were worth ten times their weight in gold. Apothecaries made many fossilized mammoth tusks into miracle-working unicorn powders.

Blumenbach, on studying the find preserved in the Town Hall of Lucerne.

In the spring of 1700, a mass of mammoth fossils was found in the German town of Cannstadt, on the River Neckar. The find included some sixty tusks. The local ruler, Duke Eberhard Ludwig of Württemberg, asked scholars to produce a "highly-reasoned" account as to "whether these horns and bones were sprung from the earth as a play of nature, or had taken shape as living creatures in their mother's belly, or whether all were the bones of men," as Herbert Wendt recounts in his "Entwicklungsgeschichte der Lebewesen."

After three years of research and scholarly wrangling, the doctor of medicine Samuel Kern burned some pieces of tusk, and concluded from the overpowering "bestial stench" they exuded that they were organic remains.

However, in the early 18th century, people did begin to study the implications of the fossil finds for natural history. Their literal interpretation of metaphorical passages in the Bible led them to assume at first that these were the remains of animals which had died in the Flood. Even the existence of the legendary unicorn was not questioned at all, and elephant tusks were attributed to these creatures.

The nature and classification of the mammoth, the source of the largest number of fossils, remained unclear until the end of the 18th century. Not until 1799 did the German zoologist, Friedrich Blumenbach, establish that the mammoth was a

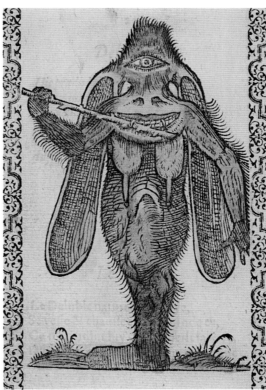

Johan Sluperius,
1572,
colored wood engraving.
Bibliothèque des Arts Décoratifs, Paris

Homer's one-eyed Cyclops, Polyphemus, was transformed by the western medieval imagination into an extraordinary monster, fitting for the role of a Beelzebub.

separate species, which differed from the living elephants of Asia and Africa. The scientific name of the mammoth, *Mammuthus primigenius*, 'first-born mammoth,' is thought to date back to the studies Blumenbach carried out.

# Excavation fever hits Europe

The science of paleontology, the study of fossils to provide information about distant events in the history of the earth, did not begin until the turn of the 18th to 19th century. Tentative descriptions were produced, still within the framework of biblical concepts, but a widespread interest had been roused concerning the mysterious remains of extinct animals, and the true age of the humans whose bones or tools had been found with the bones of these animals.

A sudden outbreak of excavation fever hit the whole of Europe. Quantities of fossil remains were unearthed in the first sixty years of the 19th century alone, and the old, literal interpretation of the biblical Creation account was shaken. The scientists involved in this research – zoologists, geologists and prehistorians – began to waver between an officially-approved adherence to the Bible and the evidence being excavated.

The 'catastrophe theory' developed by the French prehistorian Georges Cuvier (1769–1832) offered a means of subtly adapting the old interpretation of the Bible to new discoveries. This theory states that life on earth has repeatedly been destroyed and recreated, through a series of catastrophes. Following the last catastrophe, the Flood, human beings and present-day animals arose… This created a separation between humans and the distant, 'antediluvian' ages of the earth and

extinct animals, and preserved humanity's special place in Creation. William Buckland (1784–1856), professor of geology in Oxford, was one of the supporters of 'catastrophe theory' in England.

In 1823, Buckland discovered human bones in a cave in Paviland (Wales), together with remains of mammoths, woolly rhinoceroses, cave lions and others. The bones, found daubed with red ocher, were declared to be those of a woman, nicknamed 'the Red Lady' (they were in fact male).

In keeping with biblical chronology, Buckland stated that the woman had not lived at the same time as the extinct 'antediluvian' creatures; since there had once been a Roman camp in the vicinity, the 'Red Lady' was duly identified as a camp prostitute of the Roman legionaries.

The young science of paleontology was brought a decisive step forward by the work of the French pioneer of research into prehistory, Boucher de Perthes (1788–1868), in his excavations and analyses of finds. In sand and gravel deposits at Abbeville on the Somme, he found numerous remains of mammoths and other giant prehistoric creatures, as well as human tools.

Boucher recognized that the humans must have lived back at the time of the mammoth, and may have hunted these giant animals. This statement brought him nothing but derision from his contemporaries. He maintained his opinion, publishing it in a five-volume treatise 'De la création: essai sur l'origine et la progression des êtres'. After years of further rejection, his ideas were eventually confirmed by French and British scientists in 1859. Scientific investigation of the Paleolithic age began.

Illustrative proof of Boucher's ideas was provided by a sensational find in the 'Cavernes de la Madeleine' in the Département of the Dordogne; many other sites there yielded fossil remains from Paleolithic times. Amongst bones and stone implements was found a piece of mammoth tooth bearing a fine outline drawing of a mammoth, with its typical humped neck. The drawing is so lifelike that the artist must have had an extremely good knowledge of mammoths.

Near the Moravian village of Predmost, too, masses of mammoth remains and human bones were found in a hummock of clay in the mid-19th century. The Viennese prehistorian Heinrich Wankel and the geologists of the Brünner Akademie were certain that they had discovered the camp of some Stone-Age mammoth hunters.

*Georges, Baron Cuvier,*
c. 1850,
after a painting of 1826 by Nicolas Jacques (1780–1844), steel engraving.

The Frenchman Georges Cuvier is one of the pioneers of paleontology, the scientific investigation of fossils. He carried out comparative anatomical studies of living animals and fossil skeletons, bone remains. He pieced together prehistoric creatures from thousands of individual bones. He is the originator of 'catastrophe theory.'

Archeological digs in the 19th century were conducted in a vigorous and amateurish way, so much was destroyed. This illustration from 1835 shows the recovery of the famous deinotherium skull at Eppelsheim, Germany. The leader of the investigation, J. J. Kaup, stands inside the excavation to ensure that the prehistoric bones are handled carefully.

The story of the Flood

Darwin's ideas at first met with bitter rejection and vicious mockery. He was accused, in a travesty of his theory, of postulating that man was descended from apes. In this caricature from the London satirical magazine, 'Punch,' the evolutionary process leading to man runs from the worm by way of the ape, which loses its tail, on to the contemporary Victorian gentleman. Darwin did not state that man is descended from apes; he proposed different lines of development for humans and the anthropoid apes, tracing them to a common ancestor.

MAN·IS·BVT·A·WORM·

*Charles Robert Darwin,*
c. 1865,
colored wood engraving after a photograph.
Charles Robert Darwin (1809–1892), founder of the theory of natural selection, the revolutionary theory that a process of selection is at work in the hard struggle for life. His theory of the origin of species was epoch-making for research into prehistory.

## Darwin's theory of evolution

The epoch-making theory of evolution put forward by the English biologist, Charles Robert Darwin (1809–1892), founder of evolutionary biology, opened up new horizons for research into prehistory. His theories, still accepted today, revolutionized existing world views and research methods into prehistory. He said that the characteristics of living creatures have a capacity for change in the face of changing environmental conditions, and that a process of selection is at work in the struggle for life, resulting in the survival of 'the fittest'.

Darwin's book, 'On the Origin of Species,' published in 1859, came as a shock and was vigorously refuted. Scholars in the field were too firmly rooted in the idea of the immutability of species in nature; they were now asked to believe that these were the result of a long process of evolution. Society saw it as a threat to its belief in the Bible, and protested against this attack on the (biblical) special place of humanity, which was now declared part of a constant evolutionary process.

In the popular consciousness, the traditional image of the origin of the world and living beings, founded in a naive interpretation of Scripture, changed only slowly. Theologians persevered into the present century in resisting 'Darwinism,' for example giving an age for humanity based on the genealogies of the Bible, and so amounting to only around 6,000 years.

Piecing together testimony from countless fossil remains of proboscideans, excavated in large numbers across the world, has made it possible to reconstruct the family tree of our present-day elephants, a tree going back fifty million years.

No other animal has left such a rich and plentiful succession of traces of its prehistoric physical existence over a period of millions of years, nor provided deeper insights into evolutionary processes over the vast span of earth history, as the elephant.

# The mammoth:
## Europe's and America's elephant

Defying the cold of the last ice age, the woolly mammoth was the elephant of Europe, Siberia and North America. A byword for elemental animal strength and perfect mastery of the cold, it still remains universally familiar thousands of years after its extinction. Our Stone Age

The massive tusks of the mammoth, curved into an arc, could reach 16ft in length. They may have been used to scrape out grass and herbs from the snow in periods of cold.
Painting: Z.Burian

ancestors hunted this giant, with its shaggy, reddish hair and powerful, arc-shaped tusks. Numerous chance finds of its bones have occupied people's imaginations for thousands of years, and new discoveries continue to fascinate. Of all the extinct proboscideans, only the mammoth has come down to us in tangible and lifelike form. In Siberia, at the beginning of the 20th century, the most perfectly-preserved body of a mammoth so far found was successfully recovered; the Berezovka mammoth. Since then, new discoveries in the tundra have added to our knowledge of this species of animal, and the world in which it lived.

Opposite:
Reconstruction of *Mammuthus primigenius*.
Royal British Columbia Museum, Canada

## Arctic adventure: recovering the Berezovka mammoth

A hut was built over the mammoth carcass. The ground, frozen rock-hard, had to be thawed layer by layer in order to remove the body in sections.

In the spring of 1901, the Imperial Academy of Sciences in St. Petersburg received a telegraph with news that the completely preserved body of a mammoth had been found in northern Siberia. A Lamut hunter had come upon the body of this prehistoric giant, with its head and back rearing out of the stony debris, in the area of tundra near the Arctic circle. Russian zoologists had been hoping for such a find for years.

Since the 17th century, tusks, bones, and even partially-preserved bodies had been found in plenty, but it had never been possible to retrieve an entire body. The great distances involved meant that, before expeditions reached the site where the body had been found, exposed by falls of earth, it had either disintegrated, or been eaten by wolves. Now, the railway made it possible to reach the site more quickly.

The Academy immediately put together a group of experts with a support team: the head preparator, a German by the name of Pfizenmeyer, who, like so many Germans at that time, was in Russian service, the zoologist, Dr. Herz, and the young Russian geologist, Sevastianov. They set off by train for Irkutsk at the end of May, and from there by river boat, horse-drawn and reindeer-drawn transport, into the inhospitable tundra.

When, after four months, the group and their equipment eventually reached the site, an intense odor of putrefaction met them. Damage had occurred in the interim; where the body of the mammoth was exposed, carnivorous animals had eaten away the skin of the head and hump, the trunk was missing, and likewise one of the tusks, which had been taken by a hunter.

The body of the mammoth lay, in a location containing many layers of deposit, in the steep bank of the river Berezovka, a tributary of the Kolyma, some 100ft above water level. The top layer, roughly 20in thick, belonged to the swamp forest, beneath that a layer of clay permeated with ice, and finally a massive fossil ice sheet. The permafrost, a mixture of deep-frozen soil and embedded ice crystals, was as hard as concrete.

The complicated recovery work took three weeks, with the Siberian winter setting in. The expert in charge was Pfizenmeyer. The body had to be dissected; piece by piece was thawed, using the flue heat from fires, then exposed and separated off, and put to freeze in the cold of a Siberian winter, with temperatures of minus 13 degrees Fahrenheit effectively preserving it.

About 2ft below the surface, a front foot was found, bent as if pawing. Perhaps the animal had fallen into a crack just freezing over, and tried to get out. The shoulders, front and rear feet were partially scuffed, and the pelvis broken in two places. The body had a reddish-brown, shaggy coat 8–12in long, over a thick undercoat. The hair of the belly was lighter in color, and the tail, also with reddish-brown hair, was only 14in long, ending in a shaggy, 12in long tassel. Pieces of grass were still on the lower jaw, and in the stomach, twenty-five pounds of reasonably well-preserved food remains were found, revealing something about the vegetation several thousand years ago; these were species of plant that still occur there today.

The frozen, sinewy flesh of the shoulders and body, marbled with fat, looked so appetizingly like beef that the scientists thought of sampling some, but when thawed it became limp and offensive-smelling. They gave the pieces of meat to the dogs, who ate it without hesitation. Russian experts in refrigeration technology say that deep-frozen meat will keep and remain edible for a maximum of ten years, after which skin and flesh shrink, as the water in the tissues is shed as crystals. The meat undergoes a sort of freeze-drying, retaining the structure, but

not the flavor, which is dependent on the water ... So the mammoth preserved in the permafrost could be described as an 'ice mummy.'

The skeleton and the body and skin portions were sewn into animal hides and loaded onto sledges. Then came the laborious winter trek with reindeer, back to Irkutsk, where a refrigerated wagon was waiting. On February 18, 1902, the expedition arrived in St. Petersburg with its valuable cargo. The skeleton was reassembled and erected, a task of several weeks. Taxidermists produced a masterly, lifelike reconstruction of the mammoth with the original skin. Missing or excessively damaged parts were replaced using other finds from Siberia. The skeleton and the reconstruction of the Beresovka mammoth were put on display in the Zoological Museum of St. Petersburg. Various sections of the flesh and the giant's internal organs formed the subject of intensive scientific study for some time.

Dima the mammoth calf was shown as part of a touring Stone Age exhibition in various European countries and then the USA in 1992.

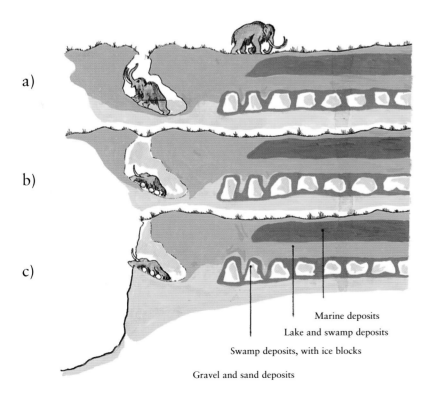

a)

b)

c)

Marine deposits

Lake and swamp deposits

Swamp deposits, with ice blocks

Gravel and sand deposits

## Dima the calf

Recently, the Siberian permafrost also afforded a sensational glimpse into the childhood of mammoths. Bulldozer work for a new gold mine in 1977 unearthed the completely preserved body of a mammoth calf, estimated to be about six months old. It was given the name Dima. Its milk tusks had not yet completely erupted, its shaggy coat had rotted off the body, and had to be dug out of the earth separately. The calf, which lived about 40,000 years ago, had fallen into a mudhole – traces of mud in its mouth show this – and had been buried by sediment.

In the laboratory of the St. Petersburg (then still known as Leningrad) Zoological Museum, scientists preserved the body in a paraffin bath, which stabilized the tear that the bulldozer shovel had made in the body. The internal organs were removed and preserved in alcohol.

In 1991, two Japanese anatomists carried out a detailed radiographic examination of the preserved heart of the calf. Slicing vertically, they created a three-dimensional image of the heart using tomography. Despite the tissue shrinkage, the essential structures inside the heart were still clearly recognizable. The investigation provided proof, among other things, of the close relationship between the mammoth and the modern Asian elephant.

A realistic reconstruction of the calf, with shaggy red coat applied (from a musk ox) is on display in the St. Petersburg Zoological Museum.

Left:
The death of a mammoth, and its preservation in the Siberian permafrost:
a) The animal has fallen into a crack.
b) Deposits of soil and ice gradually fill the 'trap' containing the frozen body.
c) Over thousands of years, a river wears away the sides of its steep bank. The body is exposed in the riverbank.

## Adapted to extreme cold

The woolly mammoth was about the size of an Asian elephant, but with a shorter, stockier body. There were, however, giants the size of the African savannah elephant. The mammoth's short rear legs gave it the characteristic, steeply sloping back, like that of a giraffe; this was emphasized by a large hump on the shoulders and on the head, fat reserves for lean times of cold. Like the yak, whose shaggy coat enables it to withstand extreme weather conditions in the steppes of Central Asia and highlands of Tibet, the mammoth was protected by a coarse, reddish-brown coat 12–16in long, and thick undercoat. Its skin was much thicker than an elephant's, and under this was a 3in layer of fat which, along with the small ears of the mammoth, reduced heat loss.

The bulls' tusks could reach enormous dimensions, arching into a circle; there was one found in Siberia which measured 16ft around its outer edge. Ridged molar teeth enabled them to deal with tough, hard foodstuffs, and the stomach contents of frozen, preserved bodies include not only grass and tundra plants, but the remains of birch and pine branches. The mammoth needed vast quantities of food, and avoided arctic winters.

In late autumn, as the herds migrated southwards, the bulls' massive, spirally curving tusks might have served as a sort of snow plow to uncover feeding grounds. During the warmer seasons, the tusks could batter a way through brush and undergrowth, the bull forging a way ahead and making food accessible for the females and young, which lacked such powerful tusks – as is observed in herds of elephants.

In Central Europe, the mammoth reached shoulder heights of 10–11 $^1/_2$ft. The species living in the harsher, subarctic regions of North America and Siberia, with less food available, was a little smaller, with shoulder heights around 9ft.

*Mammuthus primigenius* is a universally familiar symbol of perfect capacity to withstand the cold. The spirally-arching, inward-curving tusks could reach 16ft long. This shaggy giant did not die out until historic times, about 3–4,000 years ago.
Painting: Z. Burian

## "A creature that lives beneath the earth"

For thousands of years, the primitive races of Siberia knew of fossil mammoth remains, those exposed from the ice and permafrost, or by the sea on the northeastern coasts. The massive skulls, bones and parts of carcasses had no obvious place in the local fauna, so in the mental world of the Yakuts, Tungus and others, inhabited as it was by spirits of nature, the mysterious animal grew into a marvellous being which they believed had come to earth from mystic realms.

Siberian legends tell of creatures like "rats, as big as elephants, which live in the earth, and when the air or the sunlight reaches them, they die immediately." Remains of bodies had always been found deep in the earth, for example, when ground broke away from a steep riverbank. Shamans included the marvellous animal in their invocations. Huts were built as places of worship, made from mammoth bones and tusks.

The very name of the mammoth, so universal, goes back to Siberian tales. The word is made up of the Estonian word stems 'mas' = earth and 'mutt' = mole. So, if we go back to the original meaning, the mammoth's name means 'earth-mole.'

Chinese merchants, returning from the inhospitable north, also spread the Siberian legends in the Middle Kingdom, where mammoth ivory had long been a material sought after by craftsmen. A 16th-century natural history manuscript describes the strange creature of the icy northern region, 'tien-shu,' in accordance with the Siberian legends, and gives an account of its size: it looked like a mouse, but was the size of a buffalo.

In China, which had a mammoth population during the glacial periods of the Pleistocene, fossil 'dragon bones' have long been collected and ground into medicinal powders, said to be effective against all sorts of infirmities and impotence. These would have been remains of large mammals such as mammoths, woolly rhinoceroses, giant deer, and others which lived on earth at the time, not fossil remains from the Cretaceous.

The fact that deer antlers were often found with the 'dragon bones' led to the mythological dragon, frequently depicted with horns. The dragon is the traditional bringer of good fortune in China and has been the symbol of imperial dignity since the Sung Dynasty (960–1279).

The world of the mammoth, as it may have looked 20,000 years ago. When food was scarce, small family groups roamed the harsh expanses of the tundra.

The mammoth

## Prey of Stone Age hunters

For the people of the inhospitable north of Eurasia in the Paleolithic age, the place in their earth and cliff dwellings where they made their fire, their 'hearth,' was the focus of life. The women collected berries, roots, seeds and herbs; the men hunted with clubs and primitive spears, tipped with bone or sharpened stone points. The ability to use bows and arrows was also acquired early. Toolmaking sites, where implements were cut to shape and then sharpened into recognizable tools and weapons, have been found on every continent.

The woolly mammoth was a particularly desirable prey hunted by Stone Age people during the last ice age. In that dangerous environment, where prehistoric carnivores like cave bears, saber-toothed tigers, and wolves lay in wait with their murderous fangs, the mammoth hunt was a challenge for the entire tribe. The skills and few weapons possessed were tested to their limits.

The hunt had its place in the pattern of life and death of individuals and species. The mammoth, killed with such laborious effort and at risk of their lives, was heaven-sent bounty for the tribe. The mountains of flesh provided food in sufficient abundance to tide them over the periods of hunger, their bellies full from celebratory feasting.

The reddish-brown, hairy mammoth skins could be softened by beating, and used for fur garments and protection from the weather. The tendons served as string or binding twine; the tusks and bones could be made into tools and weapons, or used as hut-building material.

Times would have been hard, making life difficult for both animals and the early humans of the north. As the last glaciation, the Würm glacial period, began around 70,000 years ago, the Arctic icecap advanced across the northern latitudes of Eurasia and America. The glaciers, which extended down from the mountains into the flat lands, spread from Scandinavia into northern Germany. Environmental conditions were similar to those in the sparse tundra and swamp forest regions of northern Siberia today.

Only during the summer, which lasted three months from the end of May to the end of August, were the primitive wild game hunters able to set up camp in ice-free regions as they followed the animals. There would only have been mosses, grasses and bushes, as well as stunted pine and dwarf birch, as in Lapland today. It would have provided a meager spread for the mammoths, and for the woolly rhinoceroses, musk oxen and reindeer living alongside them; the animals that the small, nomadic tribes of Stone Age people depended on for their livelihood. In winter, when temperatures plummeted and the land disappeared under snow, both people and animals headed south to milder climes.

The dramatic end of a Stone Age mammoth hunt, which the artist has depicted as a warm, pleasant, cultivated-looking landscape. As with all these illustrations, there is a degree of artistic imagination involved. The injured animal, set upon by the whole tribe and pierced with spears and arrows, has collapsed and is being done to death. The hunting struggles were fierce and cruel.

# Ancestors of the Ice Age giant

The mammoth, descended from ancestors in the heat of Africa and adapted as it was for a life in the subarctic, stands at the end of an evolutionary process of development of a specialized species. Fossil finds in Central Europe do provide a remarkably complete sequence, revealing the structure of its immediate predecessors and intermediate forms, and these have all now been scientifically classified. The use of the mammoth's evolutionary tree gives us insights into the more recent processes of earth history.

The mammoth's immediate predecessor was the steppe mammoth (*Mammuthus trogontherii*). This lived during the Riss/Würm interglacial period, which began around 130,000 years ago and lasted until about 70,000 years ago; the start of the last (Würm) glaciation. Dry grass steppes extended across Europe and North America and seasonal temperatures were slightly lower than in today's northern temperate zone. Fossil finds (as in Darmstadt/Mosbach, in Germany's south Hessen) show that this harsh world was already populated by some typical cold region fauna, such as reindeer and musk oxen.

The steppe mammoth had thick body hair, but was by no means equipped to face the harsh subarctic temperatures. It was a huge animal, much larger even than today's African savannah elephant, and it is estimated by scientists to have had a shoulder height of between 13 and 15ft.

The steppe mammoth was the first proboscidean to adapt to the meager life of the Eurasian and North American steppes, as the climate became colder. It is the direct predecessor of the mammoth. Its domed head, and the arc of the bull's massive, inward-curving tusks, are a first hint of the mammoth. The cows had smaller tusks, with a slight inward curve. The steppe mammoth was a giant, much larger than today's African savannah elephants.
Painting: Z. Burian

*Archidiscodon imperator*, pictured by a riverbank. A well-preserved skeleton was found in tar pits near the city of Los Angeles.

The North American steppe mammoth, usually called the 'imperial mammoth' (Mammuthus imperator), had a shoulder height of 14ft. Its massive tusks were up to 16ft long. Its molar teeth already exhibited the ridged chewing surfaces, suggesting that increasing adaptation to harder foodstuffs was taking place.

The fossil remains of the steppe mammoth reveal the many different stages of evolutionary development, according to the age of the geological strata in which they are found.

The remains of skeletons found in older strata exhibit a greater similarity to the mammoth's more ancient ancestor, that is the Southern elephant (*Archidiscodon meridionalis*), which inhabited southern Europe during the northward migration of the proboscideans in the course of earth history. The more recent the geological strata in which the remains were lying, the greater the similarity in the details of its build to the later mammoth.

Fierce competition for food may have driven the steppe mammoth further and further north into colder habitats. There, over geological periods of time – which are measured in tens of thousands of years – the gradual adaptation which eventually equipped the mammoth for the cold harsh climate would have occurred. These animals demonstrated a great ability to adapt to a range of climates and conditions.

A reconstruction of the imperial mammoth, whose well-preserved skeleton was found in the tar pits of Rancho La Brea, Los Angeles, along with many other prehistoric fossils. This giant, a north American version of the steppe mammoth, had a shoulder height of 14ft, and 16ft long tusks.

## The mammoth in the New World

The mammoth had lived peaceably for tens of thousands of years on the broad steppes and savannahs of North America before the first humans arrived in the New World from Asia, between about 20,000 and 25,000 BC. America did not have an original human population of its own. Like the mammoths before them, and the many other types of proboscidean millions of years earlier, the new arrivals came across the occasional land bridge between the Kamchatka Peninsula and Alaska. During the most severe periods of glaciation, sea level sank by 330–460ft, and the Bering Strait, only 150ft deep, and 53miles wide at its narrowest point, was then dry land for hundreds of miles as a result.

The humans who set out on this trek were small groups of people of northern Asian tribes, from whom the Mongolian peoples are descended. Geological research shows that the area around the Bering Strait, and the Yukon valley in Canada, were glacier-free during the last glaciation. The Canadian ice sheet, which stretched as far as the present-day Great Lakes of America, left broad corridors free, and the migrants' southward journey would have been accomplished quite quickly and with relative ease.

There were already some Native American hunter-gatherers living in Pennsylvania 18,000 or so years ago, as finds at a Meadowcroft site prove. Caves have been discovered in Chile with signs of habitation over 15,000 years ago.

From the edge of the icecap at the Great Lakes to Mexico, the mammoth and other large Stone Age animals inhabited the expanses of what is now the USA. The mastodon, too, was represented until around 8,000 BC. Environmental conditions were fairly favorable. With no serious enemies, the proboscideans could spread without threat or disturbance. Mammoth remains have been found everywhere on the semicontinent.

Around 12,000 BC, the first Clovis hunters appeared, named after a Mexican village where the discovery of the first stone spearheads was made. Such artifacts are an indication of the stage of cultural development reached by the tribe that made them. These spearheads were of the same type as lance-shaped, flaked stone tips found amongst the fossil bone remains of mammoths wounded by hunters.

Left:
*Mammuthus columbi*, (Falconer).
Painting: Z. Burian

This massive creature lived in the warm savannahs of southeastern America in the late Pleistocene, together with camels and bison. An example was found at Melbourne, Florida. It had a shoulder height of 12ft, and remarkable, inward-curving tusks. *Mammuthus columbi* died out towards the end of the Pleistocene.

Stone knives and (lower left of picture) a typical flaked stone spearhead, the main weapon used by the first Native American mammoth hunters, who were called the Clovis hunters.

The huge skeleton of an imperial mammoth, *Mammuthus imperator*, Lincoln State Museum, Nebraska.

This sensational find is owed to a flock of hens, constantly pecking away for calcium nutrients at a certain hollow. At that spot lay the heap of huge bones, covered by just a thin layer of earth.

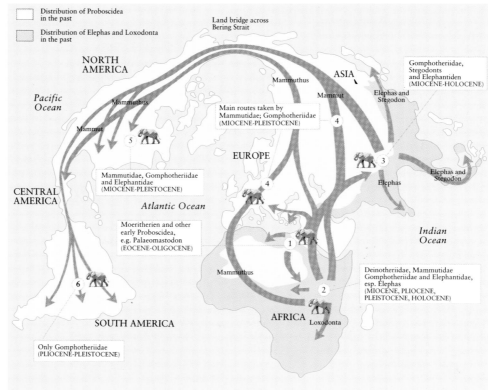

Distribution of Proboscidea in the past

Distribution of Elephas and Loxodonta in the past

Land bridge across Bering Strait

NORTH AMERICA

ASIA

Gomphotheriidae, Stegodonts and Elephantiden (MIOCENE-HOLOCENE)

Pacific Ocean

Mammuthus

Mammuthus

Mammut

Elephas and Stegodon

Mammut

Main routes taken by Mammutidae; Gomphotheriidae (MIOCENE-PLEISTOCENE)

5

4

EUROPE

3

Elephas and Stegodon

Mammutidae, Gomphotheriidae and Elephantidae (MIOCENE-PLEISTOCENE)

4

Elephas

CENTRAL AMERICA

Atlantic Ocean

Moeritherien and other early Proboscidea, e.g. Palaeomastodon (EOCENE-OLIGOCENE)

1

Indian Ocean

Mammuthus

Deinotheriidae, Mammutidae Gomphotheriidae and Elephantidae, esp. Elephas (MIOCENE, PLIOCENE, PLEISTOCENE, HOLOCENE)

6

2

SOUTH AMERICA

AFRICA

Loxodonta

Only Gomphotheriidae (PLIOCENE-PLEISTOCENE)

During the Ice Age, there were some periods when the Bering Strait was dry land. The mammoth, and later humans, made their way across this land bridge into the New World.

# European *Homo sapiens* enters the scene

Mammoth, about 30,000 years old. Ivory, length 4.9cm
Institut für Urgeschichte, Universität Tübingen

This small ivory figurine was found in 1931 in the 'Vogelherd' cave in the Schwäbische Alb. It lies 20 miles northeast of the 'Geißenklösterle' cave.

Sometime in the middle of the last glaciation, for reasons yet unexplained, the Old Stone Age Neanderthals were replaced on the European continent by a more advanced type of human. European *Homo sapiens* entered the scene.

It was the Neanderthals who had lived as hunter-gatherers in Europe during the first half of the Würm glacial period, around 70,000-27,000 years ago, and pursued the mammoth; they were about 5ft3in tall, broad and heavy-boned, low-browed, with the dome of the skull flattened. The typical heavy, protruding eyebrows, shaped by ridges of bone, were a feature shared with older hominids, *Homo erectus*. They walked with a slight stoop, as the forward inclination of the base of the spine shows. However, the volume of the brain was already equivalent to that of modern humans.

The name 'Neanderthal' comes from that of the valley where the first fragmentary skeleton of an Old Stone Age human was found in 1856, in the cave refuse of the 'Feldhofer Kirche' cave. It is the valley of the river Düssel, between Düsseldorf and Wuppertal. Since then, Neanderthal remains have been found in every part of Europe except Britain, and many other parts of the world.

Neanderthals carefully buried their dead, often in their own cave dwellings. Finds of skeletons in southwestern France, by the Dordogne, have provided the most interesting discoveries; many traces of the mammoth were also found there.

Various branches of developmentally different Neanderthals also inhabited stretches of the Near East, Africa and Asia. They disappeared 35,000–27,000 years ago, for reasons still unexplained, and Neanderthals were supplanted by a new type; Cro-Magnon man.

This new type of human was named after the Cro-Magnon cave at Les Ezyies in the Dordogne, where five human skeletons were found with fossils of mammoths and wild horses in the remains of Stone Age dwellings, in 1868. There were three men, one woman, and a fetus, characterized by a narrow face, steep forehead, narrow nose and more slender body build; without the typical features of the Neanderthals.

In the more favorable, ice-free climate of what is now France, the replacement of Neanderthal man happened so quickly and suddenly that the new type of human cannot be seen as an evolutionary development. A recent genetic study of the DNA of various races of modern humans and genes isolated from a Neanderthal bone strengthens the widely-held view that Neanderthals represented a particular evolutionary branch.

Questions remain, however. In the warm regions of the Near East and Middle East, there existed Neanderthals who differed less in appearance from modern *Homo sapiens*. A find was made in 1959, in a cave at Shanidar in the mountains of northern Iraq, of a completely preserved skeleton of a Neanderthal in which the protrusions for the eyebrows were remarkably unpronounced.

Above:
In the 'Geißenklösterle' rock cave very near to Blaubeuren in the Schwäbische Alb, Germany, which is 26ft deep and sheltered Stone Age people, ivory animal figurines and decorated plates have been found. These are some of the earliest evidence of human artistic endeavor. Radiocarbon dating of the bone charcoal from the fireplace produced an age of about 31,000 years. Painstaking excavation has been carried out there, beginning in 1974. The stone tools, fossil remains of the hunters' kill and other pieces have given us new insights into life 30,000 years ago, a time when mammoths, woolly rhinoceroses and musk oxen grazed in the southwest of Germany.

Inland ice

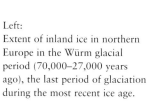

Left:
Extent of inland ice in northern Europe in the Würm glacial period (70,000–27,000 years ago), the last period of glaciation during the most recent ice age.

# The extinction of the mammoth

The strange, fairly sudden disappearance of the Old Stone Age Neanderthals 40,000 years ago was followed shortly afterwards, as geological timescales go, by that of the mammoth, as the last ice age was dying away; this extinction occurred in both Eurasia and America at the same time. The precise causes which led to the sudden extinction of this species have still not been explained.

For a long time, it was assumed that the Ice Age giants died out about 10,000 years ago, but they did in fact live on for some time after that. Russian and American investigations have since discovered that a remnant group of mammoths lived on the Wrangel islands, off the northern Siberian coast, about 3,000 to 4,000 years ago. In the far northeast of Siberia and the Kamchatka peninsula, the last refuge of the Siberian mammoth, there were still a few herds about 6,000 years ago. On the continent of America, the fossil remains of two such mammoths were found far south, at Santa Isabel Iztapan in the highlands of Mexico, with flint spearheads still in between their ribs.

The extinction of the species may have had several causes. Sudden warming, following the cold of the ice age, combined with a change in vegetation and thus food, may have been too much for even the mammoth's capacity to adapt. Bores taken of the ice in Greenland have shown, amongst other things, that the prehistoric climate change happened suddenly.

Another possibility is that natural disasters, which affect large species particularly severely, or disease, may have reduced the mammoth population, and that the remaining herds in Siberia and North America fell victim to the ever more successful hunting techniques of an expanding population of humans. In America, the mammoths disappeared first from those regions where spearheads belonging to the previously-mentioned 'Clovis hunters' were found.

The extinction of species forms a natural part of the evolutionary process, if it occurs within an ecologically intact system. If species of fauna or flora are unable to adapt quickly enough to changes in the environment, or become vulnerable as a result of over-specialization and give way to stronger competition, they disappear, and other species take their place. Modern human beings have been the first to achieve a dominance over nature, and so pose a threat to the laws of evolution and the ecological system.

As we now know, the rate of extinction of species has increased too rapidly and continues to increase. We are only now beginning to make restitution.

The evolutionary tree of the primates. American anthropologists now believe from recent fossil finds that the lines of development leading to human beings and to the anthropoid apes diverged much later than used to be supposed.

A mammoth mass grave was discovered in 1975 in the small American town of Hot Springs, South Dakota. The skeletons and tusks of over forty mammoths were unearthed in a large sinkhole, in which the warm, thermal water would not have frozen, even in a hard, ice age winter. The tempting, warm water in fact sealed the fate of these mammoths; it was easy to slither down the pit walls, but quite another matter for the giants to haul their ton-weight back out of the slippery depression. They either drowned or starved, and finally became buried. As years went by, this huge graveyard filled with yet more victims. Investigations have shown that these were mainly young, inexperienced animals, unaware of the danger.

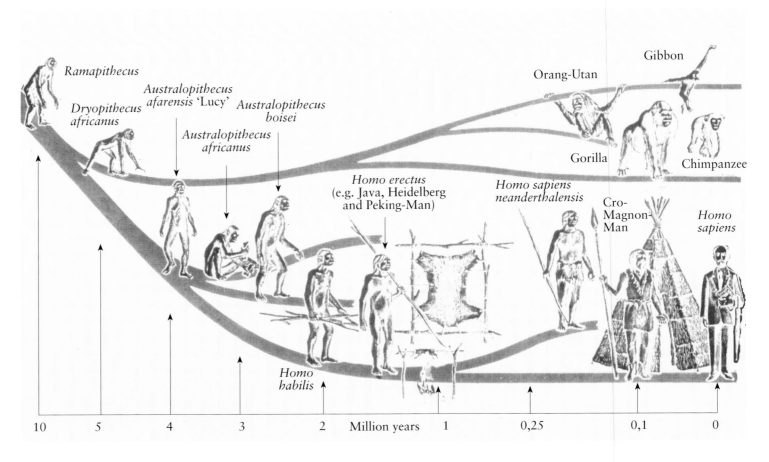

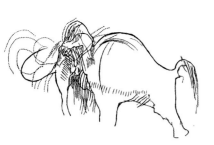

Mammoth,
c. 15,000 years old,
copied from a rock engraving.
Cave at Font-de-Gaume, on
the Dordogne

This representation of a mammoth
was found in a cave near the
village of Les Eyzies in the
Dordogne, southwest France.
Trunk and tusks have been
carefully executed.

Mammoth,
c. 12,000 years old,
rock painting.
Grotte de Pech Merle, Cabrerets

Mammoth,
c. 11,000 years old,
copied from a carving on a
piece of bone.
Musée de l'Homme, Paris

This mammoth carving,
scratched on a piece of
bone, was found in the
La Madeleine cave,
likewise on the
Dordogne. It features
the typical, sloping
back of the mammoth.

# The elephant in Stone Age art

As human beings acquired the skill of making simple implements and began to develop their powers of artistic representation, 30,000 years ago, the giant proboscideans were a constantly-recurring animal motif, and the depiction of them astonishingly lifelike. Proof that elephants and mammoths had spread across the globe at the time of man's infancy is given by copious finds in southern France and northern Spain, where ice age art blossomed, in northern and southern Africa, and also in the northern regions of Eurasia. These pictures demonstrate the amazing artistic skill of our ancestors.

The outline of the animal was first traced out with a flint tip or cutting tool on the rock walls of the cave dwelling, or of a grotto used for worship; the engraved outline was usually then retraced in black paint.

An example of this is the outline drawing of a mammoth found at El Catillo in northwestern Spain, one of the oldest known representations of an animal. Pictures of animals were also cut into the surface of horn, bone or ivory tools, using a stone knife, and were sometimes further engraved or carved. Museums of natural history across the world possess numerous finds from the earliest phase in the development of human civilization.

Between 30,000 and 10,000 BC, late ice age, a transition occurred, and animals began to be pictured in a more artistic way. This period saw the magnificent paintings of animals and hunting scenes in the caves of Altamira, near Santander, Spain, and at Lascaux in the French Dordogne, each a high point in ice age art, which provided considerable inspiration to modern painters like Picasso and Franz Marc.

The ice age artists used paints made from powdered minerals: brown and red ironstone, iron ocher and black manganese earth; charcoal

Locations of cave paintings and finds of carved animals in southwest Europe.

Right:
Mammoth,
c. 12,000 years old,
red chalk,
copied from a rock painting.
Cave, Pindal, northern Spain

The widely-known Pindal elephant picture is a red chalk sketch by Abbé Breuil of the poorly-preserved rock painting, which was 42cm x 44cm in size. He marked on his copy the position of an oval, reddish mark on the elephant's chest, a remnant

of the color with which the drawing had been filled in, or of a previous picture which had been painted over. However, when an elephant hunter suggested that this could mark the animal's heart, as the place for the hunters to aim at, he adopted the idea, and a little retouching produced the heart shape; this has even given rise to learned speculation about a possible cult of the heart amongst ice age peoples. Anyone trying to spot the sentimental symbol in the cave at Pindal will draw a blank.

and chalk were also used. Prepared paints and grinding mortars were found in various caves. The rock painting of a mammoth found at Cabrerets in the French département of Lot is executed in black and white; the famous picture of the 'elephant with a heart,' discovered in a rock cave at Pindal on the Spanish north coast and made world-famous by the French archeologist, Abbé Breuil (1877-1961), is red-brown. The figure of the animal is one of masterly, inspired simplicity. The red heart of the Pindal elephant adorns many a book and many a display illustration for a natural history museum, even lending appeal to modern-day advertising ... (see the legend to the illustration)

The subjects of the pictures were almost always animals which were hunted, on which the tribes depended for their nomadic livelihood: the aurochs, reindeer, deer, rhinoceros, and again and again the mammoth. The huntsmen's eye was sharpened for the essential features of these as they pursued them; humans and animals lived in close partnership.

The cycle of the seasons and the changing shapes of nature governed these people's image of the world. The mystical and religious imagination of humanity revolved around divine, part-animal, part-human beings until far into the historic times of antiquity. This suggests that the representation of animals and hunting scenes served mainly primitive religious purposes: hunt magic, or the rites of propitiation arising from scruple at the act of killing the animals. In this, the Stone Age artist might have had the role of intermediary to the spirit world, and to the animals in their resurrected life in the underworld, such as is played by the shamans of primitive peoples today.

The enduring legends surrounding elephants, which we shall consider later, may be an echo of prehistoric mystic ideas.

Mammoth,
c. 17,000 years old,
rock painting.
Vallon Pont d'Arc

# Anatomy of an ancient giant

The elephant, that Titan of the animal kingdom, is a miracle of nature. Through the ages, it has received the incredulous gaze of those to whom it seemed some mythical beast, and millions of years have gone

into its shaping. Its unique body structure, remarkable intelligence, and amazing social behavior have made the gentle giant adept at the art of life and survival. Zoologists have made detailed study of its physique, yet have not found all the answers. In this cultural history of the elephant, a glance at the anatomy of our modern ancient giant may help to provide a better understanding.

The elephant's trunk is its most typical feature: it is a miraculous organ, in which tens of thousands of muscles work in harmony. It serves as the elephant's hand, nose, weapon, and aid to orientation all in one; it can grasp things with enormous strength, yet in the zoo the elephant can use it to identify and pick up tiny coins thrown to it, and hand them to its keeper.

Opposite:
Despite all the differences in anatomy distinguishing the Asian, forest and savannah elephant, they have this in common: they symbolize an ancient state of the animal world, in which human beings still occupied a place within nature, and had not yet begun to assert their 'dominion' over the animals.

# Today's two surviving types: the Asian and African elephant

Above and below:
Asian elephants are considerably smaller than their cousins, the African savannah elephants. Other obvious differences are the arched back, the two humps on the animal's angular head, and the small ears.

Only two types of elephant survive today; those living now in Asia and Africa are just a tiny remnant of the many types of proboscidean which inhabited the continents over millions of years. One hundred years ago, the elephant population still numbered millions, and those we see today are an ever-shrinking remainder: some 40,000 in Asia, and about half a million in the savannahs and jungles of Africa.

Asian or African, we call both 'elephants,' but scientifically, they belong to two different groups. The word 'elephant' comes from the Greek, *Elephas*, and zoologists give this genus name to the Asian elephant. Their bigger African cousins have the scientific name *Loxodonta* (meaning diagonal, or lozenge-shaped, teeth). There are several obvious differences in appearance between the two:

The Asian elephant, *Elephas maximus*, has an arched back, an angular head with a steep forehead, quite small ears, and a fairly smooth skin, which often has a freckled look. Its trunk has only one 'finger' at the end.

The African savannah elephant, *Loxodonta africana*, on the other hand, has a saddle-shaped back which slopes away backward from the shoulders, a long head with a sloping, rounded forehead, large, fan-shaped ears which cover its neck and shoulders, and a greater body and leg length. The 'fingers' at the end of its trunk are different: it has two.

There is also a clear difference in size; the African elephant is the largest of all land animals. A fully-grown bull can reach a weight of some 6 tons, and a shoulder height of 11 feet 6in, even 12 feet and over. There was one enormous bull, shot in 1955 on the Kwando river in the former Portuguese colony of Angola, which had a shoulder height of about 13 feet, and was said to weigh around 11 tons. African cow elephants are smaller, weighing around 3–4 tons and measuring about 10 feet at the shoulder. The smaller Asian elephant grows to a shoulder height of 8 feet (10 feet at most) for a bull, and the cow elephant is on average 18in shorter.

Savannah elephants have larger tusks than Asian elephants. Some tusks have been brought in weighing around 220 pounds, and 8 feet in length, though the average weight for a tusk from a fully-grown bull is 110–175 pounds. African cow elephants also carry quite large tusks, even if these cannot compete with the ivory of the bulls. Asian elephants are more modestly endowed, with tusks weighing only 90–110 pounds. The females have only small tusks, if any, hardly protruding at all beyond the upper lip.

Ceylon elephants, from the island now called Sri Lanka, are special in that most bulls are tuskless, though they are not a separate species. This may be the result of a selection process in which, over a period of centuries, bulls with particularly large tusks were shot by ivory hunters, and had fewer offspring as a result.

A subspecies of the African elephant is the much smaller forest elephant, *Loxodonta africana cyclotis*, which inhabits the equatorial rain forests of West and Central Africa, and particularly the large jungles and swamps of the Congo Basin. These bulls attain a shoulder height of just 6–8 feet. Their small, rounded ears and darker skin are characteristic, and they have more hair than savannah elephants, especially on the chin and

An African savannah elephant at a waterhole. These giants can be up to 13 feet tall and between 6 and 8 tons in weight. Okavango Delta, Botswana

trunk. The tusks of the forest elephant are particularly strong, and downward-pointing, which is of greater use for breaking through jungle thickets, whereas in the savannah elephant, they are angled proudly forward.

A further difference between the Asian elephant, savannah and forest elephant, lies in a detail of the foot: the savannah elephant has four horny toes on each of its front feet, and three each on the rear, whereas the Asian and – surprisingly – the forest elephant have five toes on each foot, both at the front and rear.

The arrangement of the ridges on the molar teeth, an important feature for the scientific classification of elephants, differs between the Asian and the African kind. Asian elephants have parallel ridges on their teeth; in African ones the teeth are lozenge-shaped.

Savannah and forest elephants are occasionally seen in mixed herds in areas on the borders of rain forests. It was thought until recently that a cross between Asian and African elephants was not possible, but in 1978, a mixed African-Asian calf was born at Chester Zoo, England. It died fourteen days later, however; it had been born prematurely (see also the chapter "The zoo as refuge").

The familiar name, 'elephant' will continue to be used for both the Asian and the African type, but let us bear in mind that there is a distinction when seen from the point of view of zoology.

# Hand, nose and radar all in one: the trunk

When the elephant uses its 'universal organ,' the trunk, to gather food, tens of thousands of muscles operate in harmony. The 'finger' at the tip is a match for the toughest bamboo stem, and when a branch is to be broken or plants pulled up, the massive, furrowed trunk turns and coils. Curling the trunk tip, the elephant bundles grass and branches and places them in its mouth, or positions them to be held by its triangular lower lip until it is ready to chew the fresh mouthful. Then, the fleshy tongue draws in the food. The elephant can graze, hold food with its lower lip, and chew, all at the same time.

The most remarkable and characteristic feature of the elephant is its trunk, almost an extra limb, which serves it as a combined hand, nose and radar system. The animal has no need to lower its head to discover what is lying or happening at its feet; the sensitive nerve-endings in the tip of its trunk and 'finger,' and in the extended channels of its nostrils, take in all the information it needs about the composition, the smell, and the edibility of each object. In the zoo, it has no difficulty in identifying a coin amongst the titbits thrown to it, and it will pick it up and put it in the keeper's pocket. The small, prehensile fingers at the tip grasp it like a human hand: the one finger of the Asian elephant, or the African elephant's two.

The trunk is a large extension of the upper lip and nose, which are merged into a single organ. Anatomically, it is a highly complex structure, made up of successive layers of muscle running in different directions, and branching networks of nerve fibers. The muscles of the cheek, forehead, nose and upper lip work in concert, which makes the trunk extremely mobile and flexible.

An elephant's trunk is used first and foremost as a hand to gather food. It plucks or pulls up bunches of grass, wrapping each into a bundle by curling the end of its trunk backward around it, knocks the earth off, by banging it against its legs or chest, and puts the food into its relatively small mouth. The elephant may hold it there with its triangular lower lip, until it has finished chewing the current mouthful, and its molar teeth are free to deal with the next. Then, it will take the grass into its mouth with its tongue.

The giant can do all three at once: graze, hold food, and chew. Rearing up onto its hind legs and stretching its trunk, it can reach almost as high as a giraffe, which nature has endowed with a long neck for reaching lofty food sources; branches up to 19 feet high are within the elephant's grasp.

The elephant always drinks using its trunk. It sucks water into its nostrils, which can hold some 10 pints, puts the end of the trunk into its mouth, and squirts the water in. It needs 18–26 gallons a day. Its trunk effortlessly takes up moisture from puddles and rivulets in the savannah. Bathing and dust baths also require the trunk; elephants like to cool down on a hot day by showering themselves with water, followed by dust, to ward away the plague of insects.

Reports often surface of elephants squeezing water from their stomachs to cool their overheated bodies. Skeptics may say that this is just liquid from inside the trunk, which has been known to strike zoo visitors who tease too much, but the elephant expert I. T. Sanderson (b. 1911) has reported two occasions when he was hit in the face by a shower of dirty water containing scraps of food, which could only have come from the stomach.

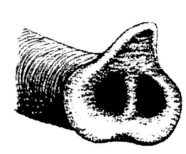

If an elephant loses its trunk through a bite from a crocodile or big cat, or cruel injury by a poacher, it is a death sentence. It cannot graze the ground with its mouth, and finds it impossible to drink or to reach enough foliage to live on.

The nostrils at the tip of the trunk are highly sensitive as regards sense of smell. When an elephant in the wild surveys its surroundings by raising and waving its trunk, it can locate water sources 12 miles away, and detect the reproductive status of another elephant from a distance. It is the trunk which enables the elephant to orientate itself and move around confidently; its eyes are weak, and not designed for night vision. Even blind animals are able to move about safely with the herd, using their trunks. This, however, is an area where science still has much to discover.

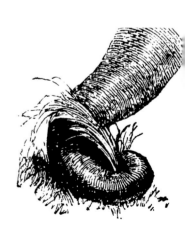

The sensitivity of the trunk to touch is enhanced by sensory hairs along its length; it is used to caress when courting, as a helping hand when caring for

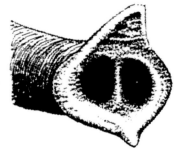

The nostrils of the Asian elephant (left), with one finger-like process, and of the African elephant (above), with two. The sensitivity of these prehensile 'fingers' is similar to that of a blind person's sense of touch. They can seize and pluck blades of grass, examine and pick up the smallest of objects, but can also apply considerable strength.

the young, and occasionally for administering discipline. This same sensitive trunk is also a hugely powerful prehensile arm; the elephant can tear down thick branches and shift entire tree trunks in the service of humans. It can deliver a fatal blow, used in anger or self-defence. Many a predatory big cat has been seized by a trunk when it became too bold, and dashed to pieces. The elephant can be a formidable creature when roused.

In Ngorongoro in Tanzania, an elephant feeds on the higher branches of an acacia. Standing on its hind legs, and stretching body and trunk, an elephant can reach food at a height of up to 19 feet, which is only otherwise accessible to a giraffe, with its extra-long neck.

# Head, mind and brain

The elephant's huge head has a bone structure that gives great stability. In the Asian elephant, the head is boxy, with two humps on the forehead; in the African elephant, elongated, with an arched forehead. A firm anchorage is needed to support the trunk, tusks, and neck muscles.

However, the skull is less heavy than it looks; the brain case is not solid bone, but contains cavities, which provide the necessary skull volume and exceptional stability without excessive weight. Solid bone would make the head far too heavy for the elephant to move easily, or would need neck muscles far more massive than they already are.

Inside this skull is the largest brain of any land mammal. It is convoluted, like the human brain. Scientists have tried to calculate an intelligence index based on the weight ratio between the brainstem (the reptilian 'old brain') and the 'new brain' (the neocortex) of mammals. This gives values of 14 for wild boar, 48 for baboons, 104 for the elephant, 121 for dolphins and 170 for humans. Although this is only a theoretical assessment, it does fit in with results of practical intelligence tests; dolphins and elephants are definitely the most intelligent animals.

Individual elephants, like humans, may be more or less gifted, but they do usually have an excellent long-term memory. Sometimes, they still recognize a person who once carried out studies with them, many decades later. They retain the memory of good and bad experiences for long periods, and often react accordingly when they meet a friend or evildoer again.

An incident at Dresden zoo in Germany is a good example. Jumbo, the African bull elephant, shared quarters with two Asian cows. He had an intestinal problem and was refusing to eat, but if the cows were offered any titbits, he would make a grab for these, and would immediately swallow the stolen morsels. The zoo used his greed to get him to take some bitter-tasting medicine; they offered the cows a crust containing the medicine, in such a way that he could reach it. He stuffed the illgotten gain into his mouth, and realized the trick too late.

The benefactor who had treated him was now viewed as an enemy, and was not allowed to approach; even if he was only spotted in the distance, the resentful elephant would pick up stones with his trunk and throw them at him.

An elephant's brain weighs 11–13 pounds. This is four or five times the weight of a human brain. The ratio of brain to body weight is 1:800 for the elephant, 1:50 for humans, and 1:18,000 for the whale.

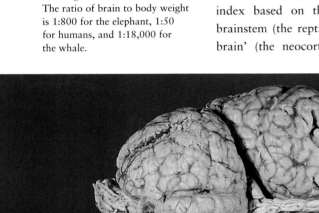

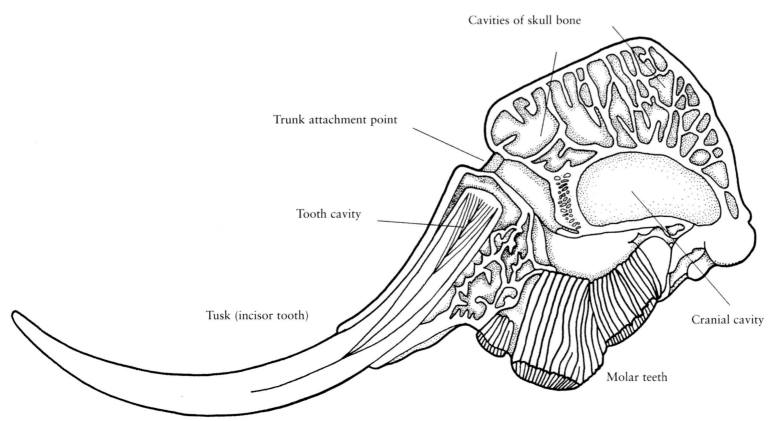

Cavities of skull bone

Trunk attachment point

Tooth cavity

Tusk (incisor tooth)

Cranial cavity

Molar teeth

Cavities in the elephant's skull make possible the size needed for the attachment of the trunk and the neck muscles, and give it high stability whilst reducing weight.

## Cooling mechanism: the African elephant's huge ears

The great, flapping ears of the African elephant have little to do with its hearing; their purpose is that of a highly efficient cooling apparatus, as the heat of the sun beats down on the elephant. The wide expanse of its earlobes is crisscrossed with a dense network of tiny blood vessels from which heat is lost through the skin surface. The greater the surface area, and the more blood flows through below it, the greater the heat loss will be. When the elephant flaps its ears or sprays them with water, it can lose a considerable amount of heat to the outside world. The savannah elephant's ears have an area equivalent to one sixth that of its body surface. Asian elephants, as well as the round-eared African forest elephants, which live in shady tropical forests, manage with much smaller ears.

Elephants have good hearing, but the sound frequencies are different from the ones heard by the human ear. Whereas bats can hear sounds up to 80,000 Hertz, dogs and apes up to 40,000, and

humans up to 20,000 Hertz, experiments at the American University of Kansas put the upper limit of the Indian elephant's hearing at 12,000 Hertz. On the other hand, elephants can hear and produce low notes in the region of 14–16 Hertz, well below the range of the human ear, whose lower limit is 20 Hertz. We cannot always listen in to elephants communicating in the wild, often indeed over great distances, as the sound is below our range.

Scientists have discovered from their studies of animals' hearing and ability to produce sounds that the limits of a mammal's hearing range depend on the size of its head, the sounding board. Other experiments suggest that elephants cannot identify the direction from which a sound is coming; some animals in the experiments even walked past hidden sound sources without locating them. The elephant's trunk is a more reliable means of precise orientation. However, elephants can distinguish individual tones, sequences of tones, and rhythms.

The face of the African elephant, with smooth, backward-sloping forehead and slightly arched skull, sail-like ears spread wide. The thick base of the trunk suggests primeval strength.
Kruger National Park, South Africa

The tusks of a cow (left) and
those of a bull (right).

## The elephant's tusks, its precious defense

The valuable ivory tusks, for which elephants have been greedily pursued for thousands of years, are massively enlarged incisor teeth of the upper jaw. The hollow shaft, which is located without a root in the bone of the upper jaw, extends for about one-third the length of the tusk, and carries a nerve. If an elephant overstrains a tusk and breaks it, the animal will feel pain, which may make it irritable and dangerous.

Baby elephants are born with tiny milk tusks, as big as a human little finger, and formed from the first pair of incisors. After about a year, these are replaced by the permanent tusks, formed from the second pair of incisors. The tusks continue to grow from then on, throughout the elephant's life, at a rate of up to 4in a year for males, and up to 3in a year for females. The weight per tusk is on average $17^1\backslash2$ pounds for an African male elephant reaching full sexual maturity, and 110–175 pounds for a bull 50–60 years old. A female elephant's tusks weigh around 9 pounds on reaching sexual maturity, and 40–44 pounds at the end of her life.

An elephant's two tusks will usually be unequal in shape and length, and will be used to differing degrees, according to whether the animal is left or right 'handed.' If damaged, a tusk will grow again as part of the constant process of growth. A spearhead was found entirely surrounded by new growth in the tusk of one African elephant. The tusks of an old African bull can become so heavy that the animal's head is bowed down by the weight, instead of being carried high. The heaviest tusks ever collected weighed over 220 pounds per tusk. Elephants with a single tusk, called 'Ganeshas,' and elephants with several, have been known among both Asian and African types. An elephant shot in Uganda in 1952 had five tusks on one side and eight on the other.

An elephant's tusks are more important to it as a tool than as a weapon. They are used together with the trunk to help expose roots and tear into the bark of trees in times of drought, and in support of the front legs and trunk in digging out waterholes; they remove obstacles, and in captivity, an elephant's trunk and tusks become lifting machinery for heavy timber.

Opposite:
Tusks of a Titan: one of these tusks weighs 224 pounds, the other, 211 pounds. This magnificent ivory comes from a massive but age-weakened bull, killed by the slave of a Swahili merchant in 1899 on Mount Kilimanjaro. The tusks were both sold in Zanzibar in 1900 for 5,000 dollars.

The molar teeth are the size of a house brick, and the grinding surface is roughened by being made up of lozenge-shaped ridges running across the width. The elephant replaces this chewing equipment six times in a full lifespan of perhaps sixty years. Tsavo National Park, Kenya

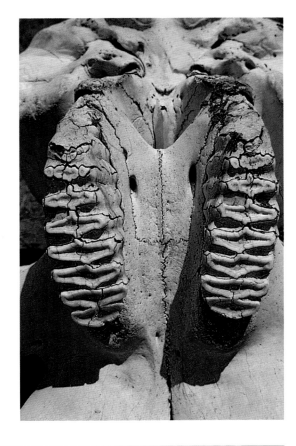

With its mouth open, the elephant seems to be laughing. The flexible, triangular lower lip, surrounded by hairs, is used to take hold of the tough vegetation passed to it by the trunk.

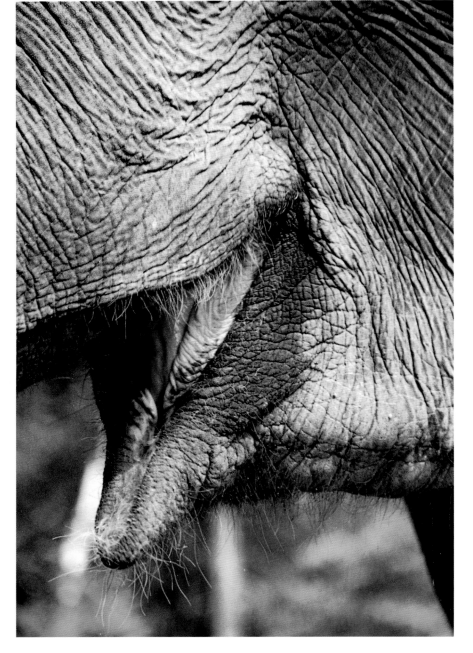

# Molars the size of a brick

The molar teeth of adult elephants are fused into plates up to a foot long, with a rough surface of parallel ridges in the Asian elephant, and a lozenge-shaped arrangement of ridges in its African cousin. Each side of the jaw has one large tooth weighing 4–4$\frac{1}{2}$ pounds. The huge tooth plates are gradually worn down, and progress toward the front of the mouth, where they break off piece by piece, finally being replaced by the following set of molars. The molar teeth are replaced six times in an elephant's lifetime. The animal uses them by moving its lower jaw backward and forward, effortlessly (though quickly and coarsely) grinding down hard food like roots, bark and branches.

At birth, elephant calves already have their first and second true molars present in each side of the jaw, as well as small milk molars. The first molar tooth falls out by the second year of life, and the second, slightly larger one, at 3–4 years old. The elephant keeps its third set until the age of ten, and chews on with its fourth set until twenty-five. The fifth set, the last but one, replaces it, and the final change happens at about 45 years of age. It may keep this last, sixth set for some twenty years, though only a few elephants reach this age. Loss of the last teeth heralds old age and death for the elephant usually aged under sixty.

Each successive set of molars is a little larger than the one before, and has more ridges; these work rather like a kitchen grater. A tooth from an Asian elephant's first set of molars will have on average four ridges, for example, and one from its final set, twenty-four. The number of lozenge-shaped ridges of an African elephant's molar increases less with each set: three in the first set, and about ten in the last.

The chewing surfaces are made of hard dental enamel, and the spaces in between are filled with the softer dental cement, so that wear is uneven. This means that the surface is never worn smooth, and will always be able to grind down hard food.

*Parinari excelsa* – Guinea plum

*Balanites wilsoniana* – Dongomakoupa

## Poor absorption of nutrients: the digestive system

The grey giant eats 330–375 pounds of vegetation each day.

Some examples of tropical fruits from the African elephant's menu.

*Panda oleosa* – Afane

*…eghemella heckelii* – Makoré

Elephants eat prodigiously, but absorb their food poorly; an elephant needs to eat 330–375 pounds of vegetation each day. Although it prefers berries and fruits, it is not choosy. It hastily chews and consumes everything, grass, roots, the stalks of dry plains grass, and all sorts of herbaceous plants, twigs and foliage from bushes, branches, and even thorn scrub. It drinks 18–40 gallons of water a day. Digestion takes about 22–46 hours, and some 60 percent of what is excreted from the 116 feet long intestines is undigested vegetable matter. Horses and sheep absorb 60–70 percent.

The small intestine is 82 feet long, the large intestine 21 feet, and a further 13 feet for the rectum. Unlike ruminants and rodents, elephants have too few symbiotic bacteria in their gut. These organisms (inside, but foreign to the animal) help break down the cellulose of plant cell walls by producing enzymes called cellulases.

A remarkable feature of the elephant's digestive system is its 5 feet long appendix, bigger than the stomach, where most of the intestinal flora, the bacteria needed for the process of digestion of plant matter, is found. Proteins, starches and sugars are digested in the appendix.

The semi-digested food remains in elephant dung, practically two hundredweight a day, provide an excellent nutrient medium for the seeds of trees and plants excreted with the dung, and for the egg deposits of beetles and insects, with their special role in nature's pattern. Tests showed that seeds of some sort were present in nine out of ten elephant dung heaps, so the elephant distributes the seed of grasses, herbaceous plants, bushes and trees on its constant travels.

The seeds of some trees and lianas of the tropical rain forest seem only to be distributed by elephants. In Africa for example, the makoré tree, whose hard, red wood is a sought-after export item, though rare today, is found only along elephant routes. The fruit of the African wood apple is disregarded by other animals, and has to date only been found in elephant dung. Elephant jaws can crack open the thickest and hardest shells of tropical fruits, releasing the seed kernels inside.

When elephants flee in panic, they can reach speeds of up to 25 m.p.h. over short distances. Heads high, they run with ears flapping and trunk swinging. If a bull elephant charges in anger, even the most athletic human runner would be hard pressed to escape at that staggering speed.

## Towering edifices: the legs

This calf looks as if it has fallen nose-first. Whatever their stiff appearance, an elephant's knees are as supple as the knees and (in the case of the forelegs) elbows of a human being.

Weighing several tons and supported by a massive frame, the elephant's large body rests on mighty, towering legs of extraordinarily simple-looking design and broad, flat feet well able to tread softly. The skeleton of the foot is set at an angle, so that the elephant in fact walks on tiptoe, with an elastic step. A pad of fat and connective tissue under the heel helps distribute the weight, as does the slant of the foot. As a result the weight rests evenly across the broad, horny sole.

It is possible to calculate from recorded actual measurements that an Asian bull elephant $9^1\!\backslash\!2$ feet high at the shoulder and weighing exactly 9,259 pounds puts just $8^1\!\backslash\!2$ pounds of weight on every square inch of its soles. This even spreading of its weight enables the elephant to move securely over swampy ground.

The elephant's knee joints are as flexible as those of a human being, so it is an excellent climber. Moving downhill is difficult, however. The angle of the slope makes the weight of the neck muscles, skull, trunk and tusks bear down on the front legs. Elephants prefer to slide down steep inclines. Jumping is more than the giants can manage; they are just too heavy to get off the ground. Even a 6 feet ditch is an insuperable barrier.

The tall legs of the African savannah elephant, designed to support a body weight of 4–6 tons, tower like columns. They are constructed to walk at a measured pace, moving along at about $2^1\!\backslash\!2$ miles per hour when the animal is grazing as it goes. If the elephant is setting out for a particular destination such as a waterhole, it settles into a nodding, regular stride, its trunk hanging, ears flat and head seesawing.
Botswana

Anatomy of an ancient giant

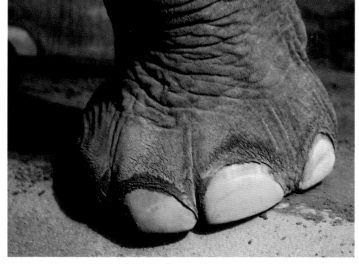

The toenails of an elephant's foot have developed into small hooves. The African elephant has four hoof nails on each front foot, and three on each hind foot; the Asian elephant has five on each front foot and four on each of the rear.

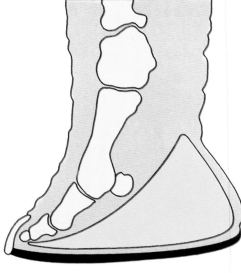

The bones of the elephant's foot are angled, and so it walks on tiptoe, giving it a pliant step. The pad of fatty tissue behind the heel distributes the body weight evenly across the horny sole of the foot.

# The tail

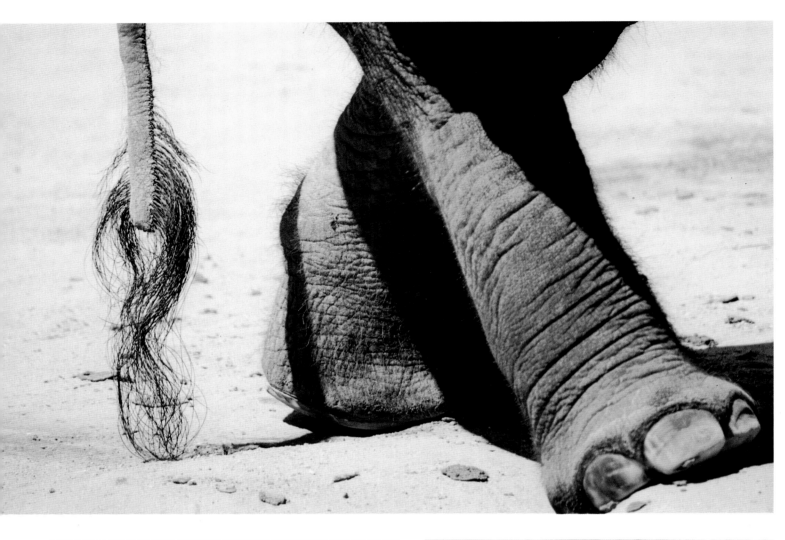

The tuft of hair at the end of the tail is often thin in elephants in captivity; hairs have been plucked out, and it may even have been bitten off by rival cows. Calves also like to chew the tails of their mothers and 'aunts.'

Headgear with tail hairs, Republic of Congo.
height 55cm
Private collection

Headgear of members of the Bwani society, which has great influence amongst the Lega people, Republic of Congo. Members of the society always wear the headdress, which is set with cowry shells. The tail tuft of elephant hair on the crown is a sign of high rank.

Far left and left:
The root of the tail is sturdy, and so can give support when fastening a harness.

The tail which adorns the elephant's huge rear is almost hairless along its length, ending in a tuft of long, black, bristly hairs. The tail is not of great use to the elephant, nor is it very efficient at flicking away flies. Elephants find that a bunch of leafy twigs wielded by the trunk is much more effective, and are able to use this tool. African peoples value the tail tuft as a love amulet, and also weave it into a bracelet.

## Primeval landscape: the elephant's skin

It seems as if eons have carved the deep creases and wrinkles into the skin of the great African savannah elephant. The wrinkles increase the surface area of the skin, which has the role of cooling the body, normally performed by sweat glands; an elephant cannot sweat. The Asian elephant, whose home is in forest, and the darker African forest elephant have a smoother body.

"Thick-skinned as an elephant" goes the saying, which can be a figure of speech or a literal statement. If we take that to imply that the elephant is physically tough or emotionally unfeeling, we are wrong. Its skin is thick, as much as $1^1\backslash2$ in thick in places, but it is in proportion to the size of its body. Thickness should not imply leathery insensibility. In fact, an elephant's skin is very sensitive, and if an elephant is curbed with a sharp instrument, it can bleed. The scattered hairs are also sensitive to touch, and flies and mosquitoes

can enrage the giant. Tending its skin is therefore a constant concern, the elephant delights in bathing, and dust baths are essential to ward off the plague of insects which are a constant irritation.

The skin around the hind legs of the elephant hangs in heavy folds, and this nether garment gives the pensive-looking animal a certain appeal as it ambles along.

Though they inhabit warm latitudes and have only a thin layer of fat beneath their skin, elephants can withstand the cold, and do make their way through cold, mountainous areas. Elephants have been seen at altitudes above 14,750 feet on Mount Kilimanjaro, and in northern climes, circus elephants walk unconcernedly in the snow.

Iain Douglas-Hamilton commented on the otherness of these intelligent creatures, and at the same time remarked on their infuriating similarity to humans in love, loyalty, and the bonds of family. The zoologist has studied many details of elephant group life and social behavior, as we see in his major study of different elephant populations.

Anatomy of an ancient giant

## Elephants' language of communication

This gray colossus stands guard as the herd bathes undisturbed, suspicious, his ears spread in warning. Constant contact is maintained. One means of contact which elephants can use over long distances is infrasound, which employs frequencies too low for the human ear to detect.

The sounds we hear an elephant make are produced in the larynx, then amplified and modulated by vibrating columns of air in the trunk. When we hear the tinny note produced by its upstretched trunk, we say that it is 'trumpeting;' in fact, the French word for the trunk is 'la trompe,' a word which also means 'trumpet.'

Elephants have a rich and varied language of communication, a range of sounds to express moods and feelings: a purring vibration denoting pleasure as they greet one of their kind; a rumbling sound in the throat, when feeling pain; a soft, moaning squeal when experiencing loneliness and boredom in captivity; and a hissing rumble of anger. Keepers say that they can also produce a remarkably melodious 'singing.' A narrow, connective strip of tissue running across some 4–5in above the nostril openings may be involved in modulating the sound, and elephants can also use the finger-like processes at the end of their trunks to close the nostrils partly or completely and thus vary the vibration of the column of air inside. Research has not yet fully explored the role of the trunk in producing sound.

### 'The air trembled'

At this point mention should be made of the strange phenomenon of vibration, a fluttering or trembling of the air, which lies behind many a tale of big game hunting in Asia.

The American zoologist, Katharine Payne, experienced this phenomenon for herself in 1984 at the zoo in Portland, Oregon. The small herd of elephants which she was observing was not 'chatty;' she could hear few if any sounds. She then became aware of a strange vibrating tension in the air. Having studied communication between whales, she attributed the vibration to inaudible sounds made by the animals in frequencies too low for the human ear, and proved her theory by tape-recording them, using special tape which brought the sounds up to a higher frequency.

In extreme cases, strong vibrations in these low infrasound frequencies can be felt physically. The old tales of a trembling of the air around elephants, capable even of sending shivers down the spines of cold-blooded hunters in certain situations, were more than just tall stories. As with many old tales modern methods have proved their basis in fact.

Affectionate greeting as elephants meet in the savannah. Elephants use a wide range of sounds to express their moods and feelings.

# Bulls in musth: the strange temporal glands

At the temples, between the eyes and the ears, bull elephants have glands whose function in the rhythm of life has not yet been fully explained. Once a year, they secrete a dark, oily substance which smells of musk. The glands are inflamed, the temples swollen, and the animal's temperament and behavior undergo a remarkable change; the bull is 'in musth,' as it is called. This mysterious condition may fade away again after a few days, though it can last longer. The animals are nervy, excitable, and unpredictable.

Musth appears in bull elephants about three years after they reach sexual maturity, which happens between the eighth and fifteenth year of life. The intensity of secretion increases gradually until the fourth decade of the animal's life, after which it declines again. Musth can occur, to a less marked degree, in African female elephants (but not Asian ones) though flow from the glands is usually absent. Zoologists think that the scent of the secretion helps to keep the herd together, rather than indicating readiness for mating, although the process is clearly of sexual origin.

The function of these glands is still unexplained. It has an unclarified place in the reproductive cycle. A scientific study of musth behavior on Sri Lanka revealed the following stages: in the early phase, signalled by a swelling of the temporal glands, bulls showed hypersexuality, with erections during breaks in work; the flow of the secretion had a sudden onset and was accompanied by a rapid rise in testosterone level, indicating increased virility. There followed a period of dribbling urine, the penis remaining in the foreskin.

At the height of musth, mating is not possible. Most elephants that have fathered young in zoos have been too young to come into musth, so it is not taken as an indicator of fertility in bulls.

Musth occurs only in strong, well-nourished animals, and Indians take the absence of musth to be a sign of poor health. Rest and a special diet of vegetation are arranged for the affected individual.

It is known from observation that bulls in the wild come into musth much later than those in captivity. The American zoologist Joyce Poole stated as a result of long-term observation of elephants in Amboseli, the small National Park by Mount Kilimanjaro, that no bull under thirty years of age had played any reproductive role; cows 'in heat' in the wild will normally not accept young bulls, whereas in the zoo, even 12–15 year-old bulls have fathered offspring.

In the wild, discoveries about the sexual rhythm of bulls in musth are very difficult to make. Observations by zoologists and rangers show that on the African savannah cows in heat follow a bull in musth, the scent of whose secretions, along with its changed behavior and particularly deep vocabulary of sounds signal strength and protection. Bulls in musth dominate the herd and are especially aggressive in fighting off rivals. Mating often takes place after the state of musth has waned. It has also been observed that musth males rub their secretion onto trees as scent markers, to signal their claim to dominance.

In the confines and emotional stress of captivity, bulls in musth can be particularly excitable and unpredictable, forgetting their training, and serious attacks can occur. When the signs of secretion begin to appear, bulls are isolated and usually chained, as a precaution.

The elephant's reproductive organs show clear differences from those of other land mammals. The vaginal opening of the female is located at the rear of the belly, as it is in sea cows, which are related to elephants, and other sea mammals. The clitoris is highly developed, up to 16in long, and can be stiffened like a penis, which can easily lead to mistakes in determining the animal's sex. The testicles of the bull are located deep inside the abdominal cavity, not externally in a bag of skin. The slightly curving, S-shaped penis is unusually long, to match the anatomy of the female.

Young bulls become sexually mature between the eighth and fifteenth year of life, cow elephants between their sixth and eighth, later if poorly nourished. A mature egg is released every three weeks, but owing to hormonal processes the cow is in season only four times a year for about 3–5 days each time. Gestation lasts 20–22 months, and the baby, weighing some 220 pounds at birth, is suckled for about two years.

Once a year, the glands situated between the eyes and the ears exude an oily secretion which smells of musk.

Anatomy of an ancient giant

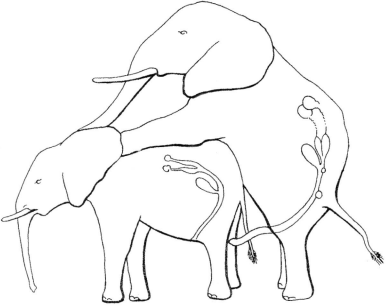

Top and above:
Mating is a complicated procedure. It lasts only about 10–15 seconds, but is repeated a number of times.

Right:
The bull elephant's penis is exceptionally long, measuring over 3 feet, to match the anatomy of the female.

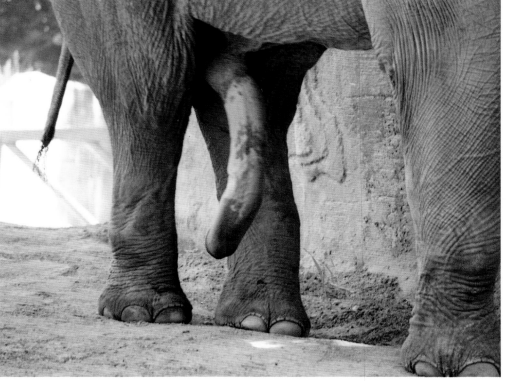

## Vision no more than moderate

The eye shown here has a peculiar feature found in some elephants, an opalescent white ring encircling the iris. Dr. E. Schäfer of the Institut für Pathologie der Gesellschaft für Strahlen- und Umweltforschung in Munich made a microscopic study of the structure, and established that this is similar to the age-ring (arcus lipoides) which sometimes appears in humans as they age. It does not affect the ability to see.

The elephant's eyes, small as they may appear in comparison to its body size, have the astonishingly large diameter of 1¹\2 inches, gazing out in a benign, almost melancholy way from beneath their long, bushy eyebrows from a face with an ancient history. They can be highly expressive of emotion; of fear and boredom, mockery, envy and determination for the fight. Yet the eye of the elephant never has the look of one observing; it is the trunk which seems to take in all the information as it twists and turns, rather than the eye.

The elephant's sense of vision is developed only to a moderate degree; recent tests put it in the same range as that of the horse. The elephant moves through savannah and bush with eyes half-closed, heads for a tree and reaches into the branches with precision, orientating itself with the aid of its trunk, not by sight. Men carrying out culls in wildlife reserves have even come across blind leaders of the herd whose ability to fulfil their role is apparently unimpaired. On an elephant's nocturnal travels, vision is of little use.

The animals' weak eyesight makes it possible to observe herds from nearby, paying due attention to the wind direction. Operating at close range, the elephant has an angle of vision which extends some way to the rear, because the eyes are situated on the side of the head. One remarkable anatomical detail is that the elephant has a 'third eyelid' as well as an upper and a lower one, a membrane which closes sideways across the eye. Another feature is the opalescent white ring encircling the iris.

The gentle, melancholy eyes behind the elephant's long eyelashes are of limited help, especially at night. It mainly uses the trunk for orientation, pointing it in the direction it is going and taking in information which the eye does not see.

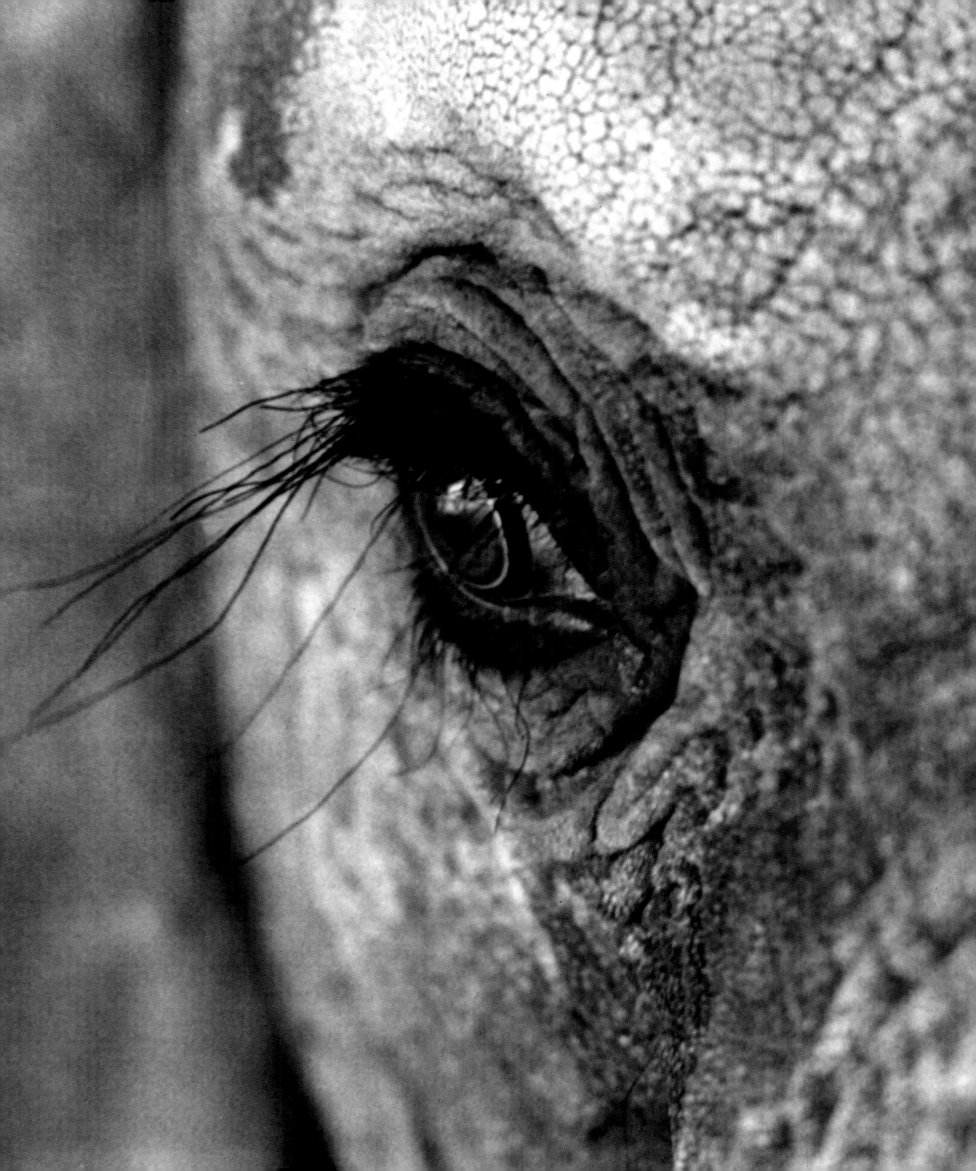

# The elephant in the wild

Elephants are herd animals. In the wild, they lead a remarkably harmonious and cohesive migratory life, with a stable social order of family and extended family groups unmatched in the world of mammals. Matriarchal authority is exercised by experienced mother elephants who lead,

protect and train the young. The herds on the open savannahs of East Africa offer the best insight into the rhythm of elephant life. There, the cycle of vegetation and the pattern of rainy and dry seasons force the elephants to undertake great, annual migrations. Their cousins in the jungles and rain forests of Asia and the African forest elephants lead their lives in similar family groups out of sight behind the barrier of green foliage which provides protection and privacy.

## The elephant matriarchy

Elephant life in the herd is governed by a matriarch; in family and clan, all authority is vested in experienced mother elephants who demand respect and are acknowledged as the herd leaders. They alone protect and lead the growing calves; they maintain order and harmony in the group; they face the foe with courage and aggression when danger threatens. The large, proud bulls also play a role in providing security, but they are not inclined to family life. They go their own way for long periods, traveling with bands of other males. They join the female groups only occasionally, at

mating times. The core group in elephant herds is the family unit, which consists of two or three older females with their offspring; this group remains together and maintains its cohesion even in larger migratory herds. The role of each cow is clearly defined, from the leader to the rear guard.

Family groups usually number up to twenty or thirty animals of different ages. The leaders are usually sisters, who retain their association for life, though other, unrelated cows can join the group if a friendly understanding is achieved. Forming family groups provides greater security for the herd.

White egrets rid the elephants of tormenting parasites. Long-term observations by the zoologist Cynthia Moss in Amboseli show an elephant population of fifty families living in the park in 1990, each numbering on average fourteen animals.

## Periodic migrations along traditional routes

A herd of elephants crossing the
Linyanti swamp.
Okavango Delta, Botswana

Each year at the beginning of the dry season, roughly between June and November, the elephant herds leave their grazing grounds on the drying savannahs, following the same migration routes, for more hospitable locations near rivers and water sources which do not dry up completely.

The family groups then separate off from the larger herd. Limited food supplies in these dry-season retreats mean that they can cope better alone, as a smaller group. One cow vigilantly leads at the front of the moving group, another follows to guard the rear. Roles are reversed if sudden withdrawal is called for. The young remain between them, under protection and supervision. If the group contains a third mother elephant, her role in the hierarchy will be to keep order among the playful youngsters.

Individual cows may travel with their calves, but individualism is not in their nature; it makes supervision and security more difficult amid the

dangers of the wild. Cows grazing alone with their calves are particularly shy and suspicious, and this can easily transmit itself to the young elephants.

Often, between two and five family units, usually related, join to form larger 'bond groups.' The cows share the leadership and supervisory responsibilities according to age, experience and temperament. Since the bond group offers more security, the leaders allow greater freedom to the adolescent bulls. These travel ahead of the herd or alongside, which gives them the opportunity of practice ready for independence in the wild. Traveling bond groups may be accompanied by bands of males, though these usually graze apart.

When, with the arrival of the rainy season from October to December and March to June, the dried-up savannahs once more become green and lush, the elephant herds return to their old grazing grounds. At this time, the bands of males and solitary old bulls join the female clans, to create

The wetland and savannah in the north of Botswana and neighboring Zimbabwe is an ideal habitat for elephants, though it too is already under threat. In this region the animals can continue to live the life of migration which is characteristic of the species and allows enough time for natural regeneration of areas exhausted by constant grazing.

herds of a few hundred animals. For them, this is the time of competion for the favor of the females.

Sometimes, entire populations of elephants may join together in mass migration. A procession of 500 huge savannah elephants is a spectacular sight (see following double-page spread) stamping out their great trail across the savannah as if the elemental power of a whirlwind had swept through the area.

The elephants' regular migrations allow time for regeneration of areas exhausted by grazing. The commercial herds of cattle, constantly increasing in size and the practice of keeping them in fixed locations, make unvarying demands on and overstretch the resources of the finely-balanced, sparse savannahs. This is a serious environmental problem for African countries.

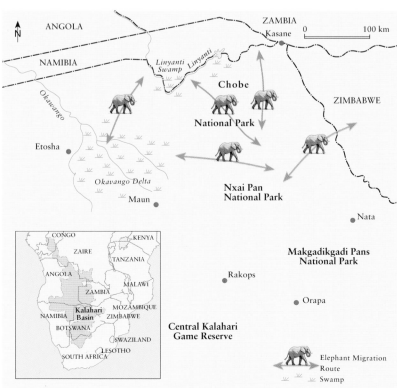

It was this robust capacity to eat anything which enabled its forebears to establish themselves in such a variety of habitats. The gray giant also drinks up to about 40 gallons of water a day.

Times of rest are amazingly short. Elephants doze for no more than around four hours a day standing under trees, usually in the searing midday heat. Late in the night, they lie down to sleep on their sides for just two or three hours, breathing noisily and often lapsing into a comfortable snore. With the dawn, they are up, their enormous digestive systems shake themselves rapidly into wakefulness, and the herd moves off into the new day, grazing as it goes.

## Salines and salt licks

Pools of water enriched with minerals are especially sought-after, and elephants' trunks are highly sensitive in locating these. Plains grass does not provide all the trace elements the animals require, so elephant herds regularly visit sites where they have found salt-containing earth. They churn up the ground with their tusks, and put the dislodged pieces of soil into their mouths with their trunks. In some places, holes several feet deep can be hollowed out in this way. This is how elephants open up salt licks, and make vital minerals accessible to other animals.

In Kenya's Mount Elgon National Park, elephants have for centuries been going to the lava caves of the mountain, a volcano on the Ugandan border, to obtain salts and minerals, and in the course of time they have hollowed out deep caverns in the mountainside. In Asia, southern India and Sumatra, too, elephants in search of salt have carved up whole hills.

This young bull is on its knees to dig deeper for ground water. Steep slopes are also negotiated on the knees, sliding with forelegs outstretched.

## Incessant foraging

It takes a long time to consume 330–375lb of forage, so elephants spend up to 18 hours daily grazing and resting between feeding sessions.

The daily life of the elephant is spent in a constant round of feeding. It takes time to fill the stomach of a fully-grown adult with the 330–375 pounds of vegetation it needs each day, and elephants spend some sixteen to eighteen hours grazing, ambling as they graze and walking for short distances between grazing sessions. Feeding even continues for half the night in an effort to fill the cavernous stomachs of the herd.

The elephant does not specialize in its choice of food plants, as do some species of mammal which are quite choosy; elephants even eat what buffalo or gazelle disdain. They will take grass and small plants, bushes, dry ripe plains grass, fruit, twigs, tree bark, and roots. Of course the giant creatures have their preferences; they can locate ripe fruit from a fair distance. If the food they prefer becomes scarce in times of drought, however, they change their feeding habits without apparent concern or harm to their digestive system.

The savannah elephants use their tusks and trunk to obtain vital minerals or ground water. Tarangire National Park, Tanzania

A savannah elephant drinks up to 40 gallons a day.

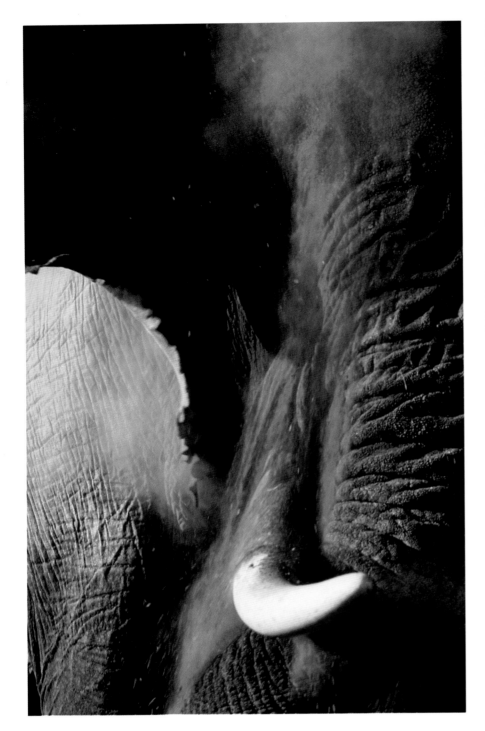

## Bathing: the elephants' greatest delight

Elephants delight in bathing. After the herd has been ambling and grazing for hours on end in the heat of the sun, the animals' steps quicken as they sense with their trunks the nearness of the water, be it river, lake or pool, which is their goal. The mighty animals are tempted on in even as they drink. Snorting, they fling the great weight of their bodies into the water, wallowing as the young splash and play.

Bathing plays an essential role for elephants in the care of their bodies. Their wrinkled, furrowed skin is by no means as coarse, protective and insensitive as it may look. When parasites bite or pierce their skin, the blood oozes. After bathing, the elephants wallow in the mud or spray their wet skin with dust, which dries to a crust and helps provide a remedy for the insect plague. They then rub the afflicted parts of their skin against a rock or tree, and a fair number of the blood-suckers can be scraped off with the mud crust.

Birds such as oxpeckers are a welcome help to the elephants. They remove and eat ticks from the folds of the animals' skin and around their eyes. Rhinoceros wallow in the mud in a very similar way, and terrapins˙ sometimes help rid them of similar parasites while the hosts lie dozing in muddy puddles. Perhaps elephants in wallows enjoy the help of similar assistants.

The sparse savannahs of East Africa cannot always offer the daily bath which elephants find so necessary. They often have to content themselves with digging out a waterhole with their tusks and front legs in order to quench their thirst.

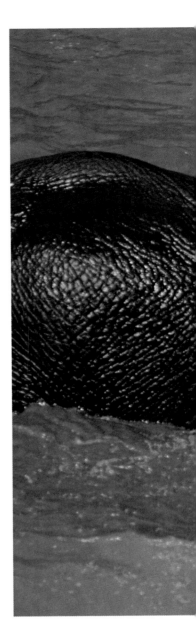

Elephant calves play in the water like children.

Pleasurable and essential: a showering of dust after bathing.

Any pool en route is a good place to pause for a good splash and playful cosmetic treatment in the cooling mud.

For elephants, bathing is followed by showering with dust to protect themselves against bloodsucking pests. Their skin is sensitive, and can bleed even when bitten by mosquitoes and other pests. Namibia

# The males' trials of strength

Although the adult bulls join the female herds only at mating times, their function is by no means only to engender offspring. Their size and strength as well as the superior, huge tusks with which they are armed make them a force to be reckoned with as guardians of traditional grazing territory and of herds on the move. They are on hand to cover the retreat or to protect a fellow member of the species in distress. They lead a quiet and exclusive life in the company of other males, aloof from the noise of the nursery, and have no wish to be disturbed. The females, knowing this, keep a cautious distance. If a youngster's attempts to play irritate a grumpy giant of a bull, the over-playful calf may end up with a box on the ears.

A strict hierarchical order operates within the male bands, which is repeatedly re-established and re-adjusted by trials of strength whenever a strange bull joins the group. The composition of the male band varies, unlike that of the female groups, which associate for life. The trials of strength are almost always carried out with moderation and without bloodshed; young bulls' head-butting sessions are early experiments.

Once a rival bull has been pushed to defeat in a duel and turns away, the victor usually only pursues him for a couple of paces. Bulls which are obviously weaker and less virile frequently refuse to duel, making gestures of submission. Bowing their heads and flattening their ears, they place their trunks in the mouth or under the chin of the superior bull. A confident, higher-ranking bull shows his superiority by proudly carrying his head high, his ears spread in warning and his trunk relaxed or reaching victoriously for the temporal gland of the subordinate animal.

In cramped habitats, where natural regeneration is no longer possible because of overgrazing, tree-fellers can cause serious damage to the vegetation. Frequently, one or two bulls in a herd specialize in this and develop it to a fine art.

Now and again, it does happen that two hostile bulls rush at each other in a furious fight to the death. The unfortunate beast which turns away first, leaving its unprotected body vulnerable for a moment to the other's cruel tusks, pays the ultimate price of an agonizing death.

Male bands, too, have herd leaders which walk on ahead and which guard the rear. It is not only brute strength or the dignity of age which earns them this rank; younger bulls can distinguish themselves by their self-confidence, courage and judicious behavior. The quiet-natured, peaceable bulls do not seek leadership rank, and provide a stabilizing element in the group, whose order can sometimes be threatened by obstinate and aggressive individuals. Less sociable animals prefer to go and lead a solitary existence.

Young, strong bulls love to try their strength at pushing over trees. Small trees of up to about 18 inches circumference can be felled by any head, trunk or foreleg, but only one or two bulls in a group seem to make tree-felling their specialty.

They perfect it to a fine art. With skill, a tree-feller can bring down trees with a circumference of maybe as much as 5ft. First of all, he pushes at the tree from different directions, testing it. Then, under the pressure of some hefty blows, he sets the tree swaying until it falls with a crash. His companions immediately come rushing up to feast on the succulent foliage and twigs which they love, as the warrior looks on unperturbed, his work completed. Bark-strippers can also do a great deal of damage in the small woods and clumps of trees of the savannahs. They carve into the trunk with a tusk, then tear off long strips with their trunks and chew them with their mighty molars. The bark is a favorite food and contains calcium and roughage, important for good digestion. Young animals quite often tear off bark for fun. In Asia, where the females have no tusks, bulls frequently perform the gentlemanly task of peeling the bark for them.

The hierarchy in the bands of males is constantly re-established by trials of strength, which are usually controlled contests without bloodshed. When one rival is forced to concede, the victor does not normally pursue him more than a few paces. Amboseli National Park, Kenya

The elephant in the wild

## Rogues and other loners

In the wild, there are many instances of solitary elephants, and these can be dangerous individuals. The lone elephants are usually old bulls which have had to leave their traditional territory after losing a leadership contest against a younger, stronger rival. Alternatively, they may be awkward-natured animals which failed to fit in with the herd and were driven out.

Bulls which have been seriously injured by a badly-aimed bullet from a hunter or poacher are particularly dangerous. They conceal themselves under cover, masters of disguise, and strike without warning. These are the much-feared 'rogues.'

However, there are also peaceable, solitary philosophers among the lone elephants, who simply enjoy being alone and prefer solitude. Not all bulls are fighting for rank and dominance.

Suspicious, testing its surroundings, ears spread wide, a lone elephant stamps his way through a desolated and overgrazed patch of woodland. Okavango Delta, Botswana

# Nuptials in the wild: elephant mating

Elephants do not go about mating pell-mell with brutish, wild abandon. Their courtship is one of affectionate companionship with its joys and games; what we might think of as a romantic engagement leading up to marriage. Asian elephants in particular seem to love with a special depth of affection.

Bull and cow elephants begin to form individual attachments before the cow comes into season, which usually happens for Asian elephants between December and February. They appear inseparable, and stand a little apart from the herd. During the pauses between times of walking and grazing, they lose themselves in loving playfulness, stroking each other with their trunks, giving each other a teasing nudge, or entwining their trunks, head to head as if in a primeval kiss.

Bull elephants are considerate and tender lovers. Rivalries between competing bulls in the wild are

Females are in heat for three weeks, but are capable of conceiving for only 3–5 days of that time. As the hormones begin to course through her body, the cow elephant becomes an accomplished vamp among animals, purposefully alternating between the taunt of half-refusal and seductive enticement. The preliminaries can last some time, leading with extraordinary suddenness to mating.

The zoologist Cynthia Moss, who spent some years observing the elephant population in Amboseli National Park, Kenya, witnessed an elephant mating in the open. She described how the bull leant his chin on the rear of the cow, then heaved himself onto his hind legs and placed his front legs on her shoulders. His penis is some 4 feet long, and is equipped with muscles enabling him to direct it. It had already assumed an S-shape. He placed the tip of his penis into her vagina, and penetration happened deeply and in one swift moment. Cynthia Moss goes on to say that Odette (the cow elephant) held quite still, and that they saw no visible movement from her for the 45 seconds until he dismounted. The excitement all happened afterwards. They heard her utter deep, pulsating noises, and her family rushed up to see the mating spectacle. They made a great deal of noise screaming and trumpeting, rumbling and roaring. The report continues that the elephants stretched out their trunks towards Odette's mouth and her vulva, and towards the fluids on the ground. While they were doing this, Odette turned round and touched Patrick's (the bull elephant's) penis with her trunk.

The sexual act is repeated a few more times away from the herd; cow elephants continue to accept bulls for an extended period of time. It may not always be the same lover that the cow accepts; there is no life-long bond between elephant pairs, as happens between some other animals.

The bull tests the cow's urine with his trunk, blowing the scent into his mouth, where a gland responds to the hormone content and establishes his partner's reproductive status.
Amboseli National Park, Kenya

normally settled forehead to forehead in a trial of strength, and the loser who is forced to retreat or bow his head quickly leaves the field. Ranking order in elephant herds is in any case established in an atmosphere of general harmony according to strength, temperament and leadership qualities. It is only occasionally that a brutal struggle for dominance and even to the death occurs, caused for example by the arrival of a strange, equally strong bull in the herd, challenging as a rival suitor. That is when the mighty giants clash, pitting their many tons, their tusks and trunks against each other, their flailing legs turned to dangerous weapons. The female for whom they are competing usually awaits the outcome of the contest grazing unconcernedly nearby, whereupon she grants her favors to the victor. She seems to have no interest in which of the two bulls is finally victorious.

The bull follows the cow in the excitement of alternating enticement and refusal.

The elephant in the wild

The herd shares in the moment of
consummation – life experience
for the younger generation.
Amboseli National Park, Kenya

# Birth

Finally the time of lovemaking is over, and the pregnant cow elephants return to grazing in their female herds, self-sufficient again. The bulls resume their traveling life along with the bands of males.

The length of pregnancy for a cow elephant is from 20–22 months. As the time of the birth approaches, she seeks the close companionship of a fellow female who remains with her to protect her once labor begins. Rangers report that in African savannah elephants, the herd sometimes forms a circle around the female giving birth to guard her from all sides, trumpeting and snorting.

The elephant gives birth standing, and the birth itself takes just a few minutes, accompanied by a great panting. The 'aunt' stands protectively behind the mother giving birth. The calf is usually born head and forelegs first, and after only a few minutes, it is able to stand up, assisted and supported by its mother and aunt, on still rather shaky diminutive elephant legs.

The afterbirth is often consumed by the mother, to avoid attracting predators; all signs are carefully removed. In the forests of Asia, one fifth of the helpless babies fall victim to tigers. In Africa, packs of hyenas lie in wait. Lions normally attack elephant calves only if there is no other prey to be had.

A newly-born elephant calf stands about 3 feet high, with quite thick body hair and weighing about 220 pounds. Its trunk is still short; the calf cannot yet use it and so drinks with its mouth. Soon after birth, it seeks out its mother's teats. She has two, between her front legs. Two days after it is born, the calf is strong enough to join the herd, which has meanwhile been waiting nearby. Twins have been known, but are rare.

Baby elephants live on their mothers' milk alone for the first 6 months. It is very high in fat, and the protein content is 100 times higher than that of cow's milk. They drink around 21 pints a day. The special composition of elephant milk meant that, for a long time, it was seldom possible to keep orphaned calves alive, but eventually a mixture was arrived at which was easily digestible and contained all the necessary nutrients for daily requirements: 9 1/2 pints raw cow's milk, 9 1/2 fl oz cream, the white of 24 hen's eggs and 4 pounds of well-boiled rice water. An Asian legend tells of another life-saving diet:

There was a wondrously white elephant calf, which was revered as holy. This calf had lost its mother and had already become too weak to stand. It was brought to the king of Burma, and the king was most concerned. He ordered twenty-four young women to be brought to the palace as wet-nurses. All was done as he commanded, and behold, the elephant calf thrived at the women's breasts, where he was suckled for five years, as the story tells us ...

In the wild, elephants almost always give birth at night. Here, we see the stages of a birth which, unusually, took place in the daytime in the African savannah.

First to emerge from the birth canal are the forelegs ...

The entire calf follows a few seconds later, still enveloped in the membrane of the amniotic sac, which protects it as it falls to the hard ground.

The mother elephant uses her trunk and forefoot to begin freeing the calf from within the amniotic sac.

The members of the family hurry to the scene, to join in helping to free the calf from the membranes and assist it to stand.

The drama of birth in the savannah: this newborn calf did not survive. The mother devotedly carries the dead calf away from the scene of the tragedy and keeps it with her for a short while.

If anything befalls the mother of a calf which is still being suckled, other cow elephants with nursing calves will frequently, though not always, adopt the youngster. In the wild, an orphaned calf (which will trot after anyone, even a human, like a puppy) that does not find an adoptive mother to look after it becomes easy prey for tigers, hyenas, lions and other predators.

Between their fourth and sixth months of life, the young elephants begin to use their fast-developing trunks, which are beginning to be a hindrance when suckling, to pick grass and leaves and feed these into their mouths. Gradual weaning follows. A female elephant is able to become pregnant again about a year after giving birth, so she may bring up to twelve calves into the world during her lifetime.

# The nursery

In the matriarchal family unit it is not simply sacrificial mother-love which surrounds the tiny calves. Young at various stages of maturity enjoy the care of the whole herd. There is a touching and harmonious cooperation on the part of mothers, aunts and sisters which continues for years to ensure the protection and training of the young, and their preparation for the hard struggle for existence ahead.

Still helpless, the suckling calf remains under the constant care of its mother, who supports, leads and caresses it with her trunk. She is there when her calf needs a push to help it down a steep embankment, she urges the youngster to overcome its fear of water and bathe, she showers it with water and dust, and she assists it across rivers where the current is flowing too strongly for it.

The mother shows endless patience when the calf becomes exhaustingly playful and curious, pushes its way under her tall legs and disturbs her peace with its unruly young trunk. The leader of the female herd adjusts the pace so that every animal in it can keep up. The calves learn from the cows which plants are good to eat, and to be aware of possible dangers. As the young become old enough to be rebellious, play too wildly and venture too far from the herd in their curiosity – which can all too easily lead to disaster – a corrective slap from an adult trunk comes on cue.

Up to the age of about 8 years, the onset of sexual maturity, young bulls too remain in the family group, under the supervision and leadership of the adult females; only at that stage are they urged towards independence and driven away. They often continue for a while to stay near the herd which afforded them such protection. Then they join a passing band of males, and go their own way from this point on.

Young bulls still in the family groups are hard to distinguish from the adult females; by the age of five, they are as tall as 15 to 20-year-old cows, with tusks of similar length.

The mother elephant uses her trunk to maintain protective and affectionate contact with the helpless suckling calf. An aunt stands by, too, to assist.

As the herd moves on, the mother's trunk is still there to guide and protect. The family group always matches its pace to the youngest, so that every member can keep up (see also following double-page spread).

The young calf relies on its mother's milk for two years, while it is still unskilled at using its trunk. A great deal of practice is needed before it can pick and bundle up grass and plants, and put them into its mouth.

The calves learn from their mothers and aunts which plants are edible. Mother's trunk is always at hand to direct.
All photographs:
Amboseli National Park, Kenya

# Mighty, but not proof against disease

Elephants in the wild enjoy robust health, but even they are not proof against disease. They can suffer and die from a range of ills, and there is an extensive literature dealing with ways of treating them. As long ago as the days of ancient India there existed a host of writings on the treatment of elephant disorders. Looking beyond this or that quack method, we find that the ancient Hindu people had a good knowledge of natural remedies. The invocation of gods and demons accompanied the practical cures and treatments, in accordance with their world-view.

The most frequently fatal disease affecting elephants is anthrax, which repeatedly kills hundreds of animals. A rod-shaped bacillus, it enters the circulation and causes high fever, shivering, blood-containing discharge from the bladder, stomach and intestines, ulcers and swellings. The disease causes horrifyingly intense suffering and is almost always fatal. It has wiped out entire elephant families and their kin.

There are illnesses specific to elephants, such as paralysis of the trunk and elephant pox, especially feared in zoo elephant houses. Pustules form in the mouth, on the trunk and on the thighs, pus and patches of decay appear between the toes; even the sole of the foot can break away. Without urgent help, death is likely.

Elephants in the wild are also at risk from foot and mouth disease and a number of tropical diseases spread by mosquitoes. They are also liable to several disorders which affect human beings, including intestinal colic, nettle rash, and pneumonia, and complaints such as constipation and even the common cold.

For those animals which fall ill in captivity, today's pharmaceutical industry does have remedies available. Once an elephant recognizes that someone is trying to help, it will endure treatment patiently, even painful procedures like lancing an abscess. The treatment must be carried out quickly, though, so that the elephant does not become fearful.

In the wild, instinct makes the animals take the right course of action in response to injury or the pain of disease. Elephants suffering from digestive disorders may fast, or fill their stomachs with plant remedies, bitter herbs and bark, or alkaline earth. They bathe wounds thoroughly and smear them with mud, which keeps away flies and limits infestation by worms, and if suffering the pain of an abscess on a tusk, an elephant will often strike the tusk against a tree and lever at it for hours until the tooth comes out. There are many examples of different ways in which elephants heal themselves with remedies passed on from one generation to the next.

An elephant encounters the bones of one of its kind, pauses as if in silent respect, and feels the skull with its trunk. Sometimes, elephants carry a bone or tusk around with them for a while.

The dead giant – in the world of nature, nothing is wasted, and the body becomes food for other forms of life: for vultures and hyenas, the health patrol of the savannah.

The calf has collapsed on the sun-baked savannah, and mother and 'aunt' try to lift it back onto its feet and out of danger.

Ahmed, once a mighty bull elephant in Kenya's Marsabit National Park, is now old and weary. Approaching journey's end, he seeks refreshment and the cool of the water ... Ahmed died in 1974 at the age of 55 years.

105

## An elephant is no Methuselah

An old female has separated from the herd, weary of life. The others pause and turn, and wait a while in concern.

Towards the end of the 19th century it was still thought in Europe that the elephant possessed a vigor in keeping with its primeval size and strength, and reached a phenomenal age, 100 years or more. But the life span given to the elephant is not one to place it in a class with the biblical forefather Methuselah, who reached the astonishing age of 969 years, according to the book of Genesis.

An elephant is old at 60 years, and easily recognizable by its wrinkled skin and the leanness of its head, sunken around the temples and eyes. Most die considerably earlier, although especially vigorous animals can occasionally live to 70 or 80 years of age.

The life span of any creature depends on the environmental conditions in which it lives. For the elephants of today, habitats in the wild are shrinking and becoming poorer. The outlook is still more dismal for animals in captivity, under the stress of circus life, and in the mental misery of confined quarters.

The idea comes across in an Indian song of praise to the elephant: The greatest joy of the elephant is the freedom from restrictions ... Whatever his heart tells him, the elephant will do; his food he chooses freely, his home is where he wills ... Fulfilment of his wishes blossoms into joy for him, and irresistibly from joy comes strength. In fullness of joy the fires of life glow bright. The consequence of harmony of the materials of his body is that illnesses have no power ... The whole is thrown into reverse the moment the elephants of the wild are brought to the dwelling-places of those known as humanity ...

Old elephants or those which are mortally ill usually die alone, away from the herd, having left to seek solitude in their weakness. When, however, an old, gray giant which has lost its last molar teeth succumbs to injury, illness or the weakness of age within the herd, its companions surround it with touching concern. Indian observers and rangers in Africa have often seen the herd pause a while

From top to bottom, left to right, the sequence of illustrations shows: The other females hurry to the scene to assist their companion. The others try to urge her on. The ailing female collapses. The herd remain standing silently for a while by their dead companion, in mute mourning. The herd has taken its farewell, and continues on its way. The life of the elephants goes on.

around their unfortunate fellow elephant, then try to help the animal to stand if there is still breath, and lay their trunks gently across the body as death finally takes hold.

Whenever in their noisy travels elephants come across skeletons of their kind, they pause in sudden silence, touch the remains with their trunks, and sometimes carry tusks or bones with them for a while as they journey on.

Tales of elephant graveyards, where old and weak or fatally injured animals withdraw to die in dignity, undisturbed and unobserved by humans, are no more than stories. The places are said to be inaccessible, secluded marshes where the huge, lifeless bodies disappear without trace. To prevent the collection of bones from being salvaged and desecrated by poachers, the saying goes, the herd guards over it, and anyone who tries to reach the graveyards risks his life ...

The fact is, the elephant dies wherever on its journeyings fate overtakes it.

# The elephant in the ancient world

The taming of the elephant was first achieved in the valley of the river Indus, where around 3500 BC the first highly advanced Oriental civilization began to emerge. Some doubt surrounds the question of how this came about, and whether those who first tried and carried out the taming of captured young elephants were settled farmers or forest hunting peoples. At that time, humans and animals lived in close

*Elephant with rider,*
India, c. birth of Christ,
Mathura stone.
32cm x 10cm x 30cm
Russek Collection, Switzerland

partnership, and the creatures had their place in the natural religions and fertility cults, honored as sacred beings and mystical symbols. As far back as 10,000 years ago and earlier, the move from hunting to agriculture and the keeping of domesticated animals, a revolutionary step in the development of civilization, had taken place in the Near East. These achievements, along with the increase in food production, also led to a tremendous rise in world population. Great cities arose as centers of flourishing advanced cultures. On the Nile and the Euphrates, the Indus and China's Yellow River, the elephant acquired a special role in everyday life and religious cult. The gray giant was tamed, trained, but not domesticated. It did not become subject to selective breeding by humans; not a domesticated creature. It remained a wild animal, even in captivity. The numbers of tame animals were maintained by the capture of young wild elephants, even into our own times.

Opposite:
Outline by La'l, painting by Sanhwala
Illustration to the *Akbarnama* (detail), Akbar inspecting a wild elephant captured near Malwa in 1564,
Mughal India, c. 1590,
Gouache on paper.
Victoria and Albert Museum, London, IS 2:39-1896

# The Mohenjo-Daro elephant seals

The oldest depictions of tame elephants date from the 3rd millennium BC. They are small seals, found during excavations in the valley of the river Indus in today's Pakistan. Here, an early advanced urban civilization grew from agricultural beginnings, with Mohenjo-Daro and Harappa as its centers. This was the period of the first Sumerian-Babylonian empires in Mesopotamia, from which, as trade flourished, spread the use of seals to indicate ownership and endorse business agreements throughout the Asia Minor region.

The seals found in the impressive ruined city of Mohenjo-Daro are mostly carved in soft steatite, and amongst the various animal symbols depicted, elephants often recur, some of them at feeding troughs. There is one particularly interesting find which depicts a very finely and realistically-carved Asian elephant with a saddle-blanket on its back and an undeciphered inscription above it, made up of a series of pictographic symbols.

As evidence of the art of taming or keeping elephants in compounds, which must surely already have been perfected, these seals cannot be ignored. In Harappa to the northeast, elephant statuettes following the pattern of the seals were found. The gray giant also seems to have entered the mythical world of animistic cults. In Mohenjo-Daro, a seal was found with a matrix depicting a mysterious composite creature. Its body is made up of a tiger at the rear and a bull at the front, with the head and trunk of an elephant. The significance of the creature is not known at present.

The extensive site of the Mohenjo-Daro ruins bears witness to an exceptionally advanced stage of urban development, of unknown ethnic origin. The two-story houses of fired brick belonging to prosperous merchants already had drainage, brickwork floors, and often baths as well. The city was divided by a right-angled grid system of streets, and there is a noticeable absence of temples and palace grounds, which characterize the cities of Mesopotamia. There were simply granaries and a large public bath.

The production of cotton cloth had already been mastered on the Indus, set weights and measures were used, and there was a system of writing using pictographs, to date undeciphered. The remarkable comfort in which people lived suggests that there was a large upper class of merchants, pursuing an active trade with the regions of the Persian Gulf, especially the cities of southern Mesopotamia, where Mohenjo-Daro seals have been found. A slave economy prevailed here, providing a high level of comfort in the lifestyles of the rich.

At the beginning of the 2nd millennium BC, decline set in. The great cities, which had stood for centuries, were deserted. Why this came about is unknown; we cannot say whether the exodus was the result of natural disasters, drought or hostile invasion. The center of economic and cultural development on the Indian subcontinent shifted to the Ganges river basin, where the first great cities and kingdoms arose around 500 BC. There is still a great deal we can learn from the study of the remains of these once great cities.

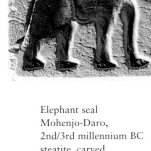

Elephant seal
Mohenjo-Daro,
2nd/3rd millennium BC
steatite, carved.
approx. 2.5cm x 2.6cm
Pakistani National Museum,
Karachi

Elephant with saddle-blanket carved into steatite seal matrix. A precious archeological exhibit from Mohenjo-Daro, a center of the early great civilization in the Indus valley.

The ruins of Mohenjo-Daro. This aerial photograph clearly shows the grid layout of the city, unusual for its time.

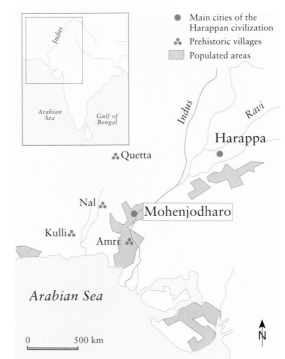

● Main cities of the Harappan civilization
⁂ Prehistoric villages
▨ Populated areas

Mohenjo-Daro and Harappa, two centers of the urban culture which developed around the Indus (modern-day Pakistan) in the 3rd millennium BC. They carried on trade with the first Sumerian-Babylonian empires in Mesopotamia.

# The white elephant of the thunder god Indra

The Aryan pastoralist warriors who conquered northern India around 1800 BC gave precedence to the horse over the elephant during the early period of their dominance. Their thunder god Indra, flinging bolts of lightning, his blond hair flying, stormed through the heavens like a military commander, driving a golden war-chariot pulled by horses. Later they were to adopt the mighty elephant of this new land, and incorporate it into their myths and legends.

By the time the Aryan warrior tribes arrived in northern India, the Indus valley civilization had already collapsed, although isolated permanently-built settlements may have continued to exist. The oldest written record, the Rig-veda, which came into being around 1200 BC, says of the victorious progress of the Aryans and their thunder god Indra: "With the all-conquering chariot-wheel you, O Indra / World-renowned, have overthrown the twice ten rulers of men. / With sixty thousand and ninety-nine companions / you stride from battle to battle without trembling. / You destroy fortress after fortress, here, full of power ..."

The Vedas, subdivided into four groups, are based on oral tradition and consist of hymns of praise, instructions for priestly rituals of sacrifice and magical spells, which provide certain insights into the life of the people during those centuries. In the canonical works of the Aryan priests, the Brahmans, mention is also made of the elephant.

The tall, fair-skinned conquerors, characterized by a long face-shape, arrived from the broad steppes of Turkestan with their horses, war-chariots and gods. They were a subgroup of the great Indo-European family of peoples whose original home is thought to be central Asia or southern Russia. In a series of migrations in successive bursts over a period of centuries, they spread in all directions to occupy the territories in which we find their historical successors: Indian and Persian, Greek and Roman, the Celts, and the Germanic and Slavic peoples.

The conquerors advanced along the Indus and Ganges river systems. The dark-skinned peoples whom they found there were disdainfully called by them 'Black' (Dasyu) or 'Noseless' (Anasah). Everywhere they encountered elephants, and learned the practicalities of taming them. Thus the emerging Aryan kingdoms were able to bring war elephants onto the battlefield against their rivals at an early date, alongside the noble warriors in double-harnessed chariots.

There is a lack of transmitted records about events in these dark centuries. The ancient Indian people had no Herodotus, and it was not the custom to write down history. Religious writings in classical Sanskrit mention the elephant only incidentally,

saying that it is wild, but faithful to humanity, and that even the tiger in the jungle fears it.

The social structure of Indian society, the unmistakable 'face of India,' developed from the hard racial contrast between the light-skinned conquerors and the various dark-skinned ethnic groups of the ancient population.

The first four castes arose, sharply distinguished from one another by prescriptions for ritual purity and set in order of rank: the Aryan Brahmans (priests), the Aryan nobility (Kshatriyas), the merchants, traders and farmers (Vaisyas) and the lowest, despised pariahs (Sudras). The caste system, which has in the meantime acquired many subdivisions, creates a rigid immobility in the Indian social structure. Caste is determined irrevocably by birth.

Indian masters passed on the art of taming and training elephants to the neighboring peoples of the regions of Southeast Asia.

*Indra riding Airavata,*
Mogul period, 16th century, gouache on paper.
New Delhi Museum, India

Indra is shown in pictures as riding through the heavens on the white elephant Airavata, which has four tusks. Airavata arose in the earliest times of the cosmos from the ocean of milk out of which the gods churned their nectar of immortality. He is the ancestor of the elephant race.

# The elephant in Mesopotamia

*Clasped hands,*
Nimrud Northwest palace,
8th century BC,
ivory.
length 5cm
British Museum, London

The Assyrian rulers hunted the elephant, which was prized in particular for its ivory, a material in which there is early demonstration of Assyrian craftsmanship.

Between the Tigris and the Euphrates, the Sumerians developed a great civilization whose legacy, cuneiform writing, inspires admiration to this day. The Sumerians were certainly familiar with elephants, but we do not know whether they made use of them. Excavations in centers of Sumerian culture such as Kish or Ur uncovered figures of elephants with riders, but these more often bore inscriptions of a Harappan master, and so were evidence of the trade which existed between the two cultures in the 3rd millennium BC.

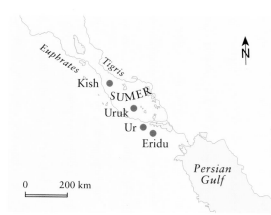

In early historical times the distribution of the Asian elephant extended from southern China to Syria, where it continued to exist in the wild until the 8th century BC. At that time, forests covered today's arid regions.

The elephant was known to the Sumerians, a creative people of unknown origin, as long ago as the end of the 4th millennium BC, the period when they developed a great civilization in southern and central Mesopotamia under the rulership of priests and princes. They also had a system of writing, called cuneiform writing. A temple economy and temple guardianship of stores held sway, under a powerful priesthood.

Among the excavation finds at former centers of Sumerian kingdoms such as Uruk, Ur and Kish, there is a terra cotta representation of an elephant with rider, dating from 2000 BC. It is not possible to deduce from this that elephants were tamed in Mesopotamia, since recorded evidence is lacking. It is possible that the figure is a product of the Indus culture which reached Mesopotamia through trade. The city of Ur in particular, which was then still a port on the Persian Gulf, carried on a lively trade with the early historical community on the Indus. Individual elephants, which still lived in the mountain forests to the north, were captured and kept in zoological gardens. However, the elephant did not play a large role in this culture.

For the later kings of Babylon, which was the dominant center of culture for the whole of the Near East from the 2nd millennium BC, and for the Assyrian rulers who dominated in the 8th and 7th centuries BC, the elephant was mainly highly prized as game. It was the ivory of the tusks which was so much desired; artists and craftsmen had early learned to make small sculptures and all manner of luxury decorative items from it. It is recorded that in 1100 BC, the Assyrian king Tiglath-pileser I killed mighty bull elephants.

We read further that "I captured four elephants alive," presumably for his zoological gardens. Elephants were also included in the booty of war brought home by the Assyrian king Shalmaneser III (858–824 BC) from a successful campaign in Syria. His triumphs and deeds of war are glorified on the 6¹\2 feet high Black Obelisk of Shalmaneser III, which can be seen today in the British Museum, London. Amongst the figures depicted on the five bands of reliefs is an elephant.

The art of taming and training elephants reached the peoples of the Near East and Mediterranean only after the overwhelming Indian campaign of Alexander the Great in the 4th century BC. The Indian mahouts (elephant keepers and riders) of the war elephants in his huge army brought the empire their expertise, which also passed to its successors, the Diadochi; in particular, the Seleucids in Syria and the Ptolemies in Egypt.

For the dynasties of the Diadochi, and after them, the Carthaginians, the elephant was above all a machine of war. A specific chapter is devoted to this stage in the unhappy history of the peaceable elephant. Many different cultures and military leaders put the gentle elephant to use in war, training it to perform tasks against its nature.

Opposite:
Detail from: *The black obelisk of Shalmaneser III* (858–824 BC),
Nimrud, c. 825 BC,
Diorite.
height 202cm
British Museum, London

The bands of reliefs which run around the obelisk each consist of four scenes, and recount the victorious Syrian campaigns of the Assyrian king. Above: an elephant is among the items of tribute paid by the conquered peoples.

# The 'abu' of the Pharaohs

Tribute scene from the tomb
of Rekhmire,
New Kingdom, 18th dynasty
c. 1450 BC,
wall painting.
Tomb of Rekhmire,
Western Thebes, Egypt

Of all the tombs of officials in
the Theban necropolis, the tomb
of Rekhmire is one of the largest.
He held the high office of vizier
for Thutmose III. One of his
official duties was to ensure that
the enormous tributes coming
into Egypt in the 18th dynasty
were paid correctly. An entire
wall section in his tomb is
devoted to this theme, showing
various foreign delegations
bearing taxes in the form of
goods typical of their countries.
The Nubian delegation can be
recognized as coming from the
south by their hair and
physiognomy, and their animal
skin loincloths. Some are carrying
elephant tusks on their shoulders,
others leading exotic animals
such as a leopard and a
hamadryas baboon.

The elephant was well-known in the kingdom of
the Pharaohs, although it played no role in
everyday life or in mythology. Even after the
foundation of the united state around 3100 BC,
and continuing well into the period of the Old
Kingdom, fairly small numbers of African
elephants are known to have lived in the Eastern
Desert area of Upper Egypt.

A deterioration in climate around the middle of
the 3rd millennium BC forced the elephants to
abandon this territory for the steppes of Nubia and
their sparse growth of trees. In the course of
history, they were forced further and further south,
so that by the time of the Ptolemies (3rd–1st
centuries BC), they were to be found either side of
the twentieth parallel, south of the equator.

In the Egyptian sphere of influence, a succession
of changing cultures with their own structures of
state developed on the upper course of the Nile.
Not until the time of the New Kingdom
(1550–1070 BC) did the Pharaohs achieve
complete control over the area of Nubia, placing it
under the control of an official, the Viceroy of
Nubia, who bore the title 'the King's Son for Kush.'
The name Kush came to be used synonymously
with Nubia from this time on. The Greeks and
Romans used the overall name Ethiopia (Greek
aithiopia) for this distant and mysterious land, as
for all lands south of the Pharaonic empire.

The kingdom of Kush was the hinterland which
above all supplied Egypt with gold, ivory and
ebony. Their military presence and the punitive
expeditions which were often necessary, also
ultimately served the purpose of securing the
economic position. The starting-point for Egypt's
Nubian expeditions was the fortified grounds of
Elephantine Island, in the Nile opposite today's
Aswan; this was for a long time the traditional
southern access route.

As early as the Sixth Dynasty (around 2230 BC)
the provincial governor of Elephantine, Herchuef,
headed southward with caravans several times. An
inscription in his tomb says that on his third
excursion, he reached the regions beyond the
Second Cataract, from where he brought back
incense, ivory and other goods.

Queen Hatshepsut (1479–1457 BC) sent ships
to the land of Punt, an area on the coast of the Red
Sea near modern-day Eritrea, to fetch incense and
ivory. The base inscription of the great obelisk of
the queen in the state temple of the god Amun-Re
deals with the handing over of tribute in the form
of 700 elephant teeth from Libya.

The successors of Hatshepsut received not only
ivory as a raw material, but also ready-made
furniture items with inlaid or applied ivory. Use of
this material was a luxury and reserved for rulers
and high officials. It was, therefore, one of the

important types of tomb objects, a fact underlined by finds among the tomb treasures of the Pharaoh Tutankhamun (c. 1330 BC).

The great Pharaoh Thutmose III (1457–1425 BC), under whom Egypt rose to become an empire in the Near East, hunted the elephant, as his grandfather Thutmose I had before him. There is a record of a hunt during a military campaign in Syria, where he and his followers killed 120 elephants "for their ivory." The king personally battled with the largest animal in the herd. A wall painting in the tomb of his vizier Rekhmire shows a Syrian elephant in a tribute scene.

There is a single Ancient Egyptian hieroglyph to represent the elephant, ivory, and the place-name Elephantine. It is 'abu.' To this was added the explanatory symbol of an elephant or a tusk. The Romans derived the Latin word 'ebur' from this, and from the Latin we have the French word 'ivoire' and the English 'ivory.'

Pharaoh Psamtik III was beaten at the battle of Pelusium, 525 BC, by the Persian King Cambyses, and dethroned. Egypt became a dependent province of the Persian Empire. Guignet's painting recalls an episode said to have occurred on the periphery of this historic event, recorded by the Greek historian Herodotus in Book Three of his Histories ('Thaleia'). The Egyptians had murdered Persian negotiators, and Cambyses decided to make an example. He had the daughters of noble Egyptians led past the Pharaoh, dressed as slaves, to fetch water. Then the sons of important Egyptians were driven past; they were to be killed. The Pharaoh is sitting in front of a pillory.

Ritual bronze,
Western Chou dynasty,
(1100-771BC),
bronze.
24cm x 28cm
City Museum, Baoji, China

The sacrificial vessel was found in 1974 in a double grave. Another nine were placed in simple coffins belonging to human sacrifices and buried alongside. The simple, humorous shape of the animal figure suggests that the artist had never seen an elephant. At the time of Western Chou China, elephants had already retreated south. Earlier elephant bronzes, from times when elephants did still exist in China, were more life-like executions.

## Elephants in ancient China

During the Bronze Age, elephants probably still lived in the forests by the Yellow River. The elephant seems to have been tamed occasionally and used as a work animal in the Shang dynasty (16th–11th centuries BC). The figure of the elephant appears in relief decorations on early ritual bronzes, and some well-proportioned three-dimensional representations from the Shang dynasty also exist.

Increasing population density drove the animals into regions south of the Yangtze-Kiang, inhabited by the Viets and other foreign peoples with whom the Chinese carried on an active exchange of goods. The elephant remained part of the everyday life of these peoples, and so it was familiar to the Chinese of the developing 'Middle Kingdom.'

All manner of elephant products reached the traditional territories of northern China by land and water, including the ivory much desired for craft work, which was also ground up and boiled in wine as a remedy for various ills; elephant skins, which were used to make arrow-proof battle armor, or were softened and used as healing bandages for wounds; and elephant meat. The trunk was considered a delicacy.

The Imperial Court had for some time had exclusive zoological gardens, reserved for the use of the ruler and the highest officials. Early historical references to zoological gardens date from the time around 1400 BC. Elephants must constantly have been showpieces of these animal collections.

Written Chinese had a character for 'elephant' at an early date; over the centuries, the original naturalistic image developed into the traditional character which stands for the elephant.

As the dynasties succeeded each other, the south was gradually infiltrated by Chinese traders and settlers, until it was finally incorporated into the Middle Kingdom, becoming effectively Chinese, under the Han dynasty (206 BC – AD 220). However, although the southern peoples, the Viets and the Thai tribes, were familiar with the taming of the elephant, it remained an exotic and unusual phenomenon in this China of peasants and administrators until Medieval times.

The Chinese character 'elephant,' an abstract development from an original pictorial form.

Elephant with pagoda, used as a censer.
5th–6th century,
bronze.

Ritual bronze with hooks and swirls,
late Shang period,
12th-11th century BC,
bronze.
Provincial Museum, Hunan,
China

Elephants still existed in central
China during this early period of
history, hence the realistic image.
As human population increased,
the animals began to retreat
southward beyond the
Yangtze-Kiang.

A carriage (possibly containing a
concubine) drawn by elephants as
part of an Imperial procession.
Painting on silk

# "Where there are elephants, there is victory ..."

Elephants were first used for military purposes in India. Their help was required when tribes turned to slaughter and life was at stake. To accustom the peaceable animals to the noise of battle, and to arouse their animal fury as the enemy army surged forward, they were subjected to a particularly brutal training. They were forced against their nature to trample people, to gore them with their tusks and to seize them with their trunks and finally kill them with a single blow.

Later, war elephants equipped with an armor consisting of fire-hardened leather coverings to protect them from arrows bore great baskets and boxes, in which sat archers, lance-throwers or men wielding slingshots. If a fortress was to be stormed, tall scaffolding was erected on their backs for scaling the walls. Their enormous strength was needed to tear down palisades and the enemy's defensive structures. There seems to be no end to the uses to which elephants were put in war.

Fragment of a war elephant,
1st century BC,
sandstone.
Great Stupa of Senehi, India

The war elephant is wearing a protective covering. Behind the mahout sits the archer. The sculpture is mounted above a gate through the enclosure of the Great Stupa of Senehi in central India.

Elephant corps were the pride of the kings. The ancient Indian manuals of the art of war praise the supreme value of the giants in battle. Their weaknesses on the battlefield were overlooked in the euphoric praise:

"The victory of the kings depends chiefly on the elephants. Huge and trained to kill, they trample to pieces battle-lines, armies, fortresses and camps of the enemy ...

"The rulers' kingdoms depend on the elephants, which, shimmering like dark clouds, dripping with the humors and odors of animal heat, break down walls with the blows of their tusks ..."

In the four divisions of the Indian battle-order – elephants, chariots, cavalry and infantry – the elephants are in the front line. Their onslaught in open battle is to "break up the closed ranks of the enemy army, and if the enemy is made to waver or flee by attack from the front, to unite with the cavalry in seizing them from behind." According to the war manuals, in mobile warfare the elephants also fulfil cavalry functions.

The speed of the elephants is also praised. The best male animals, it says with eager exaggeration, can achieve a top rate of march of 10 yojana (about 60 miles), middle-ranking ones about 7 and lesser ones, 5 yojana. The figure given for females is 4 to 7 yojana. The figure for a day's march of the entire army with baggage, war chest and the king's harem is given as only 1–2 yojana.

Elephants can also cope with ground which is difficult or impossible to tackle for horses. They are at home in the jungle, where they have to trample down thickets and force a way through. They can also cross swamps and watercourses more easily than horses, and are excellent climbers; they move intrepidly and with astonishing agility on dizzying mountain paths, in spite of their size.

In battle, elephants were considered to provide reliable backing for wavering armies, especially when they took up formation in a ring or 'pot', as the old manuals teach. Above all the book of elephant remedies sings the praises of war elephants and vividly extols their "magnificence" and "incomparability":

"Pitiless and powerful are the elephants as a sword; only they can at once protect, fight and carry at the head of the battle-lines ... an hero elephant in armor, glowing with strength and ridden by a warrior, can overcome 6,000 horses single-handed.

"They do not give up their lives easily; elephants have magnificent bodies. Man or horse will die from an ax-blow, but an elephant may survive a hundred ax-blows in battle. A warrior who abandons an elephant in battle treads the path to hell which lies in wait for the murderer of a Brahman, the murderer of father or mother, the man who betrays a girl, murders a woman or defiles the bed of a holy teacher. Where there is truth, there is justice, where there is justice, good prevails, where there is beauty, there is nobility, and where there are elephants, there is victory ..."

It was certainly known that elephants, whose value in battle was put by the ancient Indian war manual at five cavalrymen or fifteen foot soldiers, could become a danger to their own ranks; if their mahouts were killed, they milled around like rudderless ships in the midst of battle, and if they were driven to panic by the pain of injuries from arrows or javelins, they might flee and throw their own army into chaos. That, however, was ignored, so as not to tempt fate. The ancient peoples of western nations had a more sober assessment of the value of elephants in battle than the Asians.

Indian war elephant in armor,
18th century,
iron-reinforced woven raffia
and leather.
weight 260 pounds
Tower of London

The suits of armor were made
from a heavy raffia weave and
fire-hardened leather, often
reinforced with iron. This
splendid example also protects
the head and trunk. A heavy
woven iron extension around
the trunk could also serve
as a weapon.

# The elephant culture of India

Since classical Greek and Roman times the artistic portrayal of animals in Europe has concentrated upon the image of the horse. In India however, despite the fact that Aryan conquerors on horseback subdued the subcontinent, the horse could not rival the elephant. The nomadic warfaring Aryan culture was quickly submerged in the ocean of the indigenous population with its farming and trading lifestyle. When the first Indian kingdoms came into being in the 6th/5th centuries before the new era, the elephant was already a symbol of the greatness, power and rank of the rulers, and the pride of the dominant castes of the nobility and the Brahmanic priesthood. The gray giant was included in religious cults, in which the polytheistic concepts of the Aryan conquerors were blended with the indigenous fertility rites based around female deities. The Indian Olympus was inhabited by gods in human form, to whom the elephant was also of service.

*Raja Ram Singh*,
c. 1855,
Kota Collection,
Rajasthan, India

Enthroned in extravagant splendor on the backs of elephants and accompanied by an entourage of courtiers, the Indian maharajas would display their power and grandeur before the common people. Magnificently adorned elephants, to whom ancient Indian tradition attributed "consubstantiality with kings," lent particular splendor to the many official appearances.

Opposite:
Elephant with howdah,
19th century,
ivory, partly painted and gilded.
Height c. 60cm, length c. 41cm
Staatliches Museum für Völkerkunde, Munich

The sumptuous Indian carving shows the splendor of a ceremonial elephant. Even the howdah, in which two dignitaries sit beneath domed canopies supported by pillars, is a work of art.

## Taken into heavenly service by the gods

In no other country has the elephant been so integrated into everyday life, the world of work, the splendor of festivities and the myths of religious cults as in India. There is nobody able to deal more sympathetically with this animal, to be its master and at the same time its constant friend, than the mahout, the Indian elephant-driver of the old school. There is a more benevolent relationship between man and animals on the subcontinent than anywhere else in the world.

Western man seeks to control nature, both animate and inanimate, a desire with its roots in the Bible. When God created man as "male and female," he said: "... be fruitful, and multiply, and replenish the earth, and subdue it: and have dominion over the fish of the sea, and over the fowl of the air, and over every living thing that moveth upon the earth ..." (Genesis).

Of course civilized man should always avoid unnecessary cruelty to animals; nevertheless he is free to put an animal to whatever use he sees fit. According to civil law an animal is considered merely an object.

The great religions of Hinduism and Buddhism with their law of non-violence and their teaching of reincarnation and the transmigration of souls, have imbued Indians with a profound respect for nature in all its forms. Animals and man are simply different manifestations of the all-prevailing cosmic power; so too the bewildering host of deities arranged around the Hindu Trinity: Brahma, creator of the world, Vishnu, savior of the world, and Shiva, destroyer and recreator, the god of eternal becoming and passing away.

Indians are constantly aware that they come from nature and return to it after death; on the long road to complete purification the soul can also be reborn in the body of an animal at either a higher or lower level, depending on the way the previous life was lived. All life is sacred no matter how much man may sin against it. The sacred cows enjoy absolute protection amongst the bustling traffic of the modern city, but this does not prevent them from slowly dying of neglect. Hindus have built temples in honor of even rats and snakes. In the cities there are sanctuaries where old and sick animals are fed; it is forbidden to kill them. Working elephants too, when made redundant by tractors in the forests, are given lifelong care.

This animal-friendly religious background has encouraged the special esteem and veneration which the elephant enjoys, as the animal which even the gods have taken into heavenly service.

Elephants splendidly adorned for a procession in Jaipur. Colorful decorations are painted right to the tips of their trunks.

The elephant culture of India

## The winged elephants of Hindu mythology

*Indra and Sachi ride on the elephant Airavata*, Rajasthan, India, c. 1740, gouache, gold, silver on paper. 27cm x 42.5cm County Museum of Art, Los Angeles

Indra the god of war with a female companion on the divine elephant Airavata. The artist's impression shows the heavenly animal with five heads instead of the typical four tusks.

According to legend the first elephants had wings and mated with clouds. One day, however, some elephants alighted on a tree under which a holy man was instructing his pupils. Under the weight of the powerful animals a branch broke and killed some of the pupils. Furious, the holy man entreated the gods to take the elephants' wings away. The divine beings fulfilled the request. However, the elephants remained good friends with the clouds and, as a consolation, they retained the right to ask the clouds for rain on earth. Thus they became intermediaries for men suffering from drought and beseeching heaven for rain.

Another legend traces the origin of the elephant back to Brahma whom the Indian priesthood, in search of a single world ruler, had temporarily elevated to creator of the universe. One day Brahma sang a holy melody, holding half an eggshell in each hand. First from the eggshell in his right hand grew Airavata, the holy white elephant, followed by seven more bull elephants; then from the shell in his left hand came eight cow elephants. All elephants are said to be descended from these

heavenly ancestors. According to the legend the eight progenitors became the bearers and keepers of the universe.

With the unparalleled persistence which also allows the continuation of the caste system, the Indians have adhered to their mythological deities from the beginnings of their culture until the present day. The legends of the gods are a living component of the beliefs of the different religious tendencies and sects. The efforts of various priests and philosophers towards a pantheistic or a monotheistic system have not succeeded. In the course of time India's bewildering heaven has filled with ever more supernatural beings, everywhere represented in sculpture form. These deities, able to manifest in material form, ruling in the forces of nature and not too far removed from all-too-human humankind, along with their demonic adversaries, are still worshipped today. They are beseeched passionately and implored or appeased with offerings. In the flowery legends of the gods the elephant is selected again and again for many special celestial services.

# Kama the god of love

Kama, transformed by the creative spirit into the god of love, occasionally exchanges his regular mount, the parrot, for an elephant. He is accompanied by his wife Rati (Passion), his friend Vasanta (Spring) and seductive nymphs, the Apsaras. The most beautiful of the heavenly beings shoots his flowery arrows of desire, mainly in spring, at young girls, wives and ascetics, while Vasanta hands over to Kama the appropriate flower of sensual desire.

Once he shot at the meditating god Shiva, the great destroyer and recreator, the lord of eternal becoming and passing away, so Shiva burnt him to ashes with the beam from his third eye. However, since with Kama love disappeared from the earth and life began to dry up, the other gods begged Shiva for leniency for the evil-doer.

The offended divine ascetic finally allowed Kama to be reborn. The aimlessly wandering god of love has been a source of great inspiration for artists, especially painters in sensuous India.

Below:
Painting from the old south Indian artistic centre Trichinopoly (today Tiruchchirappalli).
Victoria & Albert Museum, London

Female bodies are incorporated into the body of an elephant on which Kama the god of love is enthroned.

Above:
*Indra the god of war with flaming daggers.*
Victoria & Albert Museum, London

Above:
Portrayal of the Indian 'Amor,' Kama the god of love, shooting arrows of desire in spring.

Ganesh dancing,
North India, 8th century,
gray stone.
Russeck Collection, Switzerland

Ganesh is one of the most
universal deities of India. The rat
Akhu, who serves as his mount,
is depicted on the socle.

The elephant culture of India

# Ganesh the elephant-headed Hindu god

Indians consider the elephant to be the most intelligent of all the animals, and the gods in their version of Olympus share this estimation. So it was not by chance that the protector of wisdom, erudition and well-being should have the head of a clever elephant on his shoulders; that of the popular, corpulent Ganesh. It is a good idea to call on him, the "lord of the blessed host," before any undertaking or beginning of a project, whether in business or in study.

Ganesh is represented in countless sculptures: big-bellied, the heavy elephant head with only one developed tusk above a human body of elephantine proportions, with four arms and usually shown accompanied by a slightly surprising mount and companion, the rat. This most powerful of animals shares with the small rodent the ability to remove obstacles. The giant breaks down and tramples whatever is in his way; the rat bites and wriggles through barriers the elephant does not remove.

The voluptuous, corpulent body of Ganesh is a symbol of satisfied affluence to his worshippers; the rounded paunch bears witness to his quite human susceptibility to offerings, in return for which he provides divine help.

Ganesh is the son of Shiva, the cosmic mover whose army he leads, and the beautiful Parvati. Hindu myths provide numerous imaginative explanations for the origin of his elephant head.

According to one legend, Parvati, neglected by her ascetic husband, had long yearned in vain for a son. When finally her wish was granted through the intervention of Kama the god of love, who awakened Shiva's desire with a flowery arrow, she was so proud of her beautiful child that she urged all the gods to admire him. Only Sani (Saturn), cursed by his wife to turn everything he looked at to ashes, bowed his head and did not look. But Parvati pressed him so earnestly that he too looked, and immediately the child's head turned to ashes. In her pain Parvati also cursed the wretched Sani.

Moved by pity, Brahma, the wise god of creation, promised her that he would bring the child back to life as soon as a new head could be found. Straightaway Shiva set out in search. He found an elephant sleeping on a riverbank and cut off its head for his son ...

According to another legend Shiva, hit by Kama's flowery arrow, used to surprise Parvati while she was bathing, and this displeased her very much. So one day she scraped the dirt from her body, mixed it with oil and secret ingredients, formed Ganesh from it and brought him to life by sprinkling him with water from the Ganges. Then she commanded him to stand guard in front of her bathhouse door. When Shiva next arrived for another unwelcome rendezvous, Ganesh barred his

Ganesh,
Madras, 20th century,
painting on fabric.
Private collection

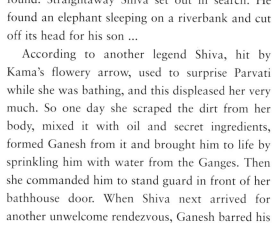

Two Brahmans worship Ganesh,
Tanjore, Tamilnadu
Marathen School,
early 19th century,
painting behind glass with stucco decoration on glass, glass mosaic.
Private collection, Madras

Above:
Ganesh relief,
Karni-Mata temple, Deshnok,
Rajasthan, India.
beaten silver

way, and this so angered the mighty god that he struck off Ganesh's head. Parvati was so grief-stricken over the fate of her creation that Shiva was moved to send out messengers to look for a new head for Ganesh. The messengers met an elephant, struck off his head and hurried back to Shiva with it. He placed the head complete with trunk on Ganesh's shoulders ...

Another legend explains why Ganesh has only one developed tusk. One day, Parasu-Rama, the sixth incarnation of Vishnu the preserver who had been commissioned to destroy the tyrannical caste of the nobility, wanted to visit Shiva who was sleeping in his palace. Ganesh would not let him enter, a fight ensued and Parasu-Rama hurled his battle-axe at his adversary. Recognizing the axe as his father's, Ganesh caught the weapon respectfully with one tusk, which broke. Parvati, his mother, then appeared, and was so furious that she wanted to curse Parasu-Rama. Brahma commanded restraint but, as a consolation promised that in compensation for his great loss Ganesh would be granted divine honor ...

Opposite:
The 15 foot high 16th century sculpture of Ganesh in Hampi, Andra Pradesh, India is much visited by pilgrims. It is situated in a shrine on the slopes of Hemakuti Hill and is hewn from the granite cliff.

Below:
Ganesh riding on a three-headed elephant. The four-armed patron of scientists, merchants and thieves holds symbolic objects in his hands: whip, fork, dagger and death's head.

Right:
Ganesh under a stylized flaming arc. The god of wisdom and well-being who helps to overcome obstacles is invoked before important projects.
Collection of the Maharaja of Mysore

Left:
Figure of Ganesh,
from Kuyperts 'De elephantis in nummis obviis,'
Hagae Comitum, 1719,
copper engraving.
Collection of the American Numismatic Society, New York

# Buddha's elephant incarnation

Elephant legends also surround Gautama Siddhartha, known as Buddha, who preached a new peaceful message of salvation in Asia half a millennium before Christ: freedom from violence, and the misery and futility of earthly existence, deliverance from the eternal cycle of birth, death and rebirth by faithfully following the "noble, eightfold path."

This path leads through right beliefs, right desires, right speech, right conduct, right livelihood, right effort, right awareness, and right contemplation to peace, enlightenment and the cool stillness of Nirvana, which eludes any earthy

*The Bodhisattva Padmapani,*
6th century AÐ,
Mural.
Cavern I, Ajanta, India

According to the birth legend of Buddha, Bodhisattvas are beings whose aim is enlightenment. They can be gods, men or animals who are seen as earlier incarnations of Buddha. The historical Buddha was also a Bodhisattva before he attained enlightenment. In the belief system of Mahajana Buddhism which came to dominance later and developed at the beginning of the Christian era, Bodhisattvas were good-natured divine beings who had indeed reached enlightenment, but had renounced the status of Buddha in order to help men to reach salvation.

explanation – for the worldly man nothingness, for the holy man fulfilment and utmost happiness.

The belief in the transmigration of souls from one life to another is common to the various belief systems of India. So the Buddha also had to pass through a series of incarnations on the long road to ever more greatness of soul, until finally, after a complete renunciation of the world and purification, he was granted enlightenment.

According to one story from the 'Jakata,' a collection of religious legends, in a previous life the holy man was incarnated as Chaddanta, the legendary snow-white elephant. He had six tusks and led a herd of 8,000 animals, endowed with various miraculous powers and the ability to fly. Chaddanta had two wives. Consumed by a desire for importance, one of them asked the gods if she could be reborn as a princess.

When, on fulfilment of her wish, she became the wife of the king of Benares, she demanded of her husband that he should go hunting for an elephant with six tusks which she wished to possess. The

hunt took place and Sonuttara the huntsman wounded Chaddanta with arrows and caught him in a pit. The elephant begged for mercy. However, when he heard that the Queen of Benares had instigated the hunt, he submitted to his fate with pious resignation. He even used his trunk to help the huntsman saw off both his tusks. Then, finally, the great elephant fell dead ...

According to the legend, the supernatural being of the future Buddha, the 'enlightened one,' entered the body of his mother in an 'immaculate' conception in the incarnation of a white elephant. King Suddhodana, who ruled over a country at the foot of the Himalayas, had been married to his wife Maya for twenty long years without being blessed with any children.

Then, one night, Queen Maya dreamt that a white elephant came over her from Heaven and touched her on the side with a white lotus blossom which he held in his trunk. She became pregnant and her body became transparent like a crystal vessel. As the day of the birth approached she had the desire to see her parents in the next country and set off on the journey. While resting in a grove of trees at Lumbini she stretched out her hand to reach a flowering twig and a little prince sprang forth from her right hip.

Joy at the court was soon clouded. Queen Maya died seven days after the birth. The prince, who had been named Siddhartha, was put in the care of Prajapati the king's younger sister. Then a pious hermit from the mountains appeared at the court. He had seen a glow over the palace and he made this prophecy to the king: if the prince remained in the palace throughout his early years he would become a great king and would rule over many lands; if, however, he renounced the courtly life and chose a religious life he would become a Buddha (old Indian, an enlightened one) and would be the savior of the world.

Concerned that in accordance with the prophecy his only son could choose a monastic life, the king offered the growing prince all the splendor and all the pleasures of courtly life and took care that Siddhartha did not set eyes on the suffering and death of his fellow creatures. The prince married his cousin Yasodhara and lived in wedded bliss. He also honed his weaponry skills. He was still aware of the poverty and misery in the world and the nagging question of the meaning of life would not leave his mind.

After his beloved wife had borne him a son and he had reached his twenty-ninth year he left the palace one night with a trusty servant, exchanged his splendid robes for beggar's rags and for seven long years devoted himself to the strictest ascetic disciplines and meditations. This finally brought him enlightenment. Then he began his great life's

work, that of proclaiming the way for man to salvation and redemption.

Soon enemies and enviers appeared. Thus the Indian fables include a legend, glorifying Buddha's spiritual power, which tells of a series of attempts on his life in which an elephant once more has a role to play:

Devadatta, who had been an envious rival of the holy man in the early years, was consumed by hatred and tried to destroy him. He sent out thirty-one of his followers to kill Buddha; but Buddha converted the assassins. Then Devadatta rolled a boulder down a mountain to crush Buddha, but the rock split in two in front of the holy preacher and rolled away on either side. Finally he made an elephant drunk to trample Buddha and all the people fled before the rampaging animal. Buddha, on the other hand, approached without fear and the elephant stopped and reverentially laid his head and trunk on the ground before him.

After this all Devadatta's followers were converted. Devadatta himself finally received his

just desserts when, feigning repentance and introspection, he sought out Buddha at the monastery with murderous intent. As he was standing before the gates and waiting for Buddha to appear before him, flames shot out of the earth and consumed him ...

The historical Buddha saw himself merely as one pointing the way to salvation. In later centuries, in a reversal of his pure teaching on virtue, he was elevated to a divine being, a deity who promotes the welfare of man surrounded by future Buddhas (Bodhisattvas). In glorifying works of art even the gods, also in need of redemption and brought from the Hindu pantheon to be associated with him, pay homage to him.

Again and again the symbolic elephant of the myths finds a place in the countless late Buddhist sculptures. The ample footprint of the elephant, which could contain the print of any other animal, has become a symbol of Buddhist teaching which holds within itself all other doctrines concerned with insight and understanding.

*Maya's dream,*
Bharhut, 2nd century BC,
red sandstone,
Indian Museum, Calcutta

Maya's dream. A white elephant comes over her from Heaven and the supernatural being of the future Buddha incarnated in him enters her body ... Relief on a pillar of the stone enclosure of the Stupa of Bharhut, 100 miles from Allahabad, today located in the Indian Museum at Calcutta.

*The taming of the raging elephant Nalagiri,*
Great Stupa of Amaravati,
2nd–3rd century AD,
limestone.
Government Museum, Madras

The legend recounts that Devadatta planned an attempt on the life of his cousin Gautama. Gautama was to be killed by a wild elephant. However, Gautama pacified the wild elephant with a single sign of his hand and the elephant bowed down at his feet. Two scenes are represented on this relief; on the left the wild elephant Nalagiri running amok, and on the right Nalagari bowing in adoration before the Buddha.

Willy Fries (born 1907)
*The light and dark elephants*
From the Indian picture series of the Swiss artist.

The painter of the Forgotten Ones of Society, the Pariahs, sketched the scene while traveling in India in 1970–71. The light or white elephant, a bringer of good luck and the rearing, dark elephant symbolize the contrast and conflict in life between rich and poor; between fortune's favorites, decreed unfathomably by divine ordinance, and pariahs, represented by the young beauty on the right and the outcast beggars on the left.

The elephant culture of India

Elephants pay homage to Buddha before his shrine, the Great Stupa of Amaravati,
2nd century AD,
stone relief.
British Museum, London

## The rainbringer

According to a further legend, Buddha spent a previous earthly existence as the son of a king before he was reborn to a final life as Prince Siddhartha and, as the enlightened one of the world, became a pointer of the way towards salvation. When he was born in this earlier incarnation, so the legend tells, a flying cow elephant added a young white elephant to his father's bond elephants. From that time onwards there was never any shortage of rain in the land. Year by year the fields brought forth a rich harvest and the people enjoyed general well-being.

When the prince was grown up there was a devastating drought in a neighboring country. In their need, the starving people beseeched the gentle prince to send them the rain-bestowing white elephant. Near to his future enlightenment, the prince had already sensed his sacred mission of redeeming the world. Inspired by pity for all beings and already free from the worldy desires of self-interest, he granted the request in "the perfect joy of giving." However, the loss of the white elephant led to drought and misery in his own land. The people grumbled and there was insurrection. So the king was forced to banish his son who, in his immeasurable goodness, had forfeited the prosperity of the land.

*Gautama Buddha receives gifts from an elephant and an ape*, Thailand, 19th century, hanging scroll, gouache on fabric. Museum Rietberg, Zürich

In the life of Gautama Buddha, even after his enlightenment, there are unpleasant experiences: at the end of his earthly life he is slandered by a beautiful courtesan, his monks quarrel and the Buddha withdraws into the forest of Parileyyaka. An elephant, who is also disgusted by the behavior of his kind, becomes his loyal companion.

## "Consubstantial with kings ..."

*The imperial elephant Ganesh
Gaj*, 1660/70,
gouache, ink, gold on paper,
32cm x 48.8cm
Collection of Howard Hodgkin,
London

The stables of the Mogul Emperor
Aurangzeb (1658–1707) contained
the most noble elephants of the
Empire. The rider shrinks into
insignificance on the back of the
imperial ceremonial elephant.

"An elephant mounted by a king is radiant; a king
mounted on an elephant is resplendent," so runs
the book of Old Indian elephant lore; "neither of
the two outshines the other, elephants are
consubstantial with kings ..."

"It is no profit if man loses in value thereby, he
is no sage who has not burnt with ardent
asceticism; he is no man towards whom women are
not well-disposed, and he is no king towards whom
elephants are not well-disposed ... The creator of
the world created the regal elephant for the
salvation of the world, and endowed him with
majestic power and splendor. A king earnestly
intent on promoting the welfare of elephants holds
victory in his grasp ... Thus elephants should be
protected like the life of a king ..." The elephant,
placed on a level with kings and, like them, lauded
in hymns throughout the centuries, has since the
earliest times shared in the lavish splendor with
which the Indian rulers have displayed their power,
their magnificence and their favor with the gods
before their admiring, subservient people.

Haidar 'Ali and Ibrahim Khan,
*Sultan Muhammad Adil Shah of
Bijapur and Iklas Khan ride a
splendidly bridled elephant,*
Bijapur, c. 1645,
gouache and gold on paper.
32cm x 44.5cm
Collection of Howard Hodgkin,
London

The Sultan holds an elephant hook,
an ankush, in his hand. In this
ceremonial portrayal the ankush was
also an insignia of royal power and
honor – a symbol of the power to
command both elephants and a state;
behind him, his Prime Minister, a
former Ethiopian slave.

The elephant culture of India   135

## The ceremonial elephant

Silver rings on the tusks complete the ceremonial finery of the riding elephant of the Mahajara of Mysore and the magnificent giant is now ready to receive royal homage. On the ninth day of the Desara festival Hindus honor the animals which serve them.

With ivory tusks beringed with gold and silver, gigantic bodies painted and hung with gold-embroidered caparisons, massive legs adorned with long silver chains and announcing their appearance with bells, the ceremonial elephants on parade during the most important excursions and processions removed the enthroned prince and his courtiers from the baseness of the world. To these chosen animals, represented in many thousands of works of art, was accrued a particular rank. This raised them above the mass of ordinary working elephants whose only fate, like that of the common people, was endless drudgery; the chosen elephants became themselves works of art.

It is still the same today, when the religious fervor of Hindu and Buddhist groups is displayed in pomp-laden processions, and magnificently bridled elephants carry idols, pagodas, temple dancers and priestly messengers of blessedness. Cultic pomp is and always was encountered in all religions which involve within their dogma a mass longing for a heavenly paradise dreamt of while living on earth.

The Oriental imagination and naive religious zeal wove around the gentle giant sundry flowery myths and an abundance of legends which, along with Buddhism and Hinduism, spread across the whole of Southeast Asia.

Sri Lanka's biggest elephant festival is celebrated every year in Kandy, the provincial capital. Over 100 splendidly-decorated elephants pass in a magical procession through lines of people in the nighttime streets.

Festively-decorated elephant,
6th century AD,
mural.
Cavern XVII, Ajanta, India

The body is covered with
caparisons and glittering
ornaments; head, trunk and legs
are painted in bright colors.

Ceremonial elephant with howdah
at the Great Exhibition in London
(Detail), 1851,
from Dickinson: 'Views of the
Exhibition,' London, 1851,
colored lithograph.
44.4cm x 59.8cm
Victoria & Albert Museum,
London

# The splendor of the howdah

Top left:
Birds entwined with vine leaves decorate the outside of the howdah, which is constructed from pieces of ivory. The seat of honor, covered with red velvet, is flanked by two lions. During processions the women held fans, symbols of princely power.

Top right:
A ceremonial howdah which elephants carried for special occasions or festivities. The wooden frame is disguised with gilded copper; the seats are covered with silk. On the front a sun wheel is flanked by sphinxes. The ceremonial pieces shown here were in the possession of the Mahajara of Benares.

During elephant rides the Indian maharajas and court society sat in howdahs, expensively worked and ornately decorated, covered with gilded copper and silk.

Riding elephant,
India, 19th century,
ivory, partly painted
and gilded.
Height 53cm, length 41cm
Staatliches Museum für
Völkerkunde, Munich

Elephant hook,
Jaipur c. 1870
gold, diamonds, enamel.
Length 54.5cm
Victoria & Albert Museum,
London

This elephant hook, or ankush, of
gold, set with diamonds and
decorated with enamel, was made
in 1870 for the Maharaja of
Jaipur; he presented it to a loyal
retainer. Reptiles holding steel
points in their mouths burst out of
the mouth of an elephant.

The Prince of Wales mounts a
magnificently bridled ceremonial
elephant during his visit to India
in April 1876. A stately throne
has been prepared for him in the
ceremonial howdah.
'The Illustrated London News'

The elephant culture of India    139

## The elephant in the Mogul empire

The Hindus bequeathed their esteem for the elephant to the Muslim conquerors who created the powerful Mogul empire in the 16th–17th centuries. Never was the intelligent giant involved in more stately pomp and circumstance than under the new masters who ruled in India until the beginning of the British colonial era.

The magnificent Mogul rulers, who resided in Agra near Delhi, were descendants of Timur (1360–1405), the ill-famed and much-feared conqueror who, in his bloody campaigns between the Volga and the Mediterranean, left a swathe of pillage, destruction and slaughter. Timur himself was descended from a Turkic branch of the descendants of Genghis Khan, the Mongolian world conqueror and nomadic ruler. The name 'Mogul' is derived from the Persian word 'Mughul' meaning Mongol.

When Timur attacked Delhi in 1398 the Indians opposed him with 30,000 foot soldiers, 10,000 horsemen and in addition a powerful phalanx of war elephants, which struck great fear into the hearts of the Mongolian cavalry. Timur had a strategy to avert the danger; he drove buffaloes and camels loaded with bundles of hay towards the ranks of war elephants and at the last moment set fire to the hay. Mad with pain the animals spread panic among the elephants which then caused chaos in their own army. A bloodbath ensued, both on the battle field and in Delhi.

About 50,000 Indians lost their lives in this incident. Craftspeople and artists, however, were spared by Timur; he took them, along with 120 captured elephants, as slaves to his residence in Samarkand, where he set up magnificent mosques, monuments and academies for Islamic studies.

# The stables of Emperor Akbar

Of special reknown are the elephant stables of Muhammad Akbar (1556–1605), the third and greatest of the Mogul emperors who, with iron fist and prudent religious tolerance towards the Hindus, brought almost the whole subcontinent under his control.

Akbar came to the throne in 1556 as a thirteen year-old boy. The throne was also claimed by equally entitled rivals in Kabul, the family's ancient ancestral seat, when Akbar's father had fallen to his death from the roof of his library. A lucky victory by Bairam Khan, Akbar's guardian, over a powerful army led by the Hindu usurper Hemu, and the expansion of his power by spoils of victory in the form of 1,000 war elephants secured the position of power of the boy-emperor in the year of his enthronement.

The head of Hemu, who had already advanced on the residence at Agra, was sent to Kabul, the old Mogul center, as a warning against further family conflict; the body was hung up in Delhi as a deterrent. The heads of slain Hindus were immured in a victory pillar with their faces turned outwards, as Timur once had done ...

Throughout his life Akbar remained a lover of elephants. He concerned himself personally with the care and training of the gray giants. At his instruction Abul Fazl, his secretary, adviser, later confidant and chronicler, wrote a compendium about elephant-keeping in the court and in the whole of the empire.

In his empire Akbar had thousands of elephants, which were divided into troops of ten, twenty and thirty animals and attached to the commanders of larger units in the provinces. Commanders of 1,000 animals had the highest rank. Every troop overseer had to report regularly on the training and characteristics of the individual animals, new acqusitions and incidents of every type.

The most noble 100 elephants stood in special stables. They were placed at the exclusive disposal of the emperor, who ranked the animals into seven classes. The highest esteem was enjoyed by the 'thoroughbreds.' Five well-paid stable attendants were assigned to each of these bloodstock animals. The less important animals had only two or three attendants each. The chosen elephants of the imperial stables received grass, foliage and hay and also a special feed for strength, about 165 pounds of cereals, rice, legumes, milk and root vegetables as well as 30 pounds of sugar cane daily.

The emperor inspected the animals in his stables according to a set timetable. For this they had to be presented formally bridled. This also included the elephants belonging to the princes and the high dignitaries at the court. He used to reward special services and honor illustrious guests with the presentation of an elephant. Suitable animals were always kept ready for this purpose. He also controlled the elephant trade.

The emperor loved hunting, daring physical activity and at times took reckless risks. Ignoring all warnings he sat on the backs of bull elephants while they fought each other over a low wall to prevent fatal injury. He also dared to ride with bulls in musth, which Abul Fazl, his chronicler, noted with incomprehension: "Even when the animals are suffering the fury of the rutting season, he puts his foot on the tusks and mounts, which astonishes many experienced people ..."

All the elephants of the court and army were trained not to be afraid of cannon and musket fire. Hunting elephants were trained not to be afraid of lions and tigers; lion and tiger skins were stuffed with straw and moved about with ropes during training. The mahout had to coax the elephant towards the dummy which it then had to trample and tear to pieces with tusks and trunk.

"When the emperor goes on a journey," wrote Abul Fazl, "comfortable structures are fastened on the backs of the best animals, and these serve as bunks during the march ... The biggest and strongest of the imperial elephants bears the title 'Elephant General.' When he appears at court adorned with costly caparisons, he is awaited in great pageantry by a line of elephants and honored with flutes, trumpets and cymbals, and a great show of flags ..."

According to Abul Fazl ten attendants were assigned to each imperial elephant: two mahouts to drive him; two to put on his chains; two lance bearers; two gunners who could intervene if difficulties occurred; a man to remove the dung and another to bring the elephant water to drink and for cooling. These attendants received twenty-five rupees a day to take care of their elephant; their own monthly pay was only four rupees per man "apart from that which each can steal from his elephant's feed ration and take away," noted Abul Fazl in his chronicle.

Apart from the 100 elephants that belonged to the Emperor, a considerable number of selected animals was kept at court for the use of the ladies of the harem, the princesses, the princes and their concubines. On forays and journeys they also served as pack animals for the tents, the luggage and the cooking utensils. Abul Fazl also notes: "During forays each elephant wears bells. These are to warn people and give them the chance to make the way clear in plenty of time, for a running or even walking elephant cannot be brought to a halt immediately like a horse can ..."

Basawan and Chitra,
*Akbar subdues the wild elephant Hawa'i* (Detail),
c. 1590,
from the 'Akbarnama' (Story of Akbar) by Abul Fazl,
gouache on paper.
34.5cm x 21.6cm
Victoria & Albert Museum,
London

As a young man Akbar feared no danger. This miniature from the biography penned by his secretary Abul Fazl tells of a particularly exciting episode. When he was barely nineteen years old, the Emperor mounted the violent, much-feared elephant Hawa'i, 'Swift as the wind,' and in spite of exhortations undertook a foolhardy test of strength with the almost equally strong bull Ran Bagha, whom he quickly put to flight. During the wild pursuit the elephants ran on to the pontoon bridge over the river Jumna. Panic ensued; boats capsized; people plunged into the river. At last Akbar managed to curb Hawa'i's wild temperament and the vanquished Ran Bagha escaped with his life.

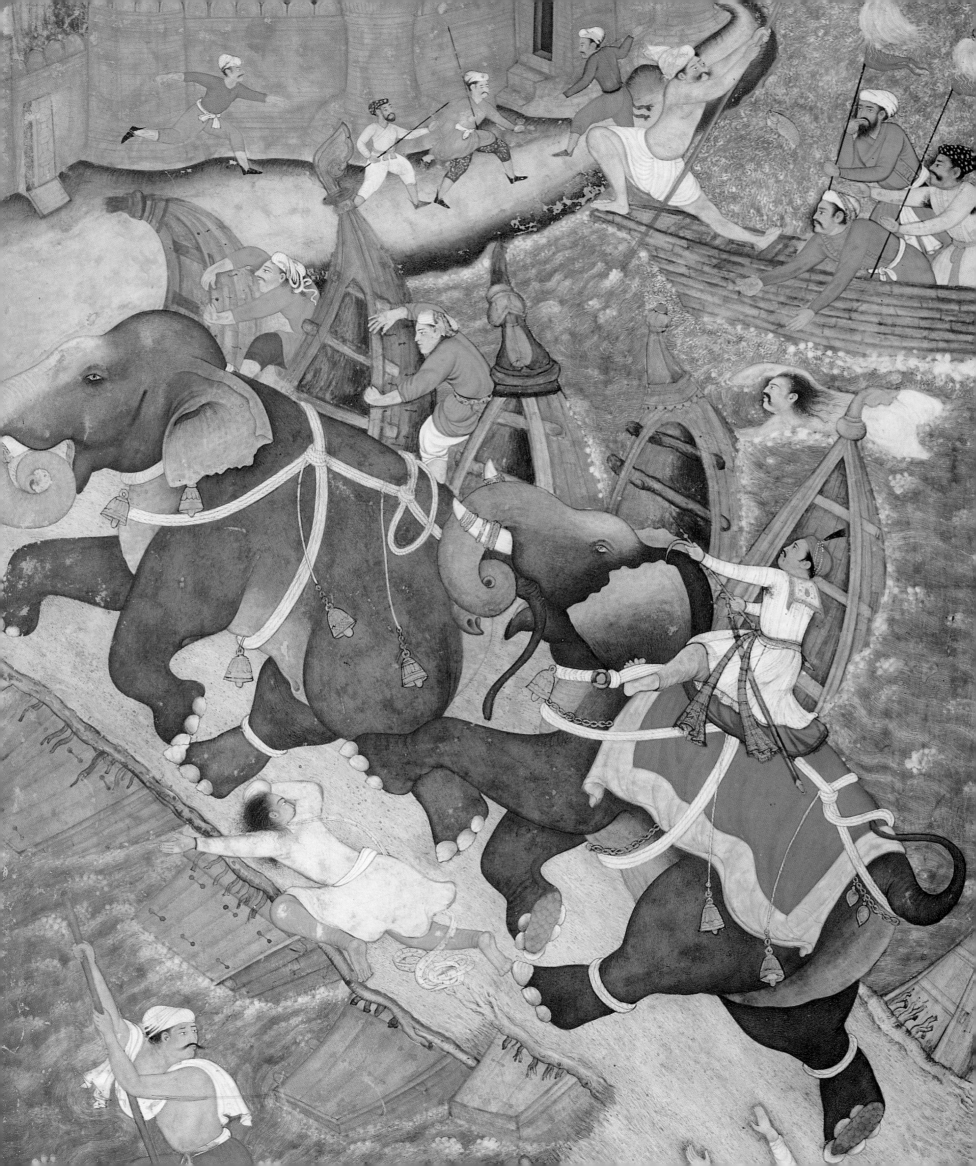

## Akbar's war elephants

*Royal elephant with mahout,*
Mogul period, c. 1660,
gouache on paper.
24cm x 28.5cm
Collection of Howard Hodgkin,
London

Elephant units were the backbone of Akbar's armies as he expanded his power, and the emperor was renowned as a lifelong lover of elephants. "The wonderful animal is like a mountain in bulk and strength" wrote Abul Fazl in his chronicle, "and like a lion in courage and ferocity. It contributes considerably to the noble representation of the king's power and to the success of a conqueror; in addition it is of the utmost use to the army. In the eyes of experienced Hindus one good elephant is worth fifty horses."

Elephants secured victory for Akbar in many battles. He even used them when, in October 1567, he attacked the vast inaccessible mountain fortress of Chitor. This was the main stronghold of the warrior tribal caste of the Rajputs who, in keeping with old Hindu tradition, still maintained a degree of independence for Rajputana from the Muslim

Mogul empire. For months 8,000 Rajputs and 1,000 serving musketeers defied the cannons and mighty forces of the Emperor. Musket fire from the stronghold prevented the advance on the steep slope. Finally Akbar ordered workers, who suffered dreadful losses, to build a beam-covered walkway, known as a 'sabah,' from the foot of the mountain up to the walls of the fortress, and this gave tolerable protection against the firing. The walkway was so big that even elephants could be taken up it. When the first breaches were blown in the walls, elephants had to make the holes larger with their tusks and were then urged to carry the attack into the fortress.

In accordance with ancient Hindu tradition the Rajputs first burnt their wives; then they fought to the death. With swords and spears they attacked the advancing war elephants. Men rashly grasped the tusks of the colossi and inflicted grievous wounds, but to little effect. The raging animals stamped down the courageous warriors, seized them in their trunks and threw them high in the air or dashed them against the walls of houses.

Furious about the heavy losses to his forces, Akbar, in contrast to his usual moderate behaviour, ordered a general massacre. The common soldiers, however, whose firing had been so devastating and against whom he particularly wanted to take revenge, escaped by a ruse. In the midst of the slaughter they hid behind their wives and children, who were being led away in fetters, and escaped from the fortress as Akbar's men counted out and led away the usual booty of slaves. Thousands of farmers, who had sought protection in the vast fortress, perished in the massacre.

Chitor, whose defences Akbar razed to the ground, was the residence of Udai Singh, the Rana of Mewar and the head of the oldest Rajput house. During the seige the prince was not in the fortress; he was organizing the devastation of the surrounding countryside so that it would be difficult for Akbar to provision his army. After the fall of the fortress he founded a new city as his residence about 60 miles to the southwest – the city of Udaipur was chosen.

Akbar loved the arts and free-thinking learned discussions and as a Muslim even allowed Hindu rituals in his palace. In the matter of his sons, however, he had little luck. In spite of all his efforts to provide a good upbringing, two died in drunkenness and depravity. Salim, the eldest, rebelliously opposed his father for years in the part of the empire ceded to him. He even risked the greatest possible challenge; he had Abul Fazl, his father's powerful secretary and confidant, treacherously murdered.

In accordance with the much-tried Mogul custom, Salim was saved from the Emperor's anger by the intercession of the older ladies of the family. His grandmother made Salim throw himself at the

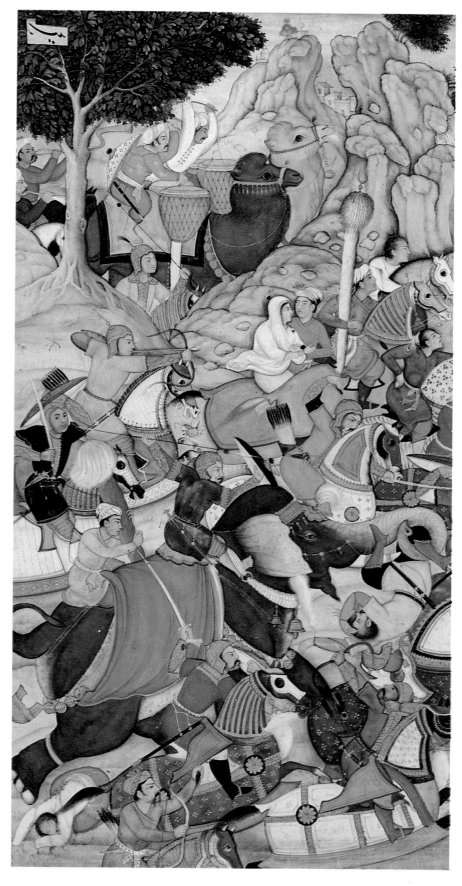

Emperor's feet and beg for forgiveness. As compensation Akbar took 350 elephants from Salim, which amounted to military disarmament. In October 1605 under the name Jehan Gir (World Conqueror) Salim succeeded the Emperor, who had done everything to bring him up as a good and tolerant ruler. In spite of his rather inglorious earlier life, Jehan Gir proved to be an able ruler. During his reign the Mogul empire enjoyed a cultural high point. Of particular report is the journal he left behind.

*Foray of a prince with a large entourage,*
Mogul period, c. 1570
gouache and gold on cotton.
34cm x 39.8cm
Collection of Howard Hodgkin, London

# Carved and hewn in stone

Hewn in stone the elephant, revered as a sacred animal, decorates the facades and portals of temples and palaces. In everyday life as a bringer of good luck he is a motif that has been used thousands of times. For the Buddhist preaching renunciation of the world he is a symbol of the all-subduing power of insight; in the Hindu myths he serves the gods and goddesses, who give graphic expression to the ancient cosmic forces and the sensual reality of life.

Indian sculpture first began to develop in the 3rd–2nd century BC under the enlivening influence of Buddhism. In the previous millennium during the rule of the Aryan aristocracy and priesthood of the 'Vedic period' ceramic objects of worship and idols were used in religious ceremonies; the epoch was stamped by religion, philosophy and literature. Stupas and many monasteries to venerate Buddha were built, and these included religious sculptures in their architecture.

The 7th century AD ushered in a new epoch of art with Hinduism which prevailed from this time onwards. Mighty temples were constructed or hewn from the rock and covered with a profusion of sculptures and reliefs.

Decorated elephant on a house facade in Jaisalmer. Rajasthan, India

Gajendramoksa, Gupta, 6th century. National Museum, Delhi

Stone guard elephant in front of a temple in Jaisalmer, 17th/18th century. Rajasthan, India

Whole armies of sculptors covered the Hindu temple buildings with a profusion of sculptures and reliefs.

The elephant culture of India

Guard elephants at the Maharana Palace of Udaipur, built on the east bank of Lake Pichola in Rajasthan, India

The elephant carved from a block of rock keeps guard in the courtyard of the Sun Temple, known as the Black Pagoda, which King Narasimhadeva I. Ganga (1259–1264) had built. Konarak, Orissa, India

Sculpture in the foreyard of the Kailasanatha Temple at Ellora in Central India, the magical likeness of Mount Kailasa, the 'Olympus' of the Indian gods. In the 8th century thousands of stone masons cut a gigantic block of stone with an area of 128 x 229 feet from a mountain and from this they carved a 90-foot-high temple with staggered terraces, pillars, towers, passages and a bewildering profusion of fully and partly three-dimensional sculptures. Elephants support the central stupa.

Sculpture decoration above the east gate of the enclosure of the Great Stupa of Sanchi, 1st century AD, an early Buddhist place of pilgrimage. A tree nymph (yaksini) embodying fertility reaches into a stylized mango tree. Her baroque form is a typical expression of Indian aesthetics.

Opposite:
A guard elephant in front of the Ranakpur Temple, one of the group of Jain temples built between 1367 and 1432 in a remote valley of the Aravalli Hills in Rajasthan, India

Bas-reliefs with elephants at the
Karni Mata Temple in Deshnok,
Rajasthan

The elephant culture of India

Opposite:
Guard elephants in front of the Rat Temple at Deshnok, Rajasthan, the destination of many pilgrims. The temple is dedicated to the tutelary goddess Karni Mata.

*The descent of the Ganga.*
The gigantic form of the elephant, who is close to the gods, dominates the fantastical mosaic of Mamallapuram, created in the 7th century, which depicts the legend of the descent of the holy water of the Ganges to earth. The sculptors used the natural channel of a diverted torrent in a 27-foot-high cliff face. The twining human-headed snakes Naga and Nagina symbolize the life-giving holy water, to which happy gods, spirits, people and animals throng.

# Masterpieces of miniature painting

The best and also most vivacious portrayals of elephants were created by the artists of the 16th–17th centuries in the era of the Muslim Mogul emperors. In particular Indo-Islamic miniature painting was at its most prolific. The great emperor Akbar was a particular promoter of the arts, and he constantly employed Persian and Hindu painters. He also held regular exibitions of their works at his court and these provided a radiant influence and increased the Emperor's reknown.

Below:
*Royal elephant with mahout,*
Mogul period, c. 1600,
gouache on paper.
24cm x 28cm
Collection of Howard Hodgkin,
London

*Bathing delight*,
Rajput style, 17th century,
gouache on paper.
County Museum of Art,
Los Angeles

Indian painting instructions recommend the use of a grid with 120 squares when doing outline drawings. The unknown painter of this picture drawn spontaneously on paper has dispensed with this method.

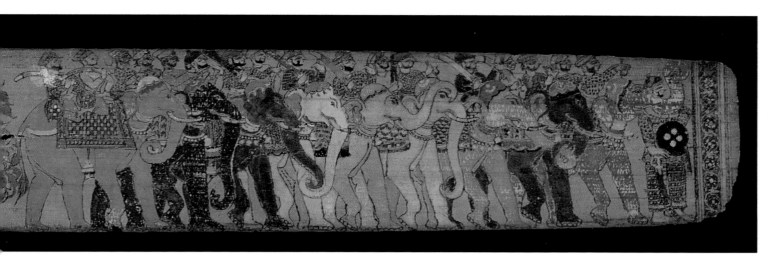

The march past of the cavalry and elephants during a procession in Puri, from 'The string of pearls for the beloved,' Orissa, c. 1800, palm leaf. Museum Rietberg, Zürich

The warrior caste of the Rajputs, who had invaded India in the 6th century and had conquered large areas of land in the northwest of the subcontinent, also cultivated the pictorial arts in the shadow of the Mogul emperors. The aristocratic lords, who soon converted to Hinduism and who can be compared with the feudal nobility of the European Middle Ages, passed their time at their courts in Rajputana in hunting and elephant fighting, music, dancing and the cultivation of the fine arts. Their sumptuous lifestyle was mirrored in a profusion of masterly, delicately sensual, miniatures.

Like the sculptors, jewelers and smiths, the Hindu painters belonged to the low Shudra caste, but they were highly regarded by their connoisseur masters. According to ancient writings, the Shudra caste can have no aspiration other than to serve the three higher classes, the priestly caste (the Brahmans), the warrior nobility and the farmers and merchants. The painters, who were mainly illiterate, often worked with scribes, who read to them from the texts or myths they were illustrating and made sure that they paid attention to the Hindu symbolism involved.

*Two elephants run out of a tent*, Kota, Rajasthan, c. 1720, gouache on paper. 24cm x 49cm Museum of Western India, Bombay

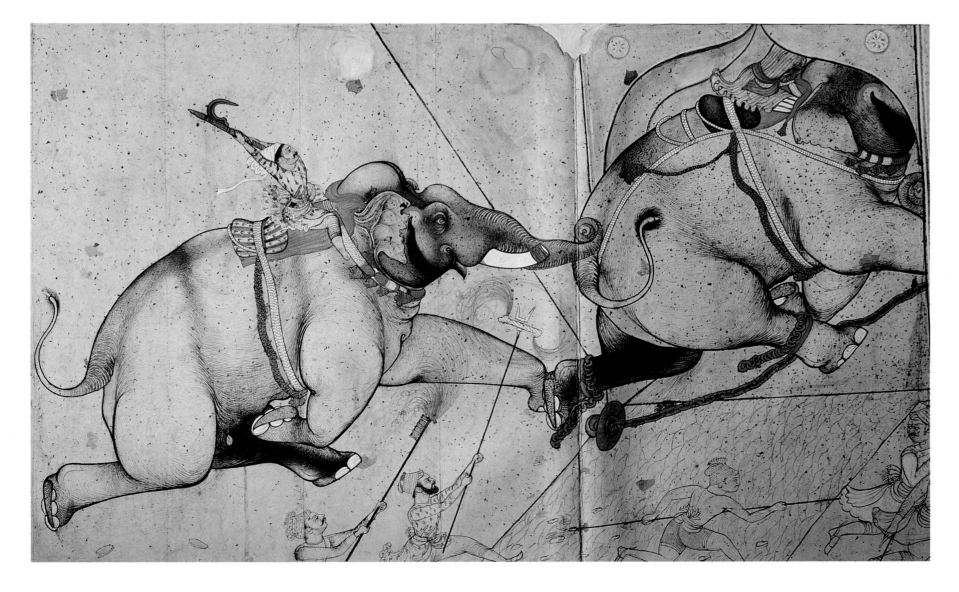

# The elephant – noble mount of dignitaries

Above:
Khem Karan,
A nobleman rides an elephant,
Mogul period, c. 1600,
gouache on paper.
31cm x 47cm
The Metropolitan Museum of Art,
New York

Top right:
Colonel James Tod on an
exploratory and surveying
expedition in Rajasthan, Udaipur,
Western India, c. 1820.
Victoria & Albert Museum,
London

The elephant culture of India

Right:
*Procession of Maharaja Ram Singh II* (Detail), Kota, c. 1850, gouache on paper.
Victoria & Albert Museum, London

Raja Ram Singh II (1826–1866) from Kota State in Rajasthan during a procession with his retainers and palace serving girls.

# Elephant murals on house walls

In many parts of Rajasthan the residents brighten bare house walls with colorful pictures of animals. A frequent motif is the elephant, whose amiable image is sometimes used to produce original decorative effects; the shrine-like structure which the ceremonial elephant carries on its back frames a small window, in which the face of a resident can be seen. Jaisalmer, Rajasthan, India

In Gorakhpur district the wives of farmers and fishermen decorate the walls of their houses with stylized figures of elephants for the goddess Lakshmi in the belief that she will be pleased.

The mahout of the riding elephant with the magnificent howdah occupied by four people is Hanuman, the monkey-god. He is holding an ornamental whisk and the elephant hook.
Navalgarh, Rajasthan, India

Navalgarh is famous for the many houses decorated with animal frescoes from the early 20th century.

The elephant culture of India

# The elephant-headed woman

The Hindu elephant-headed Ganesh has a female counterpart in the tantric Buddhism of Nepal, in Ganipatihardaya. She is a manifestation of Shakti, the mother goddess, the actual embodiment of the cosmic female force.

Around the turn of the epoch the teaching of Buddha split into two diverging doctrines: the older line, the 'Lesser Vehicle' (Hinayana) spread as a monastic religion through Ceylon, Burma, Thailand, Cambodia and Java. The predominant new doctrine, the 'Great Vehicle' (Mahayana), radiating out from northern India was received by Nepal, China, Korea, Japan and Vietnam. In an adaptation of the doctrine of renunciation of the enlightened one, which recognized no idols, Mahayana Buddhism proclaimed a belief in the grace of divine Buddhas, future or becoming Buddhas (Bodhisattvas), to mediate salvation and redemption. This included goddesses, the Taras.

In whatever direction the great religions of India advanced, and in whatever form they developed, the image of the elephant was ever-present in religious symbolism. Towards the end of the first millennium before Christ, Buddhism rapidly lost ground in India. Many monasteries returned to Hinduism. In 1193 the Muslim invasion removed almost without trace the teaching of the Prophet in the land of his birth.

In the remoteness of the Himalayan mountains, in the second half of the first millennium after Christ, there arose from Mahayana Buddhism the belief system of the 'Diamond Vehicle' (Vajrayana). According to this doctrine, celestial salvation and earthly well-being can also be attained through ritual, through incantations and holy syllables and through magical ceremonies and practices. Prayer wheels enhance the power of the beneficial incantations and holy syllables.

Hindu and Buddhist cults flowed together in tantrism, a mixture of mysticism, belief in gods and demons, magical ceremonies and ritual exercises. The Buddhist pantheon was filled with Hindu gods. Ganesh enjoyed great veneration. Magical combinations such as man-animal, woman-tree and man-woman were frequent motifs in tantric art. The elephant's head with its trunk was connected to fabulous beings. A dominating theme is the cosmic duality of the sexes. The rites of sacral sexual pleasure found creative expression in the timberwork of Nepalese temples.

Fantastical mixed beings, half man, half animal or amalgams of animal bodies, inhabit the myths and fairy tales of all races. They protect or threaten man in the form of supernatural apparitions from the world of gods and demons. In India and Southeast Asia the inventive hands of artists fused the incomparable head of the elephant, in particular, with the bodies of men and animals of all kinds. In the Middle Ages the West vied with the fabulous artists of the Far East, as exemplified by the work of Hieronymus Bosch (1450–1516) and other known artists.

The elephant-headed Ganipatihardaya, 17th century AD. Taleju Bhavani Temple, Nepal

The elephant-woman of the tantric Buddhism of Nepal corresponds to Ganesh, the Hindu god. Represented in a dancing posture, she holds a chain in one hand and an axe in the other. The main hands imitate the gesture of conversation.

Lokapala, 17th century BC. Taleju Bhavani Temple, Nepal, Unusual portrayal of a Lokapala in the form of an elephant-bird, with the horns of a bull and the mane of a horse. The ears are like fins. The Lokapalas are eight deities who support the world from eight directions. Each Lokapala has an elephant assigned to him. The piece was part of the socle of a throne.

Elephant-headed giant bird, a fabulous being from an old Singhalese legend. Sri Lanka

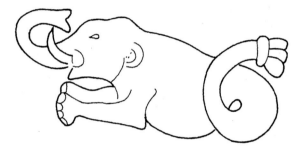

Elephant-fish, 1st century AD. India

Winged elephant-tiger after a wood sculpture. Udaipur, India

Sculpture of an anthropomorphic elephant, Quizil, Turfan, c. AD 700 air-dried clay. Height 63.5cm Museum für indische Kunst, Stiftung Museen Preußischer Kulturbesitz, Berlin

The elephant culture of India

Below:
Metal relief,
Johkang Temple.
Lhasa, Tibet

## Elephant symbols in Tibet

Opposite:
Guard elephant in front of a
temple in Bodnath, a religious
centre near the old Nepalese royal
city of Patan (near Katmandu).
A 110-foot-high stupa is the
holiest building in Nepal.

Right:
Tibetan painting in the Johkang
Temple (Master's house), the
country's most important shrine,
in Lhasa. The temple has been in
its present form since the middle
of the 17th century.

In Tibet, the theocracy of Lamaism, the image of
the elephant is found in temples as a holy symbol of
Buddha, the enlightened one. In the 6th century AD
Mahayana Buddhism was brought from Bengal
into the Himalayan region, where there developed
a purely monastic religion which also spread
throughout Mongolia.

The lamas seek redemption through meditation,
yoga exercises and ritual. In the 14th century the
monks also seized political power. Laymen practise
their beliefs by the circumambulation of temples,
the veneration of relics, and the buying of amulets;
they increase the beneficial effect of the holy
mantra "om mani padme hum" by setting prayer
wheels in motion. The holy mantra has central
importance for Buddhists. 'Om' is a sacred syllable.
Before the storm of Mao's 'cultural revolution'
passed over Tibet the country could number about
3,000 monasteries, to which the bulk of the
agricultural land belonged. The number of monks
was estimated to be about 300,000, which is an
amazingly high number in a total population of
3–4 million Tibetans.

# The 'white elephant' in Southeast Asia

The culture of India made a profound impression on the bordering countries of Southeast Asia. The mighty neighbor, with whom close trading relations had existed since olden times, exported Buddhism,

*Legend of Vishnu and the white elephant,* probably Garuda, Puri, Orissa, middle of the 20th century, Oleo-resinous paint on canvas. Private collection

which took root predominantly in Thailand, Burma, and Cambodia, and also the veneration of the elephant. The patient gray giants lent dignity to kings and religious worship and among the common people they served as useful laborers. For centuries they also performed bloody military service on the Indo-Chinese peninsula during the power struggles of rival empires. In Siam, as the land of the Thais was known for long periods, a particular cult evolved around the 'white elephant.' In 1548 the Portuguese Jesuit missionary Fernão Mendes Pinto noted that the King of Siam bore the title 'Phra Chao Chang Phuk,' the 'King of the White Elephant.' Later Siam, which never came under colonial rule, was also called the 'Land of the White Elephant.'

Opposite:
Guard elephant with two calves in front of a rebuilt temple among the extensive ruins of the former Thai capital Ayuthya, which was destroyed during a devastating invasion by the Burmese in 1767. Many pagodas have reappeared in the midst of the ruins during the long-running restoration work. Ayuthya, lying about thirty miles to the north of Bangkok, the new capital, is a popular tourist destination.

# "As beautiful as a white elephant ..."

The 'white elephant,' the exceptionally rare albino form of the elephant, was for centuries considered a priceless treasure in Southeast Asia, and reserved for the possession of kings and princes. Its exceptional nature made manifest its wondrous divine origins. The mythical Airavata was its ancestor, with four tusks and a skin as white as the

White elephant in the palace precinct of the King of Thailand, Bangkok, c. 1910. Museum für Völkerkunde, Munich

The celebrated white elephants of Siam were in no way as radiant as the immaculate white Airavata, their divine ancestor. Zoologically they are semi-albinos, animals which lack skin pigment. The historical white elephants of the royal courts of Siam and Burma represented the closest approximation to white, with pale, salmon-colored skin tones or marks and yellow-brown to reddish eyes. To the uninitiated the white elephants do not differ strikingly from normal animals. There are no truly white elephants. For religious purposes or public royal ceremonies even semi-albinos with some color were and are transformed into truly white elephants, just as they appear on coats of arms.

snowcap on Kailasa, the mountain of the gods. He was the mount of Indra, the god of thunder who imposes order on the world and who also bestows rain. If elephants, which in cosmic prehistory had mated with the clouds, were commonly considered mediators for longed-for rain, then the wondrous white type offered quite particular surety against drought and famine.

White animals enjoy special esteem and even veneration in many regions of the world, above all among the Asian peoples, who adhere to a belief in the transmigration of souls after death. In the cycle of reincarnation the soul can enter an animal's body, and white animals signify a higher level of purification. The most noble 'vestment of the soul' reserved for kings, heroes and saints, is the white elephant, which also provided for a time a noble resting place for Buddha's soul on the long road which led via complete renunciation of the world to eventual enlightenment.

In Siam and Burma particularly the white elephant appeared very early as a holy symbol. If one was caught it had to be surrendered to the king immediately. In medieval Burma not even the king was allowed to mount it, since the white elephant was considered just as great a lord as he himself: the white elephant could after all contain the soul of a previous king.

In Bangkok a pomp-laden exclusive courtly cult developed around the outsider of its species. During receptions a magnificently decorated white elephant stood constantly at the inner gate of the palace, as a symbol of royal greatness and honor. In the royal stables the stall of the white elephant, fitted out in keeping with its rank, was marked by plaques bearing extravagant homage and praise, describing him poetically as perfect in form – like a crystal of the highest value – a source of power and a bringer of rain. General veneration and deference, however, did not signify good luck for the elephant, who was usually tethered, and languishing in boredom under fine canopies.

A cousin of the king, who had led a Siamese delegation to London in the middle of the 19th century, reported, on his return, his impressions of the English court and the "wonderful appearance " of Queen Victoria: "it is impossible not to be captivated by the commanding appearance of the noble Queen of England and one cannot fail to see that she is of illustrious birth, descended from noble and powerful kings and rulers of the earth. She has the eyes, complexion and, above all, the bearing of a beautiful, majestic white elephant ..."

Even today the white elephant enjoys high esteem and cultic veneration in Thailand. In 1987 there were said to be six white elephants in the strictly shielded royal stables, and there is still the instruction to report every white elephant to the king, who knows well the stabilizing power of old traditions on his subjects.

The highly-valued white elephants are graded into four ranks by the Thais. Besides the main criteria of skin color and skin markings they evaluate: the form of the forehead and chest; the shape, length and color of the tusks; the form and length of the trunk; the color and shape of the hooves etc. An old Thai text extols in flowery terms the properties which should mark out the royal white elephant and which constitute his particular beauty as a holy symbol.

According to this, the tip of the trunk and penis, tongue and lips should be reddish, and the ears, smooth at the edges. The tusks should gleam the color of honey; the body should be fluent and the skin, with reddish marks, should be smooth. The toenails should be the color of the moon, like a tortoise. A white elephant which masters the eight rules of combat, is courageous and prepared to kill, is the king's mount in battle. For Asian connoisseurs small nuances of color or light marks are important as they promise more or less luck.

## Disenchanted in Burma

A white elephant of the royal stables in Bangkok.

General veneration certainly did not and does not mean good luck for the elephants reserved for the king, which doze away their lives in boredom or stand as fine objects under canopies.

Under Burma's founding king Anavratha and his successors, Pagan, which stretched for over 8 miles on the banks of the Irrawaddy river, became a magnificent city with 1,000 pagodas, terraces and abundant sculptures. Many hundreds of working elephants were employed during the tremendous building work; elephants whose form also enriched the Buddhist symbolism. In 1287 the magnificent royal city was destroyed by the Mongols. It remained a gigantic ruin.

Over the next 500 years Burma passed through phases of chaos, civil war and peaceful periods of prosperity. The country witnessed a new cultural flowering in the 16th–17th centuries. Exquisite

examples of painting, wood carving and sculpture have been preserved. As in the neighboring country of Thailand, a pomp-laden and ceremonial cult developed around the 'white elephant' in the royal court at Dala (today a suburb of Rangoon). The stables of the 'white' prodigies were said to have been lined with gold.

An all too turbulent history, which brought Burma into conflict with Britain at the beginning of the 19th century and led to colonial dependence in 1886, diluted and erased many of the old traditions. Today the elephant in Myanmar, as Burma is now known, is disenchanted and merely a working animal used to drag tree trunks on teak logging sites.

# The entrance of his majesty the 'White Elephant'

A colorful report about the fabulous courtly ceremony surrounding the auspicious capture of a white elephant was written by Anna Leonowens, the Englishwoman engaged by Somdech P'hra Paarmendr Maha Mongkut, the King of Siam, as governess to his children in 1862:

"When the governor of a province of Siam is notified of the appearance of a white elephant within his bailiwick, he immediately commands that prayers and offerings shall be made in all the temples, while he sends out a formidable expedition of hunters and slaves to take the precious beast ... As soon as he is informed of its capture, a special messenger is despatched to inform the king of its sex, probable age, size, complexion, deportment, looks, and ways; and in the presence of his Majesty this bearer of glorious tidings undergoes the painfully pleasant operation of having his mouth, ears, and nostrils stuffed with gold. Especially is the lucky wight ... who was first to spy the illustrious monster munificently rewarded. Orders are promptly issued to the woons and wongses of the several districts through which he must pass to prepare to receive him royally, and a wide path is cut for him through the forests he must traverse on his way to the capital. Wherever he rests he is sumptuously entertained, and everywhere he is escorted and served by a host of close attendants, who sing, dance, play upon instruments, and perform feats of strength or skill for his amusement, until he reaches the banks of the Meinam, where a great floating palace of wood, surmounted by a gorgeous roof and hung with crimson curtains, awaits him. The roof is literally thatched with flowers ingeniously arranged so as to form symbols and mottoes, which the superior beast is supposed to decipher with ease. The floor of this splendid float is laid with gilt matting curiously woven, in the centre of which his four-footed lordship is then installed in state, surrounded by an obsequious and enraptured crowd of mere bipeds, who bathe him, perfume him, fan him, feed him, sing and play to him, flatter him. His food consists of the finest herbs, the tenderest grass, the sweetest sugarcane, the mellowest plantains, the brownest cakes of wheat, served on huge trays of gold and silver ...

"Thus, in more than princely state, he is floated down the river to a point within seventy miles of the capital, where the king and his court, all the chief personages of the kingdom, and a multitude of both Buddhist and Brahmin priests, accompanied by troops of players and musicians, come out to meet him, and conduct him with all the honors to his stable-palace. A great number of cords and

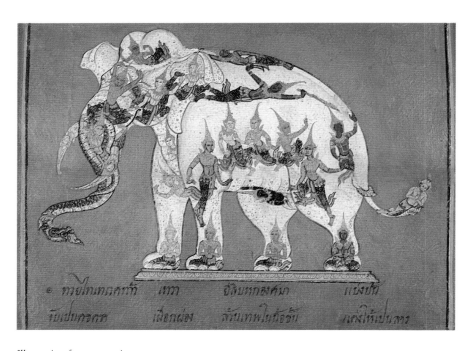

Illustration from a treatise on mythical and natural elephants, Thailand, 19th century, painting on paper.

Pictures of twenty-four deities decorate the body and tusks of the elephant; a snake forms the trunk.

Miniature by Behzad
From a collection of Indian, Turkish and Persian paintings, India, 16th–18th centuries. Bibliothèque Nationale de France, Paris

The elephant, ridden by a man with a dagger, differs from an ordinary animal only in its white or light-colored patches.

*The white elephant*, 19th century, fresco.
Great Palace, Bangkok

The legend of the 'white elephant,' the celestial mount of Indra, the Hindu god, is the subject of this mural in the colonnade of the Great Palace in Bangkok, commissioned by King Rama III (1824–51).

A white elephant in the stables of the royal palace in Bangkok tugs at his ankle chain. His physical perfection and nuances of color and markings, barely perceptible to the inexperienced eye, confer royal rank. His markings are also interpreted as good luck symbols.

The 'White Elephant' of the American circus king, Barnum, with his attendant, from 'The Illustrated London News' of December 4, 1886.

Two years after Jumbo, the circus box office hit, (see also the chapter 'The circus jumbo') the royal white elephant was to have been a sensation in New York. Barnum's agents had bought the white prodigy from King Thibau of Burma for 6,000 dollars in 1864. The elephant was certainly not the radiant white that had been imagined. It was ash grey with pale ears and light patches on its head, neck and back.

ropes of all qualities and lengths are attached to the raft, those in the center being of fine silk ... These are for the king and his noble retinue, who with their own hands make them fast to their gilded barges; the rest are secured to the great fleet of lesser boats. And so, with shouts of joy, beating of drums, blare of trumpets, the boom of cannon, a halleluja of music, and various splendid revelry, the great Chang Phoouk is conducted in triumph to the great capital city.

"Here in a pavilion, temporary but very beautiful, he is welcomed with imposing ceremonies by the custodians of the palace and the principal personages of the royal household. The king, his courtiers, and the chief priests being gathered round him, thanksgiving is offered up; and then the lordly beast is knighted, after the ancient manner of the Buddhists, by pouring upon his forehead consecrated water from a chank-shell ...

"For seven or nine days, according to certain conditions the Chang Phoouk is fêted at the temporary pavilion, and entertained with a variety of dramatic performances; and these days are observed as a general holiday throughout the land. At the expiration of this period he is conducted with great pomp to his sumptuous quarters within the precincts of the first king's palace, where he is received by his own court of officers, attendants, and slaves, who install him in his fine lodgings, and at once proceed to robe and decorate him. First the court jeweller

rings his tremendous tusks with massive gold, crowns him with a diadem of beaten gold of perfect purity, and adorns his burly neck with heavy golden chains. Next his attendants robe him with a superb velvet cloak of purple, fringed with scarlet and gold; and then his court prostrate themselves around him, and offer him royal homage ..."

Suffice to mention the Ruanweli Dagoba, built at the behest of King Dutthagamani who reigned in the 2nd century BC. Their foreheads turned towards the observer, 344 mighty elephants carry the circular 'Dagoba,' the Buddhist building for containing relics, which corresponds to the 'stupa' of India and the 'pagoda' of China. A monastic chronicle relates that during the building work particularly strong elephants, their feet protected with leather shoes, stamped down the foundations.

The Ceylonese royal chronicle tells of Kandula, the heroic war elephant, who helped Dutthagamani to overcome the periodic foreign rule of the South Indian Tamil prince Elala. With his mighty skull Kandula charged the iron-clad gate of Elala's fortress. When the enemy threw red-hot iron balls and poured boiling pitch over him from the wall he trotted to a nearby pool to cool his wounds; then he rammed the gate with redoubled force until it burst from its hinges.

In the 11th century under the pressure of Tamil invasions from South India, the Singhalese kings transferred their seat of government to their great summer residence of Polonnaruva, which was to develop into the new capital. The image of the elephant is also found in varied forms in the ruins of the second imperial and cultural centre.

After 1235 the kingdom of Polonnaruva was divided, and the Tamils controlled the north of the island. 1505 saw the beginning of the colonial era with seizure by the Portuguese, followed by the Dutch and finally the British.

Turned towards the observer, an expertly carved stone giant from the famous elephant surround of the Ruanweli Dagoba in the ruins of Anuradhapura.

Elephant surround,
Ruanweli Dagoba
2nd century BC.
Anuradhapura,
Sri Lanka

An imposing line of 344 life-size elephant sculptures surrounds the mighty rotunda of the Ruanweli Dagoba, which King Dutthagamani had built, after the Indian pattern, in Anuradhapura. The ancient capital today lies in ruins. The former royal palace, the 'Brazen Palace' was, according to tradition, a wooden building overlaid with gilded copper plate resting on granite pillars. The throne was worked in ivory and rock crystal.

## The elephants of Ceylon

The elephant has always played a special role in Ceylon, today Sri Lanka, which even in the sphere of influence of Indian culture and religion went its own insular way. As early as the 3rd century BC, at the time of Alexander the Great's Indian campaign, island princes supplied the kingdoms of the southern continent over the sea with war elephants. In the 3rd century BC missionaries were sent to the island by the renowned King Ashoka (272–232 BC) of the Indian Maurya empire to propagate Theravada Buddhism, considered the original form of the doctrine of the Enlightened One. Ashoka's son and daughter also went to Ceylon as missionaries (see also the chapter 'Elephant power in the Hellenistic period' for further reference).

The first kingdoms were founded in the 5th century BC by the Singhalese, who came from Northern India. In the ruins of Anuradhapura, the first capital, whose temple buildings, monasteries and palaces cover an area of about three square miles, there is impressive evidence of the ancient elephant culture of Ceylon. The image of the giant beasts, which lent their strength in their thousands during the construction of all the great buildings, is immortalized times without number in stone.

Tile with elephant relief,
Sri Lanka, 10th/11th century,
terra cotta.
21cm x 12.1cm x 1.3cm
County Museum of Art, Los
Angeles

Elephant frieze on the moonstone
of the 'Vatadage' Temple
(detail, top left),
Polonnaruva, Sri Lanka
12th century.

One of the four 'moonstones'
which lay before the entrances to
the 'Vatadage' Temple in
Polonnaruva, the second historical
capital of Sri Lanka. An elevated
processional path was constructed
around the circular temple which
enclosed a dagoba.

War elephant (detail),
outer gallery of 'Bayon' Temple,
c. 1200.
Angkor Thom

Military deployment with
elephants (Detail),
1st half of the 12th century,
relief.
Historical Gallery, Angkor Wat

Part of an approximately 300ft
long relief wall panel in the
western part of the 'Angkor Wat'
Temple. It shows a military
deployment of the Khmer army of
King Suryavarman II with Siamese
auxiliary troops.

Battle relief (detail),
1st half of the 12th century,
2nd level of Angkor Wat Temple.

The 'white elephant' in Southeast Asia

South end of the 'Elephant Terrace' at the temple palace of Bayon, c. 1200.
Angkor Wat

In the 13th century Bayon was the centre of power of the Khmer empire and its symbolic image. Powerful elephant reliefs stretch for 1,000 feet along the walls of the galleries which lead around the central sanctuary and the royal palace buildings. The colossi are walking in file as they would have done in their former everyday service. During festive occasions the terrace was used by the king and his court as a grandstand.

# The marvel of Angkor

The most outstanding medieval evidence of the elephant culture of Southeast Asia is found in Cambodia, in the mighty ruined city of Angkor, the former capital of the Khmer empire. Founded at the beginning of the 9th century and devastated many times by war, Angkor developed into the most glittering center of south Asia. In 1431 the Khmer empire suffered a devastating invasion by the Thais. The ravaged city of Angkor, deserted by the surviving population, was overgrown by the jungle; it was forgotten and only rediscovered in the 19th century. The mighty temple and palace buildings, which defied destruction and even the jungle, are among the most sublime cultural monuments of mankind.

At the height of the Khmer's power Angkor was a city landscape of great splendor, divided by a large checkerboard canal system which was supplied with river water via vast reservoirs. In this scene of nature transformed, the deified rulers erected gigantic temples and palaces at an expense that beggars imagination.

The mightiest architectural construction of south Asia, Angkor Wat, came into being under King Suryavarman II (1113–50), one of the most powerful rulers of Asia. The rectangular enclosure of the sacred precinct measures 5,000 feet x 4,000 feet and is surrounded by a 650 foot wide moat. Inside, the gigantic temple building rises from a base measurement of 700 feet x 650 feet and is crowned by a 150 foot high central tower. Three terraced galleries sloping down to the moat extend at the front. In a fantastic profusion of carved three-dimensional statues and mile-long reliefs on the walls and friezes, typical of Khmer art, the symbolic form of the elephant is immortalized times without number.

The elephant was the royal mount, comrade in arms in times of war and helper in everyday life; he also had his place in the ritual of the adopted Indian religions and in the worlds of divine legends. Not least, the elephant joined his enormous strength to the armies of slaves, workers and sculptors who built in a record time the gigantic and majestic holy temples and palaces gleaming with pure gold, and the shimmering towers and terraced galleries among the network of canals which supplied drinking water, provided for water transport and the carefully thought out irrigation of the hinterland. This geometric layout symbolized the cosmic world view of the Khmers.

Angkor was laid waste after its rulers lost a war against the Vietnamese. King Jayavarman VII (1161–1219) reorganized the heart of the city in a huge building program. He created his Angkor Wat surrounded by defenses; he had the colossal Bayon temple palace built. The 1,000 foot long 'Elephant Terrace' extending in front of the temple with its large elephant reliefs was used as a grandstand by the king and his entourage during festivities.

From the 9th to the 15th century the Khmer empire was a great power in southern Asia. Khmer art was influential on the whole Indo-Chinese peninsula.

The 'white elephant' in Southeast Asia

Opposite:
Festively decorated elephant monument in the ruins of Ayuthya, the capital of Thailand until its destruction by the Burmese in 1767. Today a few of the temples in Ayuthya, the destination of Bangkok tourists, have been restored.

The Buddhist shrine Wat Chang Lom built in the 13th century at Si Satchanalai is bordered by twenty-nine stucco elephants, giving the place of worship its name: 'Temple surrounded by elephants.' The Thai artists seldom worked in stone; building in brick was also the custom.

## The Elephant in Thai art

A battle scene from the Thai version of the Ramayana epic. Fresco in the 'Temple of the Emerald Buddha' (Wat Phra Keo), which is situated in the precinct of the 'Great Palace' and contains many masterpieces of Thai arts and crafts.

Below left:
Elephant relief in the 'Wat Phra That Doi Suthep' Temple in Chian Mai, 16th century.

Below right:
The 'elephant trees' of Bang Pain. Thai garden art has conjured a whole herd of elephants from living nature.

The Thais, who destroyed Angkor in 1431, accepted Buddhism, as proclaimed by Indian monks, as their state religion in about AD 600. As in all Buddhist countries, the image of the elephant, so useful in everyday working life and in war, became a religious and mythical symbol.

The first mighty empires of Sukhodaya and Ayuthya were stamped with the influence of Khmer high culture. Harking back to the monumental buildings of Angkor, they constructed, no longer in natural stone but in brick, towering shrines (prang), central stupas surrounded by small stupas, monasteries, assembly halls and extensive temples with guard elephants.

In 1767 during a phase of high cultural flowering, Ayuthya was destroyed during a devastating invasion by the Burmese. Bangkok became the new imperial center, and here Chinese influence was evident in the ornate royal palace buildings, temples, pagodas and intricately superimposed roofs covered with colorfully-glazed tiles.

# The pantheon of the 'Nats'

About eighty percent of the population of Burma (today Myanmar) profess Buddhism. However, in common with the whole of Southeast Asia, the pure doctrine of the Enlightened One is linked in the popular imagination with an ancient belief in gods, spirits and demons. In the 9th century Tibeto-Burmese conquerors from the regions on the Tibetan-Chinese border introduced the animistic cult of the 'Nats' into the country: this is the veneration of spirit deities who manifest themselves in nature and in many natural phenomena.

The invaders brought the rich rice-growing areas of Upper Burma under their control, as well as the city of Pagan on the river Irrawaddy, a nodal point on the main trade routes. They founded a kingdom that was at the height of its power and cultural development in the 11th and 12th centuries. The elephant, native to the nearby mountain forests, was of service both in war and on the building site. In 1044 King Anavathra (or Anuradha) made Pagan the capital of his far-reaching empire.

An old fable tells how the immigrant animistic Burmese became Buddhists: no sooner had a son been born to the king, than a demoness rose up out of the sea to devour the child. A troop of devils accompanied her as bodyguards, each of which had two lion's bodies and one head. It happened again just as Indian missionaries were preaching the doctrine of Buddhism. The monks summoned twice as many monsters, and the demons took flight. With such a display of superior magical powers the preachers did not find it difficult to win the astonished people for Buddha – and the gentle monks did not prevent the people from venerating their Nats in future.

The pantheon of the Nats was peopled by a great number of deities of the elements and natural forces, of trees and animals, water and fire, and in addition a very heterogeneous company of the spirits of legendary people, both good and evil, who had lost their lives in dramatic circumstances. Among the most important Nats were tree spirits worshipped on the extinct volcano Popa. There an orgiastic festival with dancing to the point of ecstasy was held annually. The Nats pictured here, carried by elephants supporting the firmament, are examples of old portrayals in folding books. The illustrations are found in 'The Thirty-Seven Nats, A Phase of Spirit-worship prevailing in Burma,' 1906.

All illustrations from 'The Thirty-Seven Nats, A Phase of Spirit-worship prevailing in Burma' London W. Griggs, Chromo-Lithographer to the King, 1906

Below left:
The exceptionally beautiful Queen Okkalabu, who was neglected by the king and forced to earn her living as a weaver, is venerated as Tonban Hla Nat. She died of grief, united in death with her daughter. She is carried by an elephant-headed Ganesh.

Mahagiri Nat, worshipped as the 'guardian of the home' is also worshipped in this incarnation: standing on the shoulders of a hobgoblin carried by an elephant.

Thagya Nat is the cosmic god of the firmament. His image is borne by four white elephants, which symbolize the four quarters of the heavens and also carry the vault of heaven.

Far left:
Ma Savme, sister of the smith and wife of the wicked king, threw herself on to her brother in the burning jasmine tree and, after her death, became Hnamadavgyi Nat. She wears courtly clothing and is supported by a hobgoblin.

As Nats, the brother and sister lived with a jasmine tree and spread much mischief among the people. So the king had the jasmine tree felled and thrown into the Irrawaddy river. From here it was recovered and then brought to Mount Popa, the volcano, where amidst great festivities sacrifices were made to the Nat siblings in December.

Left:
Mahagiri Nat venerated as the 'guardian of the home:' the deified spirit of the smith Nga Tinde, who according to a folk fable, disturbed the king with noise from his workshop, presented himself late when summoned, and was condemned to be burnt to death tied to a jasmine tree. He is represented with drawn sword and fan, and supported by three hobgoblins squatting on a kneeling elephant.

Far left:
Ngazishin Nat, the son of a king, who brought five white elephants into the country by sea. He is enthroned with four parasols, the royal insignia of Burma, on a lotus blossom carried by a five-headed elephant.

Left:
Aungbinle Sinbyushin Nat was the son of a king, who was killed. Wearing courtly clothing he is enthroned on an elephant and accompanied by hobgoblins.

# Immortalized in stone on Java

In the Indonesian archipelago today only Sumatra still has a reserve of about 3,000 elephants in the shrinking, over-felled tropical forests. The taming of wild elephants for work on logging sites has become only an occasional activity. On Java, overpopulated with about 100 million people, there has long been no room for the gray giant. In the early Middle Ages, in the powerful empires which arose on the two main islands under the strong influence of Indian culture, there were still large elephant populations in the vast forest zones and a rich elephant culture.

The oldest evidence dates from the 7th and 8th centuries. The image of the elephant has been immortalized, above all, in the countless temples built from enduring natural stone in Central Java, built incidentally with a considerable amount of heavy labor on the part of the elephant. On the island of Sumatra, where building with bricks predominated, only a few ruins of the old buildings have been preserved.

From India came Buddhism and Hinduism. Java's Hindus paid homage in their temples to Shiva, the destroyer- and creator-god, and his son, the elephant-headed Ganesh. The Javanese image of Ganesh, the luck-bringer and remover of obstacles, has been preserved in many places, including Sumatra. In addition, masks of sea monsters with trunks placed above doors are usually reminiscent of elephants.

Indo-Javanese culture experienced a high flowering from the 8th to the 10th centuries during

Scene from a relief running round the walls at the Borobudur Temple on Java, the largest Buddhist shrine outside India, built in the 9th century. It relates the life of Buddha. Here a court elephant with an escort of warriors – a reminder of the royal origin of the Enlightened One during his time as Prince Siddhartha.

the era of the great 'Shrivijaya' maritime empire, which under the Shailendra emperors controlled the Strait of Malacca and the trade route from India to China. In about AD 800, a time of growing power and profitable trade, the most impressive Buddhist shrine outside India, the hill temple of Borobudur, was built in Central Java. The seven-tiered terraced building, constructed around a hill, is 335 feet square. The first terraces, bordered by balustrades and rising in steps, are also arranged in a square. Then there is a change to circular tiers. The construction is crowned by a stupa.

The carved image of the elephant as a Buddhist religious symbol appears repeatedly on the terrace walls. The way of salvation from the depths of earthly desire to renunciation of the world and redeeming enlightment is represented in reliefs running around the walls. Other cycles tell of the life of Buddha. The mighty construction suffered a similar fate to that of Angkor Wat in Cambodia. In 1006 Borobudur was destroyed during an eruption of the nearby volcano Merapi. Abandoned by the fleeing population and left to the jungle, it was absorbed into the luxuriant tropical vegetation. The ruins were only rediscovered in 1814. There

The Hindu god Ganesh, who helps to overcome obstacles, was much venerated on Java and Sumatra. Regional artistic influences changed his appearance slightly. The plump body rests on a circular colonnade of skulls. The four arms hold an axe, a rosary, a vessel, and his own broken tusk which, according to one legend, he threw at the moon god.

Water vessel,
Eastern Java,
1st century BC,
bronze.
Height 32cm
Mpu Tantular Museum, Surabaja

A water vessel in the form of an
elephant which was perhaps used
in religious ceremonies. The 32 cm
high bronze elephant from the 1st
century BC was in a large kettle
gong which was found in Eastern
Java in 1974.

The relief from the Buddha cycle
at Borobudur shows Prince
Siddhartha in a courtly ceremonial
procession headed by a
magnificently bridled elephant.
The prince still indulges in the
joys and pleasures of life; he has
not yet encountered the misery
and suffering which before long
will prompt him completely to
renounce the world.

have been a few minor attempts at restoration, but
to little effect. Today restoration is in full swing,
financed by UNESCO which has designated
Borobudur as a World Heritage Site.

When Islam spread into the Indonesian
archipelago via Sumatra in the 13th century, at first
peacefully, and then by conquest, the Muslim rulers
of the great empire, which at times also included
part of the Malayan peninsula, also made use of the
elephant. In the 17th century the Dutch entered the
scene. The 'Dutch East India Company,' founded in
1602, acquired by treaty and conquest ever greater
territories until it finally controlled almost the
whole of the Indonesian archipelago. The elephant
was now taken under colonial management. He
helped to clear the jungle for plantation agriculture
and he served in the Dutch army, which time and
again had to crush rebellion. Only after the Second
World War, following one last fruitless 'police
action' to regain the control that had been
interrupted by the Japanese, did the Dutch release
Indonesia to independence on December 24, 1949.

Guard elephant with ornamental
decoration in front of the 'Pura
Puseh' Temple at Batubulan on
the island of Bali.

# The shadow figures of Southeast Asia

Shadow play and puppet shows, ever great favorites in Southeast Asia, maintain ancient traditions. They have an inexhaustible source of narrative material in the myths of the Hindu gods and the Ramayana saga cycle, at times with a regional flavor, in heroic stories and dramatic historical episodes. The entertainment is provided by exciting battle scenes, and here the war elephant has kept his place on the screen in regions where there have been no elephants for a long time. Artistic inventiveness is displayed in the design of the bewildering variety of gorgeously colored picture panels and figures.

Of special reknown are the Javanese shadow plays (wayang) with their delicately designed, brightly colored picture panels which are moved around on rods. The puppeteers who relate the events in the legends, with or without orchestral accompaniment, sit behind a screen on which the figures are projected. In other forms the puppeteers sit in front of the screen and offer the public an unimpeded view of the vivid colors of the picture panels.

Marionettes,
19th century,
solid wood.
Puppet theater museum in the Stadtmuseum, Munich

Moving elephant figures from a Burmese puppet theater. The holy white elephant fights against an evil black one.

Wayang figure, Balinese Hindu shadow play figure,
Indonesia,
cut, punched and painted buffalo skin.
Private collection

The 'white elephant' in Southeast Asia

Thai shadow play figure,
cut, punched and painted
buffalo skin.
Puppet theater museum in the
Stadtmuseum, Munich

The picture panel with the
elephant, moved with a rod, is a
figure from a battle scene in the
Hindu Ramayana saga cycle.

Nang screen,
scene from the Ramakien
(Ramaana), battle scene with a
three-headed elephant,
cut and punched buffalo
skin, colored.
Puppet theater museum in the
Stadtmuseum, Munich

A Javanese shadow play elephant.
The picture panel is moved
around on a rod, to fit in with the
events in the legend which is
related by the puppeteer.

179

## Asian elephant masks

In eastern Asia colorful masks are worn in theatrical performances and religious ceremonies: masks of gods and grotesque demons, of animals and human beings. The elephant's head with its trunk occupies a special place in ritual and customs. The gray giant, who according to Hindu myths had a divine ancestor, enjoys religious veneration. Ganesh, a god honored from India to Java, even has the head of an elephant. In the Thai theater dancers with elephant masks represent this friendly god, the patron of learning and helper in the adversities of existence. Elephant masks are also symbols of royalty indicating power and promising protection. During religious dances the supernatural being embodied in the mask is summoned against the powers of evil; the dancer concealed behind the elephant mask believes himself to be filled with transcendental power.

The gods and demons of the many-layered Hindu and Buddhist pantheon, who like man are subject to an eternal universal law, embody cosmic phenomena, the elemental forces of nature and ethical principles. The sun, the earth, water – the whole world in all its phenomena is a manifestation of the gods and demons who reveal themselves in countless incarnations and have their symbolic attributes in religious masked dance. In the Hindu and Buddhist concept of the world heavenly and cosmic events in the universe have their equivalents in the microcosm of our earth and in the life of man, who, with the mask, borrows the form and mysterious powers of the supernatural beings.

'Phikhánêt,' the Thai Ganesh, has the original Hindu form. The dance mask is only colored regionally. Phikhánêt represents gentleness and placability in the fullness of divine strength. In the Thai dance theater he appears as a god and the protector of art.

The 'white elephant' in Southeast Asia

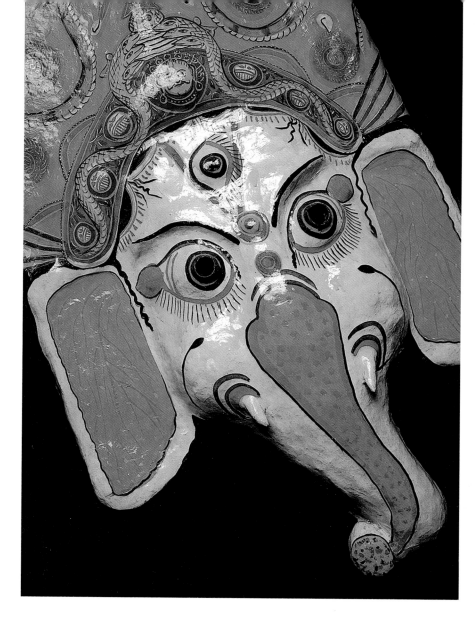

The stylized, brightly painted elephant head of 'Pulikisi,' the Nepalese Ganesh. In the spirit-inhabited Himalayan mountain region, where divine power is manifested in the violence of the elements, the good-natured god of the Indian Hindus has demonic traits. He has three eyes, around which snakes writhe.

Top right:
The mask is crowned by intertwined animal bodies and grotesque demonic beings, whose dark powers are displayed symbolically in the religious dance, in the eternal struggle of heavenly power with evil.

'Faces' from the world of India's spirits and deities. For India's Hindus animals too are incarnations of heavenly beings and demons. A large number of temples have been built in their honor and they are thanked for their help or their anger is assuaged with sacrifices and frequent festivals.

## Long-distance swimmers in the Bay of Bengal

The sensational underwater photograph was taken in the Bay of Bengal: an elephant swimming under water in the open sea. Progress is quicker under water. The flexible legs paddle; the bulky body stretches forward, supported by the water.

Elephants love water; they love to swim and they are among the best long-distance swimmers of all the mammals. In regions where there is no shortage of rivers and lakes they lead an aquatic life, reminiscent of their closest living relative, the sea cow which grazes near the shore in warm seas. On the coast of Southeast Asia it is not difficult for elephants to swim across the open sea to islands near the mainland or to swim from island to island, as they do on the Andaman Islands in the Bay of Bengal. Jacques Cousteau (1910–97), the French marine researcher famous for his wildlife documentaries and use of new filming techniques, filmed swimming elephants there.

The water supports the elephant's bulky body; the mighty feet paddle and when swimming quickly under water, the trunk serves as a snorkel. The greatest recorded distance covered by elephants is about thirty miles. Swimming speed has been measured at 1.6mph. In the coastal regions of Indonesia Sumatra's elephants have also proved to be excellent sea swimmers. But the continuing settlement and clear felling of the tropical forests, as well as the disastrous forest-clearing fires which raged out of control in 1997–98 and filled the sky over south Asia with deadly smoke, are causing the rapid disappearance of the remaining elephant herds on the island.

Towards the end of the 19th century, when there were still large elephant populations in India, G. P. Sanderson, the elephant researcher, observed the crossing of the mighty mouth of the Ganges by a herd of seventy-nine animals. The animals had to swim without a break for six hours. Then after a rest on a sandbank they had to paddle for a further three hours through the river's floods until they finally reached firm ground, an amazing journey, which was apparently easily achieved.

An elephant swimming under water. When swimming quickly under water the elephant extends its trunk like a snorkel so that it can breathe. The elephant is one of the best and most indefatigable swimmers of all the mammals.

Underwater encounter with elephant legs: an unusual tourist experience on the Andaman Islands. The elephants appear to be enjoying a sleepy bathe near to the shore.

## Elephant fighting shows

Two fighting elephants, Mogul period, c. 1625, gouache on paper. Bibliothèque Nationale de France, Paris

The trial of strength in open country has got out of control. Helpers hold crackling fireworks on long sticks between the raging animals to separate them.

During Mogul rule in the 16th–17th centuries elephant fighting shows, which existed in ancient India, were a regular form of court entertainment. Originally an imperial privilege, the spectacle of titans clashing also became a favorite titillation at the courts of the Rajput princes. The exhibition fights provided instruction and training for the elephants in preparation for their use in battle in times of war. The animals' aggressiveness was whipped up with drugs.

The exhibition fights usually took place in the courtyard so that the prince and court society could watch from the palace windows. The huge beasts were also set against each other on open spaces outside the court precinct. Usually the test of strength was carried out over a separating wall or an 8 foot high embankment. The tearing tusks often caused serious injuries. Sometimes the earth wall broke under the urgent pursuit of the victorious bull, who could easily get out of control. A thrown rider was in the utmost danger; many a rider was trampled by a raging animal.

If fighting elephants became too embroiled and a life and death battle developed, fireworks were thrown between them. Under Emperor Akbar bamboo canes filled with gunpowder, which whirled around with an infernal noise, were held between the wildly struggling animals to end the on-going fierce fight.

Sometimes an elephant was set against a rhinoceros, whose pointed horn could inflict serious injuries to the chest and neck of the elephant, causing fatal injury, even though the elephant is the stronger animal.

Traditional contest during a Thai elephant festival. Customs handed down through the ages in the elephant countries of Southeast Asia are increasingly being commercialized for tourists.

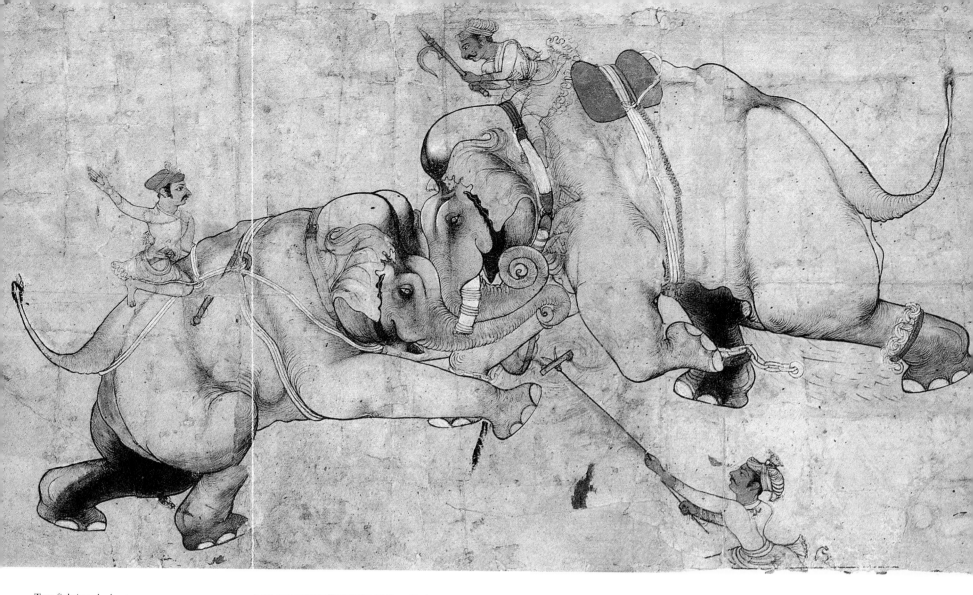

Two fighting elephants,
Kota, Rajasthan, c. 1670,
gouache and ink on paper.
34.2cm x 69cm
Bibliothèque Nationale de
France, Paris

Artist's impression of an elephant
fight in Mogul book illustration.
As on the opposite page a
firework is being used to end the
over-zealous fight.

Thousands of spectators watch
this elephant fight in Vadodara,
India on December 3, 1931.

# The biggest elephant festival in Asia

Every year on November 17 the biggest elephant festival in Asia takes place in the small town of Surin about 250 miles to the northeast of Bangkok. About 200 elephants from the teak logging sites in the forests and from elephant breeding stations gather for peaceful competition. The climax is a race between the colossal heavyweights.

At Surin and Lampang in the south of the country there are large government-sponsored breeding and training centers for working elephants. Indeed there is scarcely a need for working animals on the logging sites (there is a new generation of, for the most part, wild bulls there); however the traditional methods of elephant training should be preserved, and the experience of the old elephant clans who – like the people of Suai – live with and earn their livelihood from the elephant, should be passed on to the young elephant men who receive their wages from the state or from private enterprise.

The encouraging initiative has turned into a rewarding concern. The elephants from the stations now drag and stack tree trunks, play tug of war, kick footballs, and put on a menacing display as war elephants in tournaments, all for tourists. Since animals are of interest to people if they can bring a profit, the success of this enterprise is an inducement towards further breeding efforts.

In the neighborhood of the major tourist centers of Bangkok and Pattaya there are already some small establishments for the show training of elephants with one or two dozen animals each. The owners, however, are too intent on a quick profit; proper training is hardly possible.

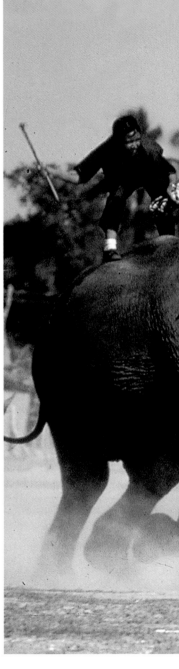

An artist draws an inventive picture of an elephant steeplechase said to have taken place in Rangoon in 1858. Elephants which jump hedges like horses exist only in fairy tales. The massive animals are indeed excellent climbers and can even get over high iron railings, but they cannot manage even the smallest jump.

Tourist show at the Crocodile Farm, Bangkok, Thailand. Posing on an elephant's back. The souvenir photograph for tourists is welcome income for the mahouts, who are needed less and less in the forests.

Elephant race,
Surin, Thailand.

The climax of the elephant events
at Surin is the spectacular 100
meter race for the heavyweight
giants, which are definitely not
built for speed. The ground
shakes; the crowd are elated.

Elephant festival,
Surin, Thailand.

The huge patient giants also have
to perform as football stars. Old
customs and ceremonial splendor
are reduced to mass spectacle for
the many tourists.

K'anghsi (1662–1722),
Porcelain dish with elephant
decoration, Ch'ing period,
porcelain.
Reemtsma Collection, Museum
für Kunst und Gewerbe, Hamburg

## The elephant in the 'Middle Kingdom'

In China where the elephant had already disappeared from the central regions in the Neolithic period, the gray giant only became a familar symbol of state power and ceremonial splendor in the 13th/14th centuries. It was the conquering far-reaching Mongolian emperors of the Yuen period (1276–1368), whose horseback armies encountered the awesome elephant corps of the kings of Annam, Burma and the East Indies on the Indo-Chinese peninsula and brought elephants in their thousands into the country.

Marco Polo (1254–1324), the famous Venetian traveler, who brought the first accurate reports about the mysterious 'Middle Kingdom' to the West, tells of a pomp-laden elephant parade on the occasion of a religious festival in Kambalu (Peking), which was the residence of the great emperor Kublai Khan:

"… On this special day all the elephants in the possession of the Great Khan – about 5,000 in number – are covered with cloths, wonderfully decorated with gold or silken animals or birds, and led past the ruler; these are followed in similar fashion by a train of camels; it is a splendid spectacle …" When the Venetian reports 5,000 elephants, he simply means a very large number. Inventive exaggeration was in keeping with the normal narrative style of his period.

Elephant with rider and chain,
China, 18th century,
ivory, length 5.6cm.
Simon Kwan Collection

An object of Chinese miniature
art: chain pendant with rider. On
the saddle cloth there is a dragon
motif in cloud decoration.

Decorated vase,
China, 19th century,
copper base with cloisonné
enamel finish,
Staatliches Museum für
Völkerkunde, Munich

This vase with elephant head
handles is shaped like a calabash
which was included in the
equipment of a Taoist holy man; it
served as a container for medicine.

Ridge turret,
Ch'ing period, 17th century,
two-colored ceramic.
Staatliches Museum für
Völkerkunde, Munich

The bodhisattva Samantabhadra
rides on an elephant, a Buddhist
symbol of wisdom and constancy.
Many bodhisattvas are venerated
in Mahayana Buddhism.
Bodhisattvas have already attained
enlightenment, but they renounce
the state and title of Buddha to
help men attain salvation. The
historical Buddha was likewise a
bodhisattva before enlightenment
came to him under the Bodhi tree.

A temple elephant from the
17th/18th century in the
'Forbidden City' in Peking
(Beijing), an enclosed, strictly
defined city within the city which,
with its magnificent palaces and
gardens, was reserved exclusively
for the emperor and court society.

Ceramic elephant as candlestick,
China, Sui dynasty (589–617),
ceramic.
Museum Rietberg, Zürich

## The 'Avenue of Spirits' of the Ming Emperors

The elephant was also well-known in the China of the Ming dynasty, which ruled from 1368–1644 following the expulsion of the Mongols, even though it was not included in the everyday life of the peasantry and officialdom. In art, which blossomed during this period, the elephant was a frequent motif, particularly as the Indian elephant myths had spread, along with Buddhism, right across the whole of China.

The gray giant appears on old scrolls and as a sculptural three-dimensional decoration on buildings; it was carved in both stone and ivory. Along with gigantic statues of people and other animals, mighty stone elephants also border the famous 'Avenue of Spirits,' which leads to the grave mounds of the Ming emperors near Peking. They stand or lie in peaceful poses, unlike the fearsome monsters which formerly kept away evil spirits in temples and on graves.

Today there are only about 250 elephants remaining in China, and they live in a small area of forest on the border with Laos and Myanmar.

Humorous ancient Chinese ink sketch. The rotund elephant, who radiates good nature like the popular, fat-bellied Buddha, seems to be chuckling about the timid woman on his back.

Stretched out in peaceful tranquillity, the mighty animal carved from a piece of rock in timeless style, keeps quiet guard.

The stone elephants of the 'Avenue of Spirits' are popular subjects for souvenir photographs for both Chinese and the many international tourists.

During the Ming period the elephant, brought into the Middle Kingdom by the conquering Mongol armies of the preceding Yuen period, was a frequent artistic motif. Powerful elephant monuments stand next to gigantic sculptures of other animals on the famous 'Avenue of Spirits,' built in 1435, which leads to the grave mounds of the Ming Emperors near Peking.

A tame elephant brought from India is scrubbed by Chinese attendants with long-handled brushes. Farcical portrayal from the 7th century.

## Kublai Khan's command post

Marco Polo's Chinese journey (see map).

In the year 1271 three Venetians, the brothers Maffeo and Nicolo Polo and Nicolo's son Marco, set off on a journey of discovery to the Far East. They took the overland route through unknown regions of Central Asia. After countless adventures they reached 'Cathay,' as China was called at that time, where they were given a friendly reception by the great Mongol emporer Kublai Khan. The Polos stayed in the Middle Kingdom until 1292, then they traveled back to Venice via the Sunda Islands, southern India and Persia. Back in Venice Marco Polo wrote down his travel reminiscences during a period as a prisoner of war. Many of his contemporaries did not take him seriously; but his travel report is a reliable documentation of the situation in the Far East of the Middle Ages.

In the Middle Ages, during Mongol rule in China (1260–1368) the great emperor Kublai Khan became acquainted with the fighting power of the South Asian war elephant when he turned his attention towards Annam (Vietnam), Burma and the East Indies. The giants were no match for his valiant steppe horsemen from Inner Asia. Thus in 1283 a mounted army of the emperor annihilated the army of the mighty king of Burma, who raised 60,000 men and hundreds of war elephants against a unit of only 12,000 men under the imperial general Nestardin. Marco Polo gave a vivid description of the battle.

Mindful of the inferiority of his mounted units and impressed by the fearsome bulk of the war elephants, Nestardin had skillfully occupied a position between two small woods, so as to ensure the possibility of retreat for his forces and to prevent the complete deployment of his opponent's superior force. Only when the enemy forces advanced did he order his cavalry to counter-attack. However, this failed because Tartar horses were afraid of elephants. Marco Polo writes:

"When the king of Mien (Chinese name for Burma) saw that the Tartars had gone down on to

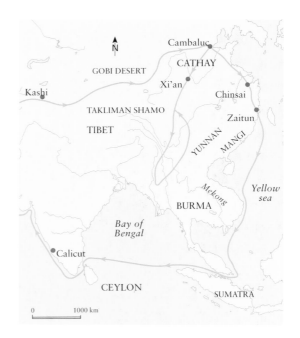

*The Great Khan hunting,* Miniature from the 'Livre des Merveilles du Monde,' c. 1400, book illustration. Bibliothèque Nationale de France, Paris

Events in the distant wonderland of China are transposed into the medieval Western world. The Great Khan is presented as an Old Testament patriarch in the style of the predominating religious paintings. The artist only knew of elephants by hearsay.

the plain he immediately set his army in motion; he advanced until he was approximately a mile from the enemy and then arranged his troops in battle order. He placed his elephants in the front line and the calvary and infantry in two extended wings behind … Thereupon he gave the order to sound the martial music and boldly advanced with his whole army against the Tartars, who made no movement, but let them draw near to the entrenchments. Then they sallied forth, but they soon saw that the Tartar horses, unused to the sight of such monstrous beasts with castles, shrank back, turned tail and tried to flee … When the clever Nestardin observed this unexpected disorder he immediately took appropriate action. He ordered his men to dismount and take their houses into the wood, where they tethered them to trees. As soon as the Tartars had dismounted, they lost no time but advanced on foot against the elephant lines and quickly loosed their arrows against them. Meanwhile the enemy soldiers in their elephant castles and the others soldiers vehemently returned fire. But their arrows were not as effective as those of the Tartars, whose bows were drawn by stronger arms. The latter fired so indefatigably, above all at the elephants, that these were soon covered with arrows and, suddenly turning about, they rushed upon their own people standing behind them."

The defeated Burma became a tributary to the Great Khan, as did neighboring Annam. However, the Mongols only exercised lax supervision and did not establish an administration of their own.

Marco Polo recorded, in addition, that the victorious Tartars seized 200 war elephants from the beaten Burmese army. "Since this time," he writes, "the Great Khan has always taken elephants along with his armies …" Before Kublai Khan incorporated war elephants into his army he had already used the giant beasts as command posts for his generals in many a battle.

Marco Polo tells of this in a report about the suppression of a rebellion by a provincial governor: "Kublai sat in a large wooden structure, carried by four elephants whose bodies were covered with armor of thick leather hardened in the fire; the armor, however, was covered with cloths interwoven with gold. Many crossbowmen and archers were posted in the structure and above fluttered the imperial standard, decorated with pictures of the sun and the moon."

*Kublai Khan* (1214–94), wood engraving. 18th century

Kublai Khan, a grandson of Genghis Khan, conquered Peking (then Hanbaligh) in 1264 after a long struggle and transferred his residence there from Karakorum. He is the founder of the Mongolian Yuen dynasty which ruled China until 1368. Conquering and extending, he incorporated the countries of the Indian hinterland into his gigantic empire. His attempts to conquer Japan via Korea failed between 1274 and 1281. Marco Polo lived at his court from 1275 to 1292.

The command post of the Mongol emperor Kublai Khan carried by four elephants. Kublai Khan's mounted army conquered China in the 13th century and forced the decaying Middle Kingdom back together again.

Painted paravent from the Shosoin treasure house in Nara, the residence of the Japanese emperor 710–94. The completely preserved, rigidly constructed building was used as a warehouse for a time in the 8th century and then became the treasure house of the emperor. It has preserved down to our time an abundance of works of art and art and craft objects, which are also typical of China during the T'ang period. China, which for its own part absorbed Indian and Persian influences, was the main model for the island empire. However with extraordinary power of assimilation, Japan stamped its own Japanese flavor on the continental style.

# Elephant legends in Japan

The elephant, which is not indigenous to Japan, only became familar to the Japanese in the 6th/7th centuries through the Chinese, who provided the stimulus for the cultural development of the island people. Discovered as fossil finds, the Asian elephant was represented temporarily on the island world in an earlier age, the Late Quaternary, when a land link existed. Later during the Ice Age the mammoth lived in North Japan.

With the Chinese script, literature, art and lifestyle, the Buddhist religion with its myths, in which the elephant has a special place, also entered the country in the early imperial period. Alongside collections of Chinese legends, familar to all at the imperial court in Kyoto, Japanese elephant stories also appeared. These included stories about Tayu, the well-known courtesan. She was frequently represented riding on a white elephant with six tusks, coming out of the clouds – a frivolous variation of the Buddhist legends.

Another widespread legend in old Japan was a Chinese legend about the deadly enmity between elephant and snake or dragon:

One night during the Chinese T'ang dynasty a gnome woke Wu, the famous warrior. He said he had come from the elephants who lived hundreds

Censer,
Meiji period, c. 1900,
bronze with remnants of gilding.
Height 63cm, length 50cm
Private collection

The elephant with the extended trunk and fang-shaped tusks carries a two-story pagoda, topped by a dragon. The pagoda, a sacred building of Buddhism in Eastern Asia, served as a censer. The bronze elephant, which has the remains of gilding, is decorated with pearl hangings; he wears a symbolic pearl gem on his head. The saddle cloth is decorated with a dragon.

Elephant figure as opium pipe,
Japan, 18th/19th century,
bronze and brass.
Height 23cm
Staatliches Museum für
Völkerkunde, Munich

The elongated trunk serves as the mouthpiece.

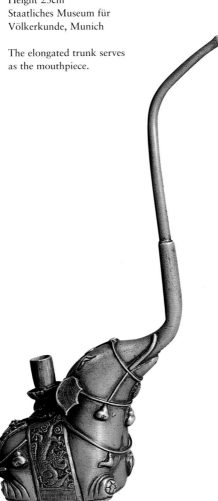

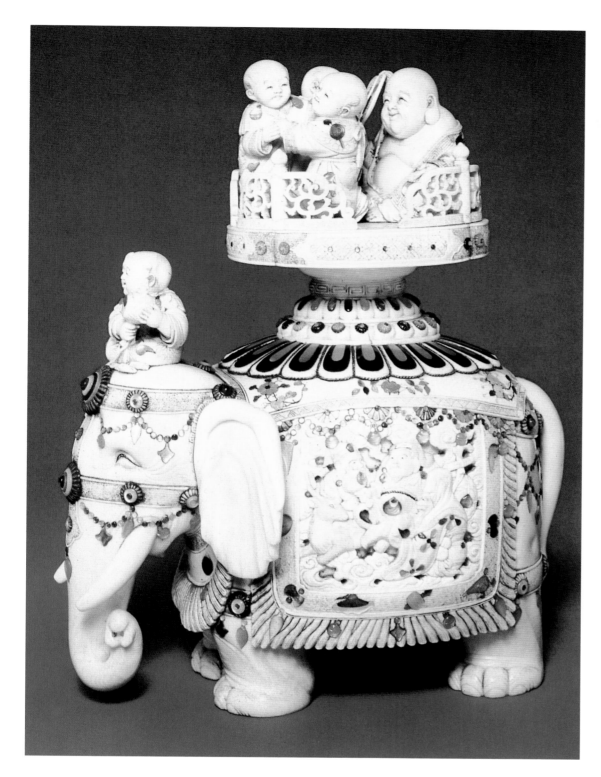

Ivory elephant,
Shibayana style.
Japan, c. 1900,
Private collection

of miles away and were asking for help against a fearsome giant dragon, who was attacking elephants in the forest and eating them. Wu set off immediately. He found the dragon lying at the entrance to a cave. He had teeth like swords, sparkling eyes and horns on his head. Wu took cover behind a rock and shot a poisoned arrow into each of the dragon's eyes. Roaring and belching out fire the monster fell twitching to the ground and perished. In the cave Wu found mountains of elephant bones. The elephants were happy and gave Wu a mountain of ivory tusks in gratitude.

The Far Eastern proverb: "the snake eats the elephant and three years later the elephant bones re-emerge from the snake," has its origins in the old Chinese story.

The elephant is also a Buddhist symbolic figure in Japan. He carries the Enlightened One or a

pagoda. He also lends his timeless likeness to comically shaped everyday items for this people, so very much concerned with the here and now.

From 1635 to 1867, during their rigorous isolation from the outside world, when apart from the Chinese only the Dutch were allowed to maintain a trading office on the artificial island of Deshima in Nagasaki harbor and the Japanese were forbidden to travel under pain of death, the image of the elephant vanished from the popular consciousness. Only a few old colored wood engravings originating from Nagasaki show one of the eccentrically-formed elephants with a Dutch rider imported by the Dutch traders.

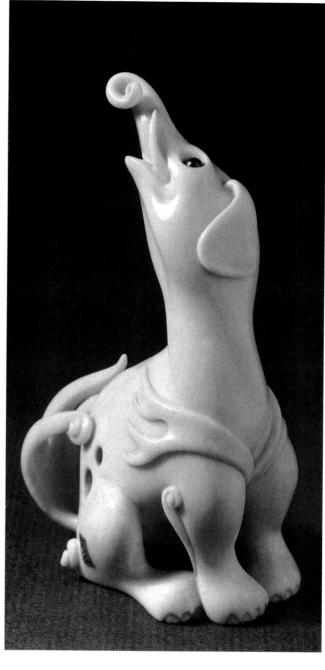

Elephant, netsuke.
Height 8.8cm
Private collection

The netsukes are a characteristic form of Japanese arts and crafts. (See also the chapter on 'Ivory art in Asia and Africa')

# Elephant power in the Hellenistic period

The elephant has had to pay a high price in war, above all in India. In the times when fighting was hand-to-hand using only muscle power, the elephant's giant strength boosted the lines of battle. The mighty beast was the 'tank' of antiquity and, in addition, an effective instrument of psychological warfare causing fear and confusion. The first test of strength between a Western warlord and an Oriental elephant fighting force took place in the 4th century BC during the bloody battle on the Hydaspes, which the Macedonian conqueror Alexander the Great (336–323 BC) fought and won in India. Detailed accounts of this world-changing event have been handed down to us by ancient historians who had access to eyewitness accounts by scholars accompanying Alexander. These have since been lost apart from fragments. After Alexander's death his generals, who divided up the conquered empire, included war elephants in the armies of their multicultural states, in which the newly established world culture of Hellenism flourished for a considerable time.

The miniature from the early Medieval French manuscript 'Secrets de l'Histoire Naturelle' (Secrets of Natural History) gives a seductive insight into "prosperous India rich in elephants." The precious collector's item was illustrated between 1480 and 1500 by an unknown master, called Maître Charles D'Angoulême.

Opposite:
François Louis Joseph Watteau (1758–1823),
*Alexander defeats Porus* (Detail), 1802,
oils on canvas.
86cm x 140cm
Musée des Beaux-Arts, Lille

Alexander the Great's victories opened the door to the Orient for the ancient Western world. The elephant appeared on the Western wartime scene. The artist who painted the stirring picture, reproduced in full on page 200, was a nephew of the 18th-century master of French painting, Antoine Watteau (1684-1721).

HECTOR · TROIANS    ALEXANDER   MACEDO    IVLIVS · CAESAR

Obverse and reverse of the Alexander commemorative coin struck after the victory over King Porus

## Alexander's elephant battle

Lucas van Leyden (1494–1533),
*Hector, Alexander and Caesar*,
1515,
wood engraving.
National Gallery of Art,
Washington

In the wood engraving cycle 'The nine heroes' the Dutch master Lucas van Leyden has depicted Alexander the Great on an elephant. In the cavalcade of fantastically adorned heroes and mounts the elephant is reduced to the size of a horse. The keenly observant artist had not yet seen an elephant with his own eyes.

In the spring of 334 BC the youthful, 22-year-old Macedonian hotspur had set out with his fighting force of 30,000 infantry and 5,000 cavalry to subdue the Persians, who had burnt down Athens in 480 BC and were a constant threat to Greece. Completely underestimated by the Persian King Darius III, he dashed from victory to victory in an unparalleled whirlwind of conquest. After four years the main Persian countries in Asia Minor, as well as Egypt and Mesopotamia, had been conquered, as also the magnificent Persian center of Persepolis, where Alexander gained vast booty of gold and silver, completely altering his financial standing in the world.

After the defeated Darius had been murdered by his own people Alexander, with world domination in mind, ascended the Persian throne himself and, to the annoyance of his Macedonian comrades in arms, also adopted the autocratic Persian court ceremonial. After sorting out the power situation he prepared to reclaim those countries on the upper Indus which 100 years earlier Darius I the great King of Persia had conquered and attached to his empire as the 20th satrapy, but which in the meantime had slipped away from under Persian control. Meanwhile three rival Indian regional kings controlled the regions – Taxiles, Porus and Abisares. Alexander enlisted one of the three, Taxiles, as a useful ally in his campaign for world domination.

In the spring of 327 BC he set out with his army from Afghanistan, spurred on by the dream of conquering the legendary country of India and uniting the Orient with the Occident. In an irresistible triumphal march he subjugated the northwest Hindu princedoms of the subcontinent, led his army over the mighty Indus on a daringly constructed pontoon bridge and advanced inland in spite of the deluges of the incipient monsoon season to take king Porus into vasallage. But Porus opposed the intruder on the Hydaspes, the border of his country, with superior military forces. It was the year 326 BC.

Porus waited for Alexander at the other side of the Hydaspes, which the monsoon rain had turned into a raging torrent. He blocked the ford which was in general use, even during high water.

His military forces numbered 50,000 infantry, 3,000 cavalry, 300 war chariots and about 200 war elephants. In addition he was expecting

The map shows the unparalleled military conquests of Alexander the Great which changed the ancient world. Hellenistic power and culture developed from the Nile to the Indus.

Tom Lovell,
*The elephant battle of Hydaspes,*
oils on canvas.
National Geographic Image
Collection, Washington

Portrayal by a historical painter.
"The elephants struck with their
trunks and trampled down
whatever got in their way, friend
or foe ..." wrote the Greek
historian Arrianus.

The youthful hero Alexander the
Great with elephant cap. At only
twenty-two the pupil of the
philosopher Aristoteles set out
against the great Persian empire.
After ten years he had laid the
foundations for a universal
empire. At only thirty-three he
had to take his ambitious plans
to the grave.

auxiliary troops from his ally Prince Abisares of
Kashmir, who was hurrying to his aid. Alexander's
army, the choice Macedonian units of which were
already lessened by many bloody battles and
untold hardships on the march, numbered only
about 30,000 men, including some lightly-armed
auxiliaries. Only his 5,000-strong cavalry had the
advantage over the enemy.

He also had at his disposal about 100 elephants.
He had gained a dozen as booty in the war against
the Persian King Darius. Darius, however had not
used the beasts, originally obtained from India, in
battle. In India tame elephants were also included
in the tribute payments of conquered princes. The
youthful ruler, ever open to new ideas, had
probably studied the character, taming practices
and usefulness of these animals in hunting and in
war. But he did not use them in battle, principally
since his cavalry horses were not trained to work
with elephants. The elephants seemed to him more
useful as beasts of burden in the supply line.

In view of the superior force on the bank,
Alexander could not risk crossing at the ford. So
he decided on an audacious flanking maneuver.

On a stormy, rainy night he took his cavalry
and the bulk of his infantry unnoticed to a place
about fifteen miles upstream. There, with luck, he
was able to cross the raging torrent at a reasonably
passable place using rafts and boats, emerging to
the rear of the enemy. Porus recognized the danger
too late. Hastily he withdrew his army from the
bank of the Hydaspes and formed it into a new
battle order. The front line was composed of a
terrifying chain of war elephants, posted at
intervals of about thirty yards, which from the
distance looked like the towers on the ramparts of
a city. This was recorded by the Greek historian
Diodorus, who lived in the 1st century BC. The
Indian infantry gathered close behind the gray
giants. The cavalry and the war chariots covered
the wider flanks.

Alexander avoided a frontal attack. He threw
the mass of his superior cavalry against the left
wing of the enemy, causing immediate confusion.
So Porus ordered his cavalry, which was supposed
to be protecting the right wing, to the endangered
sector. Now a Macedonian mounted unit rode
round the exposed right flank of the Indians and

François Louis Joseph Watteau
(1758–1823)
*Alexander defeats Porus*, 1802
Oils on canvas, 86cm x 140cm
Musée des Beaux-Arts, Lille

The Indian war elephants,
armored with castles in the
Roman fashion, tower like
mountains above the wild tumult
of battle in the historical painting.

Alexander's cavalry brings
dramatic movement into the
scene; the cavalry also ensures
a great victory.

Elephant power in the Hellenistic period

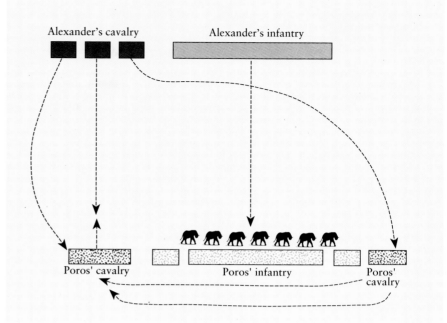

Alexander's cavalry    Alexander's infantry

Poros' cavalry    Poros' infantry    Poros' cavalry

The battle of Hydaspes. The sketch shows the deployment of the armies and the tactical maneuvers of Alexander and King Porus. The bold flank attacks of the Greek cavalry were decisive.

attacked from behind. The quickly beaten Indian cavalry, that also drew the horse-drawn war chariots into the mêlée, was thrown back onto the main force, which saw that it was being attacked from the rear. Deadly confusion ensued.

Too late Porus ordered his war elephants to attack, but they could no longer avert defeat. "Great was the fear evoked by the monsters," wrote the Roman warrior and historian Quintus Curtius Rufus, who lived in the 3rd century AD but still had access to authentic sources: "Many indeed who attacked the animals too violently brought down their fury on themselves on account of the wounds inflicted; trampled by their feet, they were a warning to others to proceed with greater caution. Above all it was dreadful to witness when the animals seized men and weapons together, with their trunks, and handed them to their drivers enthroned above them."

Alexander deployed his archers against the war elephants. They engulfed the wildly trumpeting beasts and their drivers in a hail of arrows. He also had hatchets and scimitars issued, with which fearless warriors attacked the animals' trunks and ankle tendons. The Greek Arrianus (about AD 95–175), serving under the Romans, who was familar with the records of the military leader Ptolemy and devoted his work 'Anabasis' to Alexander's conquests, reports as follows:

"So a blood bath then ensued: the elephants' commanders had for the most part already been shot, and the animals themselves, part wounded, part exhausted, and without drivers were no longer fit to put into action; completely terrified by all the horrors that had befallen them, they attacked indiscriminately both friend and foe, trying to beat a path for themselves by any means and trampling and killing everything. The Macedonians on the other hand, who had enough room and could deal with the animals quite at will, dodged out of the way when the elephants approached them and pursued them if they turned, shooting them with their long spears."

Now the choice Macedonian troops, advancing shield-to-shield, accomplished in a bloody slaughter the total defeat of the Indians, among whose chaotic mass the raging elephants caused particularly great devastation.

King Porus, who rode the finest elephant, fought courageously to the last. Wounded, he had to seek safety in flight. Stirring legends soon grew up around the faithful elephant of the beaten king. Thus Plutarch noted that when the elephant felt the wounded man on his back had collapsed he went down onto his knees and let him slide down carefully. Then he gently pulled the arrows out of the tormented body with his trunk …

Alexander had the wounded king brought before him, gained him as an ally with a noble gesture, and with far-seeing generosity restored his lands to King Porus.

The glittering victory, which should have flung open the door into new unknown distances for Alexander and should have led to a trial of strength with the Hindu empire of Magadha on the Ganges, actually became a signal for him to stop. His exhausted troops, affected by the horror of the elephant battle, refused to march any further. Thus

Charles le Téméraire,
*Story of Alexander the Great*,
14th century.
Bibliothèque Nationale de
France, Paris

In the Middle Ages Alexander's conquests inspired knightly fancies. A multitude of Alexander novels were written. This book illustration is taken from an Alexander story written in the 14th century. The battle scene in distant India is transferred to an imaginary world in the Medieval West. The war elephants have become grotesque fabulous beings.

Top view of an Alexander the Great decadrachma,
c. 300 BC,
silver.
British Museum, London

The picture on the coin shows the lance attack by Alexander on King Porus, who rode the biggest war elephant of his army, controlled by a mahout.

Charles Le Brun (1619–1690),
*The entry of Alexander the Great
into Babylon*,
1665,
oils on canvas.
450cm x 707cm
Musée du Louvre, Paris

Against a classical background the
great general and victor in
Caesarean pose returns to his new
residence of Babylon, where an
early death awaits him. Charles Le
Brun was court painter to Louis
XIV, the sun king; he also oversaw
the decoration of the famous
Palace of Versailles.

began the legendary retreat of the Greek army
through the cruel Persian desert wastes into
Mesopotamia. One unit followed later by sea.
Alexander had many elephants brought from the
re-acquired Indian satrapies on the newly-opened
trade routes, so that his army finally included
about 200 of the giant beasts.

When the bold conqueror, who still inspired the
heroic dreams of the knighthood in the Medieval
West (the early Indian acounts hardly mention
him!), succumbed to a fever in Babylon in the year
323 BC and died, barely thirty-three years old,
elephants were posted around the mourning
pavilion. Alexander's global empire was to have
been marked by a unified east-west culture and
supported by a unified people arising from the
merging of Greeks, Macedonians and Persians. A
year before his death the union of East and West
had been initiated and celebrated symbolically by
the mass marriage between Macedonian and
Persian noble families and soldiers at the famous
Marriage of Susa. Alexander himself, in keeping
with the Persian custom of polygamy, also took
another wife, Stateira, the daughter of King Darius.
He also ordered that 30,000 Persian boys be taught
the Greek language and the Macedonian art of war.

The dreams of great power ended soon after
Alexander's death. But from the legacy he left
behind there blossomed the mixed culture of
Hellenism, predominantly determined by Greece
but also including Oriental and later also Roman
elements. This culture stamped a whole epoch.

As far as Alexander's succession was concerned,
however, things went badly. He left only one son,
not yet of age, whom Roxana the Bactrian had
borne him. The rival generals packed the child and
Arrhidaeus, Alexander's incompetent half brother,
off to Macedonia under the protection of Antipater
the military leader. Antipater, who assumed control
over Macedonia and Greece, brought home seventy
elephants in the impedimenta of his company. Once
there they had to perform bloody war service
during the troubles which began after Antipater's
death in the year 319 BC.

# The elephant corps of the Diadochi

After Alexander's death his generals took over governorship in the satrapies. Ptolemy took the remains of his royal friend to be buried with dignity in Alexandria, the city of which he was most proud. He also took over Egypt. Seleucus, a leader of the Macedonian phalanx, received the satrapy of Babylonia, Antigonus received Asia Minor and Antipater, Macedonia/Greece. The generals' power struggle then began.

Alexander's seventy Greek cities, established in the conquered areas of the Middle East, ensured that Hellenistic culture extended from the Nile to India. The Indian elephant made its entry into the Mediterranean countries with the returning armies. During the bloody conflicts of the Diadochi, the successors to the great king, elephant units had an important part to play on the battle scene.

Perdiccas, Alexander's highest ranking military leader and the first to be appointed imperial administrator, was the first to attempt to seize supreme power. He began treacherously. During a religious festival of the army he brought an accusation against his rival Meleager, had him murdered and had thirty of his officers trampled by war elephants in a brutal mass execution. Then he went to Egypt to bring down Ptolemy, who had secured the rich country on the Nile for himself.

When Perdiccas reached the Nile in flood at Memphis he made particular use of his fighting elephant force; he posted a chain of the giant beasts in the raging floods to act as a breakwater so that his troops could cross more easily downstream. However, after heavy losses he brought only part of his army to the other bank, where he was forced to suffer a defeat. Forced to make a humiliating retreat from the battle, he was murdered in cold blood by his own officers.

Fragment of the head of an armored war elephant, around the birth of Christ, copy of a bronze sculpture. Staatliche Antikensammlung, Munich

The bronze sculpture served as decoration for a bed post. The veins in the ears were highlighted with silver inlays.

After bloody conflicts between the rival Diadochi there only remained three great powers: the empire of the Seleucids, the Ptolemaic empire, and the kingdom of Macedonia. And Greek-based mixed culture of Hellenism persisted in the Middle East for a long period.

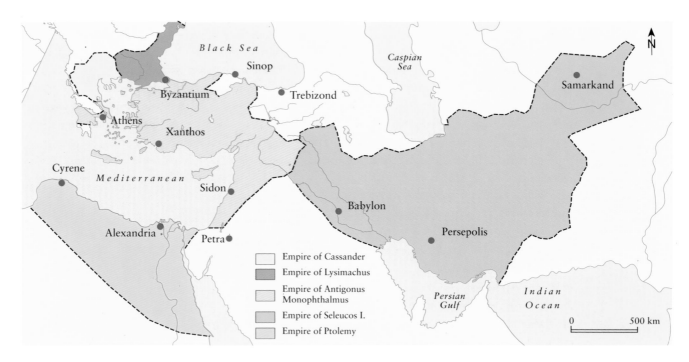

Empire of Cassander
Empire of Lysimachus
Empire of Antigonus Monophthalmus
Empire of Seleucos I.
Empire of Ptolemy

0    500 km

War elephant,
from the Picture Atlas by
Friedrich Arnold Brockhaus,
pre-1850,
colored copy.

Portrayal of an elephant battle in
antiquity. The elephant armored
with a castle wears an unusual
head plate with a spike; the
sensitive trunk is also protected
with movable plates. The whole
body is covered with a coat of
mail in the style of a knight.

Now the military leader Antigonus, who
controlled part of Asia Minor, aspired to
governorship of the whole empire. After, at first,
successful battles against his rival Eumenes, in
which each side raised dozens of war elephants, he
had to face an alliance of rivals led by Seleucus
(Eumenes had eventually fallen). The decisive battle
took place in 301 BC at Ipsus in Phrygia. The
70,000 strong army of Antigonus was slightly
superior in infantry and cavalry; he also had
seventy war elephants. His defeat was due to
Seleucus' vastly superior elephant corps. This force
cut off his cavalry, which had advanced too far
forward, and drove it to destruction at the hands of
the allied cavalry. Antigonus lost the battle and his
life. With this the fragmentation of Alexander's
empire into three great powers was complete:

Macedonia, which had disciplined the eternally
troublesome Greek city-states, the empire of the
Seleucids in Asia Minor, and the Ptolemaic empire
which, besides Egypt, had also secured for itself the
areas of southern Syria. This affected the interests
of the Seleucids.

Thus, even after the bloodily fought distribution
of power, the rivalry between the new dynasties in
the Middle East continued to exist until the
Romans appeared on the scene with their imperial
claims. And war elephants constantly played an
important part in the outcome of battle.

# The elephant trade of King Seleucus

In the gigantic Diadochi empire of the Seleucids, which stretched from Syria to India and included almost the whole of the Middle East, the elephant became a useful animal in war and peace. Relations with India, the country of the elephant, were close, even though Alexander's successors had not been able to keep control of the conquered areas on the Indus. Chandragupta Maurya (322–298 BC), the ruler of the mighty Hindu empire of Magadha on the Ganges, whose subjugation Alexander had planned, penetrated ever further into the area governed by Greece.

In 305 BC after he had conquered Bactria, King Seleucus Nicator (victor) finally marched to India with his military forces. But he and Chandragupta avoided a costly trial of strength and finally agreed on a transaction advantageous to both sides: in exchange for 500 elephants Seleucus let the Hindu king have the Indus satrapy, which he would not have been able to hold in any case. During the Diadochi wars these elephants represented a tremendous military advantage.

Chandragupta, the founder of the great Maurya empire, and Seleucus also amicably exchanged ambassadors. Seleucus sent the known Greek envoy Megasthenes to the magnificent Hindu capital, Pataliputra on the Ganges. From here he sent back to Babylon the first reliable reports about the organization and administration of the Maurya empire, which covered all the northern part of the subcontinent.

## Buddhist missionaries in Greece and Egypt

After Chandragupta's death, his grandson Ashoka, known as the Mild, who ascended the throne in 272 BC, acquired legendary reknown. He extended the empire to the south. In 262 BC he led a merciless compaign of annihilation against the Dravidian empire of Kalinga on the east coast, which claimed hundreds of thousands of lives. But shocked by the horror of war and devastation Ashoka experienced his own 'Damascus road' conversion. He immersed himself completely in the gentle teachings of Buddha and from then on charged his officials with the propagation of these teachings. Protective laws for animals curtailed slaughter and even fishing. The court cuisine was reorganized around a diet of vegetables. The king condemned war and killing of any kind. His children, Mahendra the monk and Sanghamitra the nun, went to the island of Ceylon as missionaries with some success.

Ashoka sent delegations to Asia Minor, Greece and Egypt to disseminate Buddha's teachings. Important elements of Indian wisdom flowed into the multifarious religious, philosophical and mystical trends of the Hellenistic epoch. Between Ashoka's India and the Seleucid empire there was a brisk trade over land and sea. Seleucid ships controlled the Persian Gulf; they also served the ports of western India and the elephant island of Ceylon.

*Cavalry against war elephants,* miniature from Mannuchis, 'History of India.' Bibliothèque Nationale de France, Paris

Armor made from fire-hardened leather and heavy fabrics protect the gray giants.

## A world in change

Alexander the Great, conqueror, explorer and founder of cities, radically changed the ancient world. In the new states, into which his short-lived mighty empire split, the hybrid culture of Hellenism effaced national differences in language, religion and lifestyle. In a climate of cosmopolitan openness, which promoted the free exchange of ideas and information, the change was perceptible everywhere in the ancient world.

Alexander had coins struck from the captured Persian gold and brought into circulation, and this brought about a huge upswing in the money economy, in industry and in trade. Once Alexander had opened the treasure houses of the Orient, wrote the Greek Athenaeus, the day of riches for the world dawned.

Alexander had founded about seventy cities for Greek colonists. The Diadochi emulated him as builders. Seleucus I Nicator is also said to have founded about seventy cities, in which Greek merchants and craftsmen, mercenaries and many officials, doctors and philosophers disseminated Greek culture and lifestyle. Many of the newly founded cities became large and important, like Seleucia on the Tigris and Alexandria right at the mouth of the Nile.

The absolute power of the kings, who gradually became deified, was based on mercenary armies in which the war elephant had its special place. Its strength was required in the improved siege methods, in which novel heavy machines had to be moved; and the working elephant was also needed in the continuing building boom in the Middle East.

The Seleucids, who ruled Asia Minor, obtained their war and working elephants from the friendly Hindu Maurya empire. The center of trade was the newly founded city of Seleucia on the Tigris, which grew to a city of 60,000 inhabitants and became a center of Hellenistic culture whose influence radiated far and wide. The imperial mint was also based in the city, and a modern money economy spread rapidly as far as India.

The extremely strong, well-trained Asian war elephants obtained from India gave the Seleucids a certain superiority in the continuing power struggle with the Ptolemaic empire. The Ptolemies saw themselves forced out of the Indian elephant market, and so they had to fall back on the smaller forest elephants from Africa for their military preparations. The Ptolemaic generals acquired elephants from Nubia and Ethiopia, and these were shipped via the port of Adulis.

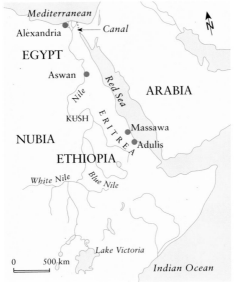

The elephants for the armies of the Ptolemaic kings came to Egypt from Nubia, Ethiopia and the Eritrean coast. The port of Adulis was the loading point.

## Ptolemaic kings hunting elephants in Ethiopia

The Ptolemies resided in Alexandria on the mouth of the Nile, where the grave of the great conqueror Alexander was maintained. Designed by the Greek architect Deinocrates, it was laid out in the form of a chessboard and was about 3 miles long and just less than a mile wide. This defensively-walled seaport quickly developed into the main centre of Hellenistic world trade, a metropolis with 600,000 inhabitants. Of these 300,000 were free citizens and an equal number, foreigners and slaves. Two huge harbor basins served navigation and the trans-shipment of goods.

With its luxurious palaces, gardens, multi-story houses and progressive supply facilities, Alexandria was the most modern and richest city of its time. Capital-based companies engaged in manufacturing; shipyards were already building 3,000-ton ships. Thus, according to a description by Athenaeus, the Greek writer, the 'Syrakosia' was 650 feet long and had 7 decks; she had a loading capacity of 60,000 bushels of grain and could accommodate 10,000 clay pots of salted fish.

Science and research were promoted on a large scale. In 315 BC Ptolemy I Soter (savior) founded the Museion, a place of learning, research and education, which comprised a famous library, an anatomical institute and a zoo, in which zoologists acquired new knowledge. Theories and discoveries abounded at the Museion.

The aesthete Ptolemy II Philadelphus (brother-loving), who ruled from 285–247 BC, made Alexandria the center of Hellenistic world culture. He established the custom, adopted from the time of the Pharaohs and subsequently practiced by almost all the Ptolemies, of marrying his own sister or a closely related princess.

At great expense the Ptolemies developed the routes to the African elephant regions on the coast of the Red Sea and in Nubia. The canal between the Upper Nile and the Red Sea – a modest forerunner of the Suez Canal – begun in the time of the Pharaohs and completed by Darius I the Great of Persia in 490 BC, but continually covered with sand, was once again made navigable. A caravan route to Arabia was also established via Palestine and southern Syria. In addition, the difficult oasis route to the land of Kush in Nubia was improved; for millennia all rulers over Egypt maintained trade links with this land.

On the Eritrean coast of the Red Sea the Ptolemies maintained the port of Adulis (not far from the present Massawa, or Mits'iwa) from which elephants and ivory from the coastal hinterland and from Ethiopia were shipped. The land link from the kingdom of Kush to Adulis was also better than the route through the inhospitable desert zones to Egypt.

The largest tusker in Sri Lanka. The photograph was taken in 1997 – at that time the mighty 53-year-old bull was working in a sawmill. From antiquity until the 19th century the elephants of the island were particularly prized. In the Hellenistic period the Seleucid rulers imported their best war elephants from there. The sea transport route led from the former 'Elephant Island' along the coast of South India to the ports on the Persian Gulf.

An old inscription discovered in Adulis bears witness to the fact that the Ptolemaic kings went on elephant hunts and organized the capture of elephants in the coastal forests of Eritrea and the Ethiopian highlands. It says: "The great king Ptolemy (III) ... took the field against Asia with ... Troglodyte and Ethiopian elephants, which his father ... and he himself ... had caught as the first in these countries." The inscription refers to Ptolemy III (246–221 BC), who successfully defended his empire against the Seleucids, and his father, Ptolemy II. By 'Troglodyte elephants' we are to understand elephants obtained from the Eritrean coastal regions (according to ancient ethnography, Troglodytes were primitive peoples living on the Red Sea). The Ptolemies had at their disposal experts experienced in the capture and taming of African forest elephants. Ptolemy I Soter, the founder of the dynasty and one-time adjutant and friend of Alexander, had also brought Indian mahouts and attendants into his new empire along with the captured Asian war elephants. These could acquaint the Nubians, who had hunting experience with elephants since time immemorial, with the Indian art of taming elephants, not so far widely practiced in the kingdom of Kush.

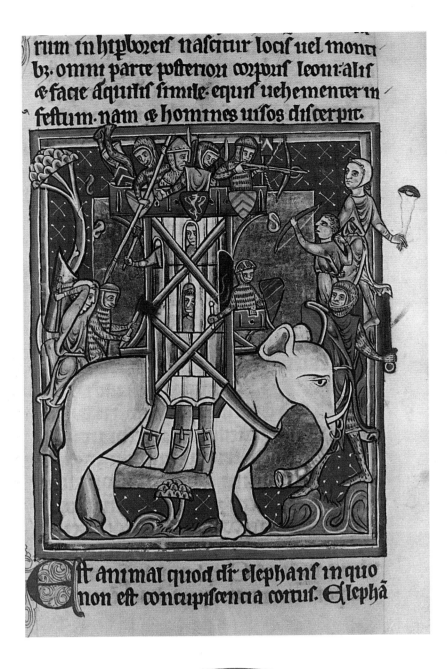

rum in hiʒboreis nascitur locis uel monti
bʒ. omni parte posterion corpus leoni. alii
ce facie aquilis simile. equis uehementer in
festum. nam ce homines uisos discerpit.

ſt animal quod dr elephans in quo
non est concupiscencia coitus. Elephā

## Asian versus African war elephants

The smaller African forest elephants had a difficult task in open battle against supremely strong war elephants trained in India. The Egyptian king Ptolemy IV (221–205 BC) found this out in the biggest elephant battle since Ipsus, fought in 217 BC to the south of Gaza.

The great Seleucid king Antiochus III (223–187 BC), who after reverses had once more expanded his empire as far as India, led 102 Indian war elephants into battle against the 73 mostly African elephants belonging to the Egyptian. The Greek historian Polybius, who lived in the 2nd century BC, has left this account:

"On their backs the occupants of the castles put up a brave fight; they engaged their lances and used them to thrust at close quarters. The animals themselves, however, proved yet more courageous, attacking forehead to forehead with all their might. The fighting style of the elephant is as follows. With locked tusks they push forward with all their strength trying to force the other to give way, until the stronger gains the upper hand and pushes the other's trunk aside. If one yields and presents his flank, the other wounds him with his tusks, just as a bull would with his horns. Most of Ptolemy's elephants, however, avoided the fight, as Lybian elephants do. They cannot endure the smell and trumpeting of the Indian elephants and doubtless are also afraid of their size and strength; they take flight immediately when they are still some distance away. And so it happened in this case also."

The Ptolemaic forces lost the battle and with it the Palestinian-South Syrian region bitterly defended for so long. When Antiochus then turned his attention to Greece he had to face the rising power of Rome. Vanquished by the Roman legions in 190 BC, he had to give up Asia Minor and Western Iran. The decline of the Seleucid dynasty had now begun.

War elephant,
Miniature from an English bestiary, 12th century.
Bodleian Library, Oxford

Warriors in the castle, pressed on all sides in the tumult of battle.

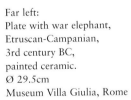

Far left:
Plate with war elephant,
Etruscan-Campanian,
3rd century BC,
painted ceramic.
Ø 29.5cm
Museum Villa Giulia, Rome

The find from an Etruscan grave near Capena probably shows one of Pyrrhus' war elephants captured by the Romans.

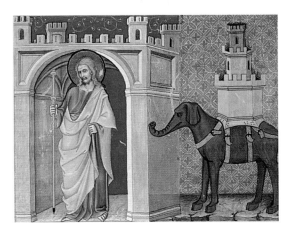

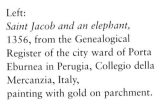

Left:
*Saint Jacob and an elephant*,
1356, from the Genealogical Register of the city ward of Porta Eburnea in Perugia, Collegio della Mercanzia, Italy,
painting with gold on parchment.

Saint Jacob is represented in a fortified stronghold of faith. He is accompanied by an elephant with castle, a symbol of the great strength of faith.

Elephant with castle,
Chapel of San Baudelio,
Berlanga, Castile
1st half 12th century,
fresco.
Private possession, USA

War elephant,
12th century,
Fresco.
Basilica in Ventaroli

In the Middle Ages the war elephant of antiquity became a Christian symbol of strong adherence to faith, suggested by the fortified castle on the elephant's back.

Elephant,
15th century,
inlay work in marble.
Duoma S. Maria, Siena, Italy

A square of the famous floor in the cathedral of Siena shows a war elephant with castle as a symbol of the city of Rome. Biblical and historical scenes are represented using various techniques in the fifty-six marble squares, on which forty artists worked for three centuries from the 14th to the 16th centuries.

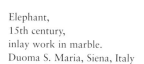

Elephant power in the Hellenistic period

# Nubians tame the African elephant

The kingdom of Kush was constantly in the power shadow and cultural sphere of influence of their great northern neighbor, Egypt. Brisk trade was pursued via various caravan routes. In spite of its peripheral position Kush was involved in the events of the ancient world.

After 1540 BC Kush was under the direct control of the Pharaohs. In 712 BC the Nubians occupied the peacock throne and established the 25th dynasty until 664 BC. When the Persian king Cambyses II (529–522 BC) subsequently conquered Egypt, for 200 years Kush came into the sphere of influence of the great Middle Eastern empire, into which Darius I the Great (521–485 BC) then also incorporated the Indus region. The influence of the Persians, who controlled the sea routes in the Red Sea, extended at this time to the elephant country of Ethiopia, the region neighboring Nubia.

According to the Greek historian Herodotus, the kingdom of Kush did not pay regular tribute to the Persians, instead every three years they sent a 'gift' to the king: about 4 pounds of gold, 200 ebony tree trunks, 5 Nubian boys and 20 elephant tusks … Ivory from Kush was also used during the building of the Persian royal residence of Susa in Asia Minor. Nubian bowmen served as mercenaries in the Persian army.

In faraway Kush they had certainly heard of Indian elephant keeping and taming techniques. The exchange of goods, knowledge and people was very brisk during the eventful phase just before Alexander's Indian campaign. All over the known world Greeks were active as merchants, teachers, architects and mercenaries, and this explains the rapid cultural and political triumph of Hellenism after Alexander's assault.

It is not known when the Nubians tried to tame the African forest elephant, but their efforts were given fresh impetus by the 'elephant rearmament' of the new Macedonian dynasties of the Ptolemies in Egypt (see also 'A world in change'). In the ruins of Meroë, the capital, and other sites in the Kush empire signs have been found that elephants were kept for war and royal pageantry.

In the remains of a temple built in the 1st century AD near Musaw-warat there is a wall-mosaic which shows an elephant decorated with caparisons holding the chains of prisoners in its trunk. In another place a mighty elephant, partly built from blocks of stone, partly carved, forms the end of a wall. Ramps and ramparts in the surrounding ruins indicate the presence of elephant stalls.

The Nubians, whose capital city Meroë was destroyed by the Ethiopians in about AD 300, bequeathed to them the art of elephant keeping. In the time of Muhammad the Ethiopians, whose empire controlled the southern part of the Arabian peninsula, were taking African elephants on their military campaigns, and Nubian elephant drivers served alongside Indian mahouts in the armies of the rival heirs to Alexander the Great.

Sketch of a symbolic pillar relief in the temple of Apedemak. A king with double crown rides an elephant. Behind him the Egyptian snake goddess Wadjit. A slave holds the trunk.

On a frieze in the Lion temple, built in the 1st century AD at Musaw-warat in modern Sudan, elephants hold the chains of prisoners of war. In the kingdom of Kush the elephant was a royal animal and a symbol of power, comparable to the lion of the Pharaohs in the iconography of power of the time.

Oil lamp in the shape of an elephant,
Meroitic, 2nd century AD, bronze.
Height 7.2cm, width 18.6cm
National Museum, Khartoum

The carefully worked bronze lamp was found in the ruins of the former Nubian capital Meroë, which was destroyed by the Ethiopians in about AD 300. The Egyptian elements of style are unmistakable.

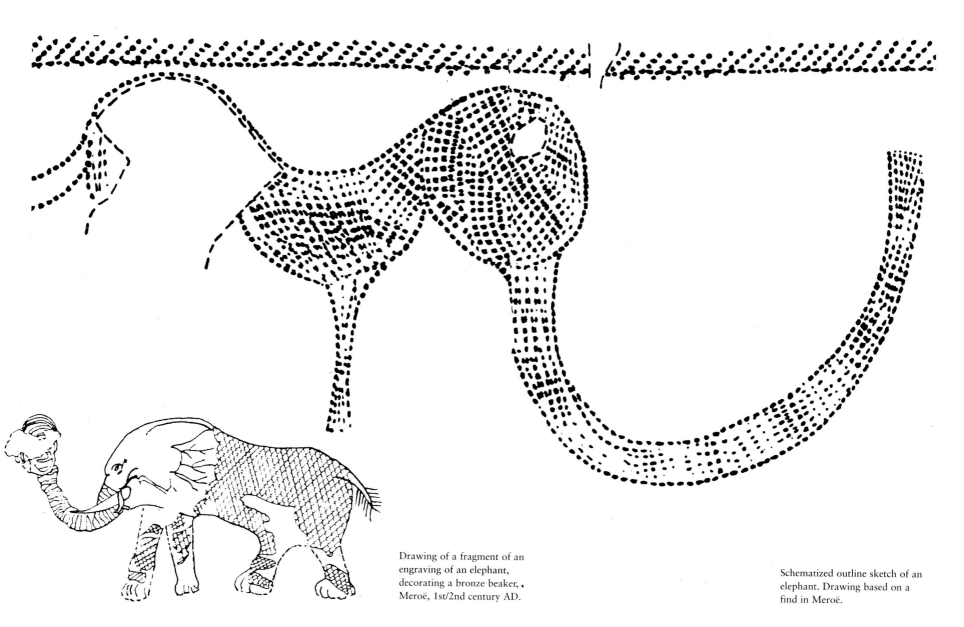

Drawing of a fragment of an engraving of an elephant, decorating a bronze beaker, Meroë, 1st/2nd century AD.

Schematized outline sketch of an elephant. Drawing based on a find in Meroë.

Elephant colossus,
Meroitic
1st/2nd century AD,
sandstone.
Temple buildings at
Musaw-warat, Sudan

The elephant, partly built from blocks of stones, partly carved, forms a powerful wall ending in the temple precinct at Musaw-warat. In Nubia the elephant was a symbol of royal power and greatness. It is not known whether it was also included in the ceremonial of religious worship.

Brixen School,
*Eleazar under the elephant*,
c. 1474,
fresco.
Parish church of St. Nicholas,
Klerant bei Brixen, South Tyrol

## The terror of the Maccabees

The perpetually disputed Palestine of the Bible, ruled since 200 BC by the Seleucid kings who reigned in Damascus, also had to face war elephants. The biblical freedom fighter Eleazar particularly distinguished himself in this respect. In 168 BC King Antiochus III plundered the temple at Jerusalem, which also housed the state treasure, and decreed a ban on worship. This decree led to an uprising under the leadership of Judas Maccabaeus. Damascus reacted with a punitive expedition, led by the imperial administrator Lysias on behalf of the young son and successor of the king, who had meanwhile died.

The events are reported with Oriental exuberance in the 'First Book of the Maccabees' which belongs to the 'Apocrypha' scripts (Greek apokryphos = hidden). Comparable in arrangement and content to the books of the Bible, these writings were, however, not included in the canon and were withheld from public consumption in the early Christian churches. Luther translated it and added it to his version of the Bible. His translation runs as follows:

"When the king heard it he became furious, and summoned all his princes and the captains of the infantry and of the cavalry, and took on foreign mercenaries from other kingdoms and from the islands, and brought together a hundred-thousand foot soldiers, twenty-thousand horsemen and thirty-two experienced war elephants. This army marched through Idumaea and besieged Beth-Zur, and fought many days, and set up battering rams; but the Jews sallied out and burnt the battering rams and fought bravely.

"And Judas left the stronghold and camped with his army at Beth-Saharia opposite the camp of the king. The king set off early in the morning before daylight and led his army to the attack on the road to Beth Saharia, he arrayed his troops for battle and let the trumpets sound, the elephants were given red wine and mulberry juice to incite them to battle and enrage them; and they distributed the elephants among the detachments, so that a thousand foot soldiers in armor and iron helmets and five hundred horsemen were attached to each elephant. The troops were already standing in the place to which the elephant was led; and wherever he went, they went also and did not leave him. And each elephant carried a strong wooden castle ...

"And when the sun rose and shone on the golden and brazen shields, the whole mountain glinted and glowed as if it were fire. And one part of the king's army spread out over the high mountains, another spread out down in the plain and they advanced carefully and in good order ... And Judas also marched against them in his array and six hundred of the king's army fell."

In this situation the biblical freedom fighter Eleazar shows true courage; he beats a path to the biggest and most magnificent elephant, which he recognizes as the center of the battle and the seat of King Antiochus. He manages to position himself underneath the elephant and strikes him down with a well-aimed blow of his sword. According to the Bible, the animal collapses immediately, mortally wounded, and dies taking with him in death the martyred hero of the people of Israel.

## The end of an era

"But because the Jews saw that the army of the king attacked with such great force, they retreated before them. Therefore the army of the king marched against them to Jerusalem and pitched camp in Judaea on Mount Zion."

Under the successors of King Antiochus IV the way was paved for the dissolution of the Seleucid empire. In 160 BC they lost rich Mesopotamia to the Parthians. In 128 BC the Jews, with the support of the Romans, fought for and finally won their independence. In 64 BC the shattered rump state of Syria was made a Roman province by Pompey.

The Ptolemies had already been under Roman control since the middle of the 2nd century BC. In the year 168 BC they had suffered a heavy defeat at the hands of the Seleucid king Antiochus IV, who had occupied parts of Egypt. The Romans intervened, forced him to withdraw and placed the weakened Egypt under their guardianship. The dynastic era came to an end in the maelstrom of Roman dramas of power and love, described and embellished a thousand times, which developed around Cleopatra, the last Ptolemaic queen. In 30 BC, during the siege of Alexandria by Octavian, later Emperor Augustus, Cleopatra committed suicide by snake bite. Rome now became the center of the ancient world.

Gustave Doré (1833–1883),
*The death of Eleazar* (Detail),
Illustration in: 'La Sainte Bible selon la Vulgate,' Tours, 1866, wood engraving.
24.7cm x 19.9cm

Eleazar sacrifices himself. "... And Eleazar Awaran noticed an elephant which was taller and better armed than the others, and he thought the king was on it ... and he placed himself under the elephant and stabbed it and it fell on to him and died and struck him dead also ..."
(1 Mac. 6, 43–46).

# Fighters and transporters
## in ancient and modern times

At the beginning of the 3rd century BC the young Roman republic came into contact with Middle Eastern war elephants. The famous King Pyrrhus (319–272 BC) crossed the Adriatic Sea with Asian elephants, who were proven in battle, and inflicted heavy defeats on the Roman legions. Rome learnt its lesson from this. On the Tiber they soon realized that this new 'weapon' was double-edged. They developed defense methods and in wars involving elephants put their trust in trained legions and the cavalry. The Romans even fought the decisive secular battle against the elephant corps and fleets of the naval power of Carthage without resorting to 'living tanks.' The Persians, on the other hand, continued to make use of elephant power during their campaigns of conquest. The elephant has been used as a military weapon, even in modern warfare.

*Elephant and Castle* (detail)
English medieval manuscript,
14th century

The elephant appears to be balancing its way across a tightrope. This is a vignette, often included in medieval bestiaries and manuscripts to brighten up the pages, without directly referring to the legends in question.

Opposite:
*The elephant battle* (detail),
Roman School, 1521,
oil on canvas.
144cm x 209cm
Pushkin Museum of Fine Arts,
Moscow

# The 'Lucanian oxen'

In ancient Greece where Macedonian supremacy was crumbling in the midst of insoluble, internal conflicts, a new and important military power arose in Epirus, opposite the foot of Italy. The leader, King Pyrrhus (whose name appears in every history book) was the first to use war elephants against the republican citizen and peasant armies of Rome, by this time a world power.

Pyrrhus was an obsessive soldier, a brilliant tactician and a great military leader. However, while he dreamt of greater power, he lacked any real political vision. In 280 BC he crossed the Adriatic Sea with 25,000 men and 20 war elephants to Tarentum, the largest Greek city-state in southern Italy, to join forces against the Romans. This was the first invasion by sea using elephants that had been specifically trained for battle.

The first engagement was at Heraclea. For a long period bitter fighting had raged, with neither side gaining victory and both sustaining heavy losses, until Pyrrhus brought his elephants. The horses of the Roman cavalry shied and fled at the sight of the frightening giants who were trumpeting furiously. The Roman phalanx which had been fighting fearlessly began to falter. Analyzing contemporary sources, Byzantine historian Zonaras reports the devastating effect of the elephants. Some Romans were killed by fighters concealed in towers mounted on the backs of elephants; others were trampled by the beasts themselves, or crushed by trunks and tusks. The Greek cavalry completed the defeat of the Roman phalanx which, armed only with short swords, was unequipped to fight even the Greek footmen and their spears. The Romans were greatly impressed by the frightening 'mythical' creatures and named the elephants 'Lucanian oxen' after the area in which the battle took place.

Pyrrhus advanced north almost to Rome, but had to retreat to the safer south with the onset of winter. The following year the Romans mustered two armies to continue the fight. As a weapon against the war elephants they took wagons harnessed with oxen, on which they erected swiveling beams fortified with iron barbs. These were to be used to hurl firebrands at the dreaded animals. The crude equipment was, though, of little use. It was positioned on the wings and not where Pyrrhus used his 'tanks' at the critical moment of the battle. In the slow ox carts those operating the swinging beams were at the mercy of the hail of arrows coming from the Greek archers. They fled and caused confusion within their own ranks. Pyrrhus triumphed once again but suffered heavy losses himself. He had not succeeded in destroying the Roman army.

Horror stories about the terrifying giants who carried a snake on their heads were now circulating in Rome. The writer Frontius mentions a specific soldier who managed to cut off an elephant's trunk, an act which supposedly proved that even the monsters were mortal.

Pyrrhus crossed to Sicily to make a stand against the Carthaginians who were attacking Greek towns. He was successful in several encounters, but did not make any decisive progress. In 275 BC he returned to Apulia where the Roman consuls Curtius and Cornelius both advanced against him; their troops marching from two different directions. In order to prevent the groups combining Pyrrhus ordered a surprise attack on Curtius' camp during the night. As they marched over inhospitable terrain the Greeks lost their way. When they finally reached the Roman camp it was daylight and the alerted legions attacked the tired, disorderly Greek units.

This time the war elephants were unable to force victory. The Romans now drove them off using pigs coated with grease and pitch which they turned into live torches. Their shrill, dying squeals made the huge pachyderms panic and put to flight.

This led to the belief that elephants could be frightened by small animals, even mice. Seneca wrote: "Elephantos porcina vox terret" – the squealing of pigs frightens elephants.

After the bloody massacre Pyrrhus, heavily defeated, retreated to Tarentum, from where he returned across the Adriatic to his kingdom with the remnants of his troops and elephants.

The sketch map shows King Pyrrhus' questionable triumphal march in southern Italy. There was only defeat at the end of it, as for many great war victors throughout history.

Floor mosaic (detail),
3rd/4th century BC.
Villa Heraclea, Casale, Sicily

A war elephant is brought on to a ship.

Fighters and transporters

Matthäus Merian Senior
(1593–1650),
*Battle at Heraclea*, 1630,
colored copperplate engraving,
Illustration Johann Ludwig
Gottfried: Historical Chronica
Frankfurt am Main, 1630.
Germany

The Romans were not yet a match
for King Pyrrhus' war elephants
who spread fear during the battle
at Heraclea in 280 BC. The
Romans suffered a crushing defeat
in this battle.

For years and with no overall political plan he
had won victory after victory, only to end up losing
almost everything. We still talk about a 'Pyrrhic
victory:' questionable triumphs won at too great a
cost. The inglorious retreat marked the end of the
powerful position of the Greek city-states at this
time in southern Italy.

In the final battle Curtius had captured several
war elephants which, on his victorious return,
were the sensation of his triumphal procession into
Rome. In Greece Pyrrhus became involved in a
gallant struggle for power with the king of
Macedonia Antigonos Gonatas (320–239 BC).
During an attempted raid on the town of Argos in
the Peloponnese in 272 BC the glittering heroic
episode came to a disastrous end. The structures
for the archers and spear throwers were removed
from the elephants so they could pass through the
narrow city gate opened at night by those close to

the king. Defenseless during the nighttime fighting
in the narrow streets the elephants panicked and
ran amok among their own advancing troops.
Pyrrhus himself met an inglorious end. A tile,
supposedly thrown by a woman from a rooftop,
knocked him to the ground and as he lay there
defenseless an enemy soldier cut off his head.

# Hannibal marches across the Alps with elephants

Bas-relief of a silver plate used for religious purposes from Cales, Campania, which shows Hannibal's war elephants. Musée du Louvre, Paris

One event in particular in the history of war elephants has fascinated and preoccupied people down the ages: Hannibal's march over the Alps. This took place during the century-long power struggle between the advancing land power of Rome and the sea and trading nation of Carthage, ruler of the western Mediterranean.

Although only a passing episode in the bold advance of the Carthaginians toward Italy, the unusual achievement deserves recognition.

The giant animals with trunks had been known to the traders of Carthage since time immemorial. Forest elephants lived in the wild, in large wooded areas of the coastal regions of northern Africa. Their ivory made them prized game animals.

The idea to tame elephants did not occur until after Alexander the Great's Indian campaign when the young Diadochi kingdom 'armed' themselves with elephants. Carthaginian mercenary units had learned of the fighting strength of war elephants during Pyrrhus' campaign in Sicily.

The pressure of the struggle with Rome led the Carthaginians to build up their own army of war elephants. They successfully tamed African forest elephants, making use of the experience gained by the Egyptians with whom they traded. They probably also acquired Indian elephants and their drivers from the Seleucid kingdom, via their Phoenician cousins in the city-states.

By the time the First Punic War broke out in 264 BC the Carthaginians were already able to ship an auxiliary unit with fifty war elephants to Sicily where the Romans were threatening their main base at Agrigentum. Deployed unwisely, most of the elephants were captured by Romans in their successful attacks outside the city walls. They were later taken to Rome to perform in circuses.

Some years later, after a series of successful naval battles the Romans attacked Carthage in Africa. The invading army, under the leadership of the consul Marcus Atilius Regulus, was confronted with a newly recruited Carthaginian elephant army consisting of around 100 animals. The Roman army, operating inefficiently, experienced the terror of a concentrated elephant attack and the expedition ended with a devastating defeat. Regulus was captured and later died in Carthage.

The success led the Carthaginians, under the command of Hasdrubal, Hannibal's brother, to ship a new army with 140 war elephants to the unremitting war in Sicily. During a battle in 250 BC, the attacking Carthaginian elephant phalanx came to a standstill at an impregnable trench which had been dug in secret. The elephants were greeted with a hail of arrows from Roman archers hidden in the trench and they fled in panic. The advancing Carthaginian mercenary units dissolved into chaos and the battle was lost. The majority of the

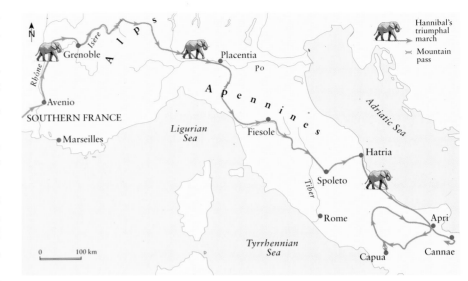

Hannibal's legendary campaign in Italy. He achieved victory after victory only to end in failure.

Terra cotta statuette, 3rd century BC. Museo Nazionale Archeologico, Naples

The elephant, fortified with a tower, is driven by an African.

Everaert Leyniers (1597–1680)
*The Defeat of Marcus Atilius Regulus* (detail), 1652/54, tapestry.
Palazzo Labia, Venice

An invading Roman army under the command of the consul Marcus Atilius Regulus, aiming to conquer the Carthaginians in Africa, succumbed to an attack by 100 war elephants in 255 BC.

elephants were captured by the Romans and taken as reinforcements for the circus in the capital. The Carthaginian elephant trappers and trainers were soon looking for replacements. A corps of about 100 elephants was available when in 242 BC a dreadful revolt broke out. The legionaries and Numidic reinforcements had taken action as a result of overdue pay. Within a few years Carthage possessed over 200 war elephants.

# A head for heights through the passes

Hannibal's star was in the ascendant when the Second Punic War broke out in 218 BC. He was to attack the Romans in Italy in an attempt to limit their expansion. He started the long march through Spain and southern France with an army of about 30,000 men and 37 war elephants, constantly under threat from hostile tribes. He had reached the Rhône when the Roman commander Scipio, who was supposed to have already stopped him in Spain, was three days' march away from him to the west. This put Hannibal in an extremely critical situation. Scipio, however, did not march back to corner the enemy; he continued towards Spain in order to cut off Hannibal's supplies. He believed he could leave the Carthaginians and their elephant corps to their fate in the inhospitable Alps.

Hannibal managed the difficult Rhône crossing using boats and rafts. Then his army made for the alpine passes upstream over the Isère valley. It is not certain which crossing he chose. According to the Hellenistic historian Polybios (circa 200–120 BC), the elephants were of great help to him in the mountains: "As when they were in the column the enemies did not venture to approach for fear of the unusual appearance of the animals." The elephants proved to be excellent climbers. Without hesitation they plodded over mountain paths, passing along precipices while the horses, used to galloping on wide plains, often had difficulty. The elephant's strength was frequently required when rocks and other obstacles had to be cleared from the path in order to carry on.

Henri Motte (1846–1922)
*Hannibal's passage over the Rhône,*
1878,
painting.

The leading cow is led first onto the raft with the other animals following. Panic suddenly breaks out in the middle of the river. Elephants fall and scramble for the rafts. Struggling to swim they all safely reach the bank.

Heinrich Leutemann (1824–1905),
*Hannibal's passage through
the Alps,*
c. 1865,
colored wood engraving.
'Pictures from antiquity' series
Münchner Bilderbogen No. 438

Hannibal's dramatic march with
elephants through the Alps has
inspired artists over the centuries.
The pachyderms proved to be
good climbers with a head for
heights. Hannibal led the army
and all thirty-seven elephants
through the pass.

The situation became perilous when a land and rock slide in the high mountain region buried the path and rendered it impassable. It took three days in blizzard conditions to clear it. The elephants showed remarkable resistance. They endured the cold, mountain storms and hunger, but by the end were greatly weakened.

Finally, in the autumn of 218 BC, Hannibal reached the Po valley with all thirty-seven elephants. His exhausted troops and animals were able to rest while the Romans, stunned by the brilliant performance in the Alps, were urgently mustering an army.

The elephants were again of help to the great commander during the initial confrontation with the enemy. During icy, foggy weather he eliminated the Roman cavalry on the Trebia, a tributary of the Po, in a clever flank maneuver. A fearless attack by the elephants completed the total defeat of the enemy phalanx. Only a few Romans escaped.

The rigors of the rain, snow and cold were, however, too much for the gentle giants from the warm regions of North Africa and they slowly wasted away. In spring 217 BC Hannibal, who had lost an eye at the battle on the Trebia, crossed the Apennines in bitterly cold weather and the last seven giants perished, leaving the powerful elephant he rode. He won the famous victory at Cannae in 216 BC over an 80,000-strong Roman army without the elephants' help.

# War elephants at Zama

For a decade Hannibal had a stronghold on the Romans in their own country, only to end in failure. The rebellion by the Italian people that had been hoped for never materialized, the Romans refused to negotiate and continued their resistance.

In 204 BC Hannibal was recalled to Carthage, which was under constant threat from a Roman expeditionary army led by Scipio. Hannibal took command of the local army which still had a corps of eighty elephants. But even Hannibal's skills as a commander could not prevent defeat. He met his match in Scipio who averted the threat from the war elephants by altering the battle formation. He arranged the three battle lines in echelon formation, so as to provide free corridors. When the animals came under fire from spears and arrows they escaped through these corridors from the chaos of the fighting.

Rome was now able to dictate terms for peace. These included Carthage giving up all of its foreign possessions abroad and handing over the fleet and war elephants.

When the final armed encounter started fifty years later Carthage no longer had any elephants to assist in its defense. The trading center was razed to the ground and Rome was confirmed as the undisputed world power.

The Romans considered war elephants to be too much of a double-edged 'weapon' to make use of them. They did send elephants they had captured into battle during subsequent colonial campaigns of conquest. However, it was the superior fighting strength of their disciplined, armored cohorts and

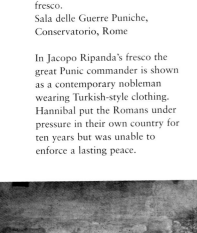

Jacopo Ripanda (active c. 1490-1530),
*Hannibal in Italy* (detail),
c. 1508
fresco.
Sala delle Guerre Puniche, Conservatorio, Rome

In Jacopo Ripanda's fresco the great Punic commander is shown as a contemporary nobleman wearing Turkish-style clothing. Hannibal put the Romans under pressure in their own country for ten years but was unable to enforce a lasting peace.

Opposite:
In 1979 an ambitious elephant crossing of the Alps was made, following in Hannibal's footsteps.

of their quick, powerful cavalry in whom they put their trust. Elephants were used predominantly as showpieces in triumphal processions.

When the Caesarean dictatorship superseded the republic war elephants began to disappear from the battle scene. Claudius, though, did send elephants to Britain to put fear into unruly tribes.

## In Hannibal's footsteps

In September 1979 a spectacular reenactment of Hannibal's historic crossing of the Alps took place. An Italian-American team completed the arduous march over steep slopes, mule tracks and passes with two powerful circus elephants.

The route chosen is believed by many historians to be that taken by Hannibal: through the valleys of the Isère and the Arc in the Savoy to the dangerous mule track of Crousta, to the St. Cenis pass and on to the 8,143 feet-high Clapier pass, and then down into the Northern Italian plain. The descent of the Col de Clapier proved to be the most difficult.

Geraert van der Strecken/Jan van Leefdael,
*Scipio and Hannibal at the battle of Zama* (detail),
17th century,
tapestry.
Sala Regia, Palazzo Quirinale, Rome

According to the historians Polybios and Titus Livius, Hannibal and Scipio Africanus supposedly held a final conversation immediately before the battle at Zama. This legend is recounted on the 17th-century tapestry.

# Persia's war elephants destroy the Christian city of Susa

While Rome ruled the Mediterranean region in imperial splendor the peoples of the East were rising up in revolt. Here the Diadochi kingdoms still owned elephants. A Persian empire developed during the Sassanid dynasty (AD 224–651). This dynasty is named after Sassan, the sovereign of the Iranian princedom of 'Persis' and high priest at the Istachir shrine to the goddess of fertility, Anahita.

Ardashir (AD 180–239), a capable commander, founded the second Persian empire. In AD 224 he rose up against his feudal lord, the Parthian king Artabanos V, who lost the battle and his life. Under the Sassanids elephants again became an essential part of the army.

The army of King Shapur II, ruler of Persia from AD 309 until AD 379 is described in detail by Ammianus Marcellinus, a Roman historian of Greek descent, who took part himself in some armed conflicts between Rome and Persia. He says:

"In the first light of dawn everything gleamed as far as the eye could see with the brightness of the weapons. The valley and hillside were packed with armored cavalry. The king himself, astride his steed and towering above the rest, rode at the head of his army; instead of a circlet, he wore a gold portrait of a ram's head studded with precious stones. The fact that his large group contained men of the highest ranks and of different national origins also made an impression …

"The Persians sent groups of armored cavalrymen towards us. They rode so close to each other that the gleam of their bodies covered with iron plating was dazzling. Furthermore all the horses were protected with leather armor.

*Fragment of a silk fabric with elephants,*
Persia, 7th-9th century.
11cm x 13cm
Parish church of St. Servatius, Siegburg, Germany

Silk had been woven in Persia since the early Sassanid dynasty. It was not until the 6th century that the Persians managed to smuggle silk mills out of China and set up their own raw silk production. In China, knowledge of silk production was a well-guarded secret and betrayal was punishable by death.

*Sassanid elephant,*
6th/7th century AD.
Metropolitan Museum of Art, New York

Miniature figure of an elephant from the period of the Persian Sassanid kingdom when war elephants were still an important part of the army. It is probably a chess piece. The game, developed in India from features of war, spread via Persia to the West.

*Silk fabric with a detailed elephant pattern,*
Persia, 9th/10th century.
54cm x 92cm
Musée du Louvre, Paris

Improved weaving technology in the latter part of the Sassanid dynasty and then under Arabic and Mongol rule allowed figures, plants and geometric patterns to be worked in. Some fabrics with elephant motifs have survived. In Europe these precious fabrics were often used to wrap relics in, as the elephant was a symbol of Christian faith. This fabric was found in a reliquary at the church of Saint-Josse-sur-Mer (Pas-de-Calais).

"Several units of footmen supported the cavalry. These soldiers, with their long, curved shields covered with interlacing and skins, advanced in close lines. Behind them came the elephants. They looked like walking hills and as they moved damaged everything around them. As a result of experiences with elephants in earlier engagements, they were generally feared ..."

Shapur II also used war elephants during the suppression of a rebellion by Christians in Susa. The old Persian city, together with the new Sassanid capital of Ktesiphon (near Baghdad), was a center of Christianity in Persia. The king needed money to maintain his large army so he doubled the taxes levied from the Christians in the empire, whom he mistrusted. This triggered the uprising. Christianity had been made into the state religion in the hated Roman empire in AD 311 by Emperor Constantine and one of Shapur's rivals, the King of Armenia, who had followed suit. As a result, Shapur saw the new religion as a threat to the interests of his empire.

In the religious counter-movement the teachings founded by Zarathustra around 600 BC, which differed from those of the polytheism of his time, gained new strength in Persia. According to these teachings the god of light Ahuramazda, creator of everything good, of the sky, truth, life and angels is involved in an eternal struggle with the god of darkness, evil, demons and hell, Ahriman. Those who lead a moral life attain salvation; sinners are destined to damnation. At the end of the world Sohsan, the Redeemer, will resurrect the dead and lead them to the decisive encounter with the powers of darkness ...

King Shapur, therefore, marched against Susa, violently suppressed the uprising and with the help of his feared war elephants razed the city, including the walls, to the ground.

Opposite:
*Royal Wild Boar Hunt,*
5th century,
rock relief.
Entrance hall to the Taq-i-Bustan
grotto, Iran

Partial view of the relief on the
left-hand side of the large grotto
at Taq-i-Bustan. It depicts a wild
boar hunt using elephants.

Left:
Elephants driving the boar (detail).
Taq-i-Bustan grotto, Iran

## Rock reliefs celebrate the glorious actions of Sassanid kings

As a reminder of their coronation and military actions, and of tournaments and great hunts, the Sassanid kings had life-sized pictures carved into rock, usually near their favorite residence. The Persian rulers built lavish cities. To date thirty rock pictures have been found, mainly in the province of Fars, the old 'Persis.' They provide historical evidence that has stood the test of time, whereas the many magnificent brick buildings fell into disrepair a long time ago.

Of particular interest are the rock reliefs that the Sassanid ruler Khurso II (AD 590–628) had carved in a grotto, in Taq-i-Bustan near Kermandschah of elephants being ridden during a wild boar hunt.

The so-called 'Iwan' – a vaulted room, closed on three sides and open at the front, created in the rock – is situated in a former park or hunting ground. The wall reliefs summarize various phases of the event. The side walls depict hunting scenes: on the left boar-hunting; on the right stag-hunting. Elephants, driven by mahouts, chase the boar out of hiding in swampland and drive them in front of the king who is standing in a boat. The ruler, surrounded by musicians, appears twice: shooting an arrow at a boar and resting. The stag-hunting is depicted similarly: musicians play on a platform; the king is immortalized three times.

On the back wall the king's investiture can be seen. He is shown standing between Ahuramazda, Zarathustra's god of light, and Anahita, the goddess of fertility. The two highest deities in the country present Khurso with a circlet as a symbol of royal dignity. Below the coronation scene: the king in armor, mounted on a charger and holding a spear; the weapon of knights. The open side is shaped like the entrance to a palace.

At the height of Persian power Khurso II overstretched the country's strength, undertaking military expeditions as far as Egypt. He destroyed Jerusalem and persecuted Christians. In the turmoil that followed he lost his power and life. In AD 642 Persia finally succumbed to the Arab onslaught.

The Persian culture spread west beyond the Hindu Kush and also later influenced European knights. The Persians adopted Islam and the Arabic alphabet but not the Arabic language or lifestyle. They also exerted an artistic and cultural influence under tolerant Arabic rulers, and later in 1220 under the Mongols.

Fighters and transporters

From 'The Journal of Indian Art and Industry,' 1914.

An elephant made up of Arabic characters – an example of the highly-developed art of calligraphy in Islam.

*The Attack on Medina*, from the Turkish manuscript 'Siyer-i-Nebi' (Life of the Prophet). Topkapi Museum, Istanbul

The attack by the people of Mecca on Medina to which Muhammad was loyally devoted failed in April AD 627 in the face of divine intervention. A violent storm spread chaos among the besiegers who retreated.

# Muhammad and elephants

The 105th sura in the Koran describes a legendary incident involving elephants which took place in the year of the prophet's birth.

"In the name of God, Most Gracious, Most Merciful. Seest thou not how thy Lord dealt with the Companions of the Elephant? Did He not make their treacherous plan go astray? And He sent against them Flights of Birds. Striking them with stones of baked clay. Then did He make them like an empty field of stalks and straw, (of which the corn) has been eaten up."

The sura, 'revealed at Mecca,' alludes to a religious legend with an historical foundation. This legend is well-known to Muslims: The Christian viceroy Abraha ibn Al-Saba had a magnificent church built in Sana, the capital of the Yemen which was under Abyssinian rule. The church was decorated with gold, silver and precious stones. Abraha then invited desert tribes to worship God in his church instead of making the pilgrimage to the holy Caaba at Mecca. Many did as he asked with the result that fewer pilgrims traveled to Mecca.

The Koreischite, the rich traders in the city, were very angry about this as it was harming their business. They sent the religious fanatic Nofail to Sana. At dead of night he smeared the altar and church walls with excrement. Infuriated by this action the viceroy swore vengeance.

With an army and thirteen war elephants Abraha then marched against Mecca to destroy the Caaba. When he reached the city he told the representative of the Koreischite, Abdal Muttalib, chosen by God to be the grandfather of the unborn prophet, that all the inhabitants had to leave Mecca. Everybody fled to the mountains in fear, and the empty, windowless cube-shape building containing the holy 'Black Stone' was surrendered to the Abyssinians without a fight.

The next morning Abraha marched into Mecca at the head of his army. As he approached the shrine his elephant dropped to its knees and refused to go any further. Abdal Muttalib had whispered the name of his expected grandson Muhammad in the elephant's ear. All the other elephants followed the example of the first. As the elephants were being beaten to make them continue the sky went dark. A large flock of birds appeared and threw baked clay stones onto the army. The warriors' faces were immediately covered in plague-spots and their limbs dropped off. The few survivors, also subject to a huge flood, had to pick their way through bodies to escape.

Allah had thus protected the Caaba which remained the shrine of his coming prophet Muhammad and of Islam … The historical foundation for the detailed Eastern legend is that an Abyssinian army advancing into the Arabian Peninsula brought in the plague and perished from it themselves. Another Arabic legend clearly shows the respect the early Muslims had for elephants which were also pleasing to Allah:

The merchant Abu-Abd-Allah al Kalamis was traveling by ship on a pilgrimage to Mecca with

Star-shaped tile with elephant lacquered ceramic.
Museo d'Arte Orientale, Rome

*The Abyssinians in front of the Caaba,*
Turkish version of the Siyer-i-Nebi (Life of the Prophet),
16th century.
Topkapi Museum, Istanbul

Shortly before Muhammad's birth the Abyssinians occupied Mecca with a contingent of elephants and tried to destroy the Caaba. According to legend the pachyderms stopped in front of the shrine. A Turkish depiction of the wondrous event.

others. As the ship passed Aden a dreadful storm suddenly blew up and everyone believed that the end was nigh. Abu-Abd-Allah al-Kalamis prayed fervently. Inspired by Allah, he promised he would never eat elephant meat again if he was saved.

The ship was then tossed onto land and dashed to pieces. The pilgrims survived, but were left to die of starvation in the middle of a desert. Suddenly, as though by a miracle, a young elephant appeared. Abu-Abd-Allah's companions immediately killed it and ate its flesh. He alone refrained from doing so, remembering his promise. During the night the elephant's mother arrived and trampled to death all those who had eaten meat from her child. Abu-Abd-Allah al Kalamis was the only one she spared. She picked him up with her trunk, carried him on her back and left him close to a village, where he was found by the inhabitants and saved ...

Since the 4th century the Abyssinians had embraced a Christian culture and in the Hellenistic period had supplied elephants to the Ptolemys in Egypt. Even when Islam was emerging they caught and tamed African elephants. The oasis cities and princedoms on the Arabian Peninsula also had elephants. They were able to obtain the animals from Abyssinian trading partners or from Mesopotamia. A traditional Arabian miniature, a reminder of Muhammad's disastrous campaign against Mecca, represents war elephants in battle with soldiers on horseback.

After the collapse of the Roman Empire European tribes again began to migrate in huge numbers. At this time the gray giants no longer played a part in the West. In the East, on the other hand, the Indian elephant continued to be used for riding by rulers and as a fighting machine in numerous wars.

The Caaba (Arabic cube) is an empty, windowless building. The eastern corner contains the holy Black Stone which was worshipped even in pagan times. The Caaba is the main objective of the pilgrimage (Hajj) to Mecca.

Traditional Arabian miniature recalling Muhammad's disastrous campaign against Mecca and the defeat at Uhud (AD 625). The prophet had to leave Mecca in AD 622 following persecution of his supporters and under pressure from the rich businessmen. He was finally able to force a return to the holy city in AD 630 with a 10,000-strong army after several clashes.

# The elephant brigade in Britain's Indian army

Despite the development of modern weapons, elephants carried out active service in Southeast Asia until recently. The pachyderms did not, though, serve as 'war machines' or 'tanks' at the front; rather they were used as transport for supplies and in the deployment of engineers. Elephants were enlisted in the building of roads and bridges. They forced their way through jungle and managed to transfer heavy equipment over inhospitable mountainous terrain. They were invaluable in these conditions, as they succeeded where horses and engines failed.

In the 19th century the British included units of elephants in their colonial army in India. The British core divisions comprised some 50,000 men, but several times this number served in the Indian unit, including soldiers with experience of elephants. Elephants were used to keep the peace in rebellions and regional conflicts, particularly in the northwest province on the border with Afghanistan where there was constant unrest.

The patient beasts were in particular demand during fighting with Burma. Here the British were up against the French who were attempting to expand from Indochina. Burma, asserting its claim to the border area of Assam, triggered the first war (1824–26) with an attack on Bengal. It misjudged the balance of power. On land the Burmese, using elephants and poorly armed, had no chance against British guns. At sea, a British naval operation in the delta estuary of the Irrawaddy led to unification. Burma relinquished its claim to Assam and granted special rights to the East India Company.

A second war (1852) led to the annexation of South Burma and a third (1885–86) to the whole of Burma being incorporated into British India. During each armed encounter elephants on both sides hauled guns, ammunition, engineering equipment and provisions for the troops over mountain paths and through swampy jungle.

Elephants in the British army, with cases of ammunition strapped to their backs, advancing during the 3rd Burmese war (1885–86). Illustration from 'The Illustrated London News.'

Departure of an elephant battery to the front from palatial barracks. Photograph c. 1890

As draught animals in artillery units elephants came into their own in difficult swamp or mountain terrain where horses failed. Photograph c. 1900

Drawing contained in a report in 'The Illustrated London News' of October 21, 1891 on the British army in India.

Eventful scene during exercises in the elephant battery in difficult mountain terrain near Madras. The British officer orders "Halt!" and the mahouts pass on the order by pressing the elephant hook on the pachyderm's forehead; a silent command to stop immediately.

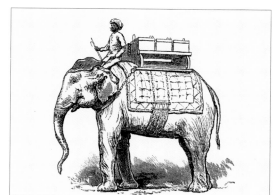

*Elephants in warfare,*
series of pictures from 'The Illustrated London News,' 1860:
1) Gun carrier
2) Munitions elephant
3) Elephants exercise in the river
4) Loading up with a gun

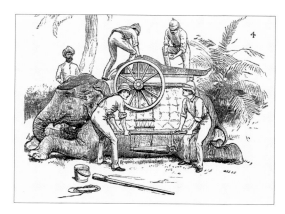

## Siam's elephant army

In the mid-19th century the king of Siam, as Thailand was called then, still had an elephant army consisting of 400 animals trained for fighting. About 100 were assigned to the artillery and carried small howitzers on their backs. Their bodies were protected by leather and rubber armor with iron plating as a precaution.

## Jenny the elephant in the German army

During the First World War the German army mobilized an elephant they called Jenny from Hamburg's Hagenbeck Zoo. Eigel Wiese describes this in his 'Hagenbeck-Buch.' The pachyderm helped with felling timber for tunnels in the trench war. The former keeper, Matthias Walter, already drafted into the navy, received a new deployment order. He took the animal by rail to the front in France. The troops could not believe their eyes when an elephant, with a marine breathing down its neck, trotted slowly out of the railroad area at Avesnes near Maubeuge. Jenny the elephant was quickly put to work to help the war effort.

Every day Jenny moved fifty heavy tree-trunks from the wood to a sawmill. She also plowed up a parade ground to be used as a field, and put her strength to use moving wagonloads of military supplies. As a reward she received special rations of rye bread. She served the German army behind the front line for two years, carrying out many heavy duties beyond the capabilities of men.

Jenny the elephant from Hamburg's Hagenbeck zoo, ridden by Matthias Walter, served in the German army during the First World War. Western front, 1916

An Anglo-Indian Gurkha squadron of elephants in 1878 deployed in battle against Afghanistan, an area disputed by England and Russia in the 19th century.
Illustration from 'The Illustrated London News.'

Fighters and transporters

A Cambodian elephant unit marches into the jungle during the Vietnam war to force out the Viet Cong who had infiltrated the country.

## The Japanese elephant squadron

During the Second World War the Japanese used an elephant squadron in their lightning campaign against the British in Burma in 1941–2. Their aim was to interrupt the supply of weapons for the Chiang Kai-shek regime in Chunking which went via the famous Burma Road; through the Irrawaddy Valley, via Mandalay, to the southern Chinese province of Yunnan. Using elephants to haul heavy military equipment through rough jungle, the Japanese managed to outflank and quickly defeat the British. As a result they captured Mandalay where they found full supply stores. Mandalay was only retaken by the allies in 1945 after a twelve-day siege, during which a large part of the city was destroyed, including the splendid royal palace containing irreplaceable works of art.

## Elephants in jungle warfare

In the French colonial empire of Indochina, embracing Vietnam, Cambodia and Laos, the regional kings were forced to hand over all their war elephants to the occupying power at the end of the 19th century. The monarchs, who were tolerated by the regime but obliged to cooperate, were allowed elephants only for show and riding during hunts. Bao Dai, king in the Vietnamese heartland of Annam from 1926, rode elephants into the jungle even during the first phase of Vietnam's ten-year struggle for independence. In 1949 Bao Dai was appointed nominal emperor of Vietnam; in 1953 he went into exile in France.

During the bloody conflicts in Vietnam working elephants were constantly brought into action. Cambodia also became involved when the Viet Cong moved its supply route south into its neutral neighbor's territory – the famous 'Ho Chi Minh Route' – because of American air attacks. The Cambodians, both concerned about peace and pressurized by America, tried to force the Viet Cong out of the country. Army units on elephantback and with little resolve to fight advanced into the jungle in the affected border areas, but did not have any effect.

Cambodia became immersed in the chaos of the bloody revolutionary regime of the Khmer Rouge. When the Vietnam war ended in 1972 and columns of Vietnamese tanks moved in against the Khmer Rouge elephants were used in the country's rough jungle in areas that vehicles could not traverse.

# Mythical creature and state gift

With the strengthening of Rome's global power the war elephant disappeared from the battlefields of the Western world. The Roman commanders had never regarded the exotic 'weapon' very highly. Before it disappeared from the West and became a mysterious, mythical creature the fate of the placid giant was to bleed to death in exhibition fights in Rome's amphitheaters for public entertainment and to increase the rulers' standing. Only when the seafaring pioneers of the early modern era rediscovered forgotten worlds did the giant with the trunk regain its real form; marveled at in the flesh in the menageries of renaissance rulers. To them the elephant was also a practical state gift happily accepted everywhere.

*Fairuz at the Pond with the King of the Elephants,*
Syria, 1354.
Illustration of a fable of the same name from an Eastern manuscript, Bodleian Library, Oxford, England

The story of Fairuz the hare and the king of the elephants who are sitting near the reflection of the moon in a lake was adopted by the Islamic-Arab world from an Indian collection of fables. Two jackals, Kalila and Dimna, are the main protagonists.

*Elephant-hunt,*
page from the 'Livre des Merveilles du Monde,' c.1400,
illumination.
29cm x 42cm
Bibliothèque Nationale de France, Paris

The Great Khan's horsemen have ridden down into a valley in the kingdom of Burma and are hunting two elephants and a unicorn.

la force des tartars. Mais se mistrent a desconfiture et tournerent a fuie. Et quit
les tartars les virent desconfis. si leur aloient derriere chassant et occiant et abatant
si malement que ce estoit vne pitie a voir. Et quant il les orent vne piece chaces
si ne les vouloient plus suir. mais retournerent arriere es bois pour prendre des
oliphans qui estoient la sous. Et leur conuenoit taillier les grans arbres
et mettre leur au deuant pour auoir les. Et auecc trestout ce ne les pouoi
ent auoir. se ne feussent les hommes meismes du roy qui auoient este pris en
la bataille qui mieur les sauoient conquoistre que les tartars. Et ainsi les
prenoient. car les oliphans sont bestes qui ont trop plus grant entendemet
que nulle autre beste. et en pristrent plus de deux cens. Et de celle bataille en a
uant commencea le grant kaan a auoir moult doliphans. Et en ceste ma
niere fu desconfist ce roy par le sens et par la maistrie des tartars. si comme
vous pouez auoir entendu cy dessus.

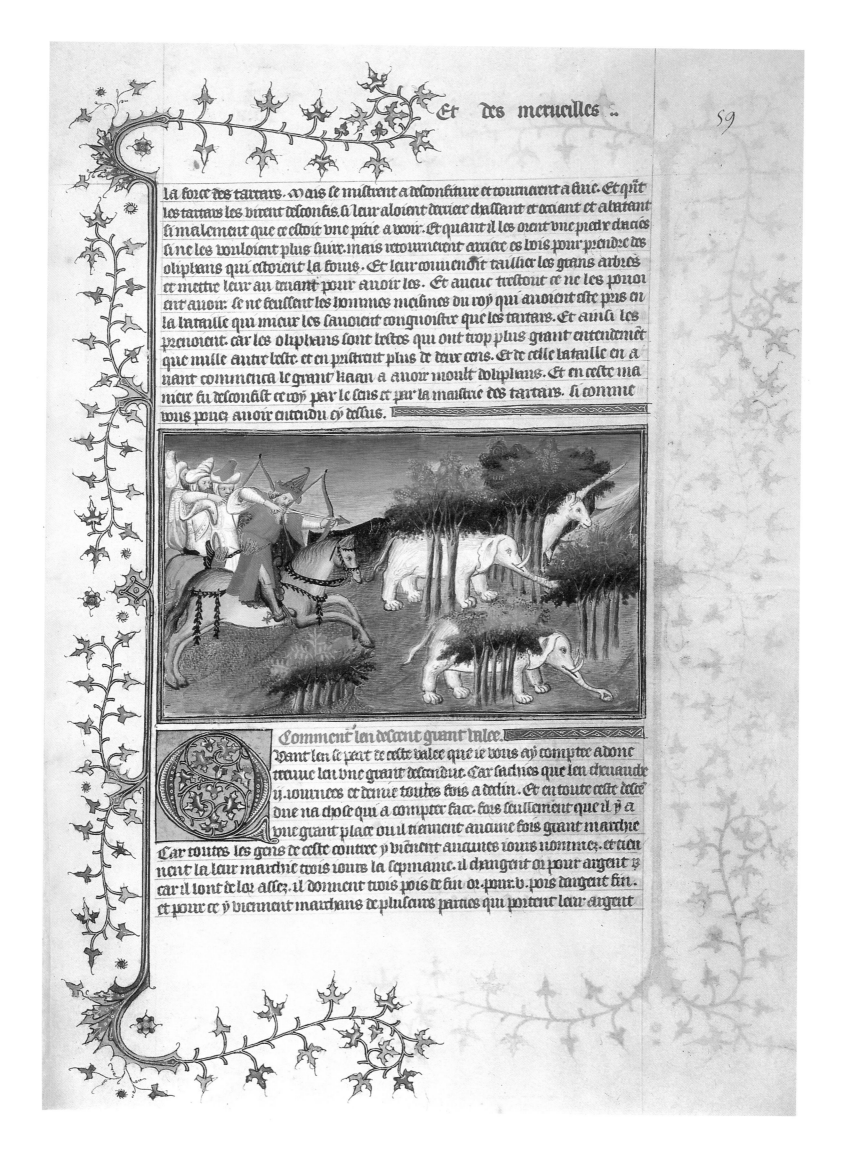

### Comment len descent grant valee.

Quant len se part de ceste valee que ie vous ay comptee adonc
treuue len vne grant descendue. Car sachies que len cheuauche
xj. iournees et demie toutes fois a declin. Et en toute ceste descen
due na chose qui a compter face. fors seulement que il y a
vne grant place ou il tiennent aucune fois grant marchie
Car toutes les gens de ceste contree y viennent aucunes iours nommez. et tien
nent la leur marchie trois iours la sepmaine. il changent or pour argent y
car il sont de lor assez. il donnent trois pois de fin or pour .v. pois dargent fin.
et pour ce y viennent marchans de plusieurs parties qui portent leur argent

Conrad Gesner,
Elephant from 'Historia
animalium' lib. 1,
Zurich 1551, p 410,
copperplate engraving.

Before the 19th century not many
artists had the opportunity to
draw from a live elephant. Even as
distinguished an author as Conrad
Gesner, therefore, had to make use
of an almost 100-year-old
engraving by Martin Schongauer
for his zoological book of 1551.
The ribbed ears and bulging
trunk, in particular, can be seen in
both artists' work and probably
come from older sources.

Elephant (detail),
illustration in Francesco Petrarca:
Artzney bayder Glück, des güten
und widerwärtigen,
Augsburg 1532,
wood engraving.
Private collection

This scene is found in a German
version of Petrarca's 16th century
book 'De Remediis utriusque
Fortunae' ('Physicke against
fortune') in the chapter devoted to
elephants and camels.

Mythical creature and state gift

'Elephantus' by Mary, Queen of Scots (1542–87), silk embroidery. Oxburgh Hall, Norfolk, England

Mary, Queen of Scots, spent her first period of imprisonment (around 1570) in Oxburgh Hall in the wilds of Norfolk. There she worked over 100 pieces of silk embroidery, including this elephant. It is part of the so-called 'Oxburgh hangings,' which show motifs from contemporary bestiary illustrations. The picture is taken from Conrad Gesner's 'Historia animalium,' Zurich 1563.

Elephant from Codex Hamilton 407 France, c. 1400, illumination on parchment. Deutsche Staatsbibliothek, Berlin

## A strange mythical creature

With the decline of the Roman Empire in the 4th century AD the elephant disappeared from sight and from the art of the young Western peoples who were embracing a new chapter in world history. In the turmoil of mass migration ancient literature about elephants was also lost. In the 4th century BC Aristotle had described the elephant's anatomy with surprising accuracy even if he had given the giant a life expectancy of 200 years.

Expanding belief Christianity pervaded and revolutionized all areas of life. In the turbulence people were swept along by new state orders. Familiar biblical stories were the main source of material for artistic work, which developed new forms of expression. For centuries people were only aware of the existence and stature of the elephant through stories handed down.

# "An animal that has no joints ..."

*Elephant,*
Illustration from 'Horus Sanitatis'
by Johannis de Cuba,
Strasbourg 1483,
wood engraving.

The 'Hortus Sanitatis' (Garden of Health) is one of the most common works from the late Middle Ages. As well as medicinal herbs, the pharmacopeia describes animals. The elephant is extolled as a placid animal easy to tame.

The 'Physiologus,' a popular compendium of early Christian animal symbolism, left its mark on the comical, medieval idea of the elephant. The work originated at the end of the 2nd century AD in Alexandria or Syria and was translated into many languages from the Greek. In the 1st millennium AD it was the source of a number of 'bestiaries.' Apart from the bible no book had a bigger distribution at that time.

The 'Physiologus,' not known as an expert text on zoology, describes familiar and legendary animals, revealing their characteristics in religious allegories. For ardent fundamentalists nature was part of the expected salvation. The treatise on the elephant is a parable of Adam and Eve's happiness in paradise before the Fall of Man. It says:

"There is an animal called the elephant whose copulating is free from wicked desire. If the elephant wishes to produce young, he goes off to the east near paradise where there is a tree called the mandrake. And he goes there with his mate, who first takes a part of the tree and gives it to her husband, and cajoles him until he eats it. After the male has eaten, [they join together] and the female immediately conceives in her womb. And when the time comes for her to give birth, she goes to a pond and where the water reaches her dugs she brings forth her offspring. Since the calf is born in the water, it swims about and finds the thighs of its mother and is suckled at her teats. The male elephant guards her while she gives birth because of the serpent who is an enemy to the elephant. If the elephant finds a serpent, he kills it by trampling on it until it dies."

For the reader who is interested in zoology 'Physiologus' mentions an anatomical peculiarity of the elephant:

"This is the nature of the elephant: if he should fall, he is unable to get up again. But how can he fall since he rests against a tree? The elephant has no knee joints enabling him to sleep lying down if he wanted to. Shortly before the beast arrives at the tree against which he is accustomed to rest, the hunter who wishes to capture the animal cuts partly through the tree. When the elephant comes and rests against the tree, both tree and beast fall at the same time ..."

*The elephant giving birth in water,*
drawing from a South German pattern book, early 13th century.

An inscription explains the Physiologus motif: "The elephant gives birth to her young in the river so that the dragon cannot kill them." The Christian moral: baptism protects souls so that the devil cannot steal them.

*Elephants and mythical creatures pay homage to a goddess,*
detail from the famous 'Gundestrup Cauldron,'
1st century BC,
silver, beaten, with gold-plating.
21cm x 40cm
National Museum, Copenhagen

The 'Gundestrup Cauldron.' The masterly work was created in the 4th century. It is probably the most important artistic work from the Celtic Iron Age. Patchy information about the elephant and its appearance probably got through to the western countries in the north first.

# On the use of the elephant: an Arabic bestiary

The Arabic counterpart of the highly imaginative representation of animals in the Western text of 'Physiologus' was the delightful bestiary, called 'Manafi'al-Haja-wan' (On the Use of Animals). The manuscript was compiled by a doctor to the caliph in Baghdad in the 11th century. It was translated into Persian 200 years later and illuminated with 94 miniatures by Persian artists. The elephant has a special place in the colorful array of mythical creatures and living animals. Two interlocked pachyderms, decorated with bells and caps, are depicted in an exotic and ornamental style in gouache paint.

The manuscript puts the life span of an elephant at 300 to 400 years. The giant, it says, is afraid of pigs and horned rams; it is particularly afraid of midges and mice. The bestiary also recommends the healing power of the elephant for all sorts of complaints. The following applications promise relief: the smoke of burned elephant fat banishes headaches; a piece of elephant skin placed on the body brings a temperature down, and ivory powder is supposedly good for the dreaded leprosy; these are among the strange uses for the elephant.

Illustration from a medieval manuscript, 12th century, illumination.
British Museum, London

Horsemen kill elephants which early medieval imagination turned into bizarre mythical creatures with clawed feet, trumpet-like trunks and the tusks of wild boar.

Aboû S'aid Oubayd Allâh ibn Baktîsh,
elephant watches over its young, illustration from the Islamic bestiary 'On the Use of Animals' (Manifi'al-Hajawan) Maragha, Persia (Iran), c. 1295, gouache on paper.
The Pierpont Morgan Library, New York

Sacrificial showpiece, mythical creature and state gift

# Elephants in early Christianity

It was only around the turn of the millennium that trade with the East and the spoils of crusades brought ideas and models for producing pictures of the weird and wonderful primeval creature across the Mediterranean. The elephant became the admonishing, Christian symbolic figure for wise level-headedness and dependable constancy, for chasteness and restrained strength – for virtues which contemporaries indulging in crude, fervently pious, superstitious and earthly pleasures lacked.

The oldest evidence of the symbolism of elephants for the early Christians dates from the 11th century and can be found in Italian and French churches. There was closer contact there with the highly-developed culture of the Islamic East than in countries north of the Alps. The elephants support fonts, adorn capitals, portals and choir stalls, and sit firmly in the filigree work of the buttresses of huge Gothic cathedrals.

Early medieval craftsmen had very little experience of elephants themselves and therefore human imagination knew no bounds. In pictorial representations the elephant, an animal that had never been seen, turned into a bizarre mythical creature, often bearing little resemblance to the real, gray giants. This was particularly the case away from the main trade routes and academic centers, where people were better informed. The elephant, like the unicorn, was a weird and wonderful animal bearing no relation to reality.

Elephant candlestick,
13th century,
bronze.

The bizarre elephant is supporting a candlestick in the form of a castle.

Romualdus,
Archbishop's throne,
11th century,
marble.
S. Sabino, Canosa di Puglia, Italy

Romualdus created this throne for Bishop Urso of Canosa, according to an inscription on the side. Elephants support the throne. The ornamental decorations are in the Byzantine style.

Elephants on a capital,
former priory church of St-Pierre et St-Benoît, Percy les Forges, Saône-et-Loire, 12th century.
France
The wealth of forms and enigmatic relief figures make the column capitals in early Romanesque churches attractive. Elephants, symbols of strength, level-headedness, and dependable constancy, support the weight of the vaults, together with comical mythical creatures.

Elephants on a capital,
St-Pierre, Aulnay-de-Saintonge,
12th century.
Charente, France.

Apart from the clawed feet, the
almost three-dimensional
elephants are very realistic. The
stonemasons probably had more
precise knowledge about the
animals' appearance.

Floor mosaic (detail), 1163–66,
Santa Maria Annunziata,
Otranto, Italy.

The floor mosaic showing
elephants and the Tree of Life was
laid in the nave in Otranto
cathedral (Apulia) around the
middle of the 13th century. In the
Old Testament the tree is the
symbol of creation and of all life.
Christianity substituted the cross
as the 'arbor vitae,' as the true
tree of life, for the original tree
symbol familiar to many cultures.
However, the old symbol, often
depicted with animals as witnesses
of living nature, was retained in a
stylized form.

# Elephants on cathedrals

Elephant, 13th century.
Rheims Cathedral, France

The elephant motif was frequently used by medieval stonemasons for decorating the outside of magnificent Gothic cathedrals. This giant, with a massive tubular trunk, sits proudly and somewhat removed from the realities of the world under the lofty towers of the high Gothic cathedral in Rheims. French monarchs were crowned here.

Elephant, 12th century.
Cathedral of Notre Dame, Paris

From the lavish, early Gothic cathedral of Notre Dame in Paris the giant with the trunk (and claws still) looks serenely and wisely out over the hustle and bustle of the city and the vanity of the world. The Gothic style was the most dominant style in the West. It was developed in France in particular with technical perfection and beauty.

Mythical creature and state gift

# Harun al-Raschid's gift to Charles the Great

In AD 802 an elephant arrived north of the Alps for the first time since Roman times. The encounter with the giant was, however, too brief and too incredible to change the almost comical medieval image the elephant had enjoyed for centuries.

This elephant was Abul Abbas, named in honor of the belligerent founder of the Abbasid dynasty (750–1258). It was given as a gift to the Frankish king, Charles the Great, by the powerful caliph of Baghdad, Harun al-Raschid. Charles the Great had just been crowned 'Emperor and Augustus' in Rome and inherited the Western Roman Empire. The gift of an elephant was a special gesture of friendship on the caliph's part. The two men were united in their opposition towards the Spanish caliphate of Cordoba and towards Eastern Roman Byzantium, which still refused to recognize the Frankish emperor as the heir to the Western Empire. Despite trade with India elephants were still a rarity and a very valuable state possession even in the Near East, not far from elephant populations.

Harun al-Raschid's delegation set off with the gray giant, which was probably a trained war elephant, in AD 801. They then crossed the Mediterranean by ship. In October the exotic group landed in Portovenere, near La Spezia and spent the winter in the small town of Vercelli, south of Lake Maggiore. Jude Isaak, a North African, led the delegation and looked after the elephant. Once the snow had melted the group crossed the Alps. They finally reached Aachen, Charles the Great's residence, in July AD 802, and the elephant, attracting much attention, was handed over with other luxurious gifts to the Frankish king.

The emperor would take the exotic weird and wonderful creature with him on state occasions and when he traveled. He wanted to emphasize his power and intimidate others. In AD 804 the terrifying giant was meant to have just that effect during a military campaign against a Frisian rebellion. But unfortunately, the elephant drowned while crossing the Rhine. A powerful hunting horn was supposedly made from one of its tusks.

At the time chroniclers paid more attention for a while to the wondrous animal than to many of the emperor's actions. There are, though, few traces of it in early Frankish art. The giant had spread fear among the ordinary people and even reinforced superstition. They suggested that the 'bogey' had been made with a monstrous body because of the atrocities it had committed before God.

# Frederick II's state elephant

In a prolonged period of power struggles, forced Christianization, and migration the memory of Charles the Great's elephant soon faded. The gray giant remained a strange mythical creature. Another 400 years passed before an elephant crossed the Mediterranean as a diplomatic gift. The sultan Al-Kamil from Cairo cemented his friendship with the last Italian-influenced Staufen emperor and king of Sicily, Frederick II (1212–50), by sending him a valuable elephant.

Frederick was a freethinker well-versed in ancient natural sciences and Arabic philosophy. He wandered between Western and Eastern cultures. He had backed the sultan instead of his brother and rival Almu-Azzam. Although excommunicated, the pope forced Frederick against his will to undertake a crusade to restore Christian rule to Jerusalem in 1227. He reached a lasting peaceful and friendly compromise with Al-Kamil.

After a century of the barbarity of crusades he wrote to the sultan: "You should not be troubled by the Christians and not be forced to shed the blood of your subjects against us …"

Because it was cared for sensibly Frederick's elephant lived for decades. The emperor took it with him on important occasions to demonstrate his power. Frederick's triumphal procession into Milan after his victory in 1237 at Cortenuova over the Lombard cities, which were allied with the pope, has gone down in history. The crowds stared in wonder at the elephant and cheered as it pulled the captured Lombard flag carriage. The animal was decorated magnificently and carried a trumpeter in a castle on its back.

The emperor apparently acquired several other elephants but this one remained his favorite. It died in Cremona in 1248. The people expected its bones to turn into ivory.

## England's first pachyderm

The elephant which the French king Louis IX or Saint Louis brought back from the failed Sixth Crusade in the 13th century is also worth mentioning for the amazement it caused.

Once the pachyderm had been admired extensively in Paris, Louis sent it as a present to his English brother-in-law, Henry III, in 1255. The English were filled with excitement. An elephant had not been seen on the island since the days of

Cesar and Emperor Claudius when their legions had crossed the Channel with elephants in an attempt to intimidate the natives.

The king immediately ordered that a house be built for the giant at the Tower of London. According to contemporary sources it was forty feet long and twenty feet wide. People flocked to marvel at the weird and wonderful animal. However, the elephant only survived until 1258 in the Tower's menagerie, probably as a result of a lack of experience on the part of its keepers and the harsh British climate.

Matthew Paris (Matthaeus Parisiensis) reports on England's first elephant in his 'Chronica majora'. An illustration in it shows an African elephant. This was one of the first realistic representations of an elephant in Northern Europe, although it was not yet commonplace in the early medieval West. For centuries the elephant was still shown as a grotesque creature with a horse's body, a trumpet-like trunk that stuck out stiffly, a sheep's face, curved tusks like those of a wild boar, and snub, pointed ears. The 'Physiologus,' along with much religious teaching, was still the source for information about the nature of the elephant.

In the 14th/15th century people began to reflect again on the great cultural heritage of antiquity, as the renaissance in art and life developed with a positive attitude to life. It was only then that the elephant stopped being a creature from the world of fables and became a real animal.

*Trade outside the city of Ormuz,* engraving after a miniature from: 'Livre des Merveilles du Monde' c. 1400, illumination. 16cm x 10.5cm Bibliothèque Nationale de France, Paris

This illustration from the sumptuous 'Livre des Merveilles du Monde' shows traders outside the Persian city of Ormuz. Ormuz (Hormoz) used to be located on the mainland but today is an island in the Persian Gulf. The Indian ships have docked in the harbor and are unloading their luxurious cargo, including an elephant.

Matthew Paris, Matthaeus Parisiensis, d. 1259, *Henry III's Elephant,* a print from the Chronica majora, England, 1255, watercolor pen-and-ink drawing. 11.8cm x 21.5cm Corpus Christi College, Cambridge

King Louis of France sent the elephant as a gift to Henry III of England in 1255. The drawing by the Benedictine monk, England's greatest 13th century painter of miniatures, is one of the first realistic animal studies since antiquity. The inscription under the giant's stomach reads: "By the size of the man portrayed here, the dimensions of the animal represented may be imagined."

## Hanno the elephant pays homage to the pope

The most famous elephant given as a gift was Hanno, an Indian elephant, presented to the Medici pope Leo X by King Manuel I of Portugal in 1515. The seafaring country of Portugal had become the richest kingdom in Europe thanks to its spice trade, colonial riches, and tribute payments. To safeguard his expansion policy Manuel sought the pope's favor. The pope encouraged him to carry out further action against 'infidels.' The king paid homage to the pontifex by sending him Hanno together with a wealth of other sumptuous gifts.

On March 12, 1515 the elephant and its entourage led by the great sailor and discoverer, Tristan da Cunha, arrived in Rome. They were greeted ceremoniously by a delegation of cardinals and taken to the Castel Sant' Angelo. There Hanno, led by an Indian and ridden by a magnificently dressed Moor, knelt before the pope. This was astonishing, particularly as the idea expressed in the 'Physiologus' that the elephant does not have any joints in its legs was still rife. The gray giant was rewarded for the respect he had previously shown to the pope with magnificent accommodation in the Vatican gardens. The pope even turned down a request from his nephew, Lorenzo, to borrow the elephant for a procession in Florence, so precious was it to the Pope.

However, just two years later Hanno died. The elephant had supposedly been covered in gold for a resplendent celebration and suffocated. According to another report the animal shied during a chaotic procession and, with a heavy castle on its back, fell into the Tiber. The inconsolable pope honored the elephant with a (no longer existing) obituary mounted on an external wall of the Vatican. He also had its picture worked into a tapestry after a sketch (also lost) by Raphael.

## The 'elephant diplomacy' of Renaissance rulers

At the beginning of the modern era Europe's seafaring pioneers reconnoitered the coasts of Africa and opened up the main sea route around the 'Cape of Good Hope' to the spice and wonderland of India, the land routes to which the Muslim kingdoms of the Near East had blocked. At this time countries in the West again became familiar with the elephant. Along with spices, silk and the booty from conquests, the windjammers returned home with live elephants.

A wide spectrum of people came into contact with the real elephant and this helped to correct fantastic early medieval ideas. The Renaissance spread from Italy and after the sacred Gothic era artists turned to the secular reality of life and made basic anatomical studies in close contact with science, with the humanistic enlightenment. They put the mythical creature back into the garden of nature. The invention of printing and the development of graphic arts and copperplate engraving techniques facilitated the duplication and distribution of artistic representations. This helped to banish previous bizarre ideas concerning elephants throughout Europe.

This was a period of lavish show, court dwarfs, grandiose processions and a passion for collecting all kinds of rarities and peculiarities which were proudly displayed in 'rooms of wonders.' The first 'menageries' were favorite showpieces. These contained cages of exotic animals imported at great expense. Like the peculiarities in the 'rooms of wonders' the animals became valued gifts presented by one ruler to another.

Elephants were top of the list of state gifts and in the 16th/17th century were shipped to the Old World more and more often. Like China's rare giant panda today, the exotic mythical creature was considered a luxurious and novel gift of friendship which flattered the recipient and at the same time emphasized the global connections and powerful position of the giver.

Unknown artist after Raphael,
*Hanno the Elephant*,
mid-16th century,
pen wash,
Copperplate cabinet.
27.7cm x 28.5cm
Stiftung Museen Preußischer
Kulturbesitz, Berlin

This drawing imitates a lost work by Raphael who had seen Pope Leo X's elephant for himself. Raphael's drawing was also used to produce Hanno's epitaph that used to be on the Vatican wall. The following inscription could be read: "Under this colossal mountain lie I a colossal elephant, whom King Emmanuel, after overcoming the East, gave as a captive to the Tenth Leo ... What nature had carried off, Raphael of Urbino reproduced with his art."

## Sulayman's remarkable march from Genoa to Vienna

On September 13, 1548 the 21-year-old crown prince Maximilian, later Emperor Maximilian II, married his cousin Maria in Spain. Maria was the daughter of the emperor Charles V on whose empire 'the sun never set.' The marriage between Maximilian, who enjoyed life to the full, and the pale, serious, and immensely pious Maria was not one of love, but a political marriage celebrated in Valladolid with suitably magnificent festivities, tournaments and entertainment.

The union was supposed to defuse the smoldering dispute between the Spanish and Austrian branches of the Habsburgs over the future distribution of power and, above all, lend solid Catholic support to the easygoing prince who was toying with Protestantism. After his marriage the prince was forced by his father to spend a good two years in Spanish 'exile' which he hated. He then received the call to return to Vienna.

Before starting out Maximilian made a final courtesy visit to the Portuguese royal court. As a sea and trading power it was held in the highest esteem in Europe. Maximilian was so impressed by the royal menagerie in Lisbon that he spent several hours there every day. He was particularly fascinated by the elephants. King John III supplied the European kings with the coveted, exotic animals, and he used this opportunity to make a friendly gesture towards Vienna. He promised the prince he would receive an elephant and team of keepers when he returned to Genoa.

When Maximilian, his wife and large entourage arrived in Genoa in the summer of 1551 to his great joy he found the elephant had been delivered by ship. King John wrote to him:

"I hope your highness will be content with this memento which your well-disposed uncle is sending to you for the homecoming of yourself and your royal wife." He then advised naming the animal after the Christian West's deadly enemy, the sultan Sulayman "so that in this way he becomes your slave and is properly humbled."

The march with Sulayman the elephant, headed by lance bearers, crossed Northern Italy towards Brenner. In Trent, where a council was to meet, a wooden reproduction was made of the weird and wonderful animal. The event started with fireworks and great festivities. The expedition, wondered at everywhere it went, did not reach Brixen until the end of December, where it rested for two weeks. The inn 'Am hohen Feld' (In the High Country) was renamed 'Gasthof zum Elefanten' (Elephant Inn) and the strange giant animal was immortalized in a life-sized picture on the outside of the building.

The winter weather forced the train to keep stopping. On January 2, 1552 it crossed the snow-covered Brenner Pass to Innsbruck, and from there traveled via Wasserburg, Passau and Linz to Vienna. Even today inn signs mark the route of Sulayman's remarkable march.

On March 7 Maximilian arrived jubilantly in Vienna. The people were more interested in the huge elephant than in the heir to the throne's young wife. The story goes that in the crush – everyone wanted to touch the weird and wonderful animal – a child was separated from its mother and fell in front of the elephant's feet. The giant carefully picked the child up with its trunk and placed it back in its mother's arms …

When Maximilian was crowned king of Hungary the people of Budapest also had the chance to see the bull, led by an Indian mahout. He was the highlight of the great procession and the people marveled at the great beast.

Elephant chair, 1553, elephant bones, wood. Benedictine Chapter House, Krems Cathedral, Austria

The end of Sulayman: The mayor of Vienna, Sebastian Hütstocker, had a macabre chair produced from the shoulder blade and bones of the right foreleg. The elephant's face is engraved in the shoulder blade that forms the seat. The chair was put in the room of art and wonders in the Benedictine Chapter House at Krems Cathedral.

Mythical creature and state gift

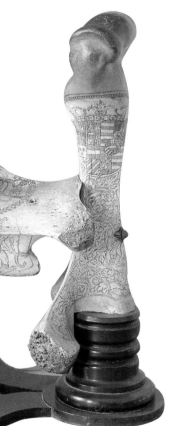

Historians have described the death, just a year later, on December 18, 1553, of the exhausted Sulayman. The giant body was preserved and stuffed. Until 1572 it was on show at Ebersdorf castle. Then Duke Albrecht of Bavaria, a collector of curiosities, received it as a gift. The stuffed animal, known as the 'Brixen elephant' could be seen in Munich's National Museum until 1941. It finally decomposed in a damp air raid shelter, a mine gallery, during the Second World War.

Many house walls in Vienna were decorated with pictures of elephants. A copperplate engraving by Solomon Kleiner shows the 'elephant house' in the street am Graben decorated with a huge head and trunk with tusks which still look more like fangs. A commemorative medallion was minted showing Sulayman the elephant being ridden.

## ... given away to Queen Elizabeth I

In 1591 King Philip II of Spain, who also wore the crown of Portugal, honored King Henry IV of France with an elephant. The animal arrived by boat at Dieppe. Henry was involved in military disputes. However, he ordered that the elephant be housed and cared for properly. According to the king, this elephant was the most precious object ever seen in his kingdom; he therefore wanted to ensure its survival.

However, the upkeep of the elephant proved too expensive for the small public purse, so King Henry decided with much regret that his prizes possession must go and he gave the animal to Queen Elizabeth I of England.

Hans Burgkmair the Elder (1473–1531), *The people of Calicut* from Maximilian I's triumphal procession, 1526, colored wood engraving of a later 18th century version.
Private collection

Hans Burgkmair's famous cycle of wood engravings from 1526 comprised 137 works. An Indian delegation with an elephant is paying homage to the emperor's greatness.

# The circus jumbo

In the circus elephants show their intelligence and aptitude in the most amazing way. Trainers are not able to demand such varied showpieces from any other animal as from the melancholy giant with the trunk,

Jumbo is the main attraction at England's Blackpool circus. He is very quick to learn and particularly fond of music.

whose powerful body seems to allow it only to trot in an ungainly manner. Even for the ancient Romans the appearance of elephants was the highlight of circus entertainment; they certainly used elephants in their hundreds in barbaric animal fights and gladiatorial bloodbaths. If an elephant has been taught by an understanding trainer and is not mistreated or overstretched it can enjoy the tricks it has learned. Elephants suffer when idle and bored. The pachyderms are also dignified and stoically resigned when they are forced to wear a jester's hat for the public's amusement. The amazed spectators who wildly applaud acrobatic performances, such as 'handstands,' are not aware of the pain felt in the joints taking the weight of the colossal body; they have no idea of the many painful hours of training which take place day after day behind closed circus doors.

Poster for 'Circus Corty-Althoff,' printed by Adolph Friedländer, Hamburg, 1913, color lithograph. 136cm x 94cm Münchner Stadtmuseum, Munich

Pièrre Althoff was one of Europe's greatest circus pioneers. At 18 he was managing the Circus Corty-Althoff. He himself juggled on horseback. Following his early death in 1924 his widow, the former circus rider Adele Rossi, continued to run the company. She also presented the big circus show with the 'marvellous musical elephants' which are advertised on the poster.

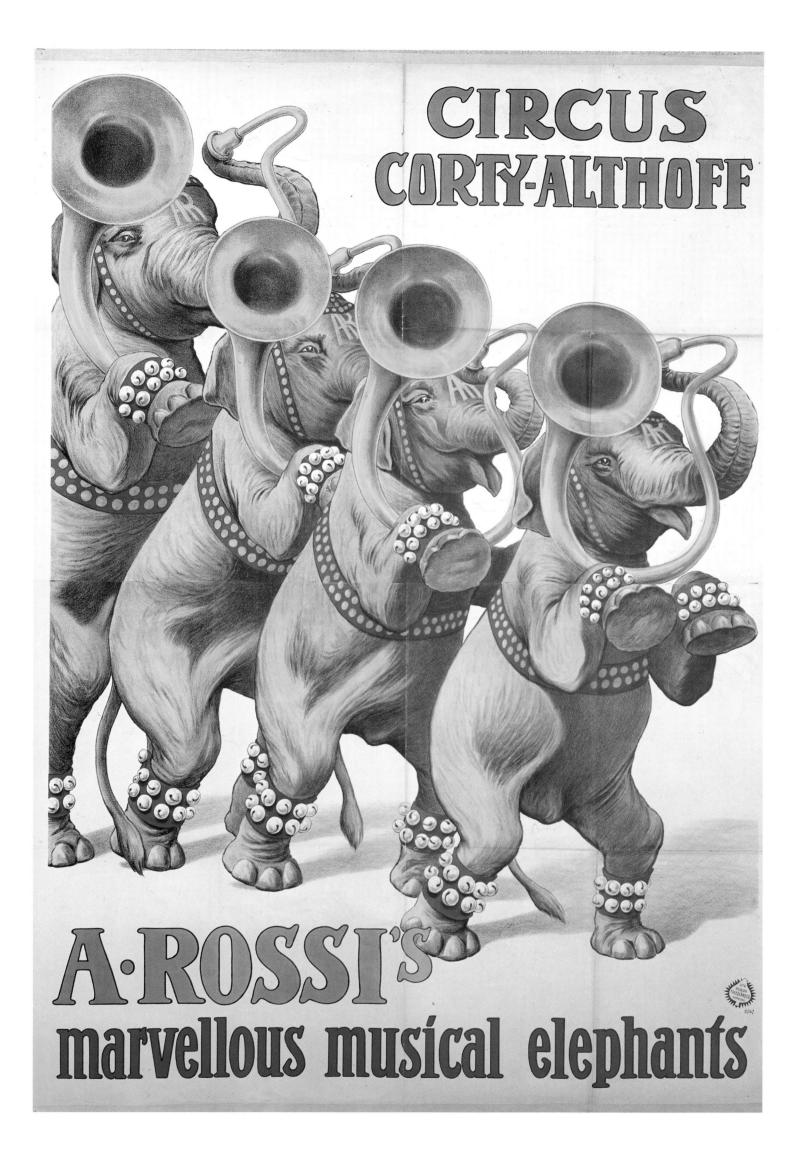

# Persecuting elephants in amphitheaters

The ancient Romans forced the elephants they had captured during battle to participate in shows in their circuses and later amphitheaters. The latter were the first places in the West where the public could fulfill its desire for sensation. The classical Rome of the republic and emperors was always a city of games, horse-racing, and shows of exotic weird and wonderful animals, but also of animal persecution and training.

The origins of the famous Circus Maximus in the valley between Palatin and Aventin supposedly date back to the legendary founder of the city, Romulus. It was, though, only under Cesar and the emperors Nero and Trajan that the Circus Maximus expanded to hold almost 50,000 spectators. In 120 BC the Circus Flaminius was erected on the Campus Martius near the Capitol. Amphitheaters were later built throughout much of the empire, the biggest of which was the Colosseum, opened in AD 80. Many ruins of these have survived.

Considered as exotic weird and wonderful creatures the elephants captured from war added to the splendor of the triumphal processions of returning victors, who would use their glorious deeds to win the people's favor. It all started with the public presentation in 275 BC of four war elephants taken during the campaign against Pyrrhus. Just 20 years later the Romans were able to admire 100 elephants which must have been surrendered by the Carthaginians in Sicily. Dark-skinned guides performed small marching movements with the heavy pachyderms for the admiring people. Elephants were later forced to take part in bloody animal fights and gladiatorial bloodbaths in the arenas to please the masses.

Elephants were first provoked into a rage with stimulants and set onto each other. The thrill of the giants crashing into each other was soon no longer enough. So in 55 BC Pompey, later a rival to Cesar, arranged for starving lions and leopards to be brought into the arena to fight against the elephants, during the official opening of a Temple of Venus. However, as the giants with the trunks were torn to pieces by the pack of big cats angry shouts of protest came from the stands.

While taking pleasure in cruel spectacles the masses did have some compassion and they took pity on the tortured creatures. The people of Rome were accustomed to the horror of death in the arena, but to them the elephant was an animal unlike any other. Its slaughter stirred deep emotions.

Despite the spectators' earlier angry reaction, on the last day of the games Pompey made a group of African prisoners of war, armed with spears, fight against twenty elephants. The crowd cheered when an elephant was killed in scenes reminiscent of war and when black bodies holding shields and spears were hurled into the air by elephants' trunks. The mood changed, however, when the giant gray animals pierced with spears fell to their knees and trumpeted pitifully. Their writhing in the throes of death was like a plea for mercy. The reaction towards Pompey, the patron of the games, was once again one of outrage and fury.

Pliny, who portrayed Roman life and customs in his works, credited the elephants with the intelligence and fairness which his contemporaries lacked. He described the incident with sympathy. Even Cicero told a friend in a letter that the people were overcome with sympathy because elephants displayed such human behavior.

However, exhibition fights involving elephants continued to be one of the highlights of Roman circuses. Cesar had prisoners of war in battle formation compete against groups of elephants. Archers were carried in castles on the elephants' backs. This made the bloody test of the elephants' strength against footmen and cavalry even more exciting. Duels between a gladiator and an enraged elephant also added spice to the circus entertainment and pleased the crowd.

Floor mosaic, 6th century. Hagia Sophia, Istanbul

Animal fight in the arena: a lion attacks an elephant. This Byzantine floor mosaic was found in the area of the former imperial residence in Constantinople (Istanbul).

Heinrich Leutemann (1824–1905), *Romans kill captured elephants,* 'Bilder aus dem Altertum' series, Münchner Bilderbogen no. 507, c. 1866, color wood engraving.

Elephants captured in battle end up in a bloodbath for sport in a Roman amphitheater.

The circus jumbo

Georges Gardet (1863–1914).
A lion held in the elephant's
trunk, bronze figure.

Monkey riding on an elephant,
1–2nd century AD,
Roman terra cotta sculpture.
Mildenberg collection

## Training elephants in ancient Rome

Drawing of a Roman state carriage.

On public occasions a magnificent state carriage pulled by four elephants and decorated with gold and ivory carried the idolized Roman emperors. Medallions showing a statue of the emperor in a state carriage were distributed during an emperor's lifetime and after his death. For example, Augustus and the tyrant Caligula were depicted traveling in a godlike pose to circus games.

Not only did bloody animal combat, dreadful gladiatorial fights and fatal battles take place in Rome's arenas – activities which thrilled the ever restless plebeians. The Romans were the first to make use of the elephant's receptive nature for very modern-looking circus entertainment with similar tricks and routines to those of today.

Knowledge of the art of animal taming and practical training ideas came from Alexandria where the most experienced in this field worked. Animal taming and training became a profession in Rome. Good-natured animals who had not been ruined by war training were taught all kinds of tricks in training schools where they received the best care. Writers of the period, such as Seneca, Pliny, Martial and the emperors' biographer Suetonius, report on the performances achieved. These stand comparison with the pièces de resistance in modern circuses.

During games organized by the emperor Domitian elephants were made to kneel by their expert guides. Dancers would perform on their backs while an elephant played the cymbals. Elephants would also sit, wearing clothes, on giant couches, imitating the Roman custom, and politely help themselves from dishes containing tidbits to the delight of the Roman crowd.

Even in ancient Rome man succumbed to the pressure to lower the animal to the level of a clown. Elephants were also made to walk tightropes. As Cesar was traveling to the Capitol during the celebrations of his victory in Gaul, celebrations which lasted several days, elephants on either side of the procession lit the way, as darkness fell, with candelabras. The Romans even tried their hand at breeding elephants in captivity, to increase numbers without the difficult journeys.

The special admiration for the gentle primeval creatures was never completely stifled by the barbaric cruelty which prevailed in the Roman amphitheaters. Commemorative medallions, for example, showing four elephants pulling the magnificent state carriage were illustrious symbols of imperial power and greatness.

Venus is pulled by elephants,
1st half of 1st century AD,
mural of the third style, Pompeii

The goddess Venus on a Roman state carriage pulled by four elephants. Mural in the entrance hall of a house on the 'Via dell' Abbondanza' in Pompeii.

Heinrich Leutemann (1824–1905)
*Criminals are thrown to wild animals,*
'Bilder aus dem Altertum' series,
Münchner Bilderbogen no. 533,
1870,
color wood engraving.

In Rome circus games started with a procession from the Capitol to the arena led by a chariot pulled by four elephants. Later, Caligula celebrated his dead sister Drusila's birthday with a procession. The fragment above of a roughly chiseled sarcophagus depicts such a scene. From the 'Dictionnaire des Antiquités' by Daremberg and Saglio.

Below right:
Dionysus on an elephant (detail),
relief on a sarcophagus.
Walters Art Gallery, Baltimore

The god of bacchanalian pleasure returns from India on an elephant. The worship of Dionysus started in the Near East and through Alexander the Great's campaign of conquest spread to the Far Eastern wonderland.

# Europe's first circus rings

Illustration from Richard Carrington's 'Elephants,' wood engraving.

In 1830 an elephant appeared at London's Adelphi Theater. This brought in a full house every evening. In a particularly well-known scene the meek giant's back was used to help a prince and his entourage escape from prison.

From ancient Rome the history of the modern circus moves on to the menageries of the 17th/18th centuries where the exotic weird and wonderful animal had an ungainly role in the shows. An African elephant from the Congo region was the sensation of the royal animal enclosure at Versailles from 1665 through 1681. It liked to drink a good 1¹/₂ gallons of wine a day and knew how to dip bread into a bucket of delicious soup politely.

When feudal glory crumbled 'democratized' and commercialized exhibition enclosures developed from the royal menageries run by the middle classes. The affable giants were kept in very cramped enclosures and would take small titbits from visitors' hands. Money was made from their clumsy skills when they appeared at shows.

In 17th century Russia, where the Czar's court kept a menagerie, tamed elephants brought from Samarkand were exhibited, along with dancing bears. Animal tamers were particularly popular among the people.

The first step towards the modern circus – popular entertainment with animal trainers and acrobats – was made around 1800, first of all in England. Circus riders, Amazons on horseback, gave action-packed performances in the permanent circus buildings that were springing up in Europe's capital cities. The elephant brought money in simply by being exhibited or ridden. At the beginning of the 19th century one of the main attractions at the famous show of Paris 'Cirque Olympique,' along with trained deer, was Baba the elephant and his routine.

In Europe and America elephants were still a rarity in the early 19th century. From the early 16th to the mid-19th century the number of pachyderms in Europe's menageries had been kept to around fifty. Then around the middle of the 19th century there was an escalation in the trade of elephants who had assumed an active role as trained performers in the circus companies that were appearing everywhere. With the emerging competition it was no longer sufficient for the exotic giants simply to appear. The audience's expectations were constantly increasing.

Continental Europe first went along the lines of the French circus and then, in the last third of the century, of the German one. The companies of Renz and Busch had set up fixed circuses in Berlin around 1850. The development into huge circuses with whole herds of elephants first took place, however, in the great 'land of unlimited opportunities,' the United States of America.

JEUNE ÉLÉPHANT DE X. ANS.

Matthäus Merian The Elder (1593–1650), *Indian elephant with rider takes bread from the basket,* illustration from 'Historiae Naturalis de Quadrapedibus Libri,' Frankfurt am Main, 1650, color copperplate engraving. Private collection

*Baba's tricks in the Cirque Franconi,* Paris, early 19th century, copperplate engraving.

Wenzel Hollar (1607–77),
*Elephas hic per Europam visus est* 1629,
etching.
Herzog-Anton-Ulrich-Museum,
Brunswick, Germany

When this elephant arrived in Europe via Amsterdam in 1629 it was a great attraction: "the whole of Europe saw it," as Wenzel Hollar noted on his copperplate engraving. In 1630 the elephant reached Italy where it was drawn by great artists, such as Pietro Testa and Bernini. In 1962 the Prague writer Johannes Urzidil included a literary tribute to Hollar's engraving in his story 'Das Elefantblatt.'

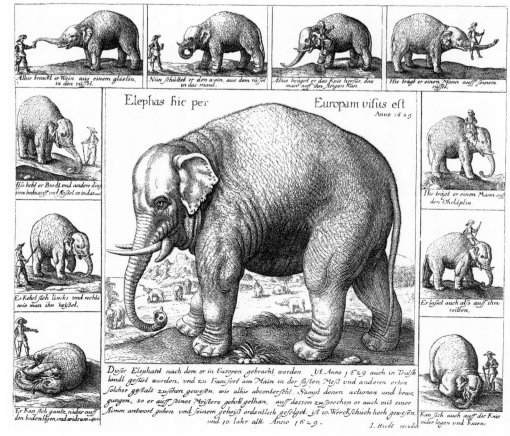

*Elephant as Marksman* (detail),
print from the four-part series
'Educable Pachyderms,'
Paris, c. 1800,
color wood engraving.
41.8cm x 61cm
Private collection

# England mourns Jumbo

In the mid-19th century an elephant called Jumbo made the headlines in England and America. His name has become an affectionate synonym for any elephant – and these days for huge passenger airplanes, 'jumbo jets.'

Jumbo, a young African elephant, arrived at London's Zoological Gardens in 1865 in exchange for a hippopotamus. The small bull was put in the stall next to another African elephant called Alice. He grew up in perfect amity with the human world. His ungainly, comical manner delighted the zoo's visitors who fed him titbits. Children and adults enjoyed the adventure of a ride on his back.

But in 1881 Jumbo, scarcely fully-grown, suddenly started to become moody. He was 'in musth' for the first time. Little was known about this at that time. Jumbo damaged his stall in a frenzied rage. His keeper was the only one who could go near him. It seemed that he would no longer be able to be ridden. Mr. Bartlett, the manager of the zoo, therefore felt it necessary to inform the Zoological Society's board of directors about the critical condition of the very popular animal. In his report published in 'The Times' he asked for the resources to kill the elephant if it became necessary. The whole of London was stunned at the news.

Then an offer arrived from the American circus owner Phineas Taylor Barnum. He expected business to bloom if he acquired an animal that was so highly thought of by the people of London. The Zoological Society saw its chance to make money out of what had become inevitable, and asked for the huge sum of 2,000 pounds. Barnum agreed and the deal was struck.

However, when the news of the sale appeared in 'The Times' in January 1882 a storm of indignation broke out. Londoners defended their Jumbo as if he were part of the national heritage. The Zoological Society was inundated with abusive letters accusing it of behaving like a slave-trader.

Jumbo is rewarded with titbits by his keeper Matthew Scott, 1882.

A ride on Jumbo's back,
c. 1882,
Zoological Gardens, London.

High stepladders were needed to
reach the saddle seats on the back
of the powerful African elephant.
London's gentlemen stood in line
to enjoy an exotic Jumbo ride at
the zoo. It was an unforgettable
experience for children. Jumbo
had come from Paris as a young
animal in exchange for a
hippopotamus.

Jumbo in the crate. A wood engraving, produced with masterly precision, of Jumbo's giant crate based on the photograph opposite.

The only photograph showing Jumbo and his keeper Matthew Scott in America. The circus king, Barnum, supposedly banned photographs being taken of his star elephant. He wanted to retain the public's curiosity so they would continue to flock to the circus box office.

Contemporary illustration for 'The Illustrated London News': the whole of New York was on the streets as Jumbo arrived on Easter Sunday 1882 aboard the 'Assyrian Monarch.' Cheering crowds lined the streets from the harbor to Madison Square Garden where Barnum's circus was situated. A team of sixteen horses pulled the truck transporting the seven-ton giant, and another elephant pushed.

## America welcomes Jumbo

Jumbo with his keeper Matthew Scott in front of the crate in which he was taken on board the 'Assyrian Monarch.'

On March 25, 1882 Jumbo put to sea aboard the 'Assyrian Monarch.' It had taken days to lure him into the box of a truck. And then he played one final trick on the transporters. He stuck his trunk through the bars and pulled some tail hairs out of a horse causing it to bolt. A serious accident was avoided thanks only to the skill of the coachman. England went into mourning.

For three years Jumbo sent the Americans into raptures just as he had done with the Londoners before. Business flourished at Barnum's circus. Then a tragic accident occurred. When the circus was loading up at the station in St. Thomas, Ontario, Jumbo was hit by a train and fatally injured. The engine was derailed and the driver killed. The railroad official on duty had watched the circus loading up and so had forgotten to change the points, causing the fatal collision.

Barnum sued the railroad company. As a result the company had to pay 10,000 dollars and transport the large traveling circus free of charge for a year. The circus owner held a funeral meal. The guests received small pieces of Jumbo's tusks as a memento. The elephant's body was preserved and stuffed and given to Tufts College in Boston. His skeleton is preserved and held in the Natural History Museum in New York.

Jumbo would not have enjoyed a long life anyway, as before the accident he had been in poor health, was refusing food and no longer lay down. The post mortem revealed his stomach to be full of coins, screws, leaden seals, wire, stones, pieces of glass and metal ...

The circus jumbo

Poster announcing a show with animals presented by the Barnum and Bailey circus company. Printed by Strobridge Lith. Co., Cincinatti, USA in 1896, color lithograph, 210cm x 290cm Deutsches Plakat-Museum, Essen, Germany

Barnum, Bailey & Hutchinson use a loud and vociferous poster to make the whole world a 100,000-dollar bet that Jumbo is the largest and heaviest elephant ever seen by a mortal, either in the wild or in captivity.

# The elephant ruled by the dollar

The first elephant, an Asian one, arrived in the New World in 1796. The business-minded Captain John Crowninshield had bought the animal, a 2-year old female named Old Bet, in Calcutta for 450 dollars. On his arrival in America he sold it to the showmen Pepin & Brechard for 10,000 dollars, which was at that time an incredible amount. The showmen traveled abroad with the exotic animal and made an even bigger profit. From this time, the circus as we know it today emerged.

The elephant was now ruled by the dollar which opened up 'unlimited opportunities.' In the cultural desert of the harsh pioneering society the people longed for entertainment and shows where they could escape from their quest for success. This led to the setting up of Phineas Taylor Barnum's giant company which was a great success.

The 'greatest show on earth,' in competition with other up-and-coming circus companies, such as Barly, Forepaugh, and Ringling, managed to integrate perfectly everything that helped to create a sensation; from the animal show and dangerous acrobatics to the hustle and bustle of the heavyweight boxing match.

The rival circus Bailey, which later merged with Barnum created the type of traveling circus which was first adopted in Europe by expanding German circus companies, such as Sarrasani, Busch, Hagenbeck, and Krone.

Two- or four-mast tents with a circular arena in the middle became the norm. Large American companies also presented their training and acrobatic programs in giant tents with several arenas holding performances at once.

Around the turn of the century some 200 large and small circuses traveled around Europe. In the New World the traveling circus reached even remote highlands in the Andes. Before the First World War Argentina had ten large and twenty small circuses; Brazil had some forty large companies. No expense was to be spared in the competition to win audiences and a market share and the trained elephant was now a big draw. No longer a rarity, elephants appeared en masse and

Poster from 'The Circus in America' by Charles Philip Fox and Tom Parkinson, Wisconsin.

The American circus pioneer Barnum once said that elephants and clowns were the linchpins on which circuses depended. He used them to fulfill the audience's expectations. Wild applause would break out in the circus tents as soon as elephants appeared in the ring. In the competition to win audiences rival companies brought on more and more elephants.

In the battle for audiences circus companies soon developed their own type of advertising: the circus poster on which the elephant was often used as the big draw.

this helped trade. Whole herds were supplied from the Far East and Africa.

In 1887 Barnum, Bailey and Forepaugh put on a special combined show in New York's Madison Square Garden and brought 160 elephants into the ring at once. By 1938 Karl Krone had already trained seventy elephants. The Swiss national circus Knie trained fifty of the giants between 1927 and 1987, and the French circus Bouglione had seventy elephants in 1950.

The huge requirement for exotic animals was accompanied by an ever increasing range of tricks. The elephant was asked to perform circus feats which were warmly applauded. As early as 1853 the first headstand was performed and the elephant stood and walked upright on its hind legs. In time the giant was even expected to perform the one-handed 'handstand.' These party pieces were much admired but were certainly contrary to the nature of the wild animal and put excessive demands on its body and strength.

Barnum toured Europe in 1900 and 1901. A varied but mediocre program took place in the same specific order, twice a day in three rings, under a huge 15,000-seater tent. The Europeans were impressed but had reservations. "A large circus, but American," wrote a respected Dutch newspaper, dissociating itself from the show.

Circus pioneers in the Old World adopted the Americans' technical and organizational concept, but padded it out with more quality: complicated spectacles and polished acrobatics. The modern circus, in which elephants played an important role, was thus formed.

Wilhelm Eigner (design),
poster for the Krone Circus,
c. 1933,
color lithograph.
65.4cm x 43cm
Museum für Kunst und Gewerbe,
Hamburg, Germany

On the poster designed by
Wilhelm Eigner the Krone Circus
uses its heraldic animal, the
elephant, as an advertisement.
Before the First World War, Karl
Krone turned his 'Menagerie
Charles' of the 1890s into an
enormous big top circus with
4,000 seats. In 1924 he could
seat 8,000 in an 8-pole tent.
He was given the name
'Master of the Elephants.'

# CIRQUE SARRASANI

Le troupeau d'éléphants du Cirque Sarrasani se baignant dans l'Elbe à Dresde

The elephants of the Sarrasani
Circus bathe in the Elbe, Dresden,
1920 poster,
color lithograph.
65cm x 89.5cm
Museum für Kunst und Gewerbe,
Hamburg, Germany

The Sarrasani Circus, founded in
Dresden in 1902, soon became a
large company and rival to the
Krone Circus.

Wilhelm Eigner (design),
the trainer Margaret Kreiser
with her elephants,
poster for the Barum Circus,
1931,
color lithograph.
66.8cm x 89cm
Museum für Kunst und Gewerbe,
Hamburg, Germany

The 'giant toy,' detail from a large Hagenbeck poster by designer Wilhelm Eigner.

# The circus pioneer Carl Hagenbeck

At the end of the 19th century Carl Hagenbeck from Hamburg made a substantial contribution to the modern circus. His concerns about the animal's psyche may have helped to bring about the new science of behaviorism.

In 1848 Gottfried Clas Carl founded a small menagerie, from the modest beginnings of a fish shop. He also put on shows with animals and traded in them. Under his son, Carl, the business expanded rapidly with worldwide connections. He bought his first African elephants in 1860. He acquired elephants from Sudan: three in 1865, twelve in 1866 and a further fourteen a year later.

In 1880 the revolt in Sudan by fanatical religious militants under the Mahdi prevented elephants being obtained via the old trade route to Cairo. Hagenbeck, therefore, bought elephants from India where British colonial rulers were issuing export

licenses liberally. In 1883 his buying agents shipped sixty-five elephants from Ceylon to Europe. His animal business was now the largest in the world. His main customers were the American circus companies Barnum and Forepaugh. In the twenty years between 1866 and 1886 the Hamburg company imported 300 Asian elephants.

Hagenbeck then moved into show business. In 1886 he traveled Europe with a 'Ceylonese caravan,' one of the first of his 'animal and people shows' which were becoming famous. The much admired stars were eight elephants led by Singhalese mahouts. In 1890 Hagenbeck added a training school to the lucrative business he had in animals of all types. This was successful and soon brought in unexpected additional income.

With the profits he built the first zoological garden with spacious open-air enclosures for the animals who, up until then, had mainly been kept in cramped cages. A zoo circus was added and soon became world famous. The training of the animals set new standards. A large traveling circus soon developed from the zoo circus. In 1913, shortly before the outbreak of war, 'Carl Hagenbeck's Wonder Zoo and Big Circus' gave a highly acclaimed performance at London's Olympia Hall. Carl Hagenbeck, the circus and zoo pioneer, died on April 14, 1913. His sons, Heinrich and Lorenz, ran the company during the difficult war and post-war period in Europe.

Heinrich Leutemann (1824-1905), arrival of Casanova's caravan of animals in Hamburg, drawn from nature.

The Italian trader and animal trapper Lorenzo Casanova worked for Carl Hagenbeck and brought the first large shipment of African wild animals to Hamburg in 1866. It was a great occasion for the city. The animal trade, which was flourishing, was based on the trading center of Kassala on the Sudanese-Ethiopian border. It took seventy to eighty days to reach Hamburg from there by land and sea. In 1872 the American circus king Phineas T. Barnum visited Carl Hagenbeck and bought 15,000 dollars worth of animals.

Parade line-up of circus elephants. After a final successful tour of England, France, and Switzerland with his 'people and animal show' Carl Hagenbeck ran his circus business along American lines. He was forced to find new sources of income to pay for the expensive upkeep of the elephant herd. On April 2, 1887 the first performance in a big top which seated 3,000 and had electric lighting took place. The first big top circus was called 'Carl Hagenbeck's International Circus and Singhalese Caravan' as a link to the great 'people shows.'

Elephant calves play just like children. The photographs were taken after the First World War. The keeper kneeling down has fun with the elephant child, August. The elephant's awkward trunk grasps the man's head; a small pillar-like leg is slipped over his shoulder, and then the human playmate is completely overpowered.

Hagenbeck's circus went on an extensive tour of East Asia in 1934/35. The Chinese poster announces its arrival in Shanghai.

## 'Tame training'

Hagenbeck practiced new, gentler methods of training that he developed from his experience with wild animals and in which he incorporated ideas from Indian mahouts. Instead of simply forcing the elephants to obey mechanically, he made use of the elephants' psyche, individuality, instincts, and responsive reactions during training. His 'tame training' became the model for elephant trainers throughout the world.

The Hagenbeck methods brought more humane treatment to the circus elephant, but not more appropriate care. The financial constraints placed on traveling companies did not make this possible. Away from the ring the gregarious animal, which in the wild moves about while grazing, had to endure the continuous nightmare of being tied up to a short chain, something that no other wild animal had to suffer. It experienced the monotony of isolation as well as being kept in a horrible pen in tent stalls and transportation boxes.

Training an elephant resigned to its fate requires an instinctive awareness and a great deal of patience. The animal must become used to the trainer who is to look after him. This is a lengthy process. The elephant's trust has to be won and unquestioning obedience taught. The trainer takes on the role of the leader of the herd and must always bear in mind each animal's individual disposition. As with people, there are intelligent and stupid, hard-working and lazy, good-natured and obstinate elephants. If the latter interrupt group work they have to be moved to zoos. In general, Asian elephants have a calm nature; they are sociable and rather thick-skinned. Their long-legged African cousins, seldom seen in circuses, are more sensitive and have to be handled particularly gently during training sessions.

Care must be taken during group training that animals equal in rank do not stand next to each other as this can trigger fierce rivalry. Gentle or

Away from the ring the naturally gregarious, roaming animal lives the nightmare of constantly being tied to a short chain in a pen in the stall tent.

young animals are put in between them. Young ones often behave in a rowdy manner and are kept under control by their elders.

The practical training work begins with roll-call exercises. The elephant must become familiar with its name. This should be short and succinct. Then it has to learn to come to its master when called and then go back. An assistant helps to guide the elephant at first and rewards encourage the animal. When it is finally successful there should be a special reward of titbits. This basic exercise can be extended into dance movements by stopping the forward movement with the counter-command 'go back.' Individual or group marching exercises can also be developed. However, 'gentle force' is needed to get an elephant to, for example, sit on a barrel by urging it to move backwards and then to raise its front legs and sit upright.

A certain amount of firmness is often needed even during 'tame' training. Elephants struggle against poses that are alien and contrary to their temperament, even if the giant bodies are not being overstretched. A painful poke behind the ears or on the sensitive trunk will result in obedience. Moderate punishments should be carried out immediately if the elephants refuse to do something or behave badly but the relationship between human and elephant is damaged if the trainer lacks self-control. Elephants can certainly distinguish between fair and unfair punishment.

The successful trainer Günther Gebel during a performance of a big number in Pittsburgh, USA, in 1977.

## Asking too much in training

Artistic feats such as head and 'hand' stands and walking upright on hind legs require lengthy training. These much admired party pieces certainly put a great strain on the animal's joints and often ask too much of its strength. Only young, adolescent animals can be expected to do these exercises; older elephants are too heavy. An animal's physical strength does not grow in proportion to its size and body measurements. In fact, the heavier an animal, the less its physical strength in relation to weight and size. Artistic pièces de resistance verge on the limit of what is reasonable for an elephant.

Even going down on its knees or elbows puts a strain on the elephant's joints and intervertebral discs, as the elephant naturally sleeps on its side. If, in addition, a heavy companion is made to stand on its back there is too much strain, causing the elephant pain. The elephant can be prevented from expressing this pain out loud.

Every trainer has his own special method for attempting to achieve the acrobatic perfection which thrills the audience. These methods are a closely guarded secret. All manner of equipment is used, such as block and tackle to heave the elephant's hindquarters up when it is practicing headstands, with the dreaded elephant hook giving a helping hand.

Things are not always so relaxed when the most difficult tricks are being rehearsed. During the critical phases of training, trainers are just as wary as show-jumpers are when they insist that their horses who, free, would go round a small obstacle, go over large jumps in enclosed halls.

Elephant learns a headstand, Ringling Brother, Barnum & Bailey Circus.

The animal observer Boris Brock watched the trainer Günther Gebel at work on a visit to the American circus Ringling Brother, Barnum & Bailey. He describes what goes on under the big top: Titschi is to do a headstand. It is not done quickly enough for Gebel. He pokes her behind the ear with the sharp point of the elephant stick. It hurts Titschi. Groaning she presses her lined forehead on the ground, carefully rolls up her trunk, and lifts her hindquarters into the air. From below she glances obsequiously at her master. A grotesque and unpleasant sight. Gebel rewards her with a banana and says: "My elephants are too impudent. Elsewhere it is a lot stricter …"

An elephant standing on its head or balancing on bottles with its hindquarters in the air are 'party pieces' which should not be performed! They put too much strain on the giant's body and go against their nature. Only a fear of sharp steel hooks and brusque corporal punishment make the gentle giants do such tricks.

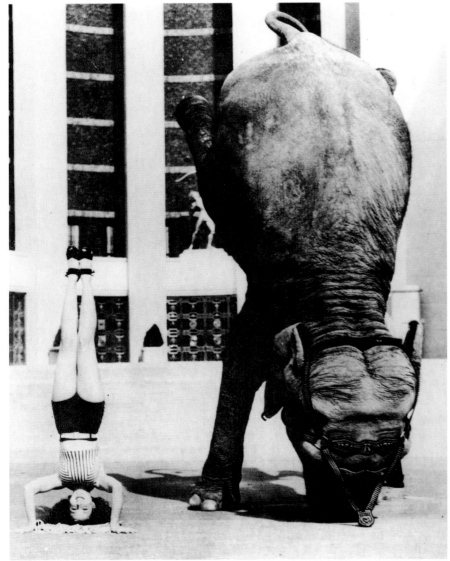

Tusko, the most chained elephant in the world, c. 1929.

The garland of chains was only show for the audience; away from the ring and public view the bull lived a life of misery.

The Asian bull, Shenka, from the Alberti Circus is a (rare) example of good treatment in a traveling company. The owner, Stefan Frank, looks after the giant himself and has close contact with him; wherever possible he lets the bull wander about and graze freely without any chains when they are touring. When Shenka became ill in 1993 he was looked after at Erfurt Zoo.

# The suffering of the bulls

Bull elephants suffer particularly badly in circuses when they are in musth. In the cramped circus accommodation they are unable to behave naturally during this critical arousal phase. Bulls in musth were and are, therefore, shackled with chains round all four feet. The chains can cut into the animal as far as the bones during desperate outbursts of rage. The bull Tusko, the most famous elephant in the USA during the first quarter of this century, is an example of mistreatment.

As 'the most chained elephant in the world' Tusko led the procession of elephants into the ring at Barnes Circus. His whole body was covered in chains. The circus manager himself would sit enthroned in a plush chair on his back. The audience loved seeing the animal secured like a monster. The extra chains were only for the show.

When Tusko was in musth he was wedged between railroad sleepers so that he could not move, let alone lie down. Since the musth dragged on for a long time as a result of the position he was in, he would stand in the torturous clamp for up to three months. During this time he broke both tusks. When the enslaved and disturbed animal finally became dangerous he was supposedly auctioned off for one dollar. The understanding keeper George 'Slim' Lewis bought Tusko. He was then well treated and became quite normal and placid again as a result.

Tortured and disturbed bulls that killed people in fits of rage were dealt with mercilessly. In 1902 neck nooses were used to strangle the 'man killer,' Mandarin, and then five years later his daughter, Columbia, because they were found responsible for a person's death.

During a march through the town of Corsana, Texas in 1929, the keeper of a bull called Black Diamond was negligent in allowing a woman to stroke the timid animal. The woman was killed. This led to a mass killing of circus bulls in order to reassure the public who were up in arms. Black Diamond, the 'murderer,' was actually executed, by Texan marksmen, who fired 170 shots at him. In 1941 police officers took 45 minutes and 107 shots to kill the bull Teddy, a 'man killer' from the Lindermann Circus. By 1952 there were only two bulls left in American circuses! However, in 1996 there were 21 Asian bulls in circus rings in the USA alongside the 158 Asian cows as well as 6 African bulls and 58 African cows.

Today the 'European Elephant Group' believes that, with few exceptions, there is no justification for keeping elephants in circuses. There is a lack of experienced handlers almost everywhere; the animals do not move about enough and care of the animals' skin and feet is unsatisfactory. The rare exceptions include the Swiss circus Knie where elephants live in spacious tent stalls when on tour and can relax in outdoor enclosures.

# A natural gift for balancing

Sketch by the American artist Bomar,
one-legged handstand, 1959.

The top-class performance which the elephant is forced to give is much admired, but for the elephant it just means painful and damaging strain on its joints. Today circus companies that are run in a more caring way do not place such inconsiderate demands on the animal.

Elephant on ball, Cirque 'Eléphants acrobates'
The huge elephant surprises the audience with its strong and supple physical control and excellent sense of balance. Visitors to the zoo can watch acrobatic stretching movements with bizarre foot positions from the edge of the elephant's enclosure when the elephant gropes for a titbit that is being offered and is particularly difficult to reach. The giants are also surprisingly skilled at balancing on balls and drums.

Drawing by Wilhelm M. Busch,
Busch-Archiv, Hamburg

Large Group, wood engraving by an unknown artist, c. 1900.

An elephant walks across a tightrope. In the 'forties the Swiss circus Knie performed this extreme exercise. Today the company sets an example with its modest tricks. Forcing an elephant to walk over rope is totally contrary to the elephant's nature and barbaric, as it damages the soles of the feet.

The elephant plays the clown on a bicycle with patience and dignity.

# Predators on elephants' backs

Even today the tiger riding on an elephant's back is one of the great achievements of circus training. Here, a showpiece of the Swiss circus Knie from 1975. It shows the extent to which the animals have been trained.

Lizzie rides a tricycle with the lion Prince, poster for Carl Hagenbeck's Zoological Circus, which performed at the trade exhibition in Berlin, 1895/96, color lithograph.
75.6cm x 56.9cm
Museum für Kunst und Gewerbe, Hamburg, Germany

The brilliant show put on by the trainer Wilhelm Philadelphia, trained at the Hagenbeck Zoological Circus, was the circus sensation of the Chicago world exhibition in 1893.

The circus jumbo

The star trainer Günther Gebel also worked with big cats. In 1975 he surprised the audience with a sensational act: his long-serving elephant Thaila trotted through the ring with Bengal the tiger on its back, and Gebel was sitting on the tiger!

Gebel poses with a partner on an elephant's shoulders. The elephant is sitting awkwardly on a stool. Photograph from 1976

The trainer Rudolf Matthies with a new attraction: a tiger on the back of an elephant who is balancing on a drum.

# Sliding and swinging

*Elephant slide*,
printed by Adolph Friedländer,
1904.
71cm x 95cm

The humorous portrayal of
athletic elephant acrobatics is an
advertisement for the circus.

These gray giants form an unusual
swing for their trainer in an
American circus c. 1930.

The elephant slide in the
permanent building at the Busch
Circus in Hamburg. In 1904 the
trainer Wilhelm Philadelphia
demonstrated the 'elephant slide,'
with the help of ten elephants,
first at the Busch Circus, and
shortly after at the London
Hippodrome.

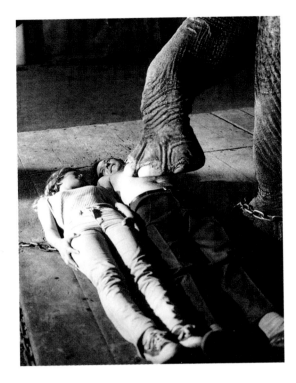

The threatening columnar leg stops over the chest. Elephants do not kill; in the wild they avoid the smallest living things.

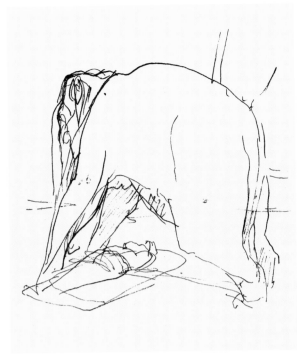

Drawing by Wilhelm M. Busch, Busch-Archiv, Hamburg, Germany

Surefooted as a sleepwalker the elephant steps over the human chain without putting it in danger. The angle of vision of the eyes does not assist the elephant very much; even the trunk 'radar' is impaired by the object it holds.

The circus jumbo

One of the elephants of the 'Hindu Village' in Paris carries his handler Vid-Hany by his feet. The Indians have set up a small village of showmen in the Bois de Boulogne.

Only a trainer who has a good relationship with his pachyderm can risk hanging by his head from the elephant's mouth – a thrill in the big top.

## Considerate towards people

Elephants are considerate animals and extremely gentle with people. If a circus elephant is ordered to put a foot on the chest of a person lying in front of him, the animal will pause just above the body, even without help from its trunk. If it is to lie over a person it holds back the bulk of its body as soon as its body hairs touch the person lying down. When there is very strong mutual trust an elephant may carefully put his master's head in its mouth and carry him hanging by his head through the ring to the audience's amazement. When it does this the elephant thoughtfully puts its lower lip between the head and its molars.

Even in the wild elephants avoid stepping on any small living things they notice. They are placid animals by nature and do not kill. Admittedly, caution is required in the case of elephants in captivity who are badly cared for and mistreated and so have become psychologically disturbed due to torture and long periods of isolation. Pent-up frustration can lead to sudden unexpected outbursts of rage. This is usually the cause of serious, often fatal, accidents.

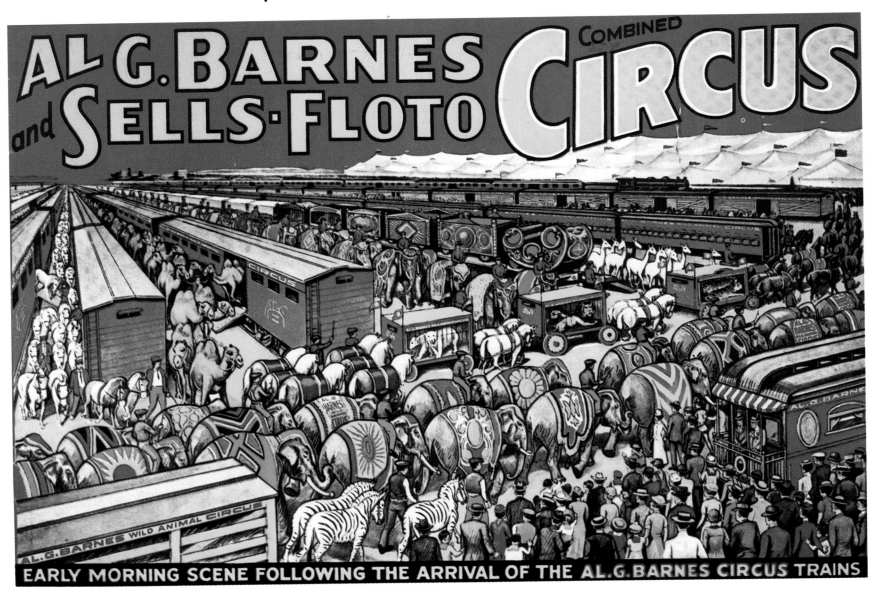

EARLY MORNING SCENE FOLLOWING THE ARRIVAL OF THE AL. G. BARNES CIRCUS TRAINS

Poster from 'The Circus in America' by Charles Philip Fox and Tom Parkinson, Wisconsin.

The large American traveling circuses had to overcome difficult organizational problems when loading their huge number of animals onto trains.

Loading onto a ship with a crane. An unpleasant experience for the elephant and always a tricky operation to carry out.
Royal Albert Docks, London

A nasty slip. It took three hours to rescue the cow elephant. Her companion in the 'bull wagon' watched on sympathetically. Bull wagons were the 'elephant houses' of traveling circuses.

Poster from 'The Circus in America' by Charles Philip Fox and Tom Parkinson, Wisconsin.

Return home of the American Cole Bros. Circus from a European tour. The poster shows the animals packed into the 'tween-decks of the huge ocean liner.

COLE BROS. CIRCUS

RETURN HOME AFTER A TRIUMPHAL CONQUEST OF THE OLD WORLD.

## "When elephants go for somebody ..."

Most fatal accidents in the circus involve not big cats, but elephants. The constant psychological stress when in captivity can trigger spontaneous outbursts of anger. Elephants panic easily when they are frightened, which means that great care is needed when they are paraded through towns. The trainer has to be vigilant at all times.

The successful German trainer Günther Gebel, who caused a stir at the end of the 'sixties with spectacular acts with tigers and elephants, once confessed that when he had nightmares they were about elephants. When he worked in the tiger cage everyone knew something might happen to him. But when elephants go for somebody ... thank God people had no idea.

The list of people killed or injured by tame elephants; by elephants running amok, in fact goes back a long way. The first small menageries at the beginning of the 19th century experienced such shocking incidents. It is said that, statistically, one person is killed or seriously injured for every bull elephant kept in captivity.

In 1824 the bull Hannibal from Issac van Amburgh's menagerie in America apparently killed seven people in an incident.

In June 1866 the small, Swiss country town of Murten witnessed a dramatic fatal incident. The showmen Bell & Meyers were performing there on market day. The evening performance had passed off without any problems and the circus was supposed to move on the next morning. However, the bull elephant refused to obey commands. When the trainer tried to make the giant kneel in an attempt to restore his authority the elephant seized him with his trunk, pressed him to the ground with his tusks, and trampled on him. A decision was taken to kill the bull and a six-pound gun was

The Munich 'elephant catastrophe' of July 31, 1888 caused a stir. The Hagenbeck circus had provided eight elephants for a carnival procession. As the group passed a steam tram decorated as a dragon, a shower of sparks was released from the dragon's nostrils at an inopportune moment. The elephants, startled, scattered. As general panic broke out, hundreds fell and others ran over them. The newspapers reported many serious injuries. One elephant supposedly forced its way into the 'Platzl' beer hall where, so the story goes, both it and the revelers behaved quite properly.

brought to the scene. It then took hours for the bull, now calmed, to finally be lured out of his accommodation with tidbits. The salvos of triumph which followed the fatal gun shot caused some damage to surroundings.

Berlin Zoo had its 'killer bulls' towards the end of the 19th century. On April 8, 1921 the cow elephant Ross crushed the trainer Wilhelm Philadelphia to death on the wall of her box at the Sarrasani Circus. Soon after this, the bull Pikkolo plunged his tusks into the back of his owner H. St. Sarrasani, who received compound fractures to his arms and legs in addition to serious internal injuries.

A particularly dreadful accident occurred in the small Canadian town of Rock Forest, near Montreal, in 1978. The experienced trainer Eloise Berchtold, famous in America, was performing with three Asian bulls from the Gatini Circus. Two of the bulls, Teak and Tunga, were just in musth and were on edge in their stalls. Despite being warned Eloise, who certainly knew that bulls in musth could be unpredictable, decided to perform with the animals in the ring in front of a few hundred spectators. Then it happened: the trainer tripped and fell in front of Teak's feet. He knelt down, pushed both tusks through her body, ripped

Using sharp spears, keepers keep an unpredictable, blind elephant at a distance. It is supposed to have already killed twenty people in Southeast Asia. Three keepers were required to look after the 56 year-old bull who is spending his old age in the Pinz Wela elephant sanctuary.

The circus jumbo

In July 1950 the young circus elephant Tuffi escaped from its keeper in the Ruhr area and jumped from a suspension railroad at a height of 46 feet into the Wupper.
(Pictorial montage)

open her stomach and, in front of the horrified spectators, hurled her gored body thirty-three feet across the ring. The keepers' attempts to stun the bull failed. The animal was finally shot by the police force.

These are only a few examples from the extensive list of fatal accidents that have occurred involving elephants under big tops and in zoological gardens; the list gets longer every year. Elephants are placid animals, but when their natural instincts are suppressed in captivity and they live a miserable life in chains, often mistreated, then aggression builds up. It is quite right to say that elephants have a long memory.

The primeval giants, whose body size is a particular burden in captivity, doze in boredom, miserable and stifled; head and trunk swing monotonously or 'weave.' The Swiss zoologist and elephant expert Fred Kurt believes that if they were human we would say they had gone mad. Almost all principles of proper care were breached when circuses and zoos added the elephant to their repertoire. Fred Kurt refers to a German guideline according to which 129 square feet is sufficient living space for a circus elephant. This does not allow it even to lie down.

During the German siege of Paris in the 1870/71 war, the last remaining elephant in the acclimatization housing was shot when it tried to escape.

Elephant runs amok, Kandy, August 1959.

In August 1959 an elephant ran amok in Kandy, Ceylon, causing fourteen deaths. An elephant was accidentally touched with a burning torch during a religious procession. The frightened animal broke through the dense crowd, killing a mother and her child. Twelve others were trampled underfoot by people in the general panic. The elephant was eventually caught and tied to a lamppost (photograph). It was finally shot when it broke loose again.

## "And every now and then a white elephant ..."

Rainer Maria Rilke (1875–1926), one of the greatest German poets of the 20th century, left a poetic memorial to the white elephant with his 1907 poem 'The Carousel.' He went to Paris in 1902 after his painful separation from the sculptress Clara Westhoff. Paris amazed and frightened him, but he stayed there for ten years nonetheless. Away from the bustle of the city, in an idyllic spot in the Jardin du Luxembourg, he encountered the carousel, which moved him to symbolic romanticizing.

*With a roof and its shadow it rotates*
*a little while, the herd of particolored*
*horses, all from the land*
*that lingers long ere it sinks out of sight.*
*Some it is true are hitched to carriages,*
*yet all of them have mettle in their mien;*
*a vicious red lion goes with them*
*and every now and then a white elephant.*

*Even a deer is there quite as in the woods,*
*save that he bears a saddle and on that*
*a little blue girl buckled up.*

*And on the lion rides all white a boy*
*and holds himself with his small hot hand,*
*the while the lion shows his teeth and tongue.*

*And every now and then a white elephant.*

*And on the horses they come passing by,*
*girls too, bright girls, who almost have outgrown*
*this leap of horses; midway in their swing*
*they look up, anywhere, across-*

*And every now and then a white elephant.*

*And this goes on and hurries that it may end,*
*and only circles and turns and has no goal.*
*A red, a green, a gray being sent by,*
*some little profile hardly yet begun.*
*And occasionally a smile, turning this way,*
*a happy one, that dazzles and dissipates*
*over this blind and breathless game.*

Rilke's famous carousel in the Jardin du Luxembourg, built by the architect of the Paris Opéra, Charles Garnier. However, if you go there today you will not find the object that inspired Rilke's thought-provoking poem. The carousel animal he eulogized was removed in the mid-1990s and replaced with an 'ordinary' gray elephant (picture left). It is said that the 'white elephant' has been in the carousel operator's garden since then ...

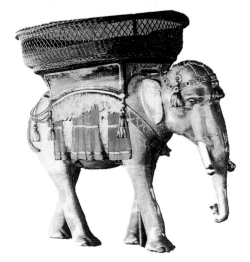

The circus jumbo

Carousel figure, made by the Allan Hearschel Company in America, 1915.

'Swinging Platform,' carousel built by 'Dare.' It was operated by hand, horse or steam and could be bought for 1,050 dollars in 1909.

# Trapping and taming elephants

From the early elephant cultures of Southeast Asia to the modern day the requirement for tamed elephants has been met exclusively by trapping them in the jungle. Fully-grown, 10 to 20 year-old animals could be integrated into work immediately after

The trunk grips like a hand, lifts and holds; the tusks hoist like cranes and support. No other large animal is more agile than the elephant – and none anatomically better equipped to help man and contribute in many different areas of work.

training and so time was not spent rearing calves. The enormous amount of food and intensive care required was too expensive for earlier feudal rulers as well as for modern companies. The mother elephants would need extra care and would also have to stop working for several years. Tamed pachyderms were, therefore, prevented from mating. Old Indian documents about elephant medicine do analyze the development of the embryo in the womb, but do not deal with the problems of rearing calves. The question of breeding did not arise. The elephant has never become a pet; it has remained a wild animal. It is only recently that the alarming decline in numbers has caused a rethink regarding possible breeding programs.

On a timber-felling site in the Thai-Burmese border region the working giant, guided by pressure from the driver's foot, brings order to the maze of felled trunks; careful of the vegetation underneath the elephant drags heavy teak trunks from the forest, stacks them and helps with floating the wood. Well-trained elephant teams carry out complete tasks on their own.

# A privilege of kings

In early times Indian peasant tribes, the founders of the first elephant cultures, captured elephants using the same methods as the first hunting tribes used for hunting big game. They used concealed pits and placed snares on elephant paths. They also, no doubt, pushed young animals away from the herd using a large number of beaters and hounded them to exhaustion, when courageous men managed to attach shackles to their feet.

Pits, which were used as early as the Paleolithic Age for hunting mammoths, were not very successful. As with snares, other animals or pachyderms that were quite unsuitable for training could be trapped. Both the risk of injury and casualty rates were very high as data from the 19th century trappings shows. At most, one elephant in ten survived the fall into the almost 10 foot-deep pits used by the Maharajas of Mysore, Southern India, and the British colonial administration.

As tamed elephants became available more effective trapping methods were developed. Elephants now provided indispensable help to man in trapping, capturing, and overwhelming their wild cousins, and still do so today. The 'kumkies,' as the willing helpers are called in India, lure the animals into ambushes with female 'scent' or force the wild giants of the woods into shackles using the bulls' brute force. Over the centuries the practices of trapping individual elephants have been passed down from one generation to the next.

When the first Hindu kingdoms came into being around the middle of the last millennium BC elephant hunting and trapping were a privilege of the warrior caste and kings. The gray giants enhanced the splendor and power of the courts and played an invaluable role in war, and in building palaces and temples. Trappers and trainers were in the service of the courts and strictly controlled by them; it was essential to protect the valuable commodities.

The situation was the same 1,000 years later, in the 16th/17th century, under the Muslim Great Moguls. They kept hundreds of war elephants and almost the whole subcontinent came under their rule. The peasant population was forbidden to kill elephants. They were allowed to use fire and trumpet alarms only to defend themselves against herds that got into their fields and to attempt to frighten away the destructive elephants.

Individual trappings could not meet the increasing demand for riding, temple and working elephants or for war elephants. The latter became the backbone of the armies of rival kings throughout Southeast Asia. Evidence from the 4th/3rd centuries BC suggests that trapping whole herds in enclosures had already been practiced. In the 3rd century BC rulers from the 'elephant island' of Ceylon supplied Indian kingdoms with particularly powerful and highly regarded war elephants for their armies.

André Thevet,
*Elephant hunt,*
from 'Cosmographia universelle,'
Paris, 1575,
wood engraving.

In Asia and Africa elephants were trapped in pits until the end of the 19th century. With animals falling into almost 10 foot-deep pits the casualty rate was alarmingly high.

An elephant that has fallen in is gradually raised from the pit, shackled and led away with the help of kumkies. The photograph was taken during a trapping expedition for Hamburg's Hagenbeck Zoo.

Miskin and Sarwan
*Elephant fight*,
from the 'Akbarnama'
(History of Emperor Akbar)
c. 1590, by Abul Fazl,
gouache on paper.
35cm x 22cm
Victoria & Albert Museum,
London

Old Indian depiction of an elephant trapping operation. At the bottom of the picture kumkies sandwich a captured wild beast. On the right above them animals trapped in an ambush. In the middle of the picture a powerful bull, being ridden by two trappers and carrying a lasso, is pushing a wild cow elephant into position for the lasso to be thrown. The cow at the top, tied to a tree, appears already to be resigned to her fate.

Two scenes from a 1746 illustrated broadsheet, copperplate engravings.

"If necessary the wild animal captured is attached to one or, if it is very wild, two tame animals ... and the tame ones will put it in its place if it is not docile ..."

"Here the captured wild animal is tied to trees by all four legs ... until the rope has cut into the flesh and the wild water run out. Then the animal is bandaged and healed. It is then tame."

Trapping and taming elephants     293

# Deadly mass trappings in Ceylon

From the 16th century European powers gradually gained sovereignty over Southeast Asian countries. The elephant also came under the new rulers' right of disposal and had to contribute to the development of colonial wealth. The foreign administrations and trading companies laid down ever more far-reaching terms for trapping and trade in the gray giants. The first strong actions taken by European powers were on the elephant island of Ceylon. Tamed elephants had been used there since early times for everyday tasks and in war. In the 3rd century BC Singhalese rulers had exported war and working elephants to India on special ships.

The Portuguese traded in spices and ivory. Around 1505 when they set up the first trading branch in Ceylon they already had bases in East Africa. About 100 years later, in 1612, a regional Singhalese ruler granted them a monopoly on trapping and trade in elephants. It entitled them to catch thirty-seven pachyderms annually. The Pannikiya, a local clan of elephant trappers, continued to trap elephants with snares for the new masters. In addition the Portuguese had them caught in so-called 'corales': small pens or corrals into which tamed cows lured wild bulls. They sold the catches to India.

In 1638 the Dutch arrived and drove out the Portuguese. Their powerful 'Dutch East India Company' required more elephants. The Dutch introduced mass trappings in so-called kraals, extensive pens fenced round with 13 foot-high

"A big stall is being made in Ceylon …"
Western idea of an elephant trapping enclosure (detail), color copperplate engraving.

*Elephant trapping with pits*,
book illustration by Peter Kolb.
Nuremberg, 1719

A plump animal falls headfirst
into a pit. Its companions trot
innocently behind in single file.

palisades to prevent the animals from escaping. Hundreds of beaters pushed whole herds into these enclosures. In one single trapping operation 100-200 elephants were brought in. According to contemporary records 13, 104, 160, and 240 wild elephants were driven in respectively in four trapping operations between 1681 and 1690. There were an enormous number of casualties during these mass trapping operations.

In 1796 the Dutch were driven out by the British who in 1815 incorporated the whole island of Ceylon into their empire. They also took control of elephant trapping and trade. All over the island huge coffee and tea plantations belonging to the 'East India Company' sprung up – as well as kraals. The elephants caused a great deal of damage to the plantations and so a rigorous mass trapping operation and mass destruction were introduced. In some operations 300–400 animals were hounded into the kraals. There were heavy casualties. These were caused by stress and injury, the destruction of family units, and inconsiderate practices in shackling and overcoming any strong resistance. According to contemporary evidence often only a third of the animals driven in survived.

Occasionally, elephants that were not suitable for training or work, or were simply not required were shot as the easiest solution.

A large number of working elephants were certainly needed for building roads, transport tasks, felling trees and so on. However, trapping operations were concerned more with reducing elephant numbers in order to protect plantations. Unrestricted 'gentlemen's hunts' were, therefore, carried out. We shall come back to these later. The working elephants were not treated particularly well either. The English naturalist Emerson Tennent noted that in 1861 out of 138 elephants caught 35 had died within a year; 37 lived for just one year; 14 died in the second year; only 16 were able to be kept longer than ten years. As well as the poor treatment, the standard of care was not good, through ignorance as much as anything.

Trapping operations provided entertainment for the colonial society. While the beaters spent days and weeks surrounding an elephant herd and driving it towards the kraal the colonists amused themselves at horse and elephant races. They then enjoyed the spectacle of the disturbed beasts being driven in from the stands at the pen.

Joel Bol and Pieter Galleus,
*Elephant hunt*,
18th century,
color copperplate engraving.
Biblioteca Nazionale, Florence

Inconsiderate mass trappings in Ceylon often developed into eradication operations. Animals that were not suitable for training and work were simply killed. Elephant numbers were systematically reduced to safeguard plantations.

All these wood engravings appeared in 'The Illustrated London News' during 1875.

An elephant drags free a launch that was stuck on a sand bank in the Sittang River. A gunboat keeps guard.

Below left:
During the Anglo-Russian Afghanistan conflict in 1885 elephants helped the British Indian army in the Himalayan region in the construction of a military narrow-gauge supply railroad. The picture shows engine parts, wagons, and French-made railroad equipment being unloaded from boats.

## Under colonial control

Even in India the British, who opened the first trading office in 1605, took control of the working elephants. The colonial forestry office had overall control and issued licenses for trapping elephants in the tropical forests. They did not, though, cut back the Maharajas' rights too much as they were essential for controlling the huge territories.

The British colonial administration had thousands of working animals and had developed a special knowledge of elephants. The animal's strength was urgently required to help with the development of the subcontinent's transport system, with building work and felling teak. Wood was desperately needed for railroad sleepers, ships, export, etc. The strong, high quality teak was a much sought-after substitute for oak which was scarce. The British, in competition with the French, therefore extended their influence to Burma tempted by vast teak forests. The king there supposedly had 6,000 working elephants which would be a great asset to the British.

As in Ceylon, the high demand for working elephants was met by mass trappings in fenced enclosures called 'kheddas' in India. Casualties were lower than in Ceylon thanks to improved trapping and taming methods. However, still only 15–20 percent of the wild animals driven in were supplied. In particular sucklings and young animals that were still dependent on their mothers were left to their fate in the wild.

Burma came under full British colonial administration in 1886. Up until the Second World War powerful trading companies overexploited the country's teak forests using thousands of elephants.

When it achieved independence in 1948 socialist Burma, today called Myanmar, nationalized the elephants. Today in India and other Southeast Asian countries they work mainly for private owners and international companies.

In 1875 the British colonial administration brought the first engine to the city of Indore in Central India. A team of five working elephants pulled the locomotive.

A British sugar plantation is prepared. Elephants pull the heavy plows.

# The kheddas

Kheddas are fenced enclosures. The entrance can be closed with a descending trapdoor. From here two palisade arms open out and lead into the wood. The animals are channeled into the trap through a camouflaged tunnel which funnels towards the pen gate. A khedda should include an area of jungle and a watering place. These do provide the minimum requirements to ensure the survival of the captured elephants, but by its very nature the khedda is a traumatic experience for elephants.

There are various types of khedda: single ones with a pen in which the animals are tied up, or double ones with a large initial enclosure and a small additional one. When large numbers are being trapped it is easier to tie up small groups of three to five elephants in this last area for transporting to taming and training areas.

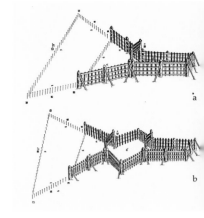

When the herds pass a certain line in the initial enclosure (marked with fine lines) torches are lit and the elephants are driven into the pen, or khedda, making an infernal noise. Shown are two types of Thai khedda:

a) a small, single trapping facility in which only a few animals are driven into a narrow palisade entrance which can be closed with a descending trapdoor and then tied up and taken away;
b) an extended trapping facility with a large kraal and a small additional enclosure, in which small groups of three to five animals can be tied up in succession.

Desperately trying to free itself from the neck noose that is choking it the young elephant falls over headfirst. The noose is tied in such a way that it cannot be pulled tight.

In panic the animals crowd together by the palisade. After letting them calm down a little the trappers on kumkies (tame elephants) ride in with ropes to tie them up.

Far left: In January 1890 Prince Albert Victor watched elephants being trapped in a khedda in India.

Left: The descending trapdoor made from heavy tree trunks is closed. The herd is in the trap. From 'The Illustrated London News.'

# Driving elephants into the khedda

One of the last operations to drive elephants into a khedda took place in 1968 in the south of the Indian state of Karnataka on the Kabani River. Fred Kurt, a Swiss zoologist and expert on Indian elephants, watched the event and reported it in his work entitled 'Das Elefantenbuch. Wie Asiens letzte Riesen leben' ('The Elephant Book. How Asia's Last Giants Live').

Weeks had been spent erecting a huge palisade pen 65,780 square yards large. Hundreds of workers had dug holes five feet deep with long-handled shovels. Dozens of working elephants rammed teak trunks up to twenty feet in length into the holes. Horizontal bamboo poles connected the trunks. A water pipe also made from tree-trunks was laid ready for the herd that was to be caught. In addition stands had been put up by the khedda for 1,700 paying tourists from all over the world. This end of an era event provided business for the tourist trade. The following account was given by Fred Kurt in his above mentioned book:

"On December 30, 1967 a Yajaman, someone who reads tracks, reported that a large elephant herd had been tracked down south of the Kabani in the Begur national forest. This herd is now surrounded. 1,500 men from the Kurumbas, the natives of the South Indian forests, are forming a living net around the herd. At night they light large fires every 65 to 100 feet; during the day they put leaves and fresh branches on them. A dense smoke-screen is supposed to prevent the elephants from escaping ... It is only open at the Kabani. The elephants go there at night to bathe and drink."

The net became tighter and tighter. It was to close in on the elephants on January 10. The Indian Tourist Board had fixed the date for driving the animals into the khedda and had advertised it worldwide to attract tourists.

"Early in the morning on the trapping day a long procession passes the stone picture of Mastiamma (the goddess of the forest): working elephants with their mahouts and khotals (assistants), forest officers, drivers. They disappear silently over the Kabani in the forest of Begur. Shortly after that it is time for the tourists to take their expensive places, among them the last reigning Maharaja of Mysore and his entourage ...

"In the jungle there is now an eerie silence, just as there is before a monsoon storm ... hours of waiting. But then the silence is suddenly broken by an unimaginable noise: the rattling of thousands of bamboo poles, the shouting of the drivers, rifle shots. The wild elephants trumpet shrilly. Hounded by working elephants and 1,500 men they try to find an escape route through the Kabani ... The herd race to the river. A newborn calf loses contact and suddenly runs between the working elephants who are storming over. Even in the confusion its mother notices it is lost. She turns towards the hordes of drivers closing in on the elephants. Shots are fired and she is wounded in the face and ears. But nothing stops her looking for her child. She finally finds it and uses her trunk to help it over the waters of the Kabani ...

"The elephants see only one way out, the entrance to the khedda. In twos or threes they rush through the funnel-shaped passage into the stockade. An inconspicuous Yajaman swings his ax and chops up a rope. 1,076 square feet of tree-trunks firmly intertwined with each other to form a descending trapdoor fall from a height of 60 feet slamming into the anchoring. The fires outside the palisades suddenly flare up. Eighty-six elephants are trapped ... A dozen or more will not survive the anguish. 'They died of a broken heart,' the mahouts will say ..."

It was two weeks before the last elephant was tied up. To make it easier to control them groups of five to eight animals were lured with sugarcane into a small closeable side kraal each night. In the morning the tourists in the stands could watch and photograph the spectacle of tying up the most frightened animals. Fred Kurt recounts the event as he saw it:

"The kumkies come into the arena. In addition to its mahout each is carrying two or three riders who are going to tie up the wild animals that have been

The last operations to drive elephants into kheddas were advertised worldwide and became spectacles for wealthy tourists. The international audience saw a wild elephant being taken between willing kumkies and moored to the palisade.

Trapped young animals are bound to kumkies to be taken to the training camp. The kumkies reassure their wild cousins and make sure they are obedient.

captured. Packed tightly together the trapped elephants stand facing their tame cousins … The old cow now strides up to the monitors, greets them on the mouth, temples, and genitals with her trunk. She is greeted too. The kumkies surround the small troop of trapped animals and thus give them a feeling of security. But this is deceptive. For men move in amongst them quick as a flash … If an animal raises a foot one of the courageous men slips the rope noose over it. Even the mahouts on the elephants' backs are involved in the tying-up process. They throw thick ropes around the wild animals' necks. The working elephants use their trunks to help put the lasso in place. Then it is tightened firmly and fastened so it cannot come open … The kumkies push each shackled animal over to the palisades. The

old cow is caught last. They want to keep agitation to a minimum. The powerful bull she greeted an hour ago now pokes her on the head and in the side with his tusks. She resists and he presses her violently onto the palisades.

The men now allow the working elephants to have a break. The wild ones pull at the ropes, trumpet, fall headfirst, hit out with their trunks at the people they can see through the palisades. Finally it is time to take them away. The wild animals are bound to the working elephants … The calves run along with them free. It is almost a mile to the Mastigudi training camp …" There is a hard and painful time ahead for the distraught animals who have to be 'broken in' before going to the special 'elephant school.'

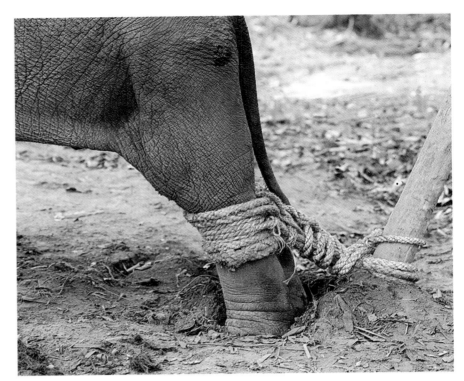

The pain and futility of pulling at the ropes that are cutting into the flesh wear the elephant down; hunger and thirst break down any remaining resistance. Resignation soon follows desperate rebellion. Resistance brings punishment, then reassuring words and tidbits. The mahout carrying out the training should remain the feared master while at the same time becoming a trusted friend.

# 'Breaking in' on the training ground

In Southeast Asia elephants are trained using methods that have been developed and refined over thousands of years. The mahouts who carry out the training come mainly from tribes and clans rooted in ancient traditions and for whom driving elephants has been a way of life for generations. Thai and Indian, Ceylonese and Burmese mahouts of the old school cannot be rivaled in their skills in training, looking after, and driving the giants of the jungle to perform useful work.

When a wild elephant is escorted to the training ground by kumkies the hard and cruel week of being 'broken in' has started. It must submit to the will of the mahout who must at the same time become a trusted friend to the animal. Tied to a timber frame or between two trees it is unable to move. The wild pachyderm pulling at the ropes and hitting out with its trunk soon becomes familiar with the pain of the elephant hook used to tame it, and the punitive stick.

Every time it refuses to obey the elephant is punished by being pricked on its sensitive trunk, behind the ears or in another painful place. A smack on the nose if the trunk moves about fiercely; a smack with sticks if it resists being touched by helpers who make a noise and sing around it. The mahout sitting in front of the shackled beast reassuringly harangues his charge who has to become familiar with the driver's voice and smell. Hunger and thirst also break the tormented animal's powers of resistance and at night the mahout brings it tidbits, such as bananas and sugarcane to mollify it.

Then again, during the day, unquestioning submission is demanded. If the elephant still rebels kumkies help to pull its stretched legs backwards and forwards. This causes the heavy body to press

down painfully on the knee and elbow joints – a shocking scene to witness.

Any elephant will soon stop putting up resistance if it is subjected to such torture. It must be spoken to reassuringly after every ordeal and tidbits given when even small progress has been made. Kindness must always prevail. The punitive human must become a friend to the elephant who will then submit to the still-feared oppressor out of affection. Rough and brutal treatment will lead only to dull obedience out of pure fear. Animals treated in this way easily become unmanageable, underhand, and dangerous.

When the elephant begins to accept its fate, away from the safety of the herd or its mother, it is taken, tied between two kumkies, to bathe every day. This is a comforting pleasure for the disturbed animal. After a few weeks the now reasonably placid pachyderm can be driven to the river, still shackled, but without needing to be accompanied by tame animals; the mahout in front, with the dreaded hook pointed at the trunk, as well as assistants to the right and left pointing their goads defensively. After first practicing at the training camp the elephant must learn to carry its mahout on its back during such expeditions. It does not yet carry him on its neck, in the driving position used later, as this is dangerously close to the trunk.

This initial training phase is shorter for 4 to 8 year-old calves, and is not required at all for young animals who were born in captivity and grew up in the human world.

Tied between trees so it cannot move, the wild, disturbed beast experiences the pain of being tamed by humans.

# The elephant school

It takes several months and a lot of patience to train an elephant to help man. The basic rule is that the same mahout must always carry out the training and look after his charge. The elephant is not like a horse, which will accept any proficient rider; it obeys one master to whom it can show the greatest devotion, and whom it considers part of its life as an elephant. A good deal of experience and an ability to understand the animal's psyche are needed to turn the giant of the jungle into a good-natured and willing helper to man. Training pets is a much simpler business.

The moment when the mahout moves from the back of a tame elephant to the driving seat, to his pupil's neck, for the first time is a critical one. Fear of the threatening hook is already so great that the elephant does not risk reaching up with its trunk whenever it is reluctant to do something.

During the first phase of basic training tame elephants set an example and are copied. Simple marching orders have to be carried out. The animal then has to learn to lift its foot or trunk, to go down on its knees and elbows, and so on, when ordered. Every individual bit of progress must be rewarded with tidbits, kind words, and stroking.

On average it takes a good six months for the pachyderm to be able to understand the three dozen or so, easy to remember, one- and two-syllable commands and immediately carry out any instruction. The elephant hook comes in useful from time to time. Later, a good mahout needs simply to threaten with the dreaded goad if the elephant does not react to a command or does not carry it out straight away.

After the basic training comes the special training, geared towards the task the elephant will carry out in the future. If the animal is to be used to pull heavy loads the preliminary training is almost all that is required. It now has only to get used to the harness and to the work. Working elephants who have to stack logs on timber felling sites and work in raging waters, or clear log-jams during the rainy season when the wood is floated, undergo much longer and more demanding training for this specialist work.

Indian elephants are very obliging, intelligent, and willing pupils once they have overcome the first difficult learning hurdles; once they have learnt to learn. As a rule it takes two to three years to train working elephants fully. They then carry out the work on the timber sites almost independently, in combination with others.

When ordered, the elephant must go down on its knees and elbows, reach for objects with its trunk, make a step up with its forefoot, and much more.

The mahout gives simple marching orders with his feet. Pressing his toes behind the elephant's left or right ear means walk in the corresponding direction. Pressing with both feet: walk quicker; tapping with his heels: slow down or stop.

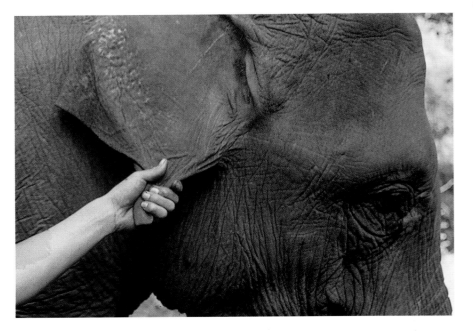

Small obedience exercises are necessary time and again with the mahout. Progress must be rewarded with tidbits and kind words.

Working elephants in towns must learn to keep calm in heavy traffic. Above all, parade and temple elephants must not shy amidst the tumult of religious ceremonies and public festivals, nor when there is a lot of noise and cannon fire.

Below:
The training of working elephants who have to stack logs and clear log-jams in rivers is much longer than that of simple draft animals.

Below right:
Displays require special training. Whole groups of elephants practice synchronizing the carrying out of commands.

The mahouts take their elephants to bathe every day. The animals must be thoroughly scrubbed on all sides so that parasites do not take root, particularly in the skin folds between the legs and hoofs, in the ears, and at the base of the tusks.

A ride in the jungle. Thai schools for working elephants in Lampang and Surin operate a profitable tourist business.

## Working on teak sites

Around the turn of the century hundreds of thousands of elephants lived in the tropical forests of Southeast Asia. Estimates put the number today at around 35,000–50,000. In Thailand alone there were some 100,000 tamed elephants 100 years ago. Today there are approximately 4,000 working elephants there, in addition to 3,500 wild ones in remote forests. This alarming trend led governments in elephant countries to introduce strict protective measures. The practice of trapping large numbers of the animals in palisade pens, carried out for thousands of years but with large numbers of casualties, was banned. In a radical rethink an attempt is being made to meet the additional requirement for working elephants through natural reproduction as far as possible using tamed elephants.

There have already been some encouraging breeding results, but in no way do they meet the demand for animals. Despite the advance of the machine, around 10,000 working elephants are still used throughout Southeast Asia. To meet the full requirement there will be restricted trapping of wild elephants in small forest kheddas as well as trapping of individual animals using kumkies, in addition to encouraging the rearing of elephants. Today it is possible to tie up animals separated from the herd in a safe and gentle way by firing shots from a safe distance to stun them.

Asia's gray giant has not yet lost the competition with the machine. New opportunities are opening up to the elephant in forestry, a field to which it is particularly suited and one which offers it as a 'working animal' the best chances of survival. The forestry authorities in Thailand and India are endeavoring to force international companies to fell teak selectively. The deforestation practices of these powerful companies are producing wide areas

Trapping and taming elephants

Hard-working elephants need other food in addition to green forage: rice balls mixed with fat, sugarcane and bread.

During selective felling the elephants have to drag the logs from the forest and stack them for transporting.

of insidious erosion. The area of Thailand covered by forest, for example, has already been reduced to just under a fifth of its original size. During selective felling, which preserves the forest, only the elephant, Asia's 'tractor,' is able to drag the individual trees released for felling through pathless jungles cost-effectively and without harming the precious undergrowth.

There are no more favorable conditions for rearing elephants than on timber sites. The animals remain in their traditional environment in the forest, and the working life in the camp gives them the opportunity to search for food in the jungle. The hard-working animals need supplementary food for extra energy: boiled rice balls mixed with fat, bread, sugarcane, etc. The elephants work six hours daily: three in the morning and three in the late afternoon. In between and during the evening there is plenty of time for bathing and scrubbing; skin-care that cannot be neglected if the animal is to remain healthy.

The elephants are regularly allowed to go into the bush after work and bathing. 'Hobbling' the animals prevents them from straying too far. This is achieved by tying the forefeet with a chain so that they can take only small steps, or by attaching a drag chain to a rear foot. Calves are free to accompany their mothers. Bells make it easier to

find them at sunset. When they graze at night in the forest the 'scent' of a cow ready to mate sometimes attracts a strong wild bull, who passes on a healthy and diverse genetic make-up.

Attaching foot chains, 'hobbling,' before letting the animals into the forest to search freely for food.

# A taming experiment in the Congo

To the indigenous peoples of equatorial and southern Africa the elephant was an animal to be hunted. Unlike in Asia, no use was made of its strength and skills. An experiment in the Congo has shown that it can be tamed just as successfully as its Asian cousin and made use of by man.

In 1879 the Belgian king Leopold II brought four Indian elephants to Dar-es-Salaam by boat. They then had to go on foot to the Congo. Young African animals were to be tamed with the help of Indian mahouts, after which they would form the nucleus of an elephant brigade to be deployed in the huge colony. However, the four Asian elephants perished during the trek. No further attempt was made until the turn of the century when King Leopold instructed Laplume, an officer with experience in Africa, to try to tame young African animals for work.

A military camp called the 'Station Api' was set up in the middle of an elephant region in the northwest of the colony, on the Uele River. The team came from the Asandeh tribe who had expert knowledge of elephant trapping. Laplume had dozens of pits laid. Finally two elephants were trapped. The African teams could not handle the animals who defended themselves furiously and did not even survive transportation.

Then an attempt was made with a palisade pen into which a cow elephant was driven with her calf. The mother was freed but kept returning to her calf so had to be shot – and the calf died too.

Unnerved, Laplume decided on cruel, radical action. During a hunt using beaters he had a number of mother animals shot and the helpless calves brought back. At least half the calves, who were still being weaned, managed to remain alive on a mixture of cow's milk and rice water. A stock of some thirty, pleasant-natured young animals was gradually built up. Then the First World War broke out and Laplume was called up. The experiment was put in jeopardy again.

After the peace agreement Laplume started again, this time on the instructions of Leopold II's successor, King Albert I. Finally appropriate steps were taken in the light of the failures and half successes. At Brussels' request India sent seven mahouts who introduced the 'elephant soldiers' from the Asandeh tribe and white officers to tried and tested elephant trapping methods. The mahouts did not get on well with their African pupils. Right up until they returned home after eight months, they are supposed to have had a fear of the lively and sensitive African elephants. According to various contemporary sources they sometimes treated them very roughly. However, their advice produced results.

The brutal killing of mothers during trapping operations stopped. Asandeh elephant soldiers, called 'cornacs,' would catch up, either on foot or horseback, with young calves (up to 4 years old) that remained behind when a herd fled in panic amidst the shots and noise. Rope nooses were thrown over the animals' rear legs. They were tied to trees, and taken to the camp in the evening with the help of tame cows. Young animals could easily be caught by good runners with staying power. The elephants' heavy bodies tire after running just 110 yards quickly. If bulls or mothers turned back, though, the athletic Asandeh trappers were in grave danger. Many lost their lives.

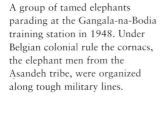

A group of tamed elephants parading at the Gangala-na-Bodia training station in 1948. Under Belgian colonial rule the cornacs, the elephant men from the Asandeh tribe, were organized along tough military lines.

Working elephants driven by cornacs plow a plantation. In 1928 there were 103 tame and trained working elephants at the Api and Wando elephant stations.

Training was also successful following advice from the Indian mahouts. The African cornacs proved to be very skillful elephant drivers. In the mid-1920s over twenty tame, reasonably trained African elephants gave useful service as draft animals during timber felling and harnessed to plows on surrounding farms. Then the elephant herds disappeared from the area. They had been harassed and over-hunted. Young animals were no longer brought in. The station had to be moved in 1927. The new station of 'Gangala-na-Bodia' was set up on the banks of the River Dongu in the middle of the Garamba National Park. The tamed elephants worked hard during the move.

## The Congo elephant school in crisis

A stock of fifty tame, well-trained and willing riding and working elephants was soon built up at the Gangala-na-Bodia elephant station. The station itself was developed into a second administration center for the Garamba National Park. The animals were soon able to be set free to graze 'hobbled,' like their Indian cousins in the jungle near the timber centers. Some elephants escaped but returned a few months later and followed their cornacs as if nothing had happened.

As is the way in Africa the taming work was often accompanied by rhythmic antiphonal singing by the leader and team; beating the young animal's back with branches in time to get it to carry out a command, and rewarding it when it obeyed.

In the 1930s the Belgian officer Raymond Lefevre ran the station along tough military lines. The colors were hoisted in the morning and the Asandeh 'elephant soldiers' wore uniforms. They did take these off on trapping operations.

Accommodation was provided for visitors who could ride into the bush on the back of an elephant. The station set its sights on the tourist business.

The station came through the turbulence of the Second World War well. In 1951 Gangala-na-Bodia had 100 trained elephants. There was then, though, a dramatic setback. When the Belgian colony gained its independence in 1960 a terrible civil war broke out in the Congo and order in the camp started to break down. Belgium lost interest in the elephant school. Shooting involving marauding soldiers occurred. Calves were no longer trapped. By 1964 the number of trained elephants had already fallen to fifteen. The old and experienced cornacs left. At the end of the 1980s there were just four tame cows, who could no longer be depended on to obey, and one calf at the station.

Since then another attempt has been made with modest resources. However, with the fragile political situation in the Congo there can be little hope of a significant, long-term safari business involving elephants.

# Safari rides on African elephants in the Okavango Delta

The American zoologist Randall Jay Moore has achieved interesting results in keeping and training African elephants in Botswana, in the famous Okavango Delta. Ten years ago he started bringing African elephants back to Africa from zoos overseas and integrating them into a community of tame riding and working animals. Today he is able to offer rides into the jungle on a number of savannah elephants driven by Africans.

The huge leading bull Abu was taken to the USA as a young animal and grew up there. One of the beasts returned to Africa from Canada, another from Sri Lanka. The other animals include a wild pachyderm from the Kruger National Park in South Africa who joined a herd that was lumped together but grew into a happy elephant family. The herd also accepted several orphans from the Kruger National Park. They are carefully looked after by the adult animals. They run along with them when the adults are being ridden; they play, tussle, and splash around just like children. The small orphans' mothers were killed during controlled shooting of whole herds where elephant populations had become too large. The gregarious animals can wander freely into the jungle near the station to look for food.

The Okavango experiment shows that it is possible to use tamed African riding elephants in

A trip on the back of an African elephant in the animal paradise of the humid and still largely untamed Okavango region. The young animals run alongside. For a long time it was wrongly thought that it was difficult to tame the giant African elephants, but they are no less suitable for riding than the Indian elephant. They can successfully be used to bring in tourists, which should safeguard their existence.
Okavango Delta, Botswana

A family unit on the move. The regularly-flooded areas in the middle of the wide steppes are an ideal environment for the elephants.
Okavango Delta, Botswana

the tourist business successfully. The elephant also has a good chance of surviving thanks to its usefulness. If the international timber companies that carry out devastating deforestation, rapidly transporting the timber away in trucks, in Africa's rain forests were to come to an agreement on sensible and selective felling, then African working elephants would also stand a chance in the forests.

The Okavango Delta is one of the last large retreats of these wild animals. The Okavango rises in the highlands of Angola. It is over 600 miles long but does not reach the sea. It ends in the steppe region north of the Kalahari desert in a huge system of lakes and islands, of channels, swamps and lagoons. The large amount of water that the river receives in Angola during the rainy season arrives in the world's largest inland delta months later when it is the dry season in Botswana, which lasts from April through September. Water supplies in the middle of the arid steppes are replenished and wide areas flooded. The animals move to the relief of the oasis. They return to the now green steppe at the beginning of the rainy season.

There are an estimated 24,000 elephants in Botswana. The Okavango Delta with the steppe nearby provides an ideal environment for them to live and roam in. There are, however, serious dangers on the horizon.

As the population of Africa increases farmers are moving into the delta. Devastating fires are lit to clear areas for cattle to graze. Following successful eradication of the tsetse fly (once the protector of the wild animals!) cattle can be kept in any biotope. The problem of poachers can scarcely be brought under control. On top of this industry is moving into the vicinity of the poor state's only large water reserve. Two open-cast diamond mines already use huge amounts of water. Copper, nickel, and coal lie in the ground. Irrigation projects are endangering the fine water balance in the delta region, and roads are being built. The future does not look bright for the elephants and the wild animals in general.

# Hunter and hunted

Even in antiquity elephant-hunts, which required special caution and cold-bloodedness, were equal to the test of royal courage provided by the stalking of tigers and lions. The fallen beast was

*Elephant-hunt,*
Brussels c. 1530,
tapestry.
Musée du Louvre, Paris

The eventfulness and colorfulness of the wall hanging which was made in a Flemish workshop brings out the joyful feeling of being alive characteristic of the renaissance period. The fallen exotic creature is woven into a sophisticated hunting scene in a landscape that has a skillful effect of depth in perspective.

seen as clear evidence of intrepidity and proud male courage. In Southeast Asia the elephant provided protection for the hunter, who rode on its back. From there he had a safe and wide view when he went into the jungle in the dangerous pursuit of stalking tigers, lions and rhinoceros. The elephant of the open African savannah and steppe has always remained a particular challenge for the passionate hunter.

Hundreds of stories have grown up around the solitary stalking expeditions of weather-beaten men who could not resist the adventure of the wild. A profit-seeking safari industry unfortunately allowed elephant hunting to degenerate into shooting entertainment.

Opposite:
*Tiger-hunt with elephant* (detail),
Patiala, Punjab, 1892,
gouache on paper.
Victoria & Albert Museum,
London

Dramatic attack by a tiger during a British gentlemen's hunt in the Indian jungle. Contemporary European painting technique overlies the old Indian style of representation.

The Prince of Wales, who visited Nepal in 1876, witnessed an attack by a tiger during a state hunt in his honor. The sketch by a reporter was published in 'The Illustrated London News' on April 1, 1876.

# Hunting tigers on elephantback

Since early times the kings and regional princes of the Indian subcontinent, the maharajas (great princes) and rajas (princes), have ridden on elephantback into the jungle to hunt tigers. They were doing so when the arrow, spear and sword were man's only defense, and the stalking of big cats a risky adventure.

The elephant remained a valued assistant as highly-accurate, modern rifles lowered tiger hunting to the level of an exclusive thrill. The hide on the elephant's back provided safety, if the tiger pounced in a surprise attack, as well as a clear view and field of fire in the high grass, bamboo thickets and wild undergrowth of the jungle. Above all the elephant can tackle the most difficult swampy terrain into which even the most modern cross-country vehicles are unable to penetrate, and so it remains the best mode of transport.

Only exceptional, powerful and fearless bulls were suitable for tiger hunters to ride; and they had to undergo special lengthy and difficult training. They were not to shy when they picked up the scent of a big cat, or let themselves be overcome by the aggression felt towards their arch-enemy. They had to obey implicitly, be able to understand a whole host of commands, and stop at close range to the tiger, so giving the hunter a good opportunity to shoot with accuracy.

In the old days when hunters had only spears and arrows they also had to rely on their elephants' defensive tusks and powerful trunks. The animals learned to run through and trample dummies of tigers. This training which went against the elephants' nature was also part of the training program for war. Rivalry between kingdoms and princedoms meant there was always a great demand for elephants which had been through the long process of training for hunting and war.

Right:
*Maharao Durjan Sal and Shri Brijnathji hunt tiger and buffalo*, Rajasthan, Kota, 18th century, painting on cotton.
102.4cm x 191.3cm
Collection of Howard Hodgkin, London

A huge contingent of beaters has pushed the game into a semicircular ring of hunters. Safe on elephantback the maharajas can get the most dangerous large animals in their sight and have the first shot.

Hunter and hunted

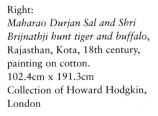

Hunter and hunted

# An invitation from the raja to a jungle dinner ...

Group picture of the ruling maharajas, India, c. 1905.

The collage of portraits of forty maharajas was put together by an unknown artist. In the middle of the front row the well-known Nizam of Hyderabad.

Until very recently India's rajas held on to the privilege of extravagant and extremely lavish tiger-hunts – even though their power was restricted following the end of British colonial rule. A contemporary report describes what happened at one of these hunts:

"In January the raja Bahadur Visvesar Singh of Radschnagar sent sixteen of his best hunting elephants and their keepers on a one month's advance expedition into the northern jungle of Bihar. A few weeks later, before it became too hot, he called together twelve followers, twenty servants, four bodyguards, and twenty-eight guests. They set off in the direction of the jungle in his private luxury railroad carriages.

"When he arrived there his men had obtained twenty more elephants together with appropriate personnel. The hunting party, now numbering 200, could set off. The party included the mahouts driving the elephants and the 'charkatas' who fed them; there were cooks, musicians, a private secretary to the raja, someone to skin the animals and even servants for more senior civil servants. Heavy equipment was also taken along, including two kitchens for Indian and Western dishes. The hunt itself seemed almost incidental.

"Every day after a sumptuous breakfast the raja and his friends would travel to the elephants by car. They would then wait on the elephants' backs until a line of beaters led game to them. After several hours a hot four-course meal was served, brought from the hunting camp. After the next phase of hunting in the afternoon came whisky and soda, then evening entertainment and lastly at a late hour a long luxurious dinner.

"Three tigers were shot in ten days. The raja killed one and gave a second, that had already been shot, the coup de grâce. He considered the cost to be reasonable as the expedition had cost him 'only' around 10,000 dollars, which was the same as the previous year's despite inflation.

"'Only' three beaters had been wounded: by hunters who had shot wildly at a leopard ..."

Hunter and hunted

The hunters view the kill in the jungle of Bihar: four tigers.

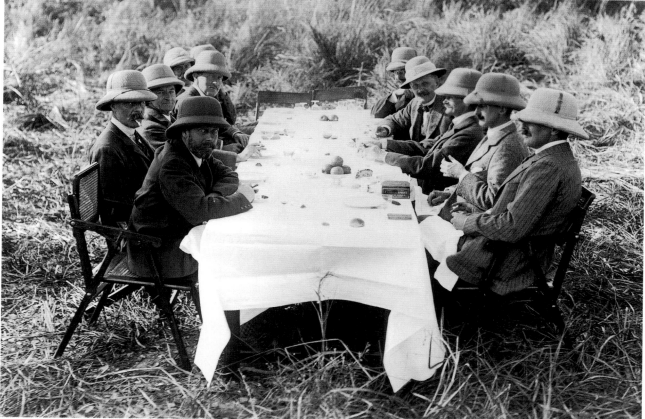

After the thrill of stalking large game a chance to relax for the grand hunting party during a snack at a table laid in a jungle clearing by servants.

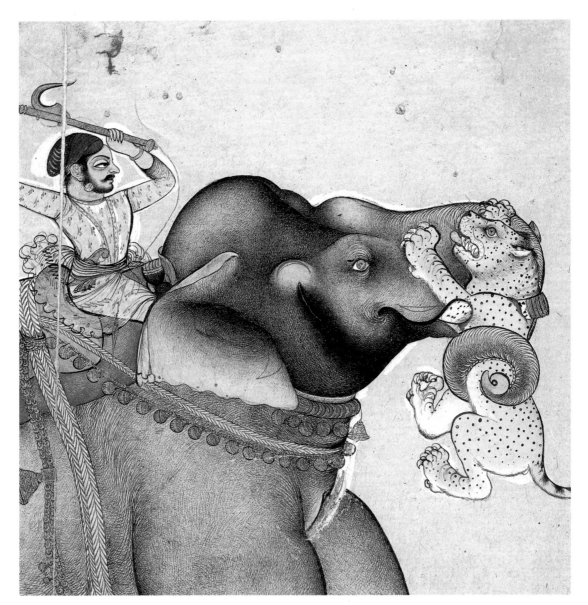

# Lion-hunting in Indian illuminations

For a prince of the belligerent Rajputs, who provided part of the imperial army in the medieval Mogul kingdom, it was a matter of honor to be the first to show cold-bloodednes and courage during the big-game hunt, to take the tiger or lion tracked down in front of the entourage. This could lead to a critical situation if he suddenly came across a lioness protecting the young in a family unit. The masters of Indian illuminations which flourished in the 16th/17th century vividly captured these dramatic scenes. They provide graphic evidence of conditions at that time and of the old Indian feudal way of life.

The painters belonged to the lowest caste, the shudra caste, but were held in high regard at the courts. They accompanied their masters on journeys, in war and hunting. They had to record their masters' actions, first in sketches and then in color when the rulers had examined them. These drawings were to increase the princes' reputation and standing. They could show their guests masterpieces of the so-called 'book painting' or illuminations or give them away as a mark of special favor. The 'books' involved were not books as understood in the West but loose leaves assembled between sheets of leather and kept wrapped in cloth.

Big-game hunting was a favorite pastime of Mogul princes, as it was for the Rajputs, India's 'knights.' It was linked to masculine pride and in a way was a substitute for war. Now and then the famous emperor Akbar (1556–1605) liked to arrange large shoots along the lines of war. With a huge number of soldiers he would use military tactics to surround the game. These shoots were a demonstration of his power and could be seen as a warning to potential adversaries.

It is said that in 1567 he had a huge zone 60 miles in diameter surrounded by 10,000 soldiers. During a two-month period they herded together all the animals in that zone into a narrow area just a few miles in diameter. For several days Akbar rode alone through the area, accompanied only by a few courtiers. He killed game using the sword, bow and arrow, spear, and musket alternately. Above all lions and tigers, the noblest game, were reserved for his thirst for action. Noblemen, court officials, and soldiers were only allowed to bag game after him, and in order of rank.

Hunter and hunted

# The Prince of Wales on a tiger-hunt

In spring 1876 the Prince of Wales made an official visit to the crown colony of India. A grandiose tiger-hunt was arranged in his honor. The illustrious party set off into the jungle with a large contingent of elephants. They shot everything that came into sight: tigers, bears and rhinoceros. 'The Illustrated London News' reported on the event in a pictorial report in its edition of March 25, 1876.

The Prince of Wales, standing in the howdah, fires at a bear. All kinds of big game come into sight.

Hunter and hunted

The Prince of Wales is sitting in the hide which Indian helpers placed in the fork of a branch in a giant tree. Below left is Prince Louis of Battenberg; right is the Indian raja Sir Jung Bahadoor. The series of pictures was published in 'The Illustrated London News' on April 8, 1876.

A tiger that has been shot is heaved up onto an elephant's back and secured there. Hunting elephants have to endure the scent of their deadly enemy without shying.

## Queen Elizabeth II rides into the jungle

In 1961 the British queen Elizabeth II and Prince Philip made a state visit to Nepal. The highlight of the grandiose program was a long ride on elephantback in order to hunt tigers. With great extravagance King Mahendra accompanied his distinguished guests into the jungle of Megauli. Dozens of hunting elephants were mustered; guests and servants numbered 2,000. In the wild, where soldiers had cleared an area $^3/_4$ square mile in size to be free of snakes and unpleasant pests, a lavish tent city was erected where the party could rest and enjoy a large hunt dinner.

When they set off Elizabeth led the elephant convoy. Reliable, specially trained elephants accompanied the hunting party to protect it against attacks from tigers. The success of this lavish country outing was, however, fairly modest in terms of game. The accompanying foreign minister missed his only chance at a tiger. The queen herself declined to shoot at game and only took photographs.

Prince Philip watches as a tiger that has been shot is fastened on the back of an elephant by some Indian helpers.

Sitting on the back of an elephant, and under a parasol, Queen Elizabeth II leads the hunting party. She is armed only with a camera. Behind on the third elephant is Prince Philip, the Duke of Edinburgh, a keen hunter.

In the middle of the hunting ground the queen moves to the gold howdah on a magnificent elephant from where there is an unrestricted view. An escort of several particularly reliable elephants protects her against attacks from tigers.

In 1911 Elizabeth's grandfather, King George V, visited Nepal where he and a large entourage spent three days hunting in the jungle. He shot one of the eighteen rhinoceros killed by the hunting party, as well as several tigers.

Right: A day's kill: four tigers and a gazelle.

# Hunting buffalo, rhinoceros and wild boar

Tara Chand, *The raja Svarup Singh of Udaypur on a wild boar hunt* (detail), Udaypur, Rajasthan, 1855, gouache on paper. Victoria & Albert Museum, London

The scene is painted in a traditional style in a wide landscape. The raja, who is firing at a boar with a muzzle-loader, is accompanied by armed men and servants as was the feudal custom.

Hunter and hunted

*Emperor Babur shoots a rhinoceros,*
Page from the 'scattered' Baburnama manuscript, attributed to the painter Bishan Das c. 1590, de Bureltt collection Basle, Switzerland post-1927, gift from Barbara and Eberhard Fischer

An enraged and hounded buffalo attacks an elephant who is not frightened by such an assault. The sketch was made by the animal painter Wilhelm Eigner while on a trip to India.

## Prince Waldemar of Prussia stalks elephants

*The prince's stalking expedition,*
Prince Waldemar of Prussia,
Ceylon 1845,
a romantic, contemporary depiction.

In 1845 Prince Waldemar of Prussia and some friends were guests of the record elephant hunter Major Rogers who organized a stalking expedition for the prominent occasional huntsmen. They set off to the jungle on horseback with a large contingent of local servants, as colonial etiquette demanded. "We would set off together fifty to sixty men strong," notes the prince in his diary. "Behind each rider a horse keeper and two or three men carrying the rifles …" They dismounted at the edge of the jungle. The major gave instructions to the local servants.

"The naked guides wound their way through the overgrown jungle, stooping and often crawling on hands and knees. We too had to walk constantly bent over; we used our rifles to forge ahead but in our clothes and broad-brimmed hats following them was no easy task for us. We got caught on something with almost every step … In the high grass we, I and Count Gröben, find an elephant. I shoot and wound it, and now we set off after it. It gets slower and unsteady; it looks round, appears as though it is thinking, beating its ears and trunk raised, turns back … and thinks we have gone away. We expect him immediately, and I press the trigger, at a distance of fifteen to twenty paces. My rifle fails to go off; the one round has come out, and I am standing there without a weapon …"

The prince seeks cover, falls over a tree, jumps further. The wounded elephant sinks onto the tree-trunk and then turns on Gröben "who, protected by a tree, aims a shot at it and it gives up the chase …"

The prince did not manage to fire a fatal shot in accordance with hunting principles on another stalking expedition either:

"We crawl and crawl for several hours. Suddenly the Singhalese creeping ahead of us leaps back: the elephant is standing fifteen paces in front of Count Oriolla. Oriolla shoots. The elephant falls, but gets up again. He shoots again. The elephant collapses once more, but turns round and comes towards us enraged … I fire my rifle; it falls onto its knees again; I press the trigger a second time – it fails to go off! The giant beast was so near us there was nothing for it but to turn back … We jump behind a particularly thick bush so the elephant cannot see us … We can hear it charging and dashing about in the bushes close by. The noise dies away. We carefully load our rifles and try to track it. Blood on all the branches, several puddles of water full of fibrin. The elephant though was unfortunately long gone …"

The prince notes: "I confess that elephants rose in my estimation from then on, and I no longer considered them as cows that run away …"

# "Elephants do not give up their lives easily ..."

The elephant who is badly injured by the hunter and escapes into the bush is condemned to a very cruel and slow death that can last many hours, or even days and weeks. The giant animal dies a more difficult and agonizing death than wounded small game. The enormous vitality of its colossal body is a painful burden to the wounded elephant.

"They do not give up their lives easily," according to an old Indian book of elephant remedies. The English writer George Orwell (1903–50) describes this from his own experience in his essay 'Shooting an Elephant.' As a young man he worked in the colonial police force in the small Burmese town of Moulmein. One day he was alerted that a working elephant was having an attack of 'musth' and had escaped into the bush. It had then returned to the town where it was causing devastation and had trampled to death an Indian coolie. The animal's mahout was looking for it in the wrong direction a long way away. So the police officer had to take control of the situation.

Orwell did not intend killing the bull, but the sight of the rifle he borrowed for his own protection made the crowd gathering round him think he was going to do so. Orwell felt forced to shoot. The actual theme of Orwell's essay is psychological coercion by an excited crowd:

"And it was at this moment, as I stood there with the rifle in my hands, that I first grasped the hollowness, the futility of the white man's dominion in the East. Here was I, the white man with his gun, standing in front of the unarmed native crowd – seemingly the leading actor of the piece; but in reality I was only an absurd puppet pushed to and fro by the will of those yellow faces behind. I perceived in this moment that when the white man turns tyrant it is his own freedom that he destroys."

He, therefore, tracks down the elephant and tries to fire the fatal shot into the elephant's brain.

However, he misses:

"... a mysterious, terrible change had come over the elephant. He neither stirred nor fell, but every line of his body had altered. He looked suddenly stricken, shrunken, immensely old ... At last, after what seemed a long time – it might have been five seconds, I dare say – he sagged flabbily to his knees. His mouth slobbered." Orwell fired a second and third time: "That was the shot that did for him. You could see the agony of it jolt his whole body and knock the last remnant of strength from his legs. But in falling he seemed for a moment to rise, for as his hind legs collapsed beneath him he seemed to tower upward like a huge rock toppling ... He trumpeted, for the first and only time. And then down he came."

The elephant, however, is still not dead.

"Finally I fired my two remaining shots into the spot where I thought his heart must be. The thick blood welled out of him like red velvet, but still he did not die. His body did not even jerk when the shots hit him, the tortured breathing continued without a pause. He was dying, very slowly ... In the end I could not stand it any longer and went away."

According to Orwell, the older Europeans thought he had acted correctly; the younger ones, on the other hand, considered an elephant to be worth more than the coolie killed and, therefore, condemned his action. He himself was glad that the elephant had killed a person; that was the legal justification for his action. Nobody, though, had guessed the real reason for his behavior: the fear of looking a fool.

*The dying giant,*
Drawing from the book 'Elephants' by John Groth. London, 1976

The artist John Groth has recorded the situation. "At last, after what seemed a long time, the elephant sagged flabbily to his knees ..."

## Record killings in Ceylon

During the colonial era elephant-hunting in Southeast Asia was a privilege of the British rulers, and of officers and government officials, who usually came from the army. Confronting the beast in the wild was a dangerous elitist pursuit. It gave the participants a thrill and made the Sahib respected amongst the natives. The local feudal rulers could match them at it.

Elephant-hunting on the island of Ceylon led to terrible mass killings. British firms and private planters carried out rigorous deforestation there, particularly in the central highlands, in order to make room for extensive coffee and tea plantations. Elephant herds that had been driven out would often return to these areas and cause enormous damage to the plantations. To the farmer the elephant was an enemy that had to be repelled and eradicated from the vicinity of the plantations he was trying to protect.

The hunting undertaken to safeguard the lucrative monocultures for the world market soon degenerated into pure sport. The 'gentlemen hunters,' who did not have to comply with any restrictions, competed for record killings. The technology of rifles improved and they became more accurate over longer ranges. This made multiple killings possible on a single stalking expedition. The men who took part in extravagant hunting parties, taking every luxury with them into the jungle, could win an elephant trophy on large expeditions into the jungle.

Romantic adventure literature grew up around elephant-hunting. It was started by the famous Sir Samuel White Baker (1821–93), who was later involved in exploring the source of the Nile and in the fight against the slave trade in East Africa. In 1845 Baker went elephant-hunting on the island of Ceylon, where he also tried his hand as a planter. In 1855 the first edition of his hunting memoirs, 'Eight Years Wanderings in Ceylon' appeared in London. The book became a bestseller. When it was reprinted in 1966 the publisher noted that during his time in Ceylon Baker had shot more elephants than exist there today.

Many officers of the British colonial army boasted of having killed many elephants. These included a Major Rogers who supposedly killed some 1,400 elephants, and a Major Skinner 700 animals. Huge bulls were the main targets because of their valuable tusks. Today most of the bulls on the island do not have tusks. As mentioned elsewhere this may be the result of a selection process within the isolation of the island, brought about by the elimination of ancestors with particularly strong tusks.

Despite all the brutality man is capable of inflicting on the gentle giant, there is a silent respect and humane affection for the animal throughout the world. In India there are even annual religious festivals at which working animals are paid homage to. Elephants made redundant by tractors are put out to grass for the rest of their lives. In the last rites the dead animal lies decorated with flowers and garlands, and surrounded by Indians silently mourning the friend who gave long service to man.

# The first hunters on the African continent

The elephant has been hunted in the south of the African continent, its original homeland, since prehistoric times. For the autochthonous peoples and tribes it was only a wild animal. It was never tamed and used for work as in Asia and its only use to man was as bag. The whole body was used. The skin was used to cover shields, drums and as protection against the weather, and belts and straps were cut out from it; the tendons were used as yarn; tail hairs could be formed into amulets with magic power, and all sorts of jewelry and ritualistic idols could be carved from the tusks. Early Africans never hunted elephants purely for ivory.

The first hunters of the African continent were the Bushmen who migrated to southern Africa in the later Palaeolithic Age, 12,000–14,000 years ago. They were small, lean people with wrinkled brownish-yellow skin who were driven into inhospitable dry regions by advancing nomadic Negroid tribes. They were good at reading tracks. They would go stalking alone with poisoned arrows or hunt and kill big game in large groups. Hunting for them was a basic necessity for survival. An elephant was a godsend for the whole clan. Survivors of this ethnic group eke out an existence today on the edge of the Kalahari desert.

The eternal dusk under the treetops of the equatorial rain forest gives rise to small forms of man and animals. Here dwarfish pygmies hunted and still hunt. Their main weapon is also the poisoned arrow with which they hit their target accurately using blowpipes. Spears are only rarely used. Today the existence of the small number of pygmies is threatened by increasing deforestation, as is that of the forest elephant, which they still sometimes kill.

In the 15th century the first Portuguese settled in West and East Africa, bringing their Western values with them. Elephant tusks became highly-priced commodities. The hunting practices of the autochthonous peoples and tribes changed. Increasingly the main purpose of hunting was to obtain ivory rather than supplies.

## Secret hunting societies

Not all the numerous ethnic and linguistic groups in southern Africa hunted elephants themselves. Secret hunting societies were formed within some tribes. They were employed as professional hunters over large regions and earned themselves a high reputation. In the kingdom of Benin, which included large parts of present-day Nigeria and had contacts with the court in Lisbon, only the most capable young men could become hunters. Before they were accepted into the society they had to undergo difficult training, demonstrate courage and endurance in the wild as well as become proficient in reading tracks, and in the use of spears, blowpipes, and bows and arrows. Initiation into the society included secret rituals and ceremonies. They learned magic formulae which were supposed to make the hunter invisible to the game and gave them confidence.

Elephant-hunting was a risky business. Wounded animals could suddenly hit out from the trap. Poisoned arrows certainly killed, but only slowly. When an elephant was killed in Benin the 'oba,' the absolute king, received a tusk; the hunter was allowed to keep the other one in addition to the head, heart and lungs.

Professional hunters in other African kingdoms were also in the ruler's service. They were organized into secret societies with their own rituals. They often wore special markings, clothes or amulets that indicated their special position and membership of a society. In the 15th century the 'Cokwe' were particularly famous. They lived in western Angola but also hunted elephants for chiefs throughout a wide area of central Africa. In East Africa the 'kamba' temporarily controlled hunting on Kenya's savannahs.

## Pits, poisoned arrows, snares

Hunting was carried out using cruel, traditional methods, according to which all primitive peoples hunted and still hunt big game:

Spears with long iron tips were hurled from trees into the back of a passing elephant. As the animal fled the long shafts acted like a lever pushing the blades deeper and deeper into the body. The same effect was produced by groups of hunters ramming spears into the body of an elephant driven away from the herd. It often took days for the wounded animal to die.

Poisoned arrows were often used. These had only a slow effect in the huge bodies. The hunters followed the trail of blood from the badly injured animals. It was often days before the elephants collapsed and died.

A common practice was – and still is today – the trapping of elephants with snares. They were laid over small, camouflaged holes and secured to tree-trunks. If the elephant tried desperately to free itself the snare would cut into it as far down as the bones. The elephant would be finished off with arrows and spears.

Africa's boldest elephant hunters were the Hamran Arabs, a dark-skinned mixed race who settled in the areas around tributaries of the Nile west of Ethiopia. They hunted on horseback. After an elephant had been driven away from the herd and hounded to exhaustion the swordsman sitting behind the rider would jump down and run his razor-sharp weapon through the animal's foot tendons above the heel. They also hunted on foot in groups, a daring method which claimed many human victims.

*Elephant-hunt,*
5th millennium BC,
tracing of a rock painting.
Mazowe, Zimbabwe

A wounded elephant is hounded
to death by a group of Bushmen.

# Elephant-hunting in Africa's savannah

A professional hunter from the pioneering age: J. A. Hunter, who lived in Kenya from 1908 until his death in 1963. He was an excellent marksman and one of the best authorities on Kenyan fauna. He went on safari with film stars and maharajas, with Denys Finch-Hatten and Karen Blixen.

In the 19th century southern Africa's animal paradise was the dream destination for Europe's keen hunters. On the open savannah and steppes the animals did not disappear into green jungle as they did in East Asia or the equatorial rain forests of West Africa. The stocks of exotic animals seemed inexhaustible. Millions of elephants populated the large expanses of subsaharan Africa. The adventure of big-game hunting was very attractive in the still-virgin wilderness.

The savannah and steppes to the north and south of Kilimanjaro were a hunting eldorado. This area, covering the present-day states of Kenya and Tanzania, was shared between the British and Germans. Hunters, discoverers and adventurers came from all corners of the globe; and many were unable to leave the magic of the wilderness and the giant herds. Robust and courageous men undertook expeditions lasting several weeks either on their own or with servants, unconcerned with hardships and danger. In the early days adventurers keen to make discoveries would set out from coastal towns over wide, roadless expanses into unexplored wild areas and often spend months in the bush. Hundreds of stories have grown up around these men.

A brotherhood of white hunters was formed. They became sought-after and well-paid guides and provided protection for prominent or rich visitors to Africa who wanted to experience a big-game hunt and proudly take home a trophy. Convoys of local carriers hauled rifles, tents and provisions. Even in the wild a certain amount of comfort was provided for the visitors.

In 1909 Theodore Roosevelt, the 26th President of the USA (1901–09) visited East Africa as the leader of a scientific expedition. He traveled by train from the coastal town of Mombasa to Kenya's animal paradises. The Mombasa – Nairobi – Uganda railroad had been opened in 1901. It was 582 miles long and crossed 162 bridges. 36,000 Indian coolies had laid the track through the

Theodore Roosevelt, President of the USA from 1901 until 1909, went big-game hunting in southeast Africa in 1909 after his term in office.

The white hunter has shot down the dangerous rogue. The mountain of flesh will feed the whole waiting clan.

jungle. The opening of the railroad to Kenya's climatically blessed highlands was the beginning of white settlement. The prominent American visitor firmly supported this colonial expansion in Africa. With 250 local carriers and with the Stars and Stripes flying, Theodore Roosevelt was the first American big-game hunter to penetrate the bush.

In the 'thirties another famous American visited Kenya's lush animal paradise, the writer Ernest Hemingway. In a dour, masculine romantic style he described the magic of the African wilderness and the coolly-executed kills.

For professional hunters the elephant ranked alongside rhinoceros, lions, leopards and buffalo as the most dangerous big game. When an elephant is frightened or wounded, or when a cow believes her calf to be in danger, it can suddenly attack. Many people, mainly primitively-armed natives, have been pierced by the tusks of an enraged elephant, trampled or crushed with the trunk.

Elephants have had bad experiences with man, the only 'predator' they fear, so they are on their guard. They have an excellent sense of smell and can detect the approach of humans from several miles away if the wind is in the right direction. The first law of hunting is always to stalk against the wind. Its direction can be determined by watching something float through the air.

When the leader of a group of elephant families innocently and noisily grazing suddenly grows suspicious, it becomes rigid and raises its trunk inquiringly. The whole herd is immediately alerted. This may be by means of a warning signal at low frequencies that cannot be detected by man. All at once the noise of eating, the rumbling of the digestive organs stops. The herd moves closer together, pauses and, if the danger is acute, disappears silently into the bush. The animals have a highly-developed camouflage instinct and are so skillful at hiding that a hunter pursuing them is often standing unawares right by an elephant.

In the 'thirties the American writer Ernest Hemingway (1899–1961) went hunting in the big-game paradises of East Africa.

The successful gentleman hunter posing like a proud victor on the body of the fallen beast. A typical souvenir scene for the desk in the study at home.

Hunter and hunted

# Only a few points to aim at for a 'humane' coup de grâce

In order to be able to sight the few small points of aim that produce an accurate fatal shot with a rifle, an elephant has to be approached at a distance of 65 to 98 feet. It is particularly difficult to fire a shot into the brain that will be immediately fatal. The elephant's colossal skull is interspersed with a network of cavities which, together with the jawbone and the tusk sockets, protect the brain. An inaccurate shot into these cavities will stun the animal for only a short time and the elephant can escape into the bush with its terrible injury.

The only points of aim for firing a fatal shot into the brain are palm-sized spots between the eyes and at the side between the eye and ear. Frontal shots into the brain are very difficult to place if an African elephant throws its very flat head up protectively or in readiness for defense. The easiest shot to fire is into the heart from the side. The point of aim is the rear spot at the top of the front left leg.

Shooting at the huge trunk of the body, the lungs, spleen or other vital organs is absolutely barbaric and cruel. Unfortunately this was done thousands of times a year until very recently. If an animal hit in this way still manages to escape it is condemned to a dreadful death in the bush. Touchingly, companions will often stand by it, supporting it and helping it when it tries to stand after having collapsed with weakness. A hunter who follows a wounded elephant into the bush would do well to exercise extreme caution.

In the wild rogues are sometimes, though certainly not always, very dangerous and malicious. They may be vicious bulls who have been driven out by stronger rivals, or harmless and placid animals who prefer to be alone. Even an experienced big-game hunter finds it demanding when aggressive rogues make an area unsafe. It is a risky undertaking to track down, in rough and uneven bush and jungle terrain, and accurately kill an elephant who can hit out maliciously against the ambush and who bears the scars of serious injuries caused by man.

Opposite: The ears are spread out wide, the tail lashes - warning gestures from a leading cow who senses danger for the herd. She does not attack blindly; she stops her warning if she does not perceive a threat.

In some countries a planned reduction in elephant numbers is carried out if too many elephants threaten the vegetation in a protected area. The cow's whole unit is shot in so-called 'controlled killings' so that helpless young animals are not abandoned in the bush.

The points of aim for the fatal shot.

Hunter and hunted

## The safari industry

After the Second World War, when African countries achieved independence, big-game hunting in East Africa was commercialized and badly corrupted. Safari companies organized comfortable shooting expeditions from off-road vehicles for well-to-do tourists seeking trophies. They were far removed from the stalking that complied with hunting principles. Many khaki-clad hunting professionals stayed in the fragile new states after the colonial powers had left. They became agents for the profitable safari industry which had good contacts with the new rulers.

Hunting was a basic activity in man's struggle for survival, but with the boasting and obsession with trophies that went with it, it has always been a sport. However, the European 'gentlemen hunters,' who in the old days would track game in the bush accompanied by experts, adhered to their own hunting practices, with some exceptions, and the colonial administrations made sure hunting

The 'splendid' trophy: an elephant's foot trash can for the study! Men who skin animals are part of the authorized Jeep safaris costing 15,000–20,000 dollars.

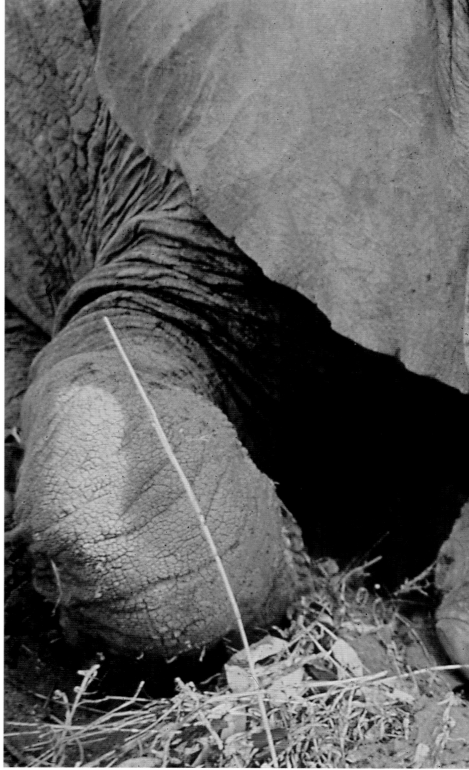

laws and licenses were complied with. The number of elephants shot during regulated hunts was limited in Africa. The alarming reduction in numbers was due to other factors.

Today elephant-hunting is banned in Kenya and most other African states. Hundreds of white hunters became unemployed or started to just accompany visitors on photo-safaris. Hunting professionals had always taken action against poachers, but because the former are no longer present in the hunting ground poachers now have a fairly free hand. It is scarcely possible for the few, badly-paid local gamekeepers to safeguard the protected areas effectively. Furthermore, some poor gamekeepers with large families succumb to the

Destroyed for his tusks. The powerful bull has collapsed; blood pours from his mouth; an open eye stares accusingly.

A sad 'hunting still life:' rifle, prized ivory and flowing blood are all that is left.

temptation themselves in order to increase their own supply of food a little.

The era of elephant-hunting has come to an end in Africa. However, killings have to be carried out when elephant herds become too large in the limited space of protected areas. Nature no longer regulates itself there, but these sad procedures are not real hunting. Passionate hunters or trophy collectors must produce a very large amount of money in order to obtain, more or less legally, a license to shoot an elephant: such as in Zimbabwe, in Botswana's Okavango swamps, or in Chad where France's former president Giscard d'Estaing used to hunt, and in some other poor states.

# The image of the elephant in Africa

The rain forests of West and Central Africa have left their mark on the appearance and way of life of forest elephants. They are smaller than their mighty cousins on the hot, dry steppes. They have thinned out the impenetrable, humid areas of equatorial regions and opened them up to man. Their fixed paths are carved through the jungle like skillfully-planned road systems, and are still used today. West and Central African tribes incorporated the highly-respected forest elephant in their myths, and their nature and ancestor worship. Its image was created in an original abstract way and frequently modified. Modern art has often been inspired by African forms of expression. The elephant has even shown unprecedented adaptability in mastering the desert. Small groups of tall animals live in barren 'corners' of the inhospitable, blazing hot desert on Namibia's north coast which medieval seafarers called the 'skeleton coast.'

Detail of a painted wooden bow of a ship, Cameroon, 19th century. Staatliches Museum für Völkerkunde, Munich

The wood-carving adorning the bow of a canoe is one of the most interesting pieces of old Duala art. The Dualas live in the mangrove swamps around the port of Douala named after them. The bow decoration, called 'tange,' was acquired by Max Buchner in 1884. He represented Germany's claim to Cameroon on Bismarck's orders.

# The kingdom of the forest elephants

The dense rain forests and swampy jungle of equatorial Africa, and above all of the Congo Basin, are the kingdom of the forest elephants (*Loxodonta africana cyclotis*). They are shy animals, and are difficult to get a glimpse of in the rampant thickets, in the eternal dusk under the canopy of leaves. Around 200,000 animals are believed to have survived the terrible culls of the 'seventies and 'eighties. Moreover they are forced into small areas and their existence is threatened just like that of the original inhabitants of the forest oceans, the pygmies.

According to the latest research forest elephants supposedly developed from the mighty savannah African elephants approximately 3.5 million years ago. As already mentioned in the chapter on the 'Anatomy of our ancient giant,' with a shoulder height of around 8 feet they are considerably smaller than the savannah elephants. They have thinner but harder tusks, small rounded ears and a darker and more hairy skin.

The social behavior of forest elephants is no different from that of their relations in the savannah. They are gregarious animals who need company, and they maintain the same solidarity. The density of the rain forests does not allow large herds to develop as they do on open grassland. Forest elephants roam in small groups of five to eight animals, but are bonded to larger units. They communicate with each other over large distances in low frequency ranges of 14 to 16 hertz, inaudible to the human ear. Like their cousins in the savannah they linger as if in mourning when they come across the remains of other elephants.

Forest elephants always have an abundance of food to choose from which allows them to be discriminating. They prefer leaves and twigs from plants that are particularly rich in calcium and protein, and their favorite food is fruit. When the giant seed capsules of the Strynos-liane, which grows in the leaf canopy of the giant trees, crash to the ground, the elephants pick up the scent from a great distance and head straight for the spoils. Only elephants are able to break open the half-inch thick shell of the fruit, the seed of which surrounds a strong-smelling, soapy mucilage. African fishermen use the mixture to stun fish; it is a medicine to witch doctors and a feast to elephants.

Forest elephants have long disappeared from the coastal regions around the Gulf of Guinea. They have been forced into the hinterland and wiped out in parts except for small groups. Devastating deforestation in Cameroon and the Congo is cutting further and further into their remaining habitat. Up until now forest elephants have only once been bred successfully, in Abidjan (Ivory Coast) although breeding programs still continue.

Forest elephants are shy animals who live together in small groups. They are difficult to make out in the dense jungle and in the half-light of the primeval forests. Leading cows attack suddenly if they think their group is threatened.

The image of the elephant in Africa

# Gardeners in the tropical jungle

Over hundreds of thousands of years a close association has developed between certain plants and animals, to their mutual benefit. This is called symbiosis. In the West African rain forests there are a number of hard-shelled fruits that can be forced open only by elephants and are broken down in their digestive tract. The animal's feces then provide ideal conditions for the seed kernels to germinate. An example of this is the huge makoré tree, the wood of which is much-sought after for export. Its large, rock-hard nuts draw elephants from a great distance as if by magic to feast on them.

With the decimation and, to a great extent, wiping out of forest elephants around the Gulf of Guinea the valuable makoré tree has also become a rarity there. Experts from the Worldwide Fund for Nature fear that about 40 percent of the giant trees that form the leaf canopy in the rain forests will disappear if forest elephants become extinct.

Elephants eat all types of fruit. They are 'gardeners in the rain forest;' they are responsible for sowing seeds of a large number of species suitable for the equatorial conditions. Scientific investigations found seeds in nine out of ten feces. The elephants that feed in the thick jungle also help to shape the environment. Their eating habits allow light to reach the undergrowth, and their well-trodden, fixed paths provided a road network for autochthonous tribes for thousands of years – and are still used today. The planners of many African roads or railroad routes were able to use the paths of elephants whose instincts had anticipated the calculations needed for laying an even track.

However, despite the usefulness of the forest elephants their future does not look bright. The ruinous deforestation policies of international timber companies are continuing in the rain forests that have already been reduced alarmingly. Soil erosion is also eating away at them. Tracks for the trucks that take away the logs are cutting up the elephants' retreats. It is difficult to prevent poaching in the vicinity of the timber sites. It can be expected that mineral resources will be exploited for profit, and a rapidly growing population – Africa is experiencing an annual growth rate of about 3 percent – requires more living space.

The Worldwide Fund for Nature and other organizations concerned with saving the rain forest and with preservation areas for forest elephants are involved in a difficult struggle with the various influential interest groups.

Only elephants can break open the rock-hard nuts of certain primeval forest trees. The seeds consumed with the flesh of the fruit are planted out in the feces.

Opposite:
The churned-up ground of the clearing in which the forest elephants dig contains essential minerals. The animals regularly go to such places to eat earth.

The image of the elephant in Africa

## 'Water' and pygmy elephants

Hunters and native peoples claim to have sighted 'water elephants' some time ago in inaccessible swamp regions in the central Congo. These animals supposedly lead hidden lives in the water and are excellent swimmers and divers. No evidence has yet been provided to support this theory.

All elephants love water and are good swimmers and divers. The Congo Basin interspersed with river courses and swampy ponds is a very suitable habitat for elephants whose forefathers led an amphibious life by and in the water. In the Congo region forest elephants certainly make the most of the opportunity to bathe.

There have also been reports from hunters and African tribes of pygmy forms of the forest elephant. The Pygmy people even have a special description of pygmy elephants distinguishing them from forest ones. Fully-grown bulls should have a maximum shoulder height of 6.2 feet and tusks that reach the ground.

The living conditions under the leafy canopy of the primeval forests favor animals that are small in stature. Are they, though, a special development of the forest elephant which is smaller in stature than their savannah cousins to adapt to their environment? Many experts believe that they may be ill or stunted animals rather than a branch of the savannah or a separate type altogether.

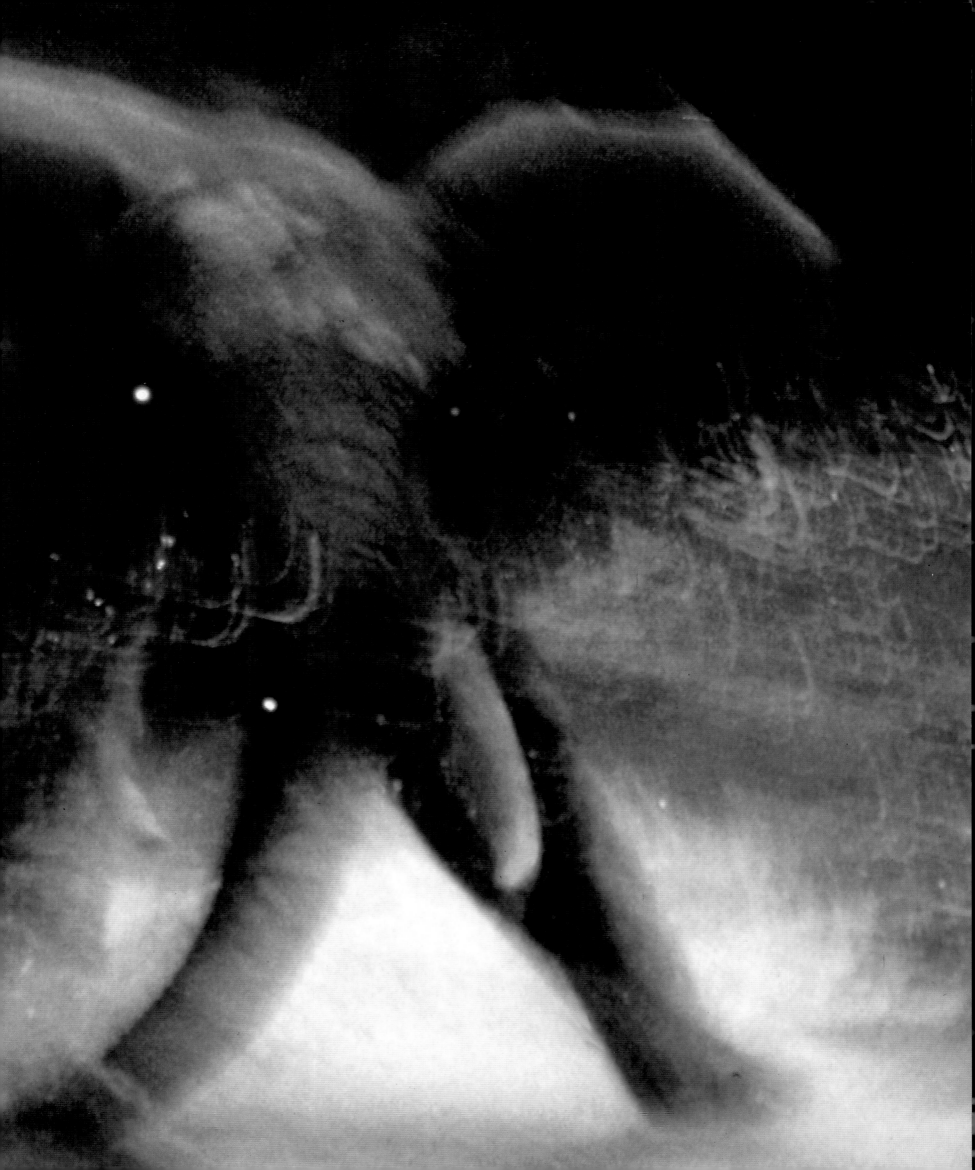

# Namibia's desert elephants

Previous double page:
In the eternal dusk of the primeval forest, forest elephants are rarely caught on camera. Their leading cows are extremely vigilant and attack suddenly if they think their group is threatened.

The elephant, who loves water above all else, has also mastered an environment that seems completely unfavorable to its needs and its nature: the swelteringly hot and inhospitable desert along the north coast of Namibia. The seafarers of the Middle Ages gave the hostile and unfriendly coastal strip the descriptive name 'skeleton coast.' The cold ocean current along the coast brings only fog and nighttime dew, which satisfy the drinking needs of many small coastal animals.

Rain falls only very rarely. When it does it fills the groundwater reservoirs and allows water to flow in the few dried-up riverbeds for a short time. This is sufficient for sparse vegetation on the banks and for the watering holes and ponds which are sometimes brackish and suitable only for bathing. The leaves of the acacia trees which elephants pick from the thorny branches are the animals' favorite food, together with tangy foliage and grasses. If they are hungry they will also make do with bitter tamarisk shrubs, if necessary.

Zoologists and animal photographers have often searched and waited for months to see desert elephants. Because they need a large amount of food and the desert offers only a meager supply the animals are always on the move. They have to undertake journeys of twelve to thirty miles a day through sand and over gravel deserts to reach another feeding or drinking place. Their reliable sense of direction helps them as they move through constantly-changing dune landscapes in which the wind soon erases any tracks. It is a stroke of luck when animal photographers manage to find an exception like the one shown here: desert elephants rushing towards the water-hole for which they have been searching.

They are tall, shy animals with a lean build. Their columnar legs seem more slender than those of the elephants in the savannah; the soles of their feet give the impression of being wide and are suitable for moving in soft sand. According to a report in the 'National Geographic Magazine' the tough beasts can survive without water for two to four days at a time.

Right:
With the scent of the nearby watering place in their trunks the two elephants increase the tempo after hours of walking through the red-hot sandy desert. Half sliding they hurry down the steep slope of the dune. Desert elephants can cover forty to fifty miles a day, and can survive without water for three to four days.

Drawing by the English naturalist Sir James Emerson Tennent from his book 'The Wild Elephant,' 1867

The elephant can descend slopes of 45 degrees. It first kneels down at the edge of the steep slope, its chest supported on the ground. Then it moves one front foot forward and digs a step if necessary. The second foot then follows …

The image of the elephant in Africa

# Skeleton Coast National Park

Today a 300 mile long and 19 to 30 mile wide strip of the inhospitable Kaoko Veld between the coast and mountain region is a strictly protected area for desert elephants: the Skeleton Coast National Park. The animals' paths naturally lead over the man-made limits of the protected area into regions in which there are also some oasis settlements, which creates various problems.

In the Namib Desert Stone Age rock engravings have been discovered that show elephants as well as other animals. It is not known whether elephants have inhabited the desert region continuously since then. European explorers first reported elephants in the Namib Desert in 1793. There can never have been a large number of such elephants in the swelteringly hot desert because of the limited amount of food.

In 1970 the number of desert elephants was estimated at around 300. They live mainly in the north of the protected area around the dry riverbeds of the Hoanib and Hoarusib. The 250 rhinoceros also shared the meager food in the carved up river channels with the elephants. The latter use their tusks, trunks and front legs to dig holes to the groundwater, not just for themselves but for other animals too. In 1980–82 poachers carried out a barbaric slaughter of the elephants and rhinoceros, at a time when they were also having to endure an extremely dry period. After the slaughter, 152 elephant carcasses were found. The number of desert elephants dwindled to around eighty. Only about sixty rhinoceros survived.

Today the numbers of the undemanding desert elephants has risen again to around 120. There are a few dozen young calves in the small herds, which is a hopeful sign. However, Namibia's desert elephant is still right at the top of the world list of endangered species.

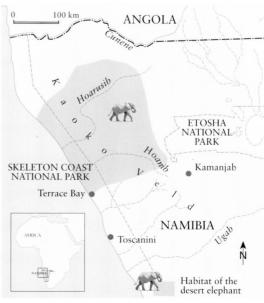

Map of the 'Skeleton Coast National Park,' the hostile world of the desert elephant surrounded by the sand dunes and stony deserts of the Namib.

# The elephant in Saharan rock pictures

During the Ice Age the Sahara was an extremely dry desert. Following the end of this cold period some 10,000 years ago it became a green area with shallow lakes, bush vegetation, trees and wadis which bore water for several months at a time. Environmental conditions were probably similar to those in today's Sahel region. Elephants and other animals inhabited the wide areas from the south.

African hunting tribes, who closely followed the animals, immortalized the image of the gray beast in rock 10,000 years ago. The forms of expression of the Stone Age artists changed over the millennia. It is only possible to date the developmental phases roughly. Research in the Sahara is still ongoing. So far, the oldest pictures of elephants are rock engravings from the so-called 'age of wild animals' or 'hunters,' the period from 12,000–8,000 years ago. A wealth of large and very lifelike pictures of animals, frequently including elephants, was found in southwest Libya, in the fissured and at that time lush Messak. The pictures had been carved into the rock by a surprisingly steady hand. The outline sketches of crocodiles and hippopotamuses suggest a rich supply of water from lakes and rivers.

Towards the end of the age of hunters a special development occurred in the mountainous region

Elephant, age of hunters,
7th/6th millennium BC,
rock engraving.
Gonoa, Tibesti Mountains, Chad

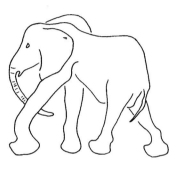

Elephant, age of hunters,
7th/6th millennium BC,
tracing of a rock engraving.
Wadi Arrechin, Fazzan, Libya

The Stone Age hunters of the Sahara, which was lush savannah, came into close contact with the wild animals. Their outline sketches of elephants carved in hard rock are surprisingly lifelike.

of Tassili-n'-Ajjer, southern Algeria, referred to by scientists as the 'roundhead period' after a stylistic element of human representations: round heads with no distinct features sitting directly on top of stylized bodies. Dwellings under overhanging rocks and in rock caves were decorated. From the scenes represented there, which are difficult to interpret, the people appear to have paid homage to animistic cults. Pictures of wild animals or of elephants are rare.

During a dry period lasting from 6000–5000 BC wild animals and hunters probably disappeared. This was followed in the Sahara, which was now full of vegetation again, by the age of 'cowherds,' which lasted until about 2400 BC. The more progressive tribes, who had migrated, mainly reproduced domestic animals and everyday scenes; they painted rock walls and also carved outlines in stone. After another dry period starting in 2000 BC there was the so-called 'age of horses' from around 1500 BC until the birth of Christ. This was characterized by stylized drawings of stick men. These were probably conquering seafaring peoples who brought metal weapons, horses and carts with them. The 'age of camels' which began around the birth of Christ was shaped by Berber tribes. Elephants inhabited the forests of the Atlas mountains up until the classical Roman period.

During the cultural phases mentioned the image of the elephant was also immortalized in rock engravings and paintings in many other regions of North Africa, for example in Tibesti (Chad) and Enndi (Niger). Outline sketches of elephants carved into rock were also produced during this Stone Age period in Nubia, present-day Sudan. They were more crude than the Saharan pictures. Rock sketches have also been preserved near Akba close to the second Nile cataract.

Elephants with a man,
Age of hunters,
7th/6th millennium BC,
copy of a rock engraving,
Tassili-n'-Ajjer, Algeria.
Collection Henri Lhote,
Musée de l'Homme, Paris

Cow elephant protects her calf
from an attacking lion,
Age of hunters,
7th/6th millennium BC,
tracing of a rock engraving.
Ain-Sfasafa, Algeria

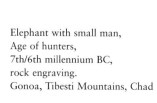

Elephant with small man,
Age of hunters,
7th/6th millennium BC,
rock engraving.
Gonoa, Tibesti Mountains, Chad

The image of the elephant in Africa

Above and below:
Elephant-hunting scenes,
6th millennium BC,
tracing of a rock painting.
Domoshawa, Zimbabwe

The elephant has already been
hounded to exhaustion by the
horde. The quickly felled beast
will feed a whole clan.

Elephant and men,
9th millennium BC,
rock painting.
Mutoko, Zimbabwe

Detail from an unfinished wall
painting discovered in a large rock
cave. The elephant has already
been hit by arrows.

Tracing of a rock painting,
7th millennium BC.
Inanke, Zimbabwe

Human figures, partly in family
groups, with an elephant outline
drawn above them.

## Stone Age art of the Bushmen

Elephant-hunt,
6th millennium BC,
rock painting.
Zombepata, Zimbabwe

Elephant-hunting by a horde.
In the midst of the action the men
surround the two animals; they
provoke them, flee and shoot. The
Stone Age artist mastered the
depiction of movement.

In subsaharan Africa, where research into the prehistoric period is still in progress, rock engravings and paintings found at several locations bear witness to Stone Age elephant-hunting. The finds are particularly widespread in Zimbabwe as well as on the wide plateau between the Limpopo River and the Zambezi, which is interspersed with caves and overhanging rock formed from granite deposits, a favored place for artists.

The hunters and rock artists were small Bushmen. According to radiocarbon dating the rock pictures were created some 5,000–13,000 years ago. Ground iron oxides were used. These produced shades of color ranging from deep red to reddish brown. White was obtained from kaolin (china clay). Animal fat and blood were used as binding agents. Upper Paleolithic artists improvised hunting scenes using their fingers, sticks, and animals' tails, unconcerned about the structure and unevenness of the rock walls, but managing to create surprisingly detailed work.

Elephants were hunted in hordes, like the mammoth was in cold Europe. At first spears with fire-hardened tips were used as weapons. Bows and arrows came later; it seems certain that they were used in hunting at least 14,000 years ago.

The oldest evidence of human artistic skills was found in East Africa. In the Upper Paleolithic period southern Europe was particularly synonymous with artistic and general progress, as the magnificent cave paintings in northern Spain and southwest France verify (see also 'The elephant in Stone Age art').

Right:
Elephant with calf
7th millennium BC
Tracing of a rock painting
Bindura, Zimbabwe

Outline sketches, which have not been colored in, of a cow elephant protecting her young. The hands below the animal group may have a magic or ritualistic significance.

## The forerunners of Yoruba artists

The history of art is difficult to uncover in tropical West Africa where the climate and insects soon destroy even hard materials. Only a few wood carvings have survived more than 100, and at the most 200 years. Looking back further we only find objects made from terra cotta and metals.

According to radiocarbon dating the oldest evidence to date of West African art comes from the period between 500 BC and AD 200. It is 'Nok terra cotta,' named after the village of Nok in northern Nigeria where it was found. At the same time fragments of an elephant's head from the 3rd century BC were also found. The elephant was a multifarious motif throughout the ages.

After the Nok period there is a 1,000-year knowledge gap until the royal cultures of the Yoruba people on the Niger which blossomed in the 15th/16th century. The art of bronze casting spread from the holy city of Ife, the seat of the 'oni,' the religious leader of the Yoruba, through the kingdom of Benin and along the Gold Coast.

Bronze heads, elephant figures and terra cotta pieces were found in the former palace of the 'oni'. They reveal a high standard of arts and crafts. Stone was only used rarely in West African art. A few roughly carved figures and slightly worked monoliths were found at holy places in the West African rain forests.

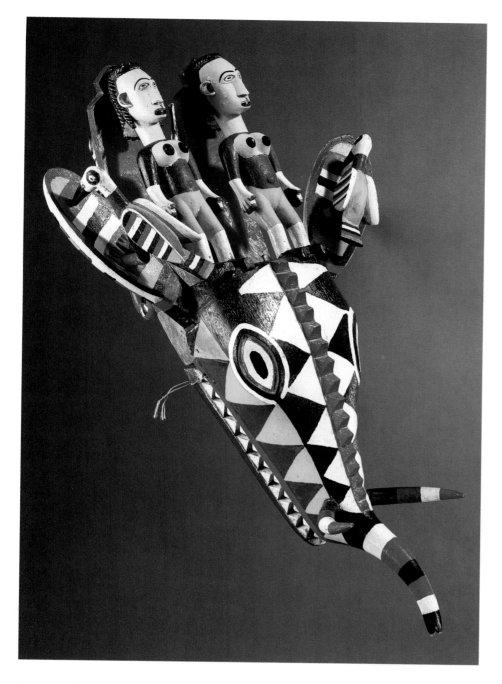

'Sama kun' elephant mask,
Bamana, Mali, modern era,
wood.
Length 95cm
Fowler Museum of Cultural
History, University of California,
Los Angeles

Masques are performed by youth
societies from the Bamana people
in Mali twice a year at the
beginning of the planting season
in May and in October during
large village festivities. The
societies are made up of young
men between the ages of fourteen
and thirty-five as well as young
girls from the age of fourteen until
they marry. Masque performances
consist of ten or more sequences,
interspersed with dance and
music. Each scene is dominated by
one character mask which finds
expression in mimed dance.

'Sama kun' elephant mask,
Bamana youth society, Mali,
modern era,
wood.
Length 80cm
James A. Monger Collection,
New Orleans

The Bamana in Central Mali are
farmers today. Earlier, when there
were still large forests and herds
of elephants, they were regarded
as experienced hunters. Today
youth societies act out
elephant-hunts.

'Sama kun' elephant mask,
Bamana, Mali,
modern era,
wood, fabric.
Length 73cm
On permanent loan from
Jerome I. Joss, Fowler Museum of
Cultural History, University of
California, Los Angeles

The Bamana 'sama kun' elephant
masks are often painted with
colorful stripy patterns. Animal
figures are added to make them
more visually attractive.

# Gold elephants of the Ashanti

Brass and gold work once flourished among the Akan peoples in the coastal region of Ghana (earlier 'Gold Coast'). The country was rich; gold was panned in abundance in rivers and streams. Gold-plated brass weights were used to weigh the gold-dust, which was used as a form of payment. The weights were shaped in the form of delicate and elaborately worked figures. Elephants were often represented, but the animals were wiped out to a large extent in the coastal area in the 19th century. Later craftsmen never saw an elephant.

The most powerful Akan territory ruled by chieftains was the Ashanti kingdom which was formed and expanded in the 17th century. To the Ashanti the elephant was a regal animal. The king's regalia included the golden state stool supported by an elephant. Elephant skin was used to produce royal drums. Only senior dignitaries were allowed to own trumpets made from tusks. Parts of the state treasury were finished with jewelry with which the king lavishly adorned himself to emphasize his position.

Gold weights worked in the shape of animals were symbols for common proverbs or parables. They were used as discreet references. The allusion to an elephant figure could, therefore, evoke the saying: "He who follows an elephant will not get wet from the dew," which means that whoever is protected by a powerful person has nothing to fear.

A counselor to the Fante chieftain with a gold-plated ceremonial staff which brings to mind the proverb: "Only the elephant can pull down the palm tree." The staff was carved by Osei Bonsu c. 1950 and is part of the state treasury of the highest Fante chieftain of Mankesim.

Gold weight,
Akan, modern era,
brass.
Length 7cm
Collection of Maurice Bonnefoy

The birds on the back of the 7cm-long elephant symbolize mutual dependency between ruler and people.

Gold weight,
Akan, modern era,
brass.
Length 13.5cm
Collection of Maurice Bonnefoy

Rigidly stylized gold weights with lavish ornamental pattern. Gold-dust was used as a means of payment among the Ashanti and other Akan peoples. As weights were not standardized people would take small gold balances and sets of weights with them when shopping at the market.

The image of the elephant in Africa

Wooden spoons,
northwest Cameroon.
Left 13.9cm
Right 26.6cm
Ernst Winkler Collection

Typical wood carvings from the
workshops of the Baoulé people,
in northwest Cameroon. The
handles are decorated with
animals' heads; on the spoon on
the left a stylized and unusual
elephant's head.

Fly-whisk,
Baoulé, Ivory Coast,
wood, gold-plated.
Length of the pommel c. 20cm
Overall length 92cm
Gift from Judith Timyan, Fowler
Museum of Cultural History,
University of California, Los
Angeles

Sumptuously worked fly-whisk
with elephant tail hairs (see
below): crown insignia of African
kings. A dainty elephant with
lattice flanks, ornamental pattern
and mini-trunk adorns the
pommel (see left).

Decorated helmet-type mask
attachment, craft work of the
Baoulé people who live on the
Ivory Coast.

## Symbol of royal power and position

Among the most beautiful elephant masks of West
Africa are those made by the Baoulé people who
live in the northwest grassland of Cameroon. The
rigidly stylized and skillfully carved dance and
helmet masks were reserved for chieftains, male
societies, and secret societies of hunters. The
elephant was regarded as a symbol of superior
power; elephant motifs revealed royal office. The
masks were worn during funeral ceremonies and
annual dance festivals.

Today they are mass-produced and fill the
souvenir shops. The original, highly imaginatively
stylized, brass or clay elephant pipe bowls, and the
elephant decorations on large groove drums show
great skill in arts and crafts.

Elephant pipe,
Bamun, Cameroon,
c. 1900,
brass.
Height 17cm
Eduard von der Heydt Collection,
Museum Rietberg, Zurich

This brass elephant pipe was probably a status symbol with no functional use. It had a metal reed mouthpiece and a wooden or ivory handle.

'Nkum nsuo' elephant mask, grassland, Cameroon, modern era, wood.
Height 79cm
Private collection

This wooden helmet mask belonged to a male society or a chieftain's family from Cameroon's grassland. During masked processions the elephant brought up the rear to provide magical protection against disaster and evil spells.

# Elephant masks in Cameroon's grassland

The tribes living in Cameroon's grassland typically used elephant representations for different shaped masks. Huge elephant constructions made from bamboo frames covered with fabric and palm bast, and often even with real tusks, were put on by two men who carried them around. Helmet masks decorated with beads were the most common.

Those attending the festival only watched during scenes with ritual significance; they did not join in the dancing. The most colorful sight was provided by dance groups in fantastically decorated elephant costumes. Scenes were often performed exclusively by secret male societies. The elephant figure adopted demonstrated strength and power.

# The glass bead masks of the elephant society

The members of the Bamileke elephant society in the northwest grasslands of Cameroon create their religious and dance masks in original, fantastic glass beadwork. In colonial Africa glass beads were a highly valued commodity and luxury possession. Glass bead jewelry was a sign of wealth and brought standing and influence, essential for admission to an exclusive secret male society. The religious high point of funeral ceremonies and masked festivals, which could last a week, was the appearance of groups armed with spears. Even today secret male societies exercise considerable influence in subsaharan Africa.

Masked dance of a secret male society in fantastic elephant costumes in Cheferie Bandjoun. Some typical examples of the glass bead culture in Cameroon's grassland. The embroidered trunks of the elephant masks are 1.5m long.

Bamileke elephant mask, Cameroon, modern era, Plant fibers, fabric with beads. Length 148.5cm Fowler Museum of Cultural History, University of California, Los Angeles

Opposite:
Fantastic elephant mask of a respected member of the 'aka,' the secret elephant society. The huge hat is decorated with red parrot feathers. A hat with a diameter of over 1m is reserved for the chieftain, the 'fon.' The trunk embroidered with glass beads hangs over the flowing garment; the ear pieces are embroidered in the shape of wheels.

Chieftain's stool, grassland, Cameroon, early 20th century, wood, fabric, glass beads. Height 30cm Diameter of seat 25.5cm On permanent loan from Jerome I. Joss, Fowler Museum of Cultural History, University of California, Los Angeles

The stool covered with fabric and glass beads has an elephant caryatid. Bamileke kingdom, grassland, Cameroon

Chieftain's stool, Cameroon, c. 1912, wood, fabric, glass beads. Height 40.6cm Field Museum of Natural History, Chicago

A two-headed, stylized elephant caryatid supports the chieftain's stool. The Bamileke craftsmen worked with rod-shaped glass beads that were highly valued.

# Elephant stools and glass bead masks

In Cameroon's grassland tribal kings and chieftains used to sit enthroned on elephant stools which were reserved for them as attributes of their position and power. There were two different styles of stool. In the northwest of the grassland rulers would sit on stools with carved, stylized elephant caryatids when they had an audience or during important public events. In the southern regions craftsmen mainly made elephant stools with fabric covers embroidered with glass beads.

Chieftain's stool, Bafoussam, Cameroon, 1905, wood, fabric, glass beads. Height 134.6cm Linden-Museum, Stuttgart

Colorful glass beads form the structure of the elephant caryatid of the chieftain's stool out of which a human figure grows, the significance of which is unknown. The figure, which serves as the stool back, is possibly meant to be a royal ancestor, or perhaps even a loyal vassal.

Elephant mask,
grassland, Cameroon, modern era,
wood, fabric, glass beads.
M. Zarember, Tambaran Gallery,
New York

Elephant-shaped stopper from a
palm wine calabash (detail).
Height with stopper 50.8cm
Field Museum of Natural
History, Chicago

The bottle gourd and the wooden
frame of the stopper are covered
in fabric which is decorated with
glass beads.

Elephant headdress,
grassland, Cameroon, modern era,
wood, fabric, glass beads.
Height 55.88cm
The Faletti Family Collection

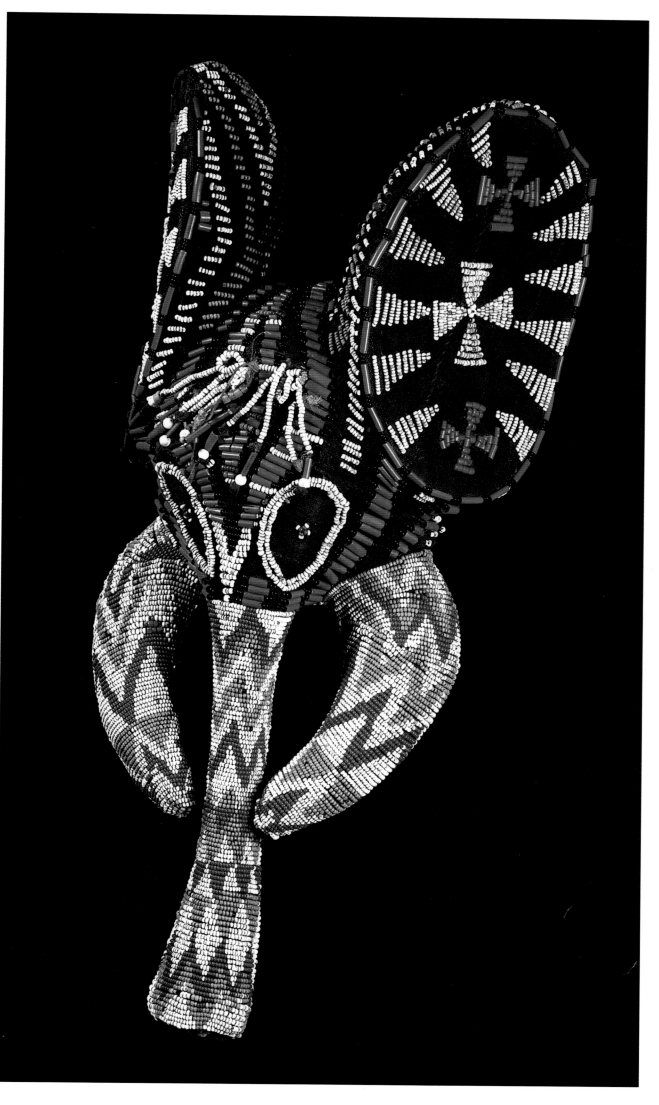

# Elephant motifs adorn house walls

Wall painting with elephants on a court house of the Mangbettu who live in the northern Congo Basin. White, black and ocher decorations with figures are the typical form of expression in paintings of these artistic people. The tall Mangbettu came from Sudan in the 18th/19th century. They founded a sultanate in the Congo.

Opposite:
Painted house wall in a village inhabited by the people of the Mbere near Fort Archambault, Chad. The depiction of the elephant with child defies interpretation. A magic symbol or general warning of danger?

The image of the elephant in Africa

# The 'white gold' trade

Ivory, always sought-after and often prized more highly than gold, has been the object of a hugely profitable trade since prehistoric times. Some exquisite works of art have been carved from this costly material. For the elephant, however, those proud, precious tusks constitute a fatal burden. The lust for 'white gold' and vast profits has repeatedly led to barbaric slaughter among the primeval giants of forest and steppe. As long as it was simply a question of keeping a small band of highly qualified ivory craftsmen in raw material, and tusk loss through natural causes was still a significant source of supply, moderate hunting represented no danger to the breed. Only recently has the trade come to threaten the elephant's very survival, as commercial greed demands vast quantities of raw ivory to fuel the lucrative and increasingly questionable mass manufacture of luxury trinkets – items for which ivory ought really to be too expensive a material. For many former uses, such as billiard balls and piano keys, other suitable materials are now available.

Ludwig Walther (1890–1972), *St. George fighting the dragon*, State gift for Queen Elizabeth II, 1965.
Height 22cm
Deutsches Elfenbeinmuseum, Erbach/Odenwald, Germany

In 1965, when Britain's Queen Elizabeth II visited Germany, the provincial government of Hesse presented its honored guest with a gift of ivory: a statuette of dragon-slayer St. George, England's patron saint, by renowned ivory-carver Ludwig Walther of the German and European Ivory Center in Erbach/Odenwald, south of Frankfurt.

Opposite:
Tusk bearer in the Congo. An international ban on the ivory trade in 1989 tried, by starving the gray market, to combat the lust for 'white gold' that during the 1970s and 1980s had led to a fearful massacre of elephants in Africa. The ban should not be seen as a general outlawing of this precious material; skilled ivory-carvers have for centuries been using ivory to produce exquisite works of art.

# Phoenician ivory for Solomon's temple

In ancient times the trade in elephant tusk was controlled by the Phoenicians, who sailed the Mediterranean and the Red Sea from their urban centers on the Lebanese-Syrian coast. Phoenicians were supplying the pharaohs with ivory from Syria and the legendary land of 'Punt' on the Red Sea as early as the 16th and 15th centuries BC. Another customer was the King of Judah and Israel, Solomon (965–926 BC), who for his famous temple purchased not only cedarwood but also 'white gold' from the Phoenicians, themselves outstanding ivory-carvers on an industrial scale. With their highly-developed mercantile spirit, these bold seafarers had an eye for maximum profit. They bequeathed their capitalistic form of economy (Phoenician money-lenders charged 33.3 percent interest) to the colonial city of Carthage, which had been founded on the north coast of Africa in 814 BC.

Around 460 BC, during the heyday of Carthage, a seafarer named Hanno took a large fleet of 'penteconters' (ships with fifty oarsmen) on a voyage of discovery down the west coast of Africa. The ships apparently also carried settlers for a colony to be founded there. It seems likely that the expedition reached the gold and elephant areas fringing the Gulf of Guinea. Following Hanno's return, a panel bearing an account of the voyage was set up in the temple of the Phoenician god Melqart, who was also the patron of seafarers. A surviving Greek translation of the panel is one of the earliest remaining geographical documents left from ancient times.

Following on from the Phoenicians, in the Hellenistic 3rd century BC the Egyptian Diadochan dynasty of the Ptolemies established trading settlements on the Eritrean-Ethiopian coast, from which they imported war elephants and ivory amongst other supplies.

The Carthaginians (called 'Punics' by the Romans) had access to their own bush elephants in the valleys of the Atlas, which they either hunted themselves, or had the indigenous Numidians hunt, for ivory as a trading commodity. The taming and training of elephants as war engines developed only much later, during the power-struggle with Rome, a long time after other nations began using them.

After the destruction of Carthage during the Third Punic War in 146 BC, the ivory trade was controlled by Rome, now master of the seas and trade routes of much of the ancient world. There was a huge demand for this luxury material in the wealthy Rome of the imperial age. Rome's shipowners and merchants bought most of their ivory from Axum, the great trading center and holy city of the Ethiopians, where Ethiopia's emperors were later crowned. The precious material was shipped from the port of Adulis, where the ships of the Ptolemaic kings of Egypt had once put in. The tusks came from the nearby hinterland of Eritrea, on whose Red Sea coast large herds of elephants were sighted as late as the 6th century, both from Somalia and from the mountain forests of Ethiopia. Rome also purchased ivory from the Atlas region of Northwest Africa, where the last elephants disappeared in the 5th–6th centuries.

Elephant, Nisa,
Greco-Iranian,
2nd century BC,
ivory.
Hermitage, St. Petersburg

The find referred to in the text also included this half-figure of a charging elephant, trunk upraised. The piece was probably a drinking-horn attachment.

Inlay, 9th century BC,
ivory.
Height 7.5cm
Israel Museum, Jerusalem

This inlay, carved from ivory, is attributed to the time of King Ahab, who ruled over the reduced kingdom of Israel a hundred years after Solomon, from 871 to 852 BC. It is thought to have belonged to a piece of intarsia furniture decoration from the palace that Ahab built near his capital, Samaria. Known as the 'House of Ivory,' the palace is even mentioned in the Bible (1 Kings 23: 39). The intarsia found there combine Egyptian and Phoenician stylistic elements. Artists and builders from Egypt and Phoenicia had earlier spent seven years erecting Solomon's temple and palace in Jerusalem.

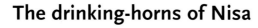

# The drinking-horns of Nisa

Other partners in the ivory business during the Hellenistic period were more recent, up-and-coming peripheral peoples of the Middle Eastern cultural region. A special part was played by the Parthians, a tribe of Iranian nomads who settled to the east of the Caspian Sea (Iran/Eran = Aryan). Under King Mithridates I (171–138 BC), the horse-riding Parthians became the dominant power on the Middle Eastern land bridge. They controlled the famous 'Great Silk Road,' the trade route to China, where there was always a large demand for ivory, put to various uses.

A find from the early Parthian period included forty large, heavy drinking-horns (rhytons) made of pieces of elephant's tusk. These were probably used for liturgical purposes. They were found in a sealed chamber in a quadrangle in the fortified city of Nisa, which lay to the east of the Caspian Sea. The carvings around the upper rim combine motives from the world of the Greek gods and heroes with Oriental decorative elements. In the Hellenistic world of the Middle East the Olympian gods of Greece became merged with local deities: distinctions between the Iranian fertility goddess Anahita and the Greek Artemis, between Mithras and Apollo, and between Zoroaster's supreme deity Ahura Mazda and Zeus gradually disappeared. Figures attached to the bottoms of rhytons include the Asiatic griffin, centaurs, and different deities.

The military might of the Parthians rested on swift bands of armored horsemen. The war elephants captured in the conquered parts of the Seleucid Kingdom were more useful as working animals. The Parthians were great builders (particularly skilled at constructing huge vaults) and needed a lot of labor. Since their ceremonial buildings were constructed in brick and the former Parthian sphere of influence was subsequently overrun by wave after wave of conquerors, only ruins of their efforts remain.

The Parthians (who lost Syria in 64 BC, when it became a Roman province), like the Seleucids before them, made a major contribution to developing east-west trade routes. The most important of these at the time was the 'Great Silk Road,' which ran from Antioch on the Mediterranean, through Seleucia on the Tigris, before turning north and skirting the Elburz Mountains on its way to the oasis city of Merv. From there a choice of two routes, south and north of the Altai Mountains, led into central Asia. To protect the caravan staging-post of Merv from raiders, the Parthians built a large wall right round the entire oasis.

A caravan journey from the Mediterranean to China and back took between six and eight years. From China came silk, gold, and a flow of artistic and technical ideas. To China the caravans took

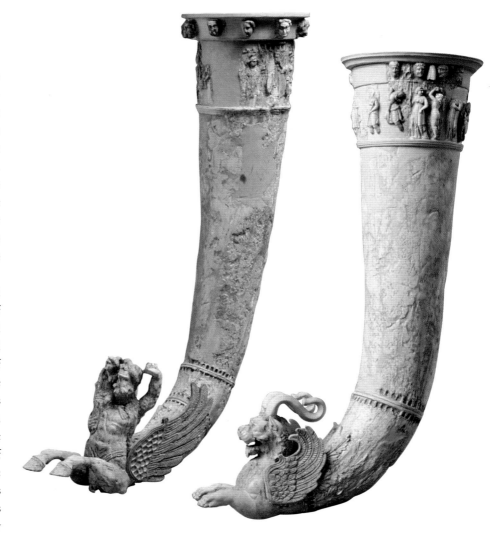

Roman glass, luxury items, ivory, Arab horses, and various useful plants including almond trees and peach trees. The Parthians made huge profits from this passing trade.

All attempts by the Romans to bring the Parthians to their knees met with failure. Cassius, who shared power in a triumvirate with Caesar and Pompey and was Governor of Syria, suffered a crushing defeat in 56 BC. Disregarding the existence of a peace treaty, he had set out with seven legions (some 40,000 men) to extend his power to India. The Parthians' mounted light archers, together with their armored cavalry (who like the later knights of the European Middle Ages wore scale armor and fought with two-handed lances), wrought havoc among the Roman army. Around 20,000 men were killed, 10,000 taken prisoner, and the rest fled. Cassius himself lost his life. Not until the time of Emperor Augustus was it possible to negotiate the eventual return of the lost standards.

In 36 BC Marcus Antonius, Cleopatra's official lover under the Ptolemaic system of polygamy, likewise failed in his attempt to force the kings of the Middle East into subjection. Having set out with 100,000 men, he brought only about 40,000 back to Syria.

In the post-Christian era, the Parthian Empire merged into the Persian kingdom of the Sasanian (Sassanid) dynasty, which succumbed to Islamic Arabs around AD 640–650.

Two elephant rhytons, Nisa, Greco-Iranian, 2nd century BC, each carved from a single tusk, Heights 53cm and 63cm Historical Museum, Ashkhabad, Turkmenistan

The carvings around the upper rims of the drinking-horns of Nisa combine motives from the world of the Greek gods and heroes with Oriental decorative elements.

# Swahili traders of East Africa

In the first centuries AD, Arab merchants in their seagoing dhows put in at cities on the East African coast, where in addition to gold, copper, and spices they also loaded elephants' tusks. Through the port of Muscat near the southeastern tip of the Arabian Peninsula, the 'white gold' made its way to India and China. East Africa became (and still is) Asia's principal supplier of ivory. Until the 6th century, India's elephant stocks continued to cover that country's ivory requirements. However, African ivory being of superior quality, it was more sought-after in Asia.

All along the coast from Eritrea to the mouth of the Zambezi, trading settlements sprang up at which Arab and Indian merchants did business. The rapid expansion of Islam provided further economic impulses. In the period around AD 1000, on the island of Zanzibar and along the coastal strip opposite, there arose a mixed culture combining Islamic-Arabic, African, and Indian elements and speaking a mixed language, namely Swahili (Arabic *sahel* = coast), which soon became the commercial lingua franca of East Africa right across to the west coast. The Portuguese with their better-designed caravels were the first of the European rivals to enter the Arab-Indian trading region in 1498, assuming control of Zanzibar and building a number of fortified settlements. They even opened a

The ivory 'Dorado' of Africa's east coast. Arab, Indian, and (later) European merchants operated in the ports, while Swahili intermediaries took care of negotiations with the African tribal kings and chieftains.

trading post in Muscat. At first the Portuguese concentrated on the gold trade, but they soon became involved in the highly profitable trade in ivory as well.

The merchants themselves stayed in the flourishing large coastal towns such as Kilwa, Mozambique, and Sofala farther to the south. Inland, just behind the coast, expert Swahili intermediaries would handle the business negotiations with self-assured tribal kings and chieftains who commanded warrior armies, were often tough negotiating partners, and usually had sole access to supplies of elephant tusk. In exchange the merchants, who avoided conflict, were able to offer textiles, knives, hooks,

Until quite recently, much raw ivory (usually contraband) was shipped out of the elephant countries of East Africa in small seagoing cutters.

The tusks exchanged inland for textiles, iron appliances, jewelry, and Asian pottery (later also guns) were brought to the coast by columns of bearers, hired men working for tribal chieftains or slaves 'belonging' to the merchants, who rarely left the coastal towns. The intermediaries were Swahili tradesmen.

decorative metalwork, beads, and Asian pottery. Transport to the coast was provided by columns of bearers hired by the chieftains or by slaves belonging to the merchants, who rarely left the coastal towns where they lived.

From time to time indigenous peoples controlled the intermediate trade in ivory. The Yao, for example, who lived to the east of what is now Lake Malawi, supplied Kilwa and Mozambique with tusks and even maintained contacts with the Lunda Kingdom of central Africa, where huge herds of elephants roamed freely.

In the mid-17th century the Portuguese suffered a reverse. With the backing of the powerful Sultan of Muscat/Oman, the Arabs drove them out of Zanzibar and from the coasts of Kenya and Tanzania. The Sultan also closed their trading post in Muscat. The Portuguese came under additional pressure from the south, where the Dutch had founded the 'Dutch East India Company' in Cape Town in 1602 and had since pushed eastward and

established themselves along the coast of Delagoa Bay. There the Ronga people supplied them with tusks from Natal and the Transvaal, areas later settled by the Boers, where by the late 18th century elephants had been virtually wiped out. Within a short time of founding their settlements, the Dutch were already sending some 20 tons of ivory across to Europe annually.

In the 18th century the ivory trade in the Portuguese-controlled ports of Mozambique and Sofala collapsed. Heavily taxed by the Portuguese authorities, many Arab merchants and Indian financiers moved north, where there was a flourishing ivory trade on the Tanzania and Kenya coast. The Yao stopped supplying the Portuguese coastal settlements, sending their ivory instead to Zanzibar, which became the main focus of the ivory and slave trades of East Africa. Meanwhile, the Indian banks that were financing the Arab merchants regularly made large profits of up to 300 and 400 percent.

A mountain of giant tusks at the central depot awaits shipment to Asia and Europe.

In the 17th century the Gulf of Guinea ivory trade was systematically exploited by the Dutch and the British. This contemporary print shows a Dutch distribution center.

# The 'black gold' of West Africa

Following the extermination of the African bush elephant in the Atlas Mountains of Morocco during the 4th–5th centuries, small quantities of ivory reached the commercial centers of Tunis, Tripoli, and Benghazi on the Mediterranean coast via the classic camel routes across the Sahara. They came from the great trading depots beyond the hostile sand barrier, namely Timbuktu, the commercial and cultural focus of Islamic West Africa, and the caravansaries on the shores of Lake Chad.

The Carthaginians and Romans had already had business contacts with the trading peoples of the desert, who in addition to gold, precious stones, spices and slaves always had ivory to offer. The tusks supplied by the desert caravans came from the elephant areas which were found around the Senegal and Gambia rivers, from equatorial central Africa, and from the Sudan.

In the 15th century the Portuguese opened up the sea route down the West African coast first discovered by Carthaginian explorer Hanno. They established trading settlements at the mouth of the Gambia and on the equatorial coasts of the Gulf of Guinea that took their names from the products they were typically involved in: Ivory Coast, Gold Coast, Slave Coast. The tropical forests had large populations of bush elephants, and tusks, whether as collector's items or as hunting trophies, were inexpensive commodities.

The Portuguese merchants remained in their fortified coastal settlements and concluded barter agreements with the tribal kings and chieftains in the neighboring hinterland. They did extensive business, for example, with the Kingdom of Benin, which controlled much of present-day Nigeria. The absolute ruler of Benin, the 'oba,' had not only large stocks of elephant tusk but also slaves for

From a Dutch map of Guinea, dated 1743. The illustration shows clearly how important the ivory trade was, alongside those in gold, slaves, and spices.

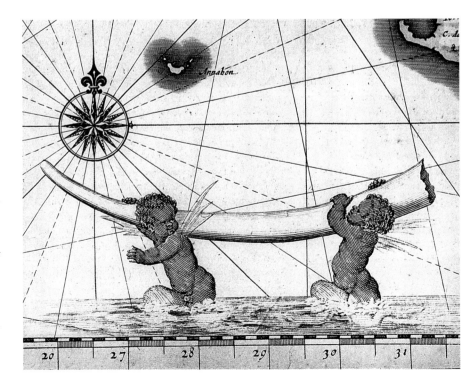

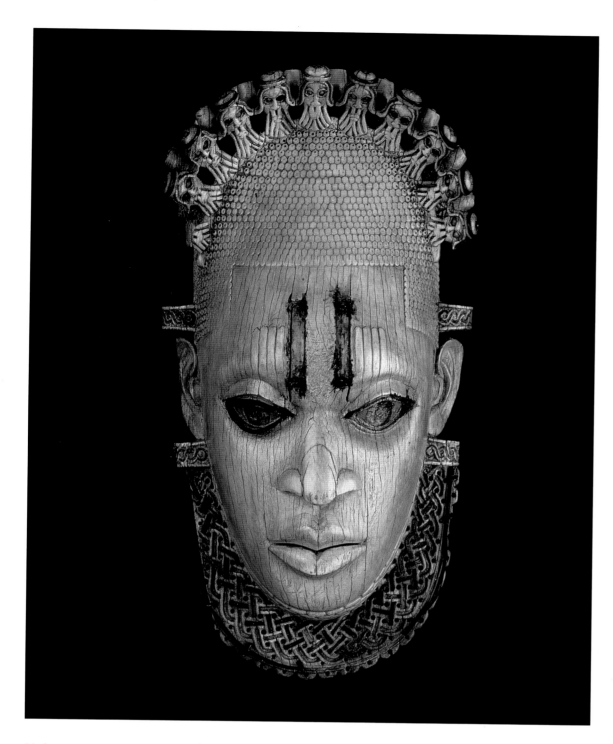

Mask,
Benin, c. 1550,
ivory.
Height 23.8cm
British Museum, London

A mask from the Kingdom of Benin. A crown of Portuguese heads surmounts the forehead. The mask was probably used during religious ceremonies to mark royal ancestral feasts and may represent the mother of 'oba' Esigie, who ruled Benin at the time of the arrival of the Portuguese.

barter, captured in regular campaigns. The oba had first refusal of all tusks hunted. To foster trust, the merchants arranged a goodwill visit by a deputation from the 'oba' to the court of the King of Portugal in Lisbon.

The Portuguese and the British, Dutch, and French traders who followed them combined the trade in ivory with the new and rapidly expanding slave trade. Slavery existed already in the native kingdoms of Africa. The human 'commodities' acquired by native chieftains or African-Arab Swahili traders laboriously carried the tusks down to the coast free of charge, there to be shipped out themselves as slave labor for the early-capitalistic plantation economies of Brazil and the southern states of America.

Major ivory supplies came from what is now Cameroon as well as from the savannahs of Angola. In the 18th century supplies of elephant tusk from areas near the coast dried up, as

elephants just disappeared from many regions. Caravans had to be fitted out for expeditions deep inland. The struggle for markets intensified, and rival traders sought to outbid one another with offers of guns in exchange for goods. Guns were highly prized among African tribesmen, and their spread accelerated the extermination of elephants over large areas.

From the late-17th century onwards, there was more money to be made in West Africa from the slave trade than from ivory. According to international estimates, between 1520 and the abolition of the slave trade in 1850 something like eight to ten million slaves were transported to South America and the southern states of the USA in Portuguese, Dutch, British, French, and Danish ships. Just prior to the outbreak of the American War of Independence in 1776, 162 British ships carried some 48,000 slaves across the ocean to these countries in a single year.

Ivory pectoral,
c. 1600,
ivory.
Height c. 12cm
Museum of Mankind, London

This piece shows the 'oba', supported by servants, wearing his traditional coral adornments. All tusks hunted had to be presented to the 'oba.' One he kept for himself, according to ancient custom; on the other he had first refusal. A hunter who tried to cheat him faced torture and execution. Craftsmen in ivory and bronze were organized in guilds and lived in specific quarters, where it was easier to keep an eye on them.

# The ivory trade in the colonial era

Once the ivory resources of areas near the coast had been exhausted in the 19th century, merchants turned their attention to the dark interior of the largely unexplored African continent. Caravans fitted out by east-coast businessmen reached Lake Tanganyika in the years 1825–30. Tabora was founded as an inland supply base, and from there further expeditions moved north into the elephant-rich areas around Kilimanjaro and (lured by reports of particularly rich tusk stocks) west to the kingdoms of the interlacustrine region. With the spread of the modern breech-loading gun, which was capable of firing more than one shot, the mass destruction of elephant herds proceeded apace.

The sultanates of southern Ethiopia purchased ivory from Swahili traders who brought it from the region watered by the tributaries of the Nile. Tusks from this area and from the savannahs of Darfur were borne by caravans as far as Cairo, where the Mameluke governors ruling under nominal Turkish overlordship themselves developed a taste for 'white gold.' The Mamelukes were descendents of freed former slaves (Arabic mamluk = taken into possession, slave) of Cherkassian origin who had done military service in Egypt and Syria in the 12th century, occupied Cairo in 1252, and remained influential even after the Osmanic conquest of Egypt in 1516–17. Not until 1811 were they disempowered by Mehmed Ali.

In 1882 Egyptian troops established a base at Khartoum in the Sudan, which quickly became a cosmopolitan trading center. At Khartoum, the Egyptians exercized a strict state monopoly over the ivory trade.

Cairo developed into the principal market for both ivory and menagerie elephants in the Mediterranean region. It was from Cairo that the Hamburg animal dealer Hagenbeck obtained his first exhibition elephants. Pressure from Britain and France forced Egypt to lift its ivory monopoly in 1850. However, unrestricted elephant shooting by hunting parties reduced stocks in Upper Sudan and Darfur so rapidly that the trading monopoly had to be reintroduced. Then in 1880 the Mahdi Uprising in the Sudan cut off access to the elephant grounds on the banks of the Nile tributaries.

On the other side of Africa envoys from King Leopold II of the Belgians, instructed to ensure the 'political development' of the country, were pushing east along the Congo River. They reached Katanga, where copper had already been mined for centuries. The ivory trade was sucked into the wake of the political and commercial struggles of rival European powers over raw materials and colonial possessions. Dominating the scene was the overwhelming maritime power of Great Britain, which controlled India and in 1806 drove the Dutch out of the Cape. In 1834 Britain abolished the slave trade within its own sphere of influence, thus gaining a moral advantage over advocates of the slave economy in the pursuit of its own policy of imperialist expansion.

In 1856 the Sultan of Muscat/Oman was forced to relinquish Zanzibar, the largest ivory and slave market on Africa's eastern seaboard. Under Anglo-Indian administration, the European powers now opened trading-posts on the island. In 1891 Zanzibar came under full British sovereignty. Meanwhile, to control the Suez Canal (opened in 1869) and the direct sea route to India, in 1881 Egypt had been occupied. In 1898 it was the turn of the French to submit to British pressure as they were obliged to take down the tricolor they had raised in Fashoda and abandon their claim to the Sudan as well as to shared rule in Cairo.

At the 1885 Africa conference in Berlin Britain, France, Portugal, and latecomer Germany had sat down with ruler and compasses to divide the 'dark continent' up between them – using maps that were still covered with white areas denoting unexplored regions. The vast area of what is now the People's Republic of the Congo became the personal property of King Leopold II of the Belgians, and ruthless exploitation by Brussels-based mining companies was sanctioned. What was mainly implemented in Berlin was the grand imperial design of British colonial strategist Cecil Rhodes, namely a corridor of colonial possessions stretching from Cairo to the Cape, disturbed only by subsequent German acquisitions on its flanks.

In West Africa the slave trade accounted for larger turnovers than the trade in ivory. Britain's ban on the former within its own sphere of influence was followed in 1850 by an international ban (with transitional deadlines). This led to a radical restructuring of markets.

Agricultural products (coffee, cocoa, sisal, etc.) became commercially profitable, and an early-capitalistic plantation economy began to emerge in equitorial coastal zones. Huge areas of tropical forest were cleared for agricultural purposes, while at the same time extermination programs were mounted against elephants, which disappeared from the coastal hinterland. Mass slaughter of elephants brought a short-term boom in the ivory trade on the west coast, partly under the aegis of German merchants in Cameroon. Boom was followed by bust – until expeditions in Angola and the Congo tapped fresh resources deep in the interior.

This was the age of the great explorers, men filled with humanitarian ideals, in whose footsteps ivory dealers and colonial pioneers followed.

Scottish missionary and anti-slavery campaigner David Livingstone (1813–73) penetrated the unknown center of the continent as he crossed from coast to coast in search of the sources of the

Journalist Henry Morton Stanley set out on behalf of the 'New York Herald' to look for David Livingstone, the British missionary and explorer who since the last report received from him in 1869 had disappeared in the wilderness of the interior. On November 3, 1871 he found Livingstone in a village near Udji on Lake Tanganyika.

Nile. What he actually discovered were the head waters of the Congo River.

Livingstone was the first European (this was between 1869 and 1871) to spend any time in the unexplored regions to the west of Lake Tanganyika, where he discovered exceptionally dense elephant populations. Collecting tusks there was like "gold digging," he noted; they simply lay around in the vast forests where the elephants had died. If dealers came into the area, the inhabitants would, if treated with respect, bring them tusks in exchange for cheap copper armbands. Dealers were not long in coming.

A German doctor and traveler, Heinrich Barth, explored North Africa between the Mediterranean, Niger, and Chad. Frenchman Savorgnan de Brazza sailed up the Ogowe River, reaching the Congo. There he concluded a treaty of friendship with Chief Mukoko, who gave him a present of a piece of land on the Congo River; in return the chief received a tricolor. Today the piece of land is occupied by the city of Brazzaville – a classic example of typical colonial appropriation.

In the 19th century, relations between ivory traders and the African tribal kings and chieftains coarsened. Expeditions with armed escorts and columns of bearers, fitted out by merchants at enormous expense, brought pressure to bear on trading negotiations, by either threatening or actually using force. Formal agreements were disregarded, conflicts among native populations stirred up. Above all, the practice of colonial appropriation corrupted relations by deploying troops.

In a climate of ruthless competition and general lawlessness, there was unrestrained slaughter of elephants, particularly in the Congo region. According to contemporary sources (the French publications 'L'Ivoire' and 'Le Commerce de l'Ivoire),' quantities of elephant tusk from this region coming onto the world market shot up from 87 tons in 1884 to 375 tons in 1895. In the same two years, total supplies from the west coast amounted to 299 and 480 tons respectively. From the east-coast regions, between 1879 and 1883 the following quantities of ivory (in tons per year) reached the world market: from Zanzibar 216 tons, Mozambique 157 tons, Egypt/Khartoum yielded 188 tons, Ethiopia/Somalia 29 tons, and from the Cape 32 tons.

Only with the demarcation of power relations and the establishment of colonial administrations were elephant stocks taken under state control. Indigenous populations were banned from owning weapons and hunting. The trading organizations of the Swahili merchants, who offered armed resistance, were defeated by troops from the Congo Free State. Hunting legislation patterned on European models curbed illegal shooting. The age of the 'white hunter' had arrived.

His formal greeting in this remote spot ("Dr. Livingstone, I presume?") was soon known all around the world. Stanley had his story – and became an explorer himself. He plotted the course of the Congo and was enlisted as an adviser and aide to Belgian King Leopold II in the latter's acquisition of the Congo region.

Thomas Baines,
*The 'Ma Roberts' and elephant in the shallows, Shire River, Lower Zambesi,* 1859,
oil on canvas.
65cm x 44cm
Royal Geographic Society, London

The steam launch 'Ma Roberts,' with which David Livingstone explored the lower reaches of the Zambezi in 1858, one day encountered a giant elephant. Rifles and a cannon were swiftly deployed in a senseless attack. The boat did not get far; Livingstone abandoned it and continued on foot with a column of bearers.

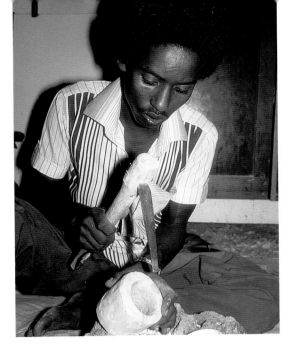

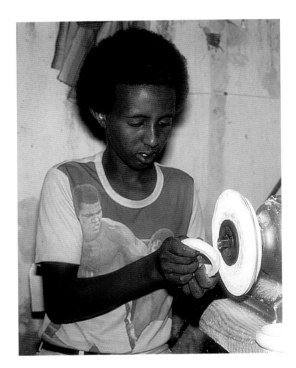

In a workshop in Mogadishu, Somalia, an ivory bangle is roughed out with a hand tool.

A simple wheel is used to polish the finished product.

## Ivory as a material

The term ivory refers to the bone matter of the tusks of elephant and mammoth. This hard yet slightly elastic and easily-worked material is a mixture of dentine, gristle, and calcium salts. Mammoth tusk, having lain in the earth for thousands of years, is dark in color and often brittle. Elephant ivory is similar to the tooth material of several other animals: the tusk developing from the left tooth (the right is stunted) of the male narwhal in a left-handed spiral between 7 and 10 feet in length; the tusks of the walrus, which measure between 24 and 28 inches in length; and those of the hippopotamus, between 16 and 24 inches. To the non-expert, all are difficult to distinguish from elephant ivory.

The grain and color of ivory vary according to where the tusk comes from. Asian ivory is more brittle than African ivory, which also occurs in larger quantities. Ivory from bush elephants living in the rain forests of West Africa has a faint brownish gleam and is slightly harder than the creamy-white tusk matter produced by its mighty cousin from the hot dry steppes and savannahs of East Africa. Ivory from the elephants that once inhabited the bamboo forests of China has a reddish gleam; the now-extinct Chinese elephant is therefore assumed to have belonged to a subspecies: *Elephas maximus rubidens*. Ancient ivory from Ceylon and Thailand also frequently has a reddish gleam to it. Prolonged exposure to light bleaches ivory; kept in the dark, it turns brown.

There are two distinct processing techniques: the older carving method and the more modern turning. The same tools are used to work ivory as craftsmen use to work wood, the only difference

Sawn piece of tusk for manufacturing bead blanks.

An ivory workshop on the Congo River, where ancient African motives are today turned out in series production for the tourist trade. A popular item are whole tusks with African decoration. Ivory workshop, Zaire

Carving an 'Erbach rose.' This internationally successful decorative motive was developed in 1873 by craftsmen from the Odenwald region, the center of the ivory-carving industry in Germany. It was particularly in tune with late-19th century fashion. At the World Fair in Vienna in that same year, the design was even awarded a medal.

being that ivory is harder and the tools need more frequent sharpening. Simple forms of lathe existed in ancient Egypt, but only with the introduction of wheel drive during the late Middle Ages did sophisticated turning become possible. Before ivory is worked, it can be softened in boiling water containing soda. A key criterion for assessing artistic merit is 'one-piece manufacture.' Also important, however, is that structure and grain should be taken account of in design.

As we have already seen in another context, the English term 'ivory,' likewise the French 'ivoire' and the Italian 'avorio,' is derived from the ancient Egyptian word 'abu' (see for instance 'The 'abu' of the Pharaohs'), while the German 'Elfenbein' (Old German 'helfantbein') comes from the Greek word 'elephas.'

Female head,
Assyrian, 8th century BC,
ivory.
15.8cm x 13.5cm
Iraq Museum, Baghdad.

This ivory panel once adorned a
piece of furniture in the palace of
King Sargon II (721–705 BC) in
Kalhu (Nimrud). It was found in
an excellent state of preservation
in the mud at the bottom of a 80
foot-deep well-shaft. Only
the nose needed restoring.

Below right:
Mycenaean snake goddess,
Knossos, Crete, c. 1500 BC,
ivory and gold.
Height 16.1cm

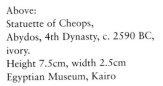

Above:
Statuette of Cheops,
Abydos, 4th Dynasty, c. 2590 BC,
ivory.
Height 7.5cm, width 2.5cm
Egyptian Museum, Kairo

This miniature portrait of Cheops
is the only documented image of
the man who built the Great
Pyramid at Giza. The king is
shown wearing the crown of
Lower Egypt and a short
loincloth. In his right hand he
holds a whip, symbol of his
power. The Horus name of
Cheops is inscribed on the front of
the simple throne.

# The magic of ivory

Ivory is one of the oldest and most precious materials used by artists and craftsmen. This softly gleaming material, which has been credited with magical powers, has fascinated the human race for millennia. The exquisite works of ivory art occupy a special place in the history of civilization.

In Egypt, the development of ivory art can be followed from the Stone Age. A great many works have survived, recovered from the tombs of the Pharaohs in an excellent state of preservation. They include statuettes, models of animals, cultic objects, burial idols, furniture decoration, and jars and combs for women's dressing-tables. Ivory was often painted or treated in dye-baths. The works of the Egyptian masters provided a fertile source of prototypes for the ancient civilizations of the Mediterranean region, where from the 3rd millennium BC they were joined by stylistic elements from the Middle East and Mesopotamia.

Under Egyptian influence, ivory was being worked in Crete as early as the Minoan period (2100–1580 BC). Statuettes of snake goddesses and bull jumpers have been found in the palace of Knossos. The Cretans bequeathed their techniques to the ancient Greeks, whose skill in turn inspired the ivory art of the Etruscans and the Romans. The Greeks developed special ways of processing the precious material. Take, for example, the more-than-life-sized gold and ivory standing figure of Athene by the sculptor Phidias (born c. 500 BC). The flesh parts over the wooden core were carved from sheets of ivory obtained by peeling – not unlike the modern technique of veneer. A sophisticated network of tubes constantly moistened the ivory parts with oil to prevent them from drying out, losing fat, and fissuring.

Elsewhere within the sphere of influence of Egyptian civilization, the Phoenician city-states on the Lebanese and Syrian coasts developed a flourishing ivory industry that mainly turned out luxury items. The Phoenicians were also, as we have seen, responsible for supplying the material for Solomon's throne of gold and ivory.

A major consumer of luxury items carved from ivory was wealthy imperial Rome. The highly prized material was processed in a variety of forms in both private and public spheres, whether for statuettes and jewelry, low reliefs and intarsia work, cosmetic utensils, or public displays of magnificence. Cesar's triumphal chariot, for example, was clad in ivory. In Byzantium in the Eastern Empire, ivory craftsmen transformed hunting scenes into pious religious motives for the dawn of Christianity (e.g. the Good Shepherd). Jewelry boxes became receptacles for consecrated wafers. There followed the period of stylized low reliefs for the covers of Gospels and priceless manuscripts with miniature paintings.

Portrait head, *King Philip II*,
4th century BC,
ivory.
c. 3cm
Archeological Museum,
Thessaloniki

The father of Alexander the Great
united and ruled Macedonia from
359 to 336 BC. During a military
campaign three years before his
murder at the hands of one of his
bodyguards, a spear wounded him
in the right eye. On this ivory
portrait the scar has been notched
in above the eyebrow.

The carving of ivory book covers continued in the Carolingian period. Byzantine artists working in Charlemagne's court college in Aachen (Aix-la-Chapelle) as well as at Metz, Lorsch, and Trier imported eastern stylistic elements.

The Romanesque era was a time of stagnation for ivory art. Ivory carvers were chiefly occupied producing devotional objects. The Gothic period that followed was dominated by French craftsmen. This was the heyday of religious ivory art, during which the famous workshops of Dieppe, Paris, and Soissons manufactured elegantly sinuous statuettes of the Madonna, crucifixes, reliquaries adorned with reliefs, and diptychs illustrating the Passion. At the same time, secular jewelry boxes were adorned with portrayals of loving couples and scenes from romances of chivalry.

During the Renaissance, the great masters of sculpture preferred other materials, but with the advent of the Baroque style ivory-carving came back into fashion. German, Flemish, and Dutch masters led the way, artists who were now known and celebrated by name. Naked bodies of Rubensesque voluptuousness, radiating sensual enjoyment, frolicked in high relief on tankards, jugs, table decorations, and caskets. Statuettes of considerable artistic merit were produced. Famous workshops grew up in Antwerp, Augsburg, Nuremberg, Geislingen, and Vienna.

The carving and turning of ivory became fashionable at many European courts. Habsburg Emperor Rudolph II, for example, had Peter Zick of Nuremberg initiate him in the art of ivory-turning. Emperor Ferdinand III, Peter the Great, Carl II of Sweden, and George II of Great Britain were among other monarchs who tried their hands at the creation of ivory art.

In 19th century France the tone was set by the Dieppe School, founded in 1808. Work shown by members of the school at the 1834 Paris World Fair won great acclaim.

Around the same time, in Biedermeier Germany, a new cultural center for ivory art was set up at Erbach/Odenwald under Count Erbach, a qualified master ivory-carver. In the 19th century, ivory art also flourished in Britain, which imported vast quantities of elephant tusk from its colonial empire.

Towards the end of the 19th century the tradition of carving that had characterized Dieppe for hundred of years came to an end. In the 20th century the center of European ivory art shifted to Erbach/Odenwald, where a specialist college of elephant-ivory carving had been established in 1892. The general trend was toward series production, which at the same time had to bear the marks of individual artistic creation. For economic reasons, part of the Erbach factory was also obliged to take some account of the souvenir business.

The interim ban on the entire ivory trade imposed in 1989 and the further restrictions enacted since have had serious repercussions for the craft of ivory-carving throughout the Western world. With awareness of the plight of elephants increasing, the market for ivory has dwindled.

Christ as 'The Good Shepherd' (detail),
Goa, India, c. 1700,
ivory.
Height 43.5cm
Victoria & Albert Museum,
London

This piece blends European and Indian stylistic elements. It was manufactured in the former Portuguese colony of Goa on India's west coast. A whole collection of similar figures suggests a sort of series production for export.

Center:
Seated Madonna,
Paris, c. 1325,
carved single block of ivory.
Height 25.3cm
Treasury of Church of St. Francis,
Assisi (Italy)

Below:
Baroque statuette of Venus,
Flemish c. 1700,
ivory.
Height 17.5cm
Private collection

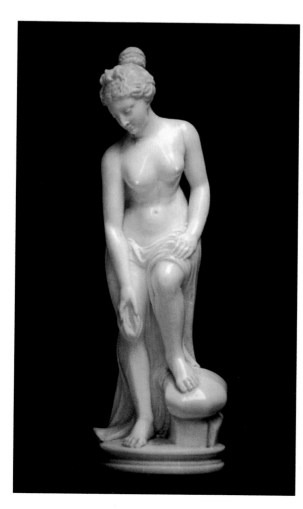

Medieval ivory horn carved with
Christian symbols and bands of
ornament.

## Oliphants

'Olifant' meant in Old French first 'ivory' and then
'horn of ivory'. The best-known oliphant is the one
associated with Roland, hero of the saga cycle that
grew up around the figure of Charlemagne
(742–814). In 778 the emperor marched back
across the Pyrenees after a campaign against the
Spanish Moors. According to the French national
epic 'Song of Roland,' the rearguard was attacked
by Basques in the valley of Roncesvalles and cut off
from the main body of the army. Roland, fatally
wounded, reached for his oliphant to call the army
back. The sound is said to have been so powerful
that the heathen took fright and speech became

thereafter impossible. From then on oliphants were
widely used as signal horns and then later also as
powder horns.

Historical note: According to Einhard's 'Vita
Caroli Magni,' during Emperor Charlemagne's
retreat from Spain Margrave Roland of Brittany
('britanici limitis praefectus') did indeed, together
with other noblemen, lose his life.

Some seventy-five ivory horns have survived
from the Early Middle Ages. Most of them come
from the Islamic civilization of Sicily, which
between 940 and 1040 enjoyed a century of high
culture under Arab rule.

Powder horn from the armory of
Maharaja Madhu Singh II, which
was set up in 1720.
18th century,
ivory.

Bell of an oliphant surrounded
with animal carving,
southern Italy, 11th century,
ivory.
Length c. 70cm
Herzog Anton Ulrich-Museum,
Braunschweig Brunswick,
Germany

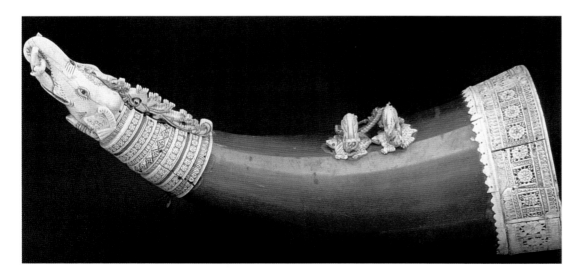

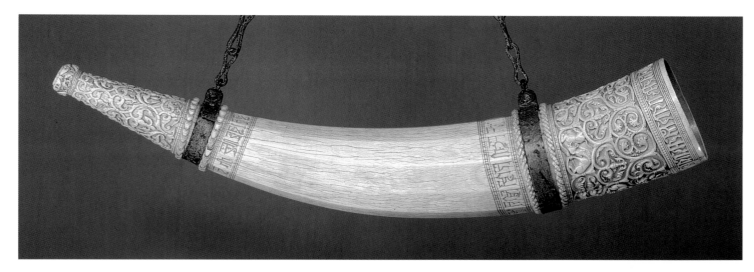

*Oliphant*,
Sicily, Saracen, 13th century,
ivory.
Length 72cm
Kunstgewerbe Museum,
Staatliche Museen Preussischer
Kulturbesitz, Berlin

This signal horn has a plain
central portion and relief
decoration at the bell and mouth
ends. It is the work of Arab ivory-
carvers, who blended stylistic
influences from their homeland
with southern-Italian forms.

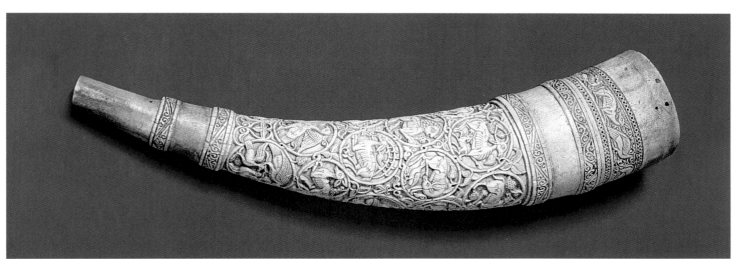

*Oliphant*,
southern Italy, late 11th century,
ivory.
Length 69cm
Royal Scottish Museum,
Edinburgh

# Ivory art in Asia and Africa

In China, craftsmen began carving ivory during the Shang Dynasty (16th–11th centuries BC). A number of saddle pommels and small human and animal figurines have survived from that time. Ivory-carving first achieved high artistic quality during the Ming period (AD 1368–1644). Ming craftsmen produced statuettes of goddesses (Kuan Yin), monks, and heroes of legend that were distinguished by a noble simplicity. The Chi'ing Dynasty (1646–1912) brought a more playful style of figure-carving, with many luxury articles such as boxes, jars decorated in low relief, games, and so on, made more for decorative than functional purposes.

In India, ivory art flourished mainly in the 16th and 17th centuries, during the heyday of the Islamic Mogul overlords. Ivory workshops turned out large quantities of ornamental carving, much of it featuring gods from the Hindu pantheon. Indian and Chinese stylistic elements infiltrated the ivory art of Southeast Asia from Burma across to Vietnam during this period.

There was a strong Chinese influence in the early days of ivory art in Japan. Later, Japan developed a distinctive indigenous form in the netsuke. These tiny carvings, incorporating a hole to thread a lace through, were used to attach tobacco pouches, or stamps, or medicine boxes to men's sashes (traditional Japanese garments having no pockets). Nowadays these exquisite marvellous miniatures (average size 1$^1$/2–2in) are much sought-after as collector's items the world over.

Okimonos, slightly larger figures with no hole but similarly imaginative in design, were for purely decorative purposes. In the 19th century, famous schools of ivory-carving operated in Kyoto, Edo (Tokyo), and Osaka.

In the Middle Ages, the leader in the carving of ivory of African origin was the kingdom of Benin. A major export were whole tusks carved in the round with an engraved decoration of stylized human and animal figures. Bleaching was achieved with acid-bearing plant juices. Benin craftsmen were particularly good at combining ivory with bronze and other materials, a process that called for great technical skill.

Old man with carrier,
Japan, 19th century,
ivory.
Height 15cm
Private collection

Powder horn,
India, 19th century,
Nautilus shell, ivory inlays.
Height c. 23cm
Victoria and Albert Museum,
London

This powder horn is made from the iridescent shell of a nautilus snail inlaid with ivory leaves and flowers. The lid, also of ivory, is elaborately decorated with coded signs and symbols.

Ivory panel from an ancient Indian throne. South India

Splendidly caparisoned elephant accompanied by courtiers. Bengal, 19th century

*Doctor's Lady,*
China,
ivory.
Length 17.5cm
Private collection

A Chinese ivory speciality are the reclining female nudes called 'doctor's ladies' or 'medical figures.' The traditional interpretation is that they were used by women visiting the doctor to describe their symptoms, physical examination being taboo. Nowadays, they are regarded as discreetly labeled erotica.

Elephant carving decorated with gold, jewels, and pearls.
Thailand, 20th century

Ivory statuette of a Chinese court lady,
China, 20th century.
Height 20cm
Private collection

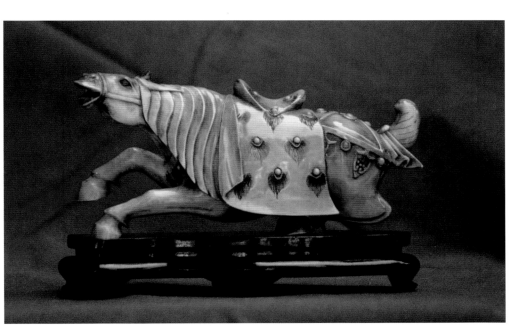

Horse,
China, 19th century,
stained ivory with
inlaid turquoises.
Length 18cm
Private collection

# Elephants in the realm of the imagination

Elephants have fuelled the human imagination for thousands of years. In the Western world, where the animal is not indigenous and can be seen only in zoos, it has traditionally enjoyed the status of a mythical creature from nature's magic garden. People have a large place in their hearts for the stout exotic foreigner, whose affecting image is familiar to us in a wide variety of manifestations. The elephant is at home in the nursery, whether as picture-book hero or as cuddly toy; it has also 'sat' for some of the world's greatest painters. It has been widely used as a chess piece, and goldsmiths have turned its dumpy figure into costly trinkets. It lends its weight to advertizing campaigns, while in joke books it wears the jester's cap. Everyone adores the good-humored giant. In fact, so deeply do we love and prize the symbol that we tend to lose sight of the actual animal, this highly endangered species.

Johann Joachim Kändler (1706–75),
*Sultan riding on an elephant*,
Meissen, c. 1743–50,
Meissen porcelain.
Height 25.8cm, length c. 28cm
Schloss Ricklingen, Germany

Trumpeter riding on a decorated elephant, c. 1700, woven under the direction of Philipp Behagie from designs by Jean Berain, Beauvais Factory, northern France Wall-hanging, wool and silk Badisches Landesmuseum, Schloss Bruchsal, Germany.

# Images of elephants by great masters

Rembrandt van Rijn (1606–69),
*Hansken the elephant*, 1637,
black chalk.
23cm x 34cm
Graphische Sammlung
Albertina, Vienna

Hansken was a young elephant
from Ceylon whom the great
master of 17th-century Dutch
painting saw in Amsterdam in
1637. The animal was exhibited
at fairs in Holland and Germany
for a number of years.

Salnave Philippe-Auguste
(b. 1908)
*Animals in the jungle*, 1963,
oil on board.
61cm x 91cm
Kurt Beckmann Collection,
New York

Like many former slaves in Haiti,
Salnave Philippe-Auguste's
ancestors adopted a French slave
name as their surname. The
artist's work is thoroughly imbued
with memories of his African
roots (there are of course no wild
elephants in his country). Philippe-
Auguste's paintings are among the
most highly-prized examples of
naive art in Haiti.

Elephants in the realm of the imagination

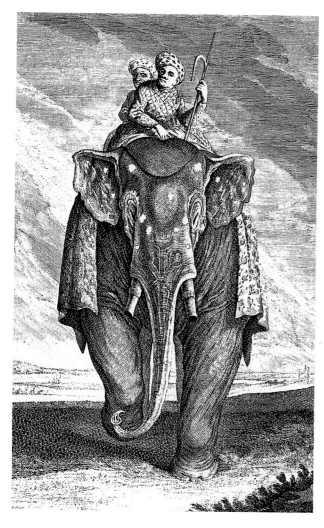

Johann Elias Riedinger
(1698–1767),
*Elephant in full finery,*
Augsburg, post-1741,
copperplate engraving.
27.8cm x 19.2cm
Graphische Sammlung, Staatsgalerie,
Stuttgart Germany

Franz Marc (1880-1916),
*Elephant*, 1907,
chalk on paper.
41.5cm x 32.8cm
Kunsthalle, Hamburg
A powerful sketch by Franz Marc,
co-founder of the 'Blue Rider'
group of artists in Munich.

Francisco Goya (1746–1828),
*Disparate de bestia* ('Foolish act
of an animal'), c. 1815–24,
etching and aquatint.
24.5cm x 35cm
Graphische Sammlung der
ETH, Zurich

This etching by the great Spanish
artist is from his 'Los disparates'
('Foolish acts') series, based on
proverbs. The enormous animal is
arching its back almost like a cat
as, with a blend of fear and
inquisitiveness, it regards the
objects the figures in the left are
showing it (a book and a collar
with bells attached). The Spanish
saying "Pondra el cascabel al
gato" ('Tying bells on the cat')
refers to any particularly
dangerous enterprise. Here the
elephant stands for the mass of
the people – clumsy, cautious, and
at the same time dangerous –
whom the power-hungry must
first tame.

# How modern artists see elephants

Andy Warhol (1928–87),
*African elephant*, 1983,
silk-screen print,
96.5cm x 96.5cm
Courtesy Ronald Feldman
Fine Arts, New York

Probably the best-known representative of Pop Art, Andy Warhol devoted a whole series ('Endangered species') to animals under threat. Each picture was based on a photograph, which Warhol then drew over and colored. This 'pop' treatment exacted a price in that, as a result of the doubling of the outline, the elephant lost much of its stability. Both superficially and subtly, the artist thus highlighted the precariousness of the balance of nature. Warhol donated ten copies of the series to various animal-protection organizations worldwide.

Elephants in the realm of the imagination

Walasse Ting (b. 1929),
*Elephants.*
87.5cm x 156.6cm
Yves Rivière

The Chinese background of
painter and illustrator Walasse
Ting is evident in his penchant for
brilliant, pop-art-type colors. Here
a naively-drawn pair of elephants
stroll through a tranquil jungle – a
picture straight out of the brave
new world of that consumer
paradise, the shopping mall.

*Grazing elephant,*
picture by a handicapped child.
MhB Menschen helfen
Behinderten e.V.

David Hockney (b. 1937),
*The cruel elephant*, 1962,
oil on canvas.
121.9cm x 152.4cm
Private collection
(Lady D'Avigdor-Goldsmith)

Trained as a draftsman, Hockney
here reduces everything pictorial
to childlike forms. The elephant of
our childhood disappoints the
artistic expectations of the adult
world in a process that is 'cruel,'
as the title suggests, but also
ironic. The fact is, this elephant is
no less 'true' for being childlike.

Elephants in the realm of the imagination

Elephants in the realm of the imagination

Max Ernst (1891–1976),
*The elephant of Celebes*, 1921,
oil on canvas.
125cm x 108cm
Tate Gallery, London

In this famous picture the most disparate elements, with no rational connection whatsoever, are surprisingly combined. The huge elephant looks like an assemblage of mechanical components. The body resembles a gasholder, while the tail, suggesting both a trunk and a length of stovepipe, ends unaccountably in a cuff protector and a sort of bull's head. Two tusks are just visible on the extreme left. Clearly Max Ernst was not aiming at a realistic image here but using dream elements to create their own world of association. As a result, his elephant is reinvested with all the strangeness, menace, but also dignity that scientifically thinking man appears to have robbed it of.

Salvador Dali (1904–89),
*The temptation of St. Anthony*,
1946,
oil on canvas,
89.7cm x 119.5cm
Musées Royaux des Beaux-Arts
de Belgique, Brussels

The first elephant tempts with the cup of lust. Those behind bear symbols of wealth, power, and finally gluttony.

Boyd Webb,
*Subcontinent*, 1963,
mural, saw, bicycle.
112cm x 152cm

This humorous work by the New Zealand artist Webb tells a little story. An elephant painted in a corner of a room 'steals' the saddle of an actual bicycle. The boundaries of art and reality seem to have become playfully blurred. The mind is permitted to roam free, enjoying the memory of circus scenes or alternatively the reality of the piece.

# From garden of monsters to urban plinth

Emmanuel Frémiet (1824–1910), *Elephant*, 1878, sandstone. Jardin du Trocadero, Paris

Visitors to Paris's Trocadero Gardens are greeted by this lifelike giant roaring in protest at his captivity – a cry for freedom captured in stone by French sculptor Emmanuel Frémiet.

War elephant, post-1550, sandstone. Parco dei Monstri, Bomarzo, near Viterbo, Italy

The 'Garden of Monsters' that, beginning in 1550, Prince Vicino Orsini laid out around his 400-room palace near Viterbo is filled with dragons, giants, and other fearsome creatures, including this war elephant carved from a single rock. It bears a castle on its back and is kitted out for battle. Wrapped in its trunk is an apparently lifeless warrior. The masters who created these mysterious sculptures remain anonymous, and we shall probably never know what obsessions tormented the prince.

Elephants in the realm of the imagination

Ercole Ferrata, after Giovanni
Lorenzo Bernini (1598–1680),
elephant obelisk,
Egypt, 6th century BC,
granite.
Elephant, 1667,
marble.
Height (with plinth) c. 8m
Piazza della Minerva, Rome

High on a grandiose plinth
outside the church of Santa Maria
sopra Minerva in Rome, its trunk
pointing mockingly at the obelisk
on its back, stands this elephant
carved by Ercole Ferrata from
plans drawn up by Giovanni
Lorenzo Bernini, the great master
of Italian Baroque. The already
ancient obelisk had been brought
from Egypt by the Romans and
set up in honor of the goddess
Minerva. The monolith (long since
toppled) having been rediscovered
in the Campus Martius, Pope
Alexander VII gave orders in 1667
that it should be re-erected to the
glory of the Church – this time as
a symbol, in the midst of the
urban everyday, of the
steadfastness of the spiritual
power, which the elephant was
required to support. An
inscription reminds passers-by
that it takes great strength to
uphold wisdom.

# Elephant carvings on gateways and façades

Jochen Ihle (1919–96),
elephant gateway,
sandstone,
Height 12.7m
Budapester Strasse, Berlin

The much-photographed entrance
to Berlin's zoological gardens. The
two sandstone elephants by
animal sculptor Ihle, destroyed in
the war, were restored in 1985
from old plans.

Top left:
Elephant's head door-knocker,
Birmingham, England

Above:
Elephant carving on the corner
of a house.
Neue-Welt-Gasse, Graz Austria

Top right:
Josef Pallenberg (1882–1946),
Elephant head, 1907,
sandstone.
Main gate of Hagenbeck Animal
Park, Hamburg

Elephant carving on the famous
entrance to the Hamburg zoo
where pioneering work in
elephant keeping has been done
for the last hundred years.

Above:
Bronze sculpture on the union
building opposite Hamburg's
Musikhalle,
c. 1930.

Horst Rellecke (b. 1951),
*Glass elephant*,
1981–84,
glass, concrete.
Height 39m
Maximilianpark, Hamm-Werries,
Westphalia, Germany

Architect Horst Rellecke added
this giant glass elephant in
Postmodernist Pop Art style to the
former 'Maximilian' mine (disused
since 1914) in Hamm, north-east
of Dortmund. The concrete body
is the old coal-washing plant, onto
which the architect built a glass
head and trunk (containing an
elevator), which are used as an
exhibition space. Rellecke was a
pupil of famous American
architect Charles Moore
(b. 1925), who enlivened the
mirror façade of the Best building
in San Francisco with a dozen
glass elephants.

# Elephant architecture

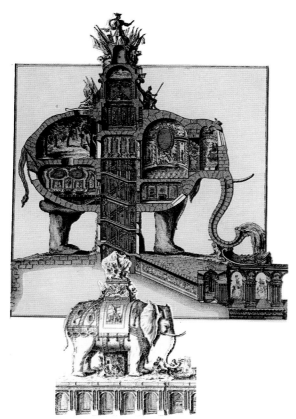

Charles-François Ribart, design for an elephant monument in honor of the king, 1758, copperplate engraving. Louvre, Paris

In 1758 Ribart, a member of France's Academy of Sciences, produced this design for a vast elephant monument for Louis XV. It was to occupy the Place de l'Étoile and to be built of bronze. The body of the giant was to include a ceremonial throne room. Water was to gush from the trunk into a basin, while an elaborate superstructure would be surmounted by a splendid statue of the king. However, Ribert's idea was greeted with derision. The magazine 'L'Année littéraire' wrote that the project was fit only to be cast in icing-sugar as decoration for a baker's shop.

*Lucy,* 1884, timber construction, clad in sheet metal. Height 37m Coney Island, USA

The colossus of Coney Island. This gigantic structure, affectionately known as 'Lucy,' served as a 37-room hotel. The howdah on its back was a popular viewing-platform. Inside were shops and a coffee bar, and people queued to spend the night in one of the rooms that occupied the legs and belly of the elephant. James V. Lafferty commissioned the building on a piece of wasteland with the idea that it should boost economic development in the area. Opened in 1884, the elephant hotel was destroyed by fire twelve years later.

Sketches for the proposed elephant hotel on Coney Island. The tip of the monster's trunk disappeared into a large water tank.

# On walls and paneling

François Mansart (1598–1666), mural decoration, 1635–38, gilded.
Hôtel de la Vrillière, Paris

Mansart, who designed this gilded mural decoration for Paris's Hôtel de la Vrillière (now the head office of the Banque de France) is credited with having 'invented' the mansard roof, though all that this required was extending the roof truss with dormers. His great-nephew, Jules Hardouin Mansart, was court architect to 'Sun King' Louis XIV.

Plaster animal relief,
17th century,
great hall of the medieval castle of Weikersheim
Taubertal, Württemberg, Germany

Amusing mural depiction of an elephant in the great hall of the former residence of Prince and Count Hohenlohe. Life-sized animal sculptures on the walls and hunting scenes on the panels of the coffered ceiling still convey something of the full-blooded atmosphere of feudal hunting parties. The mighty elephant, dominating one whole section of wall, offers an exotic contrast to these indigenous portrayals. The great hall or 'Rittersaal' of Schloss Weikersheim is one of the few stylistically consistent banqueting halls to have survived from the great age of German château-building around 1600.

A dignitary rides out on a magnificently caparisoned elephant, accompanied by his servants.
Detail from the wallpaper panorama 'Hindustan,' handprinted in 85 colors, Alsace, 1806.
Deutsches Tapeten-Museum, Kassel, Germany

Elephants in the realm of the imagination

# An elephant from Dresden's magic garden

Johann Melchior Dinglinger,
(1664–1731),
*Dignitaries with elephant*,
1701–08,
gold, enamel, diamonds.
Grünes Gewölbe, Staatliche
Kunstsammlungen, Dresden

Together with two dignitaries, a
splendidly caparisoned elephant
bows before Great Mogul
Aurangzeb (reigned 1658–1707).
This treasure from Dresden's
'Green Vault,' which houses the
largest historical collection of
precious objects in Europe,
belongs to a scene that court
jeweler Dinglinger made for
Augustus the Strong (1670–1733),
Prince of Saxony and King of
Poland. In a miniature palace of
silver, gold, and precious stones
the Delhi court celebrates the
Great Mogul's birthday.
Dinglinger used a total of 133
figures to conjure up a scene from
'The Thousand and One Nights.'
Up in the howdah are two
squabbling Moorish boys, one
holding a parasol and the other a
parrot stand. The clothes are
rendered in enamel on gold, as is
the diamond-studded shabrack on
the elephant's back, where two
monkeys romp.

Peter Carl Fabergé (1846–1920),
*Pine-cone egg*,
Easter 1900,
gold work.
Height (egg) 9.5cm, length
(elephant) 5cm

This precious Easter egg from
Czarist Russia gleams in royal-blue
enamel. Garlands of gold and silver,
set with diamonds, suggest the
structure of a pine cone. Inside the
egg is a tiny elephant wearing a red
cover set with diamonds and
topped by a smaller green
saddlecloth on which a turbaned
mahout sits cross-legged. One of
the diamonds conceals a keyhole.

Careful winding with a tiny key
sets a miniature clockwork motor
in motion, and the elephant trudges
forward, moving its head and tail.
Fabergé, the czar's court jeweler,
designed this expensive plaything
for Russian goldmine owner
Alexander Kelch, who gave it to his
wife Petrovna as an Easter present.
On the top of the egg, framed in
diamonds, is the date '1900.' The
piece is thought to be worth
between three and four million
dollars. In the period 1885–1917
Fabergé made fifty such Easter gifts
for the Czar's family. When the
Bolshevik Revolution broke out,
Fabergé fled to Switzerland, where
he died in 1920.

Hans Reimer (attrib.),
gold pendant in the shape of an
elephant, with diamond roses,
ruby spinel, and baroque pearl,

c. 1555.
Height 0.56cm
Residenz Treasury, Munich

Elephants in the realm of the imagination

# Tableware and drinking-vessels

Tableware in animal designs was enormously popular in the 16th and 17th centuries. Each animal possessed a symbolic significance that would be familiar to every member of polite society. A particularly popular figure was that of the stag, favorite animal of Diana, goddess of hunting. Goldsmiths were also fond of representing the elephant, that invitation to exotic reverie. To adorn royal and aristocratic tables, huge sums were spent on fine metals and precious stones.

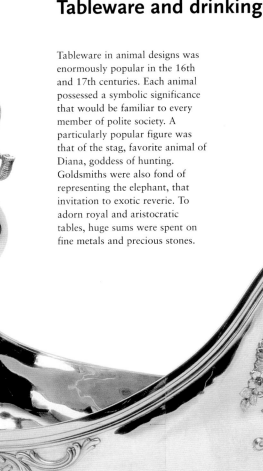

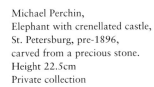

Michael Perchin,
Elephant with crenellated castle,
St. Petersburg, pre-1896,
carved from a precious stone.
Height 22.5cm
Private collection

Russian drinking vessel known as a kovsh. This monumental piece of tableware (length 88.2cm) was a golden-wedding present from Russia's Czar Alexander III to the Danish royal couple, Christian IX and Queen Louise. Made of silver, partly gold-plated, the kovsh is decorated with the Danish royal coat of arms and the Hessian coat of arms and inscribed with the date 26 May 1842–1892. The handle is surmounted by the Danish ceremonial elephant bearing a castle enameled in white and red and a pair of blue saddlebags.

Far left:
Gilded bottle with elephant decor,
Indian, 18th century.
Museum für Kunsthandwerk,
Frankfurt

Left:
Max Esser,
Elephant candelabrum, 1924,
Meissen porcelain.
Height 68.5cm
Schauhalle Staatliche
Porzellanmanufaktur,
Meissen Germany

Opposite:
Christoph Jamnitzer (1563–1618),
Elephant pourer, c. 1600,
Silver, gold-plated partly, painted.
Height 43cm, length 29cm
Kunstgewerbemuseum, Staatliche
Museen Preussischer Kulturbesitz,
Berlin

# Chinoiseries and elephant clocks

In the late 17th and early 18th centuries, a wave of enthusiasm for the great civilizations of Asia swept through Europe. Particularly in France, where a splendid delegation from Siam to the court of Louis XIV caused a sensation, the decorative arts succumbed to a fashion for all things oriental. The French king ordered six French Jesuits to travel via Siam to China in order to counter the influence of Portuguese Jesuits at the Imperial court. However, when the Emperor learned that these highly-respected scholars from the West were also missionaries who questioned the moral foundations of the Empire as well as being agents of specific political interests, he banned all Jesuits from the country in 1718.

Along with chinoiseries and the silk-weaving industry that flourished in Lyon, the elephant, too, which could be admired in the flesh in the Sun King's menagerie, found its way into the nation's salons in a wide variety of forms. Goldsmiths and porcelain manufacturers collaborated with clockmakers to create exquisite pieces combining exquisite craftsmanship with a high degree of mechanical precision.

Georg Jungmeier (1563–1634),
Elephant clock,
Augsburg, 17th century,
bronze, gilded copper.
Height (without base) 31cm
Bayrisches Nationalmuseum,
Munich

This mechanical masterpiece was built by a clockmaker from the free imperial city of Augsburg, where the Fugger and Welser families cultivated international relations. The openwork base contains a musical box. The superstructure houses the clock movement.

Right:
Baroque clock,
c. 1770,
Gilded and patinated bronze.

This Louis XV-style elephant
clock strikes the hour and the
half-hour.

Far right:
Clock automaton,
workshop of James Cox
(1740–88),
London, c. 1810
gilded brass, enamel.
93cm x 39cm x 33.5cm
Musée de l'Horlogerie, Geneva

This valuable piece skillfully
combines decorative elements
from Europe and Asia. It was
made by Genevan craftsmen in the
London workshop of a renowned
clockmaker, the late James Cox.
The client was an Asian prince.

Right:
Jewelry casket,
17th century.
Topkapi Museum, Istanbul

This jewelry casket, surmounted
by a golden elephant, was a gift to
an Ottoman sultan.

Far right:
Nikolaus Schmidt,
Elephant clock,
Augsburg, c. 1580,
bronze, gilded copper.
Height 43cm
Private collection, Munich

Elephant bearing the burden of
time. The 'stress' makes the
animal's eyes move.

Elephants in the realm of the imagination

# Orders, coats of arms, inn signs

*Order of the Elephant,*
1617,
gold, diamonds, enamel.
Height of elephant 5.6cm,
height of sword arm 6.8cm
Rosenborg Palace, Copenhagen

The Danish Order of the Elephant and (attached by a chain) Order of the Sword-in-Hand. This gem from Copenhagen's Rosenborg Palace is crafted in gold and enamel and embellished with diamonds. The castle on the elephant's back carries a miniature portrait of King Christian IV, while the arm bears the king's monogram and the date '1617.' The Order of the Elephant, donated by King Christian I in 1462 and revived with its own statutes by Christian V in 1693, is Denmark's highest decoration. It is awarded only to Protestant potentates, members of the Danish Privy Council, ministers, generals, and knights of the Order of Danebrog.

Otto Hupp (b. 1859),
*Helfenstein* (old family of Swabian counts that died out in 1627), color print from a drawing, 1908. 'Münchener Kalender,' 14th series. Munich and Regensburg, Germany

Center:
National coat of arms of the young Republic of Ivory Coast. The rising sun symbolizes freedom, while the elephant's head (like the name of the country) is a reminder of the coveted material obtained from the vast herds of elephant that once roamed this coast.

Center below:
National coat of arms of the Kingdom of Swaziland, an enclave within the Republic of South Africa. The lion stands for the king, the elephant for the queen mother. The shield showing traditional weapons is surmounted by the headdress of a Swazi warrior, decorated with bundles of feathers from the indigenous widowbird. Swaziland achieved formal independence in 1968.

Top and above:
Royal standard and flag of Laos. The legendary founder of the former Kingdom of Laos, Khoun Borom, is believed to have entered the country on a white elephant, sheltered by a white parasol, so both items were adopted as symbols of state. The old name for Laos is 'Lane Xang' ('land of a million elephants'). The three-headed elephant is a reference to the kingdom's three principalities.

Inn sign in Münster in northwest Germany, inviting passers-by to rest and relax at 'The Elephant.'

An 'elephant and castle,' widely used on British inn signs, here adorn the headquarters of the London cutlers' guild.

Elephant sign over the door of an English inn.

This inn sign in Bressanone (formerly Brixen) in Italy's South Tyrol commemorates the visit of 'Sulayman,' an elephant that King John III of Portugal gave to Austrian crown prince and future Emperor Maximilian II.

# On the chessboard

Early Indian chess-set,
19th century.
Jodhpur, India

Scene of play on an early-Indian chessboard. The game symbolized the deployment of two armies of equal strength, the object being to maneuver the foreign king into a position from which he could not escape. Chess used the same terminology as the army: infantry, elephants, cavalry, and chariots. Chess pieces in the form of elephants corresponded to military realities.

Chess, the royal game with sixteen white and sixteen black pieces, has millions of fans the world over. Local championships are held worldwide, culminating in the final duels for the crown (and purse) of the World Championship. Craftsmen have traditionally produced chess pieces that are minor works of art in their own right, carving them in wood or ivory in a wide variety of forms, often incorporating elephants.

This demanding game grew out of tactical war games, emerging in India during the 6th century BC. In the early Middle Ages, Arabs introduced it via North Africa into their possessions in Spain. From there it spread as far as central Europe around AD 1000, although for hundreds of years after that it remained a rarity in the homes of aristocrats and bourgeois alike. In 1283 Spanish author Alfonso el Sabio published the first chess manual, complete with ninety-seven illustrations. The earliest mention of a chess tournament in Germany is in a Dutch chronicle dating from 1467.

The first unofficial world championship was played in the USA in 1868 between the Russian Zuckertort (then living in the New World) and the German Steinitz, who won. In recent years Russian players have dominated the chess scene.

King piece,
20th century,
enamel, with pearls hanging from the parasol.
Jaipur, Rajasthan, India

King piece,
North India, 19th/20th century,
ivory.
Museum für Völkerkunde,
Munich

Elephants in the realm of the imagination

Castle pieces from the 'Munich Chess-set,'
North India, late-19th/early 20th century,
carved ivory.
Museum für Völkerkunde, Munich

Much-used ivory elephant
chess piece.
Collection of Dr. Jaeger,
Neu-Ulm, Germany

Indian chess-set,
c. 1820,
ivory.

The elephants with canopies are
the kings. The elephant with three
riders is a queen; those with two
riders are castles. As symbols of
power, elephants usually represent
officers in Indian chess-sets.

Early Indian playing-cards were usually circular. This one, from a pack that dates from the Mogul period (16th–17th centuries), shows an archer surrounded by elephants.

## On beermats, matchboxes, and postage stamps

The beermat, that small cardboard disk that is the barfly's 'tablecloth,' is a now valued collector's item. Some breweries go to enormous trouble to dress up what is basically designed to absorb the foamy overflowing 'head' as an advertisement for their particular brew, providing the silent drinker, whose mind is alive to matters metaphysical, with (they hope) some welcome food for thought. The portly figure of the elephant is clearly thought a great encouragement to down another glass.

Of course Nietzsche, who may have had a nasty experience with beer, opined that Germans' minds were being held back by their beer and newspapers; he recommended some herb tea and defamatory pamphlets instead ...

Hundreds of different elephant images adorn postage stamps, particularly in tropical countries where the giant pachyderm is at home.

Elephants in the realm of the imagination

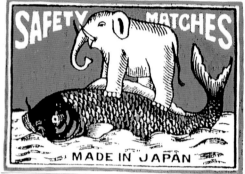

In Japan, with its sophisticated approach to packaging, the ordinary matchbox is an amazingly rich vehicle for graphic design – charming, ever-changing, and open to a thousand playful variations. Up until the First World War, box decorations were engraved on copper plates for printing. For the export trade, motives appropriate to the customer country would be selected. The Southeast Asian market invited use of the friendly image of the elephant. Japanese matchboxes are valued collector's items worldwide.

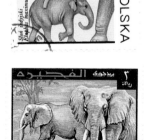

Elephants feature on whole sets of stamps from the countries of Africa or Asia where the animals still live or did until recently. Their familiar, friendly form is also used to adorn the stamps of countries that know elephants only from the circus or the zoo.

Elephants in the realm of the imagination

*Adoration of the Magi*,
two crib scenes from Bavaria,
c. 1800,
wire figures with wax heads
and fabric clothing.
Bayerisches Nationalmuseum,
Munich

It was considered in keeping
with the exotic appearance of the
"wise men from the East" that
one of them should be mounted
on an elephant.

Elephants in the realm of the imagination

# The Christmas crib

In 1223, so the story goes, St. Francis of Assisi set up a manger or 'crib' in the Forest of Greccio and brought ox and ass to celebrate Christmas in the open air. For Francis, whose 'Canticle of the sun' paid homage to all of life, animals belonged to the "brotherhood of living creatures."

This lifelike form of the Christmas liturgy, which the Franciscan Order continued to practice, received a further boost in the 15th and 16th centuries from the emerging custom of displaying groups of figures from the Bethlehem story. As early as 1567 the Duchess of Amalfi owned a collection of 167 figures representing the birth of Christ, the Adoration of the Shepherds, and the procession of the Three Wise Men. The center of crib art was Naples in southern Italy. Very much in

the spirit of St. Francis, ox and ass were joined at the cribside by elephant, camel, and horse. Beginning in the 16th century, a small number of mechanical cribs with moving figures were manufactured (Augsburg in Germany was one source of these pieces.)

In the 17th and 18th centuries, the custom of the Christmas crib spread throughout Europe. In nunneries in particular small cribs were set up to provide a focal point for mystical Jesus-worship, not just at Christmas. Growing secularization during the Renaissance and Baroque periods gave rise to some colorful works of art incorporating large numbers of figures. The Christmas story was set amid the bustle of public life in the cities, or in scenes of courtly splendor.

# The Elephant's Child
*by Rudyard Kipling*

## How the elephant got its trunk

'Just So Stories' is a collection of children's stories by Rudyard Kipling (1865–1936) in which he writes with great imagination about various peculiarities in the animal kingdom. One of the things he explains is how the elephant got its trunk. Apparently it happened like this:

"In the high and far-off Times the Elephant, O Best Beloved [Kipling always addresses the reader thus], had no trunk. He had only a blackish, bulgy nose, as big as a boot, that he could wriggle about from side to side; but he couldn't pick things up with it. But there was one Elephant – a new Elephant – an Elephant's Child – who was full of 'satiable curtiosity, and that means he asked ever so many questions. And he lived in Africa, and he filled all Africa with his 'satiable curtiosities. He asked his tall aunt, the Ostrich, why her tail-feathers grew just so, and his tall aunt the Ostrich spanked him with her hard, hard claw. [...] He asked his broad aunt, the Hippopotamus, why her eyes were red, and his broad aunt, the Hippopotamus, spanked him with her broad, broad hoof."

Another thing the Elephant's Child wanted to know was what the Crocodile had for dinner.

"Then everybody said 'Hush!' in a loud and dretful tone, and they spanked him immediately and directly, without stopping, for a long time.

"By and by [...] he came upon Kolokolo Bird [...] and he said, 'My father has spanked me, and my mother has spanked me; all my aunts and uncles have spanked me for my 'satiable curtiosity; and still I want to know what the Crocodile has for dinner!'

"Then Kolokolo Bird said, with a mournful cry, 'Go to the banks of the great gray-green, greasy Limpopo River, all set about with fever-trees, and find out.'

"The Elephant's Child made his way to the Limpopo River and politely asked the first animal he came across to direct him to the crocodile.

"The Crocodile caught him by his little nose ... " Original illustration by Rudyard Kipling.

Elephants in the realm of the imagination

Gustave Doré (1832–83),
*The elephant and the rat*,
illustration from 'Fables' by Jean
de la Fontaine, Fable XV, Book 8,
Paris, 1868,
colored wood engraving.
24cm x 19cm

In his fable 'The elephant and the rat,' La Fontaine (1621–95) held up a mirror to contemporaries who were happy to pose as gentlemen of rank but were in fact little people. The rat arrogantly mocks the elephant's bulk until a cat comes along and proves that "a rat ain't no elephant."

" 'Come hither, Little One,' said the Crocodile, 'for I am the Crocodile,' and he wept crocodile-tears to show it was quite true.

"Then the Elephant's Child grew all breathless, and panted, and kneeled down on the bank and said, 'You are the very person I have been looking for all these long days. Will you please tell me what you have for dinner?'

" 'Come hither, Little One,' said the Crocodile, 'and I'll whisper.'

"Then the Elephant's Child put his head down close to the Crocodile's musky, tusky mouth, and the Crocodile caught him by his little nose [...] and pulled, and pulled, and pulled.

"And the Elephant's Child's nose kept on stretching; and the Elephant's Child spread all his little four legs and pulled, and pulled, and pulled, and his nose kept on stretching; and the Crocodile threshed his tail like an oar, and he pulled, and pulled, and pulled, and at each pull the Elephant's Child's nose grew longer and longer – and it hurt him hijjus!"

Eventually, with the help of a recent acquaintance, the Bi-Colored-Python-Rock-Snake, the Elephant's Child pulls harder and the Crocodile lets go. The disconsolate young pachyderm, his

nose badly out of shape, sits there for three days waiting in vain for it to shrink. Again, the Bi-Colored-Python-Rock-Snake comes to his aid, pointing out the advantages of such an extended member. The Elephant's Child does indeed find to his delight that he can use to swat flies, pluck grass to eat, and make himself cooling mud-caps against the heat of the day. He is also, on reaching home, able to return some of the spanking formerly meted out to him. Indeed, so astonished are the members of his family and so intrigued by the merits of the new appendage that they all hurry off to the river "to borrow new noses from the Crocodile. When they came back nobody spanked anybody any more; and ever since that day, O Best Beloved, all the elephants you will ever see, besides all those that you won't, have trunks precisely like the trunk of the 'satiable Elephant's Child."

Kipling, who was born and grew up in India, also wrote many stories and autobiographical works that together give a detailed picture of Anglo-Indian colonial society, of the country, and of its animals. His 'Jungle Book' and 'Second Jungle Book'are known all over the world. In 1907 Kipling was awarded the Nobel Prize for Literature.

Ignace-Isidore Gérard, known as
Grandville (1803–47),
*The elephant*,
illustration from 'Scènes de la vie privé et publique des animaux,'
Paris, 1842,
wood engraving.
18.3cm x 13.2cm

"Sir, you're too fat to be a conspirator!" One of Grandville's satirical illustrations from his 'Scenes from the private and public lives of animals,' a collection of malicious parables lampooning the rotten socio-political conditions that caused the France of 'bourgeois king' Louis-Philippe of Orleans finally to slide into the February Revolution of 1848.

Above:
Steiff elephant on wheels, c. 1920.

Top right:
Title page of a children's book by Walter Trier, the great German illustrator of the 1920s.

Center right:
Toy elephant, India, c. 1910.

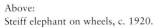

Elephants large and small. Two-year-old Jane, accompanied by her toy elephant, watches the 'Jumbos' of the Bertram Mills Circus parade through London on December 11, 1963.

African elephant calf Plastic educational toy.

Far right:
Tin elephant riding a tricycle.

Toys based on circus acts, manufactured from old designs, can still be found in the shops.

# Elephants in the nursery

It is said that an elephant will never harm a child. Many are the stories about how well this gentle giant treats children who, for their part, adore the kindly, clumsy colossus who carries them off into the world of fantasy.

The elephant, which lends itself so good-naturedly to trivialization by the artist's hand, is the hero of countless children's stories. French author and illustrator Jean de Brunhoff created a particularly lovable specimen, found in nurseries the world over: he is the little orphan elephant 'Babar,' who arrives in the human city and there, under the protection of a nice old lady, becomes a well-behaved member of the family, always correctly attired, diligent, and well-mannered, and so a good role model.

At the end of the story, which has been translated into many languages, Babar returns to the animal kingdom and is there made king, showing his hosts of small admirers how far even an elephant child can get by being good, and so hopefully providing food for thought.

The humanized elephant: Babar in formal attire and driving a sports car.

Tin war elephants are still manufactured today from patterns dating from the 19th century.

## Actors in film and theater

Elephant scene in Johann Kresnik's (b. 1939) production of *Rosa Luxemburg – Red roses for you* from a libretto by George Tabori at the Volksbühne am Rosa Luxemburg Platz, October 29, 1993, with Susanne Ibanez as Rosa and René Steinke as the elephant.

The wider public's taste for spectacle makes the elephant a sought-after extra for film, opera, theater, even the musical. It has also served on occasion as an intelligent actor whose exceptional circus skills are capable of lending weight to the thinnest scenario. It can use its trunk to carry its partner gently out of harm's way, trumpet at precisely the right moment, and tolerate every kind of prank with dignity. If its gigantic bulk imposes certain restrictions as regards stage appearances, in film there are no such limits. In exotic adventure stories particularly, elephant actors can make a notable contribution.

*Mahabharata,*
A Peter Brook film,
Joinville Studios France,
1988.

The film is taken from the great Hindu national epic of that name, whose 100,000 couplets narrate a whole range of stories and episodes. The photograph, taken during shooting, shows Vyasa the poet telling his story, the story of mankind, to a child. The god Ganesh offers his services as scribe. And since the child enquires about his fate, the legend of how Ganesh came by his elephant's head also finds a place in the epic.

Elephants featured as heavyweight extras in the gigantic 1987 production of Verdi's opera 'Aida' in the Luxor temple complex in Egypt. Under the direction of Giuseppe Raffa, this 'operama'drew on the services of 120 musicians, 150 singers, 50 dancers, and 1,000 extras.

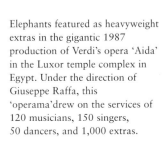

Elephants in the realm of the imagination

In the comedy film 'Operation Dumbo,' US soldiers have to replace a village's lost sacred elephant during the Vietnam War. The animal, weighing several tons, has to be dropped by parachute.

In the cartoon film of 'The Jungle Book,' the elephants (pictured) take the tiny hero Mowgli into their midst to protect him from predatory wild animals.

The Indian youngster Sabu in the role of elephant boy Tumai with his faithful friend Kala Nag.

Sporting his red cap, elephant Benjamin Blümchen ('little flower') and his tiny witch companion Bibi Blocksberg fly back into the Stone Age on a magic broomstick to rescue a baby mammoth.

The 100,000 frames of this cartoon film bring author Elfi Donelly's amusing adventure story to vibrant life, delighting millions of children.

## The elephant boy

British colonial writer Rudyard Kipling, who grew up in India, paid homage to the loyalty and reliability of the elephant in his world-famous 'Jungle Book.' His story of the Indian boy Tumai, who experiences the legendary nocturnal dance of the wild elephants in a jungle clearing, perched safely on the back of his gray friend Kala Nag, was filmed by Hollywood as 'The elephant boy,' which became an international hit.

When director Robert Flaherty (1884–1951) went into the jungle in 1936 to look for a suitable animal, he found one who would obey only his tiny master, an Indian boy named Sabu. Flaherty signed up his 'dream team,' and as 'Tumai, darling of the elephants' Sabu became a Hollywood star. He died suddenly of a heart attack in 1963 at the age of only thirty-nine.

# The elephant and the donkey

Political parties have traditionally used the elephant as a symbol of irresistible drive and outstanding intelligence. In the USA it is the mascot of the Republicans, the 'Grand Old Party' that emerged in the industrialized northern states in 1834 as a political movement opposed to slavery and rival British imports (and political influence) in the cotton states of the south. In 1861 the new political force carried Abraham Lincoln, the champion of liberalism and American unity, into the Presidency (which he occupied until his assassination in 1865).

Following the victory of the North over the agrarian South, a powerful Republican Party organization emerged that deliberately chose the mightiest of all land animals as its mascot. The mascot of the Southern Democrats, the donkey, lagged far behind. However, after many triumphs the elephant did eventually lose ground to the donkey of the reforming Democratic Party, which reached the summit of its power before and during the Second World War under the presidency of Franklin D. Roosevelt (1933–45).

More recently, the programs of the two major parties have moved closer together. Elephant and donkey are now mere party labels, their physical weight no longer bearing any symbolic relation to power and influence.

During the 1876 election campaign the Republican giant tramples the Democrat candidates for the presidency and vice-presidency, Tilden and Hendricks, underfoot. They are portrayed as a deformed, two-headed tiger bcause, as a team, they represented contradictory policies – in favor of 'hard' and 'soft' money.

After the 1876 election the elephant, though crowned with the laurels of victory, was badly wounded. The Republicans had only just scraped together a majority for their own candidate, Hayes, against the Democrat Tilden. "Another victory like that and I'm done for," groaned Hayes, echoing King Pyrrhus when he famously won the battle but lost the war.

The elephant, longtime symbol and mascot of the Republican Party in the USA.

Elephants in the realm of the imagination

Young elephant campaigning for the Republicans. "I like Ike" was the slogan of Dwight David Eisenhower, who on November 4, 1952 was elected President by a substantial majority.

'Stars and stripes' surround the Republican Party's elephant symbol and mascot.

Dressed as elephants, the children of conference delegates elicit support for the Republican Party.

Elephants in the realm of the imagination

# From the sketchbook of Heinrich Kley

Heinrich Kley (1863–1945),
Elephants,
1909,
Lithographs from pen drawings.

The sketchbook of German painter and illustrator Heinrich Kley was published in Munich in 1909. It includes these magical drawings, which place elephants in our 'human, all-too-human' world. Together, they make a warm-hearted plea for the threatened giant.

Elephants in the realm of the imagination

Elephants in the realm of the imagination

# The zoo as refuge

The peaceful primordial giant, trunk reaching out over the perimeter ditch for tidbits, is constantly besieged by visitors. Elephant rides round zoos and pachyderms appearing in romantic 'Jungle Nights' shows are an unforgettable experience for young and old. The mighty pachyderm is a major

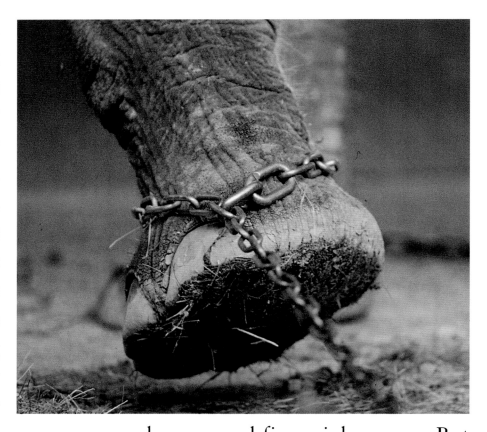

Chained up for long periods and only occasionally allowed to roam free in their compounds, elephants can fall victim to mental illness. There is a great need for modernization in those elephant houses where groups of cows must stand at night and be confined throughout the winter, usually in chains or isolated in individual stalls. Only a few of the world's largest zoos have communal indoor spaces where elephant cows are able to move about unchained.

attraction, the pride of many zoos, and zoos need financial success. But do there have to be elephants in every zoo, no matter how restricted the space or how tight the budget? In a world in which people are becoming increasingly alienated from animals, a number of zoos are already trying to turn themselves into islands of protection for nature and its endangered species, though with so many other barred cages the human race continues to sin gravely against the animal world. It is right that the threatened elephant should be offered a friendly refuge. Yet its gigantic bulk, its anatomy, and its character all demand an extraordinary amount of care. The elephant is a herd animal. In solitary confinement, its movements constrained and its mind a prey to boredom, it suffers psychologically. Proper, species-friendly elephant care can be provided only by well-equipped zoos cooperating on a supra-regional basis.

'Husein', senior bull elephant of Hamburg's Hagenbeck Animal Park, with friend. Twenty-year-old Husein is a fine example of good bull keeping, the basic prerequisite of successful elephant-breeding. He has his own house and his own compound, with access to the communal enclosure where the cows roam. This reproduces something of a herd atmosphere.

Paris's *Palais des Pachydermes*. A scene from the old menagerie days: elephants behind bars in the 'Jardin des Plantes.'

## Cages and free compounds

When around the mid-19th century the first zoological gardens evolved from menageries and animal shows with their rows of cages, the people of Europe and North America had the sensational experience of seeing with their own eyes exotic creatures from far-off lands: the mighty elephant and the ominous big cats, reassuringly behind bars. Zoos vied with one another to present the public with the greatest possible variety of species, despite conditions of severe confinement that sometimes amounted to torture. Animals were objects; species protection was not on the agenda. These were dreadful times for the 'true' wild animal.

Nowadays, animal rarities from the tropics are no longer a novelty. People no longer visit zoos in search of exotic sensations. They are looking for a congenial encounter with familiar creatures kept in open compounds, a few hours' rest and recreation in an oasis of nature.

Chainsaws and fire clearance have destroyed nearly two-thirds of the world's rain forests, once the source of replenishment of the wild-animal requirements of circuses and zoos. Every day, more than seventy species disappear for all time. The elephant itself is now on the list of endangered species. In a dramatically altered world, zoos now have the task of providing active species protection.

The majority of the world's zoos have begun to rethink and re-equip. By deciding not to keep certain species, they have made room even on restricted inner-city sites for suitably large compounds for threatened species unable to thrive in cages. Wild animals that have room to move, and whose behavior and characteristics are allowed for, offer visitors a more rewarding experience than a wide variety of rarities living in less congenial conditions. This is particularly true of elephants, which it ought to be illegal to keep in confined spaces.

The message has got through. Change is apparent all over the world, not least in the USA, where the major zoos have done pioneering work in this field. In Europe, Berlin Zoo once boasted the continent's largest variety of species. However, since its inner-city location allows no room for expansion, for large-animal breeding it has agreed a division of responsibilities with Friedrichsfelde

Species-friendly elephant keeping in Hamburg's Hagenbeck Animal Park. In the spacious maternity compound with its bathing pools and in the even larger herd compound with its indispensable mud wallows, a healthy social life is able to develop.

Ghastly dreariness and loneliness in an elephant house. Cow and calf doze apathetically in 'solitary.'

Zoo in the eastern suburbs, which has extensive free-range compounds. Hagenbeck Animal Park in Hamburg has decided to stop keeping rhinos, freeing up another compound for its herd of elephants. Frankfurt Zoo, which had only one elephant, has given up the keeping of elephants altogether because it lacks sufficient space.

Holland has expanded its zoos on a grand scale; Basel and Zurich in Switzerland both have the latest facilities; while Vincennes (Paris) and Chester (UK) are undergoing thorough renovation. Once performed in a rather haphazard fashion in too many poorly equipped locations, elephant-breeding is now practiced only in large zoos employing seasoned experts.

There is still a great need for modernization in many elephant houses, where animals have to spend every night and the whole of the winter. In the few zoos with systematic elephant-breeding programs, it is usually only the bulls that have their own territory where they can go unchained. With one or two exceptions, zoos lack large, communal indoor spaces where groups of cows are free to roam. Most elephant cows in captivity spend an average of sixteen to eighteen hours standing chained in spaces that are too small for them.

How much time animals are able to spend in free-range compounds, how much exercise they get, whether there are opportunities for them to work within the zoo – all these things are limited by the statutory working-hours of their keepers. For safety reasons, casual labor cannot be used to chain the animals up for their evening feed and for the night. Groups of cows are governed by a strict hierarchy, and chaining at feeding-times is essential if the lowest-ranking animal is also to get her share.

Many of the world's zoos now have tropical houses where big cats, monkeys, etc. are provided with more appropriate living-space in a jungle atmosphere. One thinks of the spectacular facilities in Arnheim (Holland), for example, or in New York's Bronx district, where the zoo is called a 'Wildlife Conservation Park.' Communal indoor spaces suitable for elephants need to be very large to accommodate these gigantic animals. Expensive to build, they are well beyond the means of most privately-financed zoos. Fine examples exist in Vienna's Schönbrunn Zoo as well as in Münster in northwest Germany, where at a cost of over DM 6 million the group of elephant cows is housed in a building covering some 5,400 square feet, which is certainly sufficient for their needs.

# Bull-keeping is the key

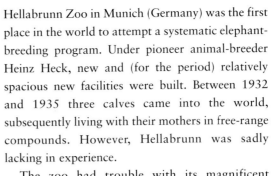

'Boy,' the magnificent bull elephant of Munich's Hellabrunn Zoo, who fathered five calves in the 1930s.

Hellabrunn Zoo in Munich (Germany) was the first place in the world to attempt a systematic elephant-breeding program. Under pioneer animal-breeder Heinz Heck, new and (for the period) relatively spacious new facilities were built. Between 1932 and 1935 three calves came into the world, subsequently living with their mothers in free-range compounds. However, Hellabrunn was sadly lacking in experience.

The zoo had trouble with its magnificent breeding bull 'Boy' who, as a result of being inappropriately chained up, developed behavioral problems and one day seriously wounded Heck and an assistant keeper. When Boy later fell into the moat and broke both tusks, exposing the nerve-ends, the animal was destroyed. A further breeding attempt in 1951 led to the stillbirth of twins, after which breeding in Munich was halted.

Now, however, Munich's Hellabrunn Zoo is preparing for a fresh try at producing its own young. Five-year-old bull 'Gajendra' has nearly reached mating age. There are six cows in the herd, with an additional youngster on order. The facilities of the pioneering days have been generously extended and modernized. The old concrete moats were V-shaped, which meant that any elephant falling in had little chance of survival. These have now been replaced by broad moats with sloping sides, making it easier for animals that take a tumble to regain their feet. And the herd now spends the night in a communal indoor space rather than individually chained. Following the bitter experiences of those early attempts in the 1930s, Hellabrunn has drawn the consequences.

Hellabrunn in the 1930s. The first attempt at controlled elephant breeding failed because of the problems of keeping bulls in appropriate conditions.

'Schari,' Hellabrunn's first breeding bull. The picture was taken in 1942, when Schari was already an old animal.

The zoo as refuge

## Partner selection in captivity

There was a great stir at Vincennes Zoo in Paris when 'Caveri,' a young cow of only 4 1/2 years, became pregnant. Three months after this photograph was taken in February 1988, the gigantic 41 year-old Asian bull 'Siam' mated with little Caveri, who in March 1990 gave birth to and nurtured a healthy bull calf. Siam was Europe's most successful breeding bull Asian elephant ever. In 1997, aged about 52 years, he developed foot problems and had to be put down.

Elephants need to be young when they first give birth, say between 10 and 20 years of age. First pregnancies in cows over 25 can lead to problems and stillbirths. Bulls are most likely to retain their mating instinct and their normal behavior when not regimented by humans – that is to say, if mature males are able to satisfy their sex drive even with cows that do not 'take.' If a bull dips his trunk in a cow's urine and blows the scent into his own mouth, this is regarded as a sign that the cow is about to come into heat. The bull must be able to move about the compound unhindered, at liberty to visit the cows or stay in the peace and quiet of his private domain, all of which helps to foster a natural herd atmosphere.

The world's greatest breeding success with twenty-three births and only one stillbirth has been achieved in the USA, where Roman Schmitt has been working with his group of elephants at the Ringling Circus breeding station in Polk City, Florida, since 1995. His breeding bull 'Vance' has always been able to select his own partners and has

also been excused duties in the ring. Vance has fathered twenty calves! Schmitt's father, formerly Ringling's celebrated 'elephant man,' had learned his trade at Hagenbeck Animal Park in Hamburg.

At Hagenbeck, which has the largest breeding group in Europe, 23 year-old bull 'Husein' also selects his own partners. He has mated successfully six times: four calves have grown up healthy, while two stillbirths were from cows over 30 years of age. So far Husein has not experienced a prolonged or dangerous 'musth' phase (see 'Bulls in musth: the strange temporal glands), which experts put down to his balanced sex life. In the wild, musth causes bulls to dominate the herd and shield it from rivals. Evidently Husein does not need a strong musth impulse, since his dominance of the group of cows is permanent and he has no rivals.

Concerning the musth phenomenon, many questions remain unanswered. Blood tests offer an interesting insight. When Husein's testosterone level rises, a cow comes into heat between one and two days later.

# Breeding problems

The recent International Convention on Species Protection bans capture of elephants living in the wild and any trade in such animals. In future, zoos may no longer 'consume' wild elephants; they must now supply their own young animals. However, experience has shown that elephant-breeding is an extremely difficult and expensive undertaking.

According to figures released by the 'European Elephant Group,' which concerns itself with the protection and proper keeping of elephants, of 120 Asian elephants born in Europe between the years 1902 and 1992, 43 were either stillborn, were killed immediately by their mothers, or died shortly after birth; only 44 lived long enough (eight years) to become sexually mature. This dismal breeding result is due to inappropriate keeping in wretchedly cramped conditions as well as to sheer lack of experience of keepers.

Elephants are herd animals; they need company. The basic prerequisite for successful breeding is an intact social group in the compound. Elephants take time to get to know and like one another. Cows sent to strange bulls in makeshift breeding attempts have failed to come into heat.

A confined breeding group requires spacious, appropriately laid-out free-range compounds and costly buildings. Hamburg's Hagenbeck Animal

Hagenbeck Animal Park, Hamburg. An 'aunt' with three calves born in 1995–96 in the maternity compound. Calves remain in the care of mothers and 'aunts' until the age of three, when they are transferred to other suitable breeding groups.

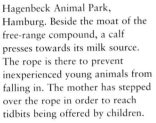

Hagenbeck Animal Park, Hamburg. Beside the moat of the free-range compound, a calf presses towards its milk source. The rope is there to prevent inexperienced young animals from falling in. The mother has stepped over the rope in order to reach tidbits being offered by children.

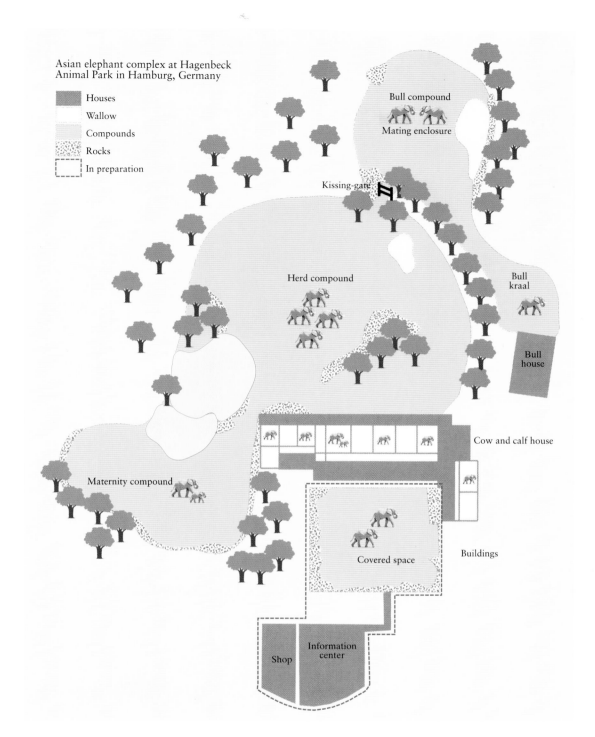

Asian elephant complex at Hagenbeck
Animal Park in Hamburg, Germany

- Houses
- Wallow
- Compounds
- Rocks
- In preparation

Bull compound
Mating enclosure
Kissing-gate
Herd compound
Bull kraal
Bull house
Cow and calf house
Buildings
Covered space
Maternity compound
Shop
Information center

The extended elephant facilities at Hagenbeck Animal Park.

Park has fine compounds capable of serving as international models. It also boasts the best breeding results in Europe. Until completion of a projected communal indoor space, cows will spend the night standing in chain-free boxes.

Keeping a bull calls for special facilities. In the wild, the bull leads a life of his own away from the cows; in captivity, he must have his own house and his own free-range compound. Once a year an adult bull comes into musth – a critical state of arousal that usually lasts for about three days but may go on for much longer. Zoo animals are particularly irritable and dangerous during this phase. They must be kept in undisturbed isolation and tended from a safe distance. The bull house needs to contain a double stall consisting of two separate stand boxes with doors operated from outside. The bull can thus be lured into one or the other box with tidbits whenever fodder needs

replenishing or mucking-out is required. Part of the bull's free-range compound can be sealed off as a small kraal for exercise during musth. Only after several days, when the bull once more responds to orders, can he be treated normally again.

Cows also need their own house as well as a large communal compound. The presence of a bull at night would keep them in a constant state of stress. Also required is a separate maternity compound, where mothers and 'aunts' can tend and nurture suckling calves undisturbed. In captivity, cows sometimes react in a hostile manner to being crowded together. Only when the babies have grown up a bit are they introduced to the other cows of the group.

When young Vietnamese cow 'Lai Sinh' arrived at Hagenbeck in 1994 she was an orphan with behavioral problems. As a result of living in a group and receiving proper treatment, she has become so good-natured that she enjoys playing with her familiar keeper. Lai Sinh has lost the prehensile tip of her trunk. This scarcely hinders her while feeding, though she is unable to grasp small objects such as grass stems or coins.

Top:
The kissing-gate between the herd and bull compounds.

# An elephant is born in captivity

**8 minutes old**

Eight minutes after birth, little Chamundi has, with human help, been freed from the amniotic sac. The mother's probing trunk checks what is happening.

In the wild, the birth of an elephant calf is watched over by an 'aunt,' an experienced older cow who is herself suckling a baby or has previously given birth. Young calves in a group of cows, most of whom will be sisters, are able to witness the birthing process and the tending of the newborn animal. They are thus familiar with the youngster from the very first moment, and later they will be involved in looking after it. When young cows first become pregnant, they already know something of what they must do.

In the 'unnatural' elephant groups kept in zoos, the difficult task of rendering assistance at a birth falls to humans, who can only ever be a poor substitute. Critical situations may quickly arise, particularly at a young cow's first birth when she has not been able to learn from older cows and often has no idea how to deal with a newborn baby. Instinct does not cover everything.

Elephant keeper Karl Kock, who in ten years' employment at Hagenbeck Animal Park in Hamburg had been able to gather a wealth of experience, described in his 1994 book 'My Life with Elephants' the difficult first parturition of a young cow named 'Thura,' who suddenly became restless one evening, passing a great deal of water and dung. A careful watch was kept on her throughout the night. Towards morning she calmed down again and was slowly led around the compound. After a while she wished to return to her stall, where she was fastened by one foreleg and

one hind leg – a precautionary measure since first-time elephant mothers in captivity often refuse to accept the baby, pushing it away. Eventually Thura was ready. Karl Kock takes up the story:

"At twenty to eleven that evening, Thura suddenly threw up her head and spread her hind legs. Beneath her tail appeared a large swelling, she shuffled lower and lower, the amniotic sac began to emerge, it burst open, and the baby slid out of the vagina onto the floor. The whole thing was over in less than two minutes … The baby lay half in, half out of the box, and Thura was already attempting to step towards it."

The newborn was quickly dragged away, and in half an hour's time it was helped to its feet. It was a female, weighing around 190 pounds. An hour later, when the calf was carefully presented to the teat, its mother had to be prevented from stepping on it.

After several days of constant supervision to protect the youngster, an experienced 59 year-old cow called 'Kiri' was brought into the maternity compound. Kiri accepted the baby straight away, looked after it fondly, gave it a helping trunk and foot when it fell over, and pacified Thura when the little one went for the teat. If Thura, still rejecting her youngster, became nervous when it suckled, the 'aunt' threatened warningly with movements of her trunk and head. In this case it proved possible, even under zoo conditions, to mobilize and make use of an element of herd solidarity and natural 'aunt' care as would occur in the wild.

**20 minutes old**

After twenty minutes, the calf raises its head for a first, wide-eyed look at the world.

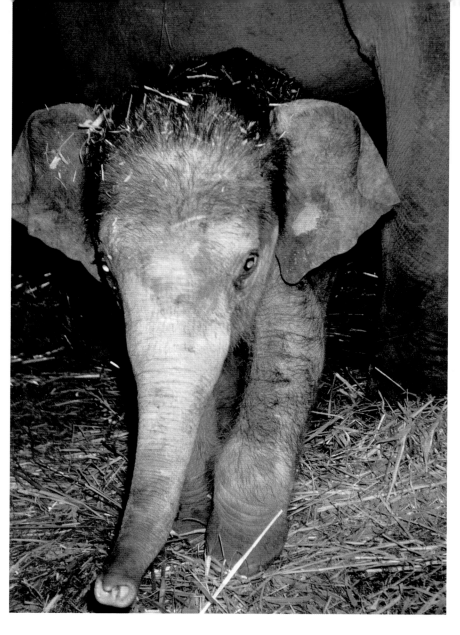

## Motty the crossbreed

**30 minutes old**

After half an hour Chamundi is able to stand unaided.

In July 1978, in Britain's Chester Zoo, an African-Asian crossbred elephant calf was born. This caused an international sensation. Most people had thought that crossbreeding between the two species was simply not possible. Like its Asian-elephant mother 'Sheba,' the calf had only a single prehensile 'finger' on its trunk and the same number of toes as the Asian species. The large ears and other features had been inherited from 15 year-old African bull 'Jumbolino.'

Sheba and Jumbolino had mated on several occasions. No one, however, believed in the possibility of a crossbreed being conceived. When the mother's abdomen began to swell, pregnancy was not diagnosed. The result, on July 11, 1978, was a surprise premature birth in the free-range compound at Chester Zoo.

The male calf, despite having been accepted by the mother and surrounded with care, died after fourteen days. The skin was stuffed and put on show in London's Natural History Museum. To this day, there has been no successful attempt to cross Asian and African elephants.

## An aging population

Captive breeding in zoos operates on a very narrow base. According to data gathered by the European Elephant Group, of 450 Asian-elephant cows kept in zoos in 1992, only 19 were fit for breeding. That means a breeding base of only 4 percent!

Elephants off-loaded onto zoos by circuses are usually of no use for breeding purposes. In conditions of long-term physical and mental stress, both female and male animals cease to function sexually. As a result, few animals that up to the age of fifteen or over have been trained in circus rings, and have spent the rest of the time dozing in chains inside narrow canvas stalls or crowded behind electric fences, will be fit for breeding.

In the USA, too, the aging of the elephant population in zoos, circuses, and animal shows is well advanced. Even the zoo in Portland, Oregon which, in the two decades between 1962 and 1991, achieved the world's best breeding result with twenty births, managed only another five births in the period 1982–96. Moreover, Portland's experiments with artificial insemination had a negative effect on natural reproduction: forcing breeding bulls to donate semen actually dulled their natural mating instinct!

**one day old**

Day-old Chamundi already enjoys a firm footing between mother's rear 'columns' and has begun playing with that trunk!

An elephant in Los Angeles Zoo makes an acrobatic attempt to reach some greenery outside the enclosure. Elephants are difficult to confine; they are good climbers and do not, like rhinos, need to keep all four feet on the ground.

African elephant in Vincennes Zoo in Paris. There is no excuse for such barbaric 'defenses;' these iron spikes set in concrete often cause serious foot injuries.

## Dangerous moats

Feeding by members of the public reduces boredom, which elephants find hard to tolerate. It also creates opportunities for friendly contact between people and animals. However, extreme stretching for a child's tidbit can lead to a tumble into the moat.

One problem encountered in zoos is the use of moats around elephant compounds, because animals are forever falling in, injuring themselves badly and sometimes even fatally. However, no one has yet come up with a better solution. Heavy iron bars would destroy the impression of relative freedom, erecting a barrier between humans and animals. Nor would such a solution be in the elephants' interests: in the friendly surroundings of the open animal park, the animals make more endearing ambassadors for their threatened cousins in the wild.

Particularly dangerous (but still often to be found) are concrete moats that taper downwards. These give elephants little chance of surviving a fall. If the bottom of the moat is kept wide and presents a soft landing, an elephant is better able to get to its feet again and be helped out. Iron spikes set in concrete along the edge of a moat are a nasty, barbaric solution capable of inflicting serious foot injuries.

The elephant compounds in Israel's model Ramat Gan Zoo in Tel Aviv are surrounded by walls; there are no moats. Terraces give visitors an unimpeded view from above. However, such a solution rules out the ever-popular practice of 'feeding the elephants' – members of the public holding out tidbits for trunks to reach for – which gives the animals something to do and combats boredom.

When African elephant 'Dixie' fell into the moat surrounding the free-range enclosure in London Zoo, the incident proved fatal; all attempts to save the unfortunate animal were in vain.

The zoo as refuge

## When elephants cry ...

It is said that elephants, in torment and despair, will occasionally cry. This has been reported by experienced zoologists. Ivan T. Sanderson, for instance, in his book 'The Dynasty of Abu' mentions a moving incident that occurred in Lancaster, Missouri:

Two experienced animal-trainers were trying to teach the young elephant cow 'Sadie' a circus trick. Sadie could not understand what was expected of her and tried to walk out of the ring. She was hauled back and moderately, without cruelty, punished for her refusal. Whereupon Sadie, we are told, sank to her knees, rolled over onto her side, and cried like a baby.

In half a century of living and working with elephants, Sanderson wrote, nothing had ever moved him so deeply. Anyone pointing a gun at an animal might expect it to flinch – even if only as a mechanical reflex. It was quite a different matter when the animal (particularly one weighing 3 tons) lay right down and actually wept. "Are we men, who give ourselves such airs, not in fact the only creatures to have mood swings and experience the higher emotions?"

According to Sylvia K. Sikes, author of 'The Natural History of the African Elephant,' wild elephants seldom cry, while captive animals will do so quite often.

In 'The Expression of the Emotions in Men and Animals,' Charles Darwin quoted fellow Briton Sir James Emerson Tennent on the capture and shackling of elephants in Ceylon (Sri Lanka): "Some lay motionless on the ground; only the tears wetting their cheeks revealed the fact that they were suffering." Of one animal he wrote: "When he had been overpowered and bound, his distress was touching. What had been resistance turned to total submission. Lying on the ground, he uttered muffled cries, tears running down his cheeks."

Karl Kock (whom we have already met) also describes a moving experience in his book 'My Life with Elephants.' In the 1980s, Augsburg Zoo sent him to Mallorca to buy the only elephant from a small animal park that had closed down and been sold into private hands. He found the animal in a small walled pen. A woman brought kitchen waste daily, and every three days a man came to muck out. Kock: "The elephant stretched out its trunk towards us and chirped like a canary. I had never heard an elephant utter such sounds before."

Keen to free the elephant from its misery, Kock tried everything to persuade the owner to sell the animal. But the owner firmly refused: the elephant was his sole hobby! Kock reports again: "When, hours later, we had to go, the elephant reached after us with its trunk and chirped again. Since that day it has been my conviction that elephants are capable of crying."

In surroundings of cruel bleakness, bored, held in chains, these elephant cows, migratory animals by nature, doze in perpetual confinement.

# Elephant hygiene in the zoo

In the wild – in steppe, bush, and forest – elephants attend to their hygiene needs as part of their daily rhythm. For skin-care, they wallow in mud-holes, rub against trees and rocks, bathe whenever they can, and take regular dust-baths; while simply strolling along, feeding all the time, provides natural exercise and chiropody. In captivity, human improvisation has to take the place of such natural health care. Looking after the gentle giant is an expensive business and one that calls for a great deal of expertise.

Elephants cannot be looked after by casual workers who are always changing. They need to have contact with and confidence in people to whom they have grown accustomed. "Humans do not pick their elephants," the official Hagenbeck Animal Park guide explains, "elephants pick their humans. [It is] important to think like an elephant ..."

Elephants in the wild cover more than 12 miles a day. In captivity, they do not get enough exercise in free-range compounds; they need to be walked around the zoo or ridden by their keepers. A welcome change – because elephants suffer from boredom – is to have elephants give rides to children. However, not every zoo elephant is suitable for this, and easily frightened animals should not be exposed to noise and bustle. It is also good for elephants when there is work to do around the place and heavy burdens need shifting.

An elephant's feet, in particular, require constant monitoring and regular care. After all, they are expected to carry a weight of several tons for something like twenty hours a day!

During their brief nightly sleep elephants tend to roll in their own dung, so first thing in the morning they need to be hosed down with warm water and given steam showers. To rub off dry skin, animals must have access to an overhanging concrete wall in the free-range compound as well as to a block for dealing with the stomach parts. In Asian countries, mahouts sand working animals down after their daily bath – a laborious task that would be prohibitively expensive in Europe.

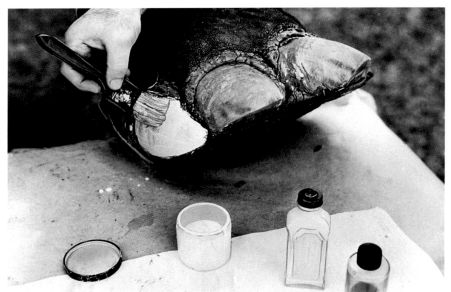

To round off her six-monthly pedicure, 29 year-old 'Anna May' receives a protective covering for her toenails. The final coat is applied with an ordinary household paintbrush.

## Medical attention

Regular full medical checks and treatment are both indispensable for zoo elephants. Indeed, elephants in captivity will probably have changed owners several times. They are therefore more vulnerable to illnesses (often behavioral disturbances) than elephants living in the wild. The different diseases that humans suffer from can be a torment to animals (see 'The elephant in the wild'). One that is particularly feared is elephant smallpox, although recently an effective vaccine has been found against this.

In the USA, treatments involving only minor discomfort are carried out in 'crush cages,' also known as 'elephant restraint chutes' or ERCs for short. This piece of equipment, use of which may be made compulsory in the USA, consists of a series of heavy sliding grilles that, when open, point the way to freedom (thus allaying the pachyderm's suspicions). Once the animal has been introduced, the exits are closed off and the sides brought in tight against the body. Depending on the part to be treated, individual bars can be removed.

'Elephant men' and vets approve of crush cages since they avoid the necessity for more violent methods of restraint. Elephants with previous experience of the ERC soon realize their helplessness and become quietly resigned. The device has also proved invaluable for dealing with major chiropody problems.

## Plenty of food – plenty of dung

Elephants in captivity need a balanced diet. They are not choosy; they will throw anything down their throats, and what they throw their digestive system will push out again half-digested. But proper, regulated feeding calls for careful selection and dosage. Particular account must be taken of the highly nutritious tidbits that members of the public like to offer. Too much concentrated feed (excessive quantities of good-quality hay, for instance) would be harmful and could endanger the animals' health and well being.

Elephants, whose massive molars are capable (in the wild) of crushing bark, small branches, and undergrowth, need roughage and bulk. At Hamburg's Hagenbeck Animal Park their diet includes hay made from the reeds that grow on the banks of rivers and lakes. Farmers dismiss these as being of inferior value, and they are not easy to come by. The Hagenbeck herd of a dozen animals gets through about 100 tons a year.

It takes a lot of work and considerable expense to look after (and clean up after) elephants. Each one eats up to 330 pounds of greenstuff and hay a day – and drops well over 200 pounds of dung! 'Elephant men' work hard, with a great deal of idealism and fondness for their animals. For many of them, looking after these loyal, friendly giants is more than just a job: it is a vocation.

A powerful jet of water is not only a useful hygiene aid – clearly it is also a pleasurable experience.

From the fifth or sixth year on, an elephant's nails should be tended quarterly. They should never make contact with the ground under a full load; if they do, they may split, and to prevent this the bottoms must be filed down with a hoof rasp. Nail fissures will close up again. A finger-width gap needs to be kept or filed free between the nails; otherwise there is a risk of nail rot. Rotten spots need to be removed by an expert and afterwards treated to a daily rinse with disinfectant solutions. Dry, loose cuticle is removed with a hoof knife and irregularities in the nail surface filed flat. No special care of the sole of the foot-pad is required if the animal gets enough exercise; if it does not, the sole needs to be peeled once a year. It is essential that elephants' feet are washed daily in warm water to keep them healthy.

# Elephants like variety

Afternoon pastimes in the gardens of the London Zoological Society. Engraving from the 'Illustrated London News,' September 23, 1871.

Elephant rides in Hamburg's Hagenbeck Animal Park.

Below:
An elephant-drawn sled ride. Former 'elephant man' Karl Kock leads the friendly cow.

Bottom:
Winter in Hagenbeck Animal Park. Even elephants enjoy a roll in the snow.

Boys used to haul the drinking water into the elephant house at London Zoo. Their reward was a free elephant ride.

Being allowed to handle the gentle giant and ride on its back constitute an unforgettable experience for children.

On summer evenings, Hagenbeck Animal Park organizes elephant shows with a touch of Indian magic. These draw large crowds and are an effective way of putting across the animal-protection message. The elephants perform little tricks, and for them too such shows add a bit of playful variety to their lives.

## The zoo generation

Born in Hamburg's Hagenbeck Animal Park on March 23, 1992, little 'Ratna' is growing up in the harmonious care of both humans and elephants. Mother 'Thura' is on the left; the animal on the right is 36 year-old lead cow 'Mala.'

Rotterdam Zoo, having expanded its elephant accommodation very generously, now maintains a continuous breeding program. Here Europe's first baby elephants of the second generation living in captivity were born; 'Bernhardini' and 'Jasmin' entered the world in 1984 and 1990 respectively. The two cows, who share the same parents, are already adult animals. In fact, the older one can soon be expected to start producing the third zoo generation of calves.

The efforts of forward-looking zoos to foster a 'herd atmosphere' in suitably spacious compounds has led recently to the successful development of intact groups of cows and some good breeding results. What had been an alarmingly high death rate among new born elephants has come down dramatically, and in many of the world's more modern zoos healthy calves are growing up in the proper care of mothers and 'aunts.' Here are some examples of this gratifying trend:

In Hamburg's Hagenbeck Animal Park, five healthy calves have been born since 1992, three of them in 1995–96. In the model zoo in Emmen, Holland, which purchased a breeding group of 11 to 13 year-old cows and one bull in Burma in 1988, the first calves are already romping around. There are calves, too, at the modern zoo in Basel, Switzerland, which breeds African elephants. Israel's Ramat Gan Zoo in Tel Aviv is proud of its twelve African elephant births up to 1992; the zoo maintains breeding groups of African and Asian elephants in two large free-range compounds. But the world record up to 1996 was held by the zoo in

Portland, Oregon, which had successfully bred twenty-five calves.

The zoo-born elephant that grows up in human care is no longer a wild animal that has been 'broken in' by humans and put to work – a practice dating back thousands of years. Like a pet, such an elephant is conceived in accordance with the rules of human breeding selection. The suckling animal, through playing with its keepers, grows into the human world. Humans feed it, care for it, and walk it around like its herd leader. Elephants of the zoo generation need the company and affection of the humans in whose world they are involved.

Elephant-breeding in zoos does not set out to create new wild stocks; a zoo is not a sort of Noah's Ark.

The elephant born in captivity grows up as a domestic pet. However, because of its enormous size it can hardly be harnessed as a working animal like an ox or a horse. For all its strength, it cannot compete with the machine. The earth's mightiest land animal must, for its own sake and in order to give pleasure to people living far from its tropical 'home,' find a small niche in which it can survive. We have the ability, through international cooperation, to build up small populations of zoo elephants that with proper keeping will replenish themselves. All we need is the determination. The elephant has proved its exceptional adaptability over millions of years.

Everyone loves the gentle giant. If estimates are to be believed, some 500 million people visit zoos annually. Clearly, as one of the main attractions, the elephant has its economic uses too.

'Corny,' born in Hagenbeck Animal Park on June 4, 1996, gets several helping hands as it stands up for the first time.

In the spacious surroundings of Hagenbeck Animal Park, three young elephants enjoy a romp in the pool.

# Retreat into the reserve

In the early years of the 20th century, millions of elephants roamed the tropical forests and savannahs of Africa and Southeast Asia. As the second millennium dawns, the elephant is an

J.M. Bernatz, *Herd of elephants in Chad,* September 25, 1851, colored lithograph. Staatliches Museum für Völkerkunde, Munich

Romantic scene of a formerly intact elephant world. Only a century ago, the African continent was home to ten million of these gentle giants.

endangered species. Man's lust for ivory has decimated elephant stocks. More and more people, clamoring for land, encroach on the gray giant's living-space, while unchecked exploitation of natural resources is destroying the environment for humans and animals alike. Everywhere, elephants and other not immediately useful wild animals are on the retreat, forced back by the tide of humanity. They enjoy a degree of security only in a generous allocation of reserves and national parks. Guarding these protected areas against the spread of economic land-use and dedicating them as a permanent home for elephants and other large mammals are key objectives of international efforts at species protection.

In the glow of evening, a solitary elephant near the bank of the Chobe River provides an easy camera target for a boatload of tourists. The melancholy scene serves to remind us of the sad state of East Africa's national parks in the wake of the devastating elephant massacres of the 1970s and 1980s. Whole herds, entire family groups were slaughtered, while forest and savannah were laid waste by a combination of panicky mass migrations and drought.

## From grassy savannah to barren desert

A network of state-owned and private reserves covers the countries of eastern and southern Africa. Between 5 and 10 percent of national territories have been set aside for this purpose. With those reserves, more has been done for endangered animal species than the industrialized countries have ever dreamed of doing in their latitudes. In Europe, every scrap of land is put to economic use; only a handful of wild animals that lend themselves to being hunted for sport are kept on timber plantations.

The peoples of East Africa have been forced into making many sacrifices to allow these often vast animal-protection zones, devoted to photo-tourism, to become established. Thousands were resettled to make room for – among others – the Kruger National Park in South Africa (7,500 square miles), Tanzania's famous Serengeti (5,700 square miles), or the Tsavo National Park in Kenya (a major destination of safari tourism lying some 90 miles north west of Mombasa's Beach Hotel),

which at over 8,000 square miles is almost as large as the island of Sicily.

Through the many ramifications of a tourist industry that accounts for much of the national income of these economically weaker countries, millions of visitors a year are able to experience the unique richness of Africa's animal kingdom. And when species protection in national parks serves financial interests as well, animals will be safer than any number of international conventions could make them.

Wildlife reserves are artificially demarcated segments of more extensive ecosystems featuring the same flora and fauna. They are islands of relative safety – within which, however, the ecological balance, that natural regulator of animal stocks, has been disturbed. As a result, in crisis situations they can prove highly vulnerable.

This emerged during the 1960s, when the former colonial countries, unprepared and lacking administrative infrastructures of their own, were

When fear or hunger drive too many elephant herds into protected areas, appalling damage to vegetation can result. Elephants, whose appetite is vast, can even chew wood. Nature is no longer able to recover, which is why in the 1970s whole parks were reduced to desert.

released into an unstable independence. Large sections of Africa were suddenly plunged into the choppy waters of civil unrest. It was a period of generalized lawlessness, leading in many places to unrestrained shooting of elephants by poachers and marauding soldiers. Herds fled from the danger zones into the greater safety of the reserves. Animals already living there tolerated this mass invasion, for elephants are not in the habit of defending ancestral territories.

Nature, however, was no longer able to deal with the hugely increased numbers now occupying national parks. When elephant populations get out of control – that is to say, when the requisite 0.4 of a square mile per animal is no longer available – devastation ensues. In the 1970s, several years of drought compounded the catastrophe. Tens of thousands of elephants died of hunger and thirst in Africa's burnt-out steppes, trampled forests, and ravaged savannahs as a result of natural disaster and mismanagement.

In Tsavo National Park, immigration pushed elephant numbers above 30,000 animals. The park's tropical grasslands, interspersed with river forests, were reduced to barren desert. In the smaller, scenically delightful Amboseli Park at the foot of Mount Kilimanjaro, what had once been forest and bush degenerated into steppe. The high plateau of the Serengeti saw an influx of herds from the lowlands, where human settlements were becoming established. In 1977, elephant numbers rose from around 450 to over 3,000 animals. Arboreal cover was largely destroyed as the hungry giants stripped the bark off standing trees and pushed others over. In Mozambique, where the Gorongoza National Park (1,500 square miles) provides ideal living conditions for elephants, park administration collapsed completely as civil war broke out.

When the price of ivory then climbed to unprecedented heights, the greatest elephant massacre of the century began.

## The 'ivory rush' and the great elephant massacre

In the decade 1979–89, ivory poaching in Africa's savannahs and rain forests intensified, bringing about a barbaric slaughter of elephants. Every year, between 50,000 and 100,000 of the peaceful pachyderms fell victim to well-armed teams of poachers enjoying the protection of influential backers. Using machine guns, the poachers mowed down animals indiscriminately. The 1973 Washington Convention (CITES), which had laid down strict controls for the import and export of ivory, proved ineffective.

Towards the end of the 19th century, there were apparently some 10 million elephants left in Africa. In 1979 their number was put at 1.3 million; by 1989 perhaps 600,000 remained. That may still sound a lot, but behind the figures lies an ominous process whereby the very basis of the animal's livelihood is being undermined. The worst-case scenario suggests that the species may become extinct by the year 2020.

Zoologist J. Douglas-Hamilton, who in the late 1980s took an inventory in Africa on behalf of the Worldwide Fund for Nature, witnessed an elephant massacre while flying low over a national park one day. Poachers ambushed a herd of elephants as it strolled peacefully along and opened fire with automatic weapons. He watched helplessly as the giant animals, measuring over 13 feet in height and weighing several tons, sank to their knees, blood gushing through their trunks from punctured lungs. He saw others, fatally wounded, stagger a few feet further into the undergrowth before collapsing in their turn. With axes and chainsaws the tusks were then ripped from their mouths and loaded onto waiting trucks. Douglas-Hamilton spoke of "the greatest mammalian tragedy of the century."

The unscrupulous hunt for 'white gold' was spurred on during the 1970s and 1980s by a phenomenal rise in the price of ivory, itself triggered by monetary instability springing from international political tensions. Whereas in the 1960s the price per kilo lay around 5.50 dollars, by 1978 it had reached 52 dollars and ten years later people were paying 200 and even 300 dollars. Of the 600–1,000 tons of ivory sold annually, international organizations involved in species protection tell us that some 94 percent was derived from poaching. As these figures show, animal reserves were no longer providing the protection required to halt the decline in elephant numbers.

Back in 1960, tusks confiscated from poachers had weighed an average of 55 pounds each; by 1979, that figure was down to between 25 pounds and 35 pounds, indicating an ominous reduction in numbers of elephants aged between twenty-five and forty-five – the crucial years for reproduction. Around eighty elephants must now die to yield a ton of ivory. Mountains of meat that might have fed whole villages lay rotting in the steppe.

The extent of the slaughter, which continued until 1989, emerges from some figures based on the findings and estimates of international observers. No precise statistics exist.

In Tanzania, which is thought to have had approximately 300,000 elephants in 1970, by 1987 there were only 30,000 left. In Kenya, where in 1970 the elephant population stood at 130,000, numbers had shrunk to 18,000. Of 30,000 animals in Tsavo National Park, around 7,000 survived. In Zambia, elephant numbers dropped from 150,000 to a mere 40,000 animals. In Uganda, marauding troops of toppled dictator Idi Amin, together with Tanzanian peace-keeping forces, exterminated the country's once abundant elephant stocks until no more than 10 percent remained. Observers found animal parks strewn with corpses.

By contrast, there are well-preserved elephant stocks in South Africa, where 90 percent of the country's 8,000 or so pachyderms live in the Kruger National Park, and in Zimbabwe, where poaching has been rigorously combated. During the critical period, some 150 poachers were shot dead. The

An East African 'Golgotha' dating from the worst days of the slaughter by international gangs of ivory poachers.

controlled, hugely expensive trophy hunting in the company of official game wardens that Zimbabwe continued to allow (in contravention of blanket international bans) and that has brought and continues to bring in a large slice of the national income does not threaten stocks. Much the same policy was pursued in Botswana, where the elephant paradise of the Okavango Delta remained unharmed.

A similar massacre to that seen on the East African steppes took place in West Africa, particularly in the rain forests of the Congo Basin, where bush-elephant stocks were decimated. In former Zaire, elephant numbers dropped from around 300,000 in 1977 to a paltry 85,000 ten years later. Of the Central African Republic's 70,000 animals, only 19,000 survived. In Cameroon, there are said to be as few as 5,000 survivors.

The main safari countries of East Africa, namely Kenya and Tanzania, where gangs of poachers had organized the most appalling massacres with the connivance of influential backers, eventually asked for international intervention and the imposition of an embargo on the ivory trade. The devastation being caused in their national parks was threatening the tourist industry, which contributes essential revenue to the national coffers! That, in the end, is what brought them to the negotiating table.

An elephant carcass is butchered with spear blades in a scene of poverty-inspired poaching in Africa. International gangs of ivory poachers would massacre their prey with automatic weapons before ripping out the tusks with chainsaws and then trucking them away.

# Appendix 1: 'Threatened with extinction'

On October 15, 1989 the many signatories of the Washington Convention on International Trade in Endangered Species (known as CITES for short) agreed to place elephants in 'Appendix 1,' which comprises the list of species facing possible extinction. Countries exporting and importing ivory and live elephants now had to prove that the trade did not constitute a threat to the species.

Some signatory countries seemed to be in no hurry to ratify the convention, so the USA, the EU countries, and Switzerland agreed an immediate, total ban on ivory imports. The big importers that had been dragging their feet, namely Japan and Hong Kong, now at least had to commit themselves to importing only 'legal ivory,' however this was to be controlled. In 1984–85, more than half the ivory traded internationally went to Japan, which every year manufactured (among other trinkets) a million 'hankos,' the personal seals with which the Japanese like to validate legal documents. Most hankos were made of precious ivory.

The strict import ban, coupled with international ostracism of the trade in illegal ivory, had its effect. The price of tusks fell through the floor, and a degree of calm returned to the 'killing fields' of Africa. Large-scale slaughter, occasionally using helicopters to locate migrating herds, was no longer such a money-spinner. The few poorly-paid game wardens were unable to stamp out poaching completely. Even with reduced profits, 'white gold' was still an attractive proposition. However, elephant stocks could at last make something of a recovery.

## 'Eco-colonialism?'

Yet a mere eight years later, in June 1997, the strict embargo on the ivory trade was (with reservations) lifted at the conference on species protection held in the Zimbabwean capital Harare. The African elephant was downgraded from CITES Appendix 1 (threatened with extinction) to Appendix 2 (potentially threatened unless trading restrictions are introduced). From 1999 it would once again be legal to sell and trade in tusks derived from natural deaths and officially approved shoots designed to cull excessive stocks. If poaching again became widespread, however, a strict trading ban should be reimposed without delay.

The African elephant countries of Zimbabwe, Botswana, Namibia, and Malawi prevailed. When a vote was taken among the 136 delegations, they carried the day in alliance with Japan, Canada, and Norway – countries that themselves also market 'species-protection goods' such as whales. The EU countries, which had previously been against

New York's Museum of Natural History boasts what it calls "the most lifelike dead elephants." A special dermoplastic process makes it possible to reproduce even the giant's muscle play.

relaxing the strict trade embargo, helped by abstaining on the day.

When various CITES countries urged a complete ban on the ivory trade, the African delegations objected. There was talk of 'eco-colonialism.' Zimbabwe's environment minister suggested sarcastically that the West wished to keep Africa as an under-developed zoo for vacationers.

Some adjustment of the strict embargo was inevitable. In the main exporting countries, accumulated quantities of elephant tusk were estimated at well over 600 tons. These were of course resources belonging to poor countries in urgent need of capital. Trade on a restricted scale is possible without jeopardizing elephant stocks, provided that the rules, once codified, are very rigidly adhered to.

Without help, the younger African states are in no position to carry out thorough checks. International criminal syndicates, with a member of the relevant government in their pocket to provide cover, have always ridden roughshod over species-protection provisions. Moreover, Japanese trading companies, the 3,000–4,000 craftsmen employed in ivory processing, and the many dealers marketing their wares never accepted the strict embargo in reality.

A few examples will indicate the true position regarding controls and statistics. Tiny Burundi has had no elephants for a long time, yet up until 1989 the country exported, complete with certificates of origin and export licences, annual totals of between 20,000 and 30,000 tusks! In 1976, Kenya's official export statistics recorded a figure of 55 tons of ivory dispatched to the intermediate market of Hong Kong, while Hong Kong's own import statistics indicated that 235 tons had arrived from Kenya! In the late summer of 1996, during the strict embargo on trade in products from endangered species, the London police seized 127 rhino horns from South Africa.

To rule out the possibility of making forged declarations of ivory exports, work is being done at the universities of Cape Town in South Africa and Saarbrücken in Germany to develop a process whereby the origin of tusks can be determined from their chemical composition. From samples, measurements are taken of the quantities of sodium, magnesium, silicon, phosphorus, strontium, and sulphur present. Those quantities, together with their relative proportions, provide very precise data patterns for ivory originating in the main exporting countries.

The Harare compromise has not improved the situation of the African elephant. Even if it is successful in preventing a revival of organized poaching, illegal hunting of elephants for their tusks is only one of the deadly dangers facing the gentle giant in the future.

# Culling

It is a shocking sight when whole herds of elephants are wiped out during controlled culls. Yet if elephants become too numerous within the restricted living-space of a national park, threatening to destroy the very foundations of their existence, humans have to take corrective action.

In national parks that are well secured against poachers, problems arise as a result of excessive natural regeneration of elephant stocks. In remote areas, food cover becomes too thin. Nature, overtaxed, is unable to renew itself. Left to their own devices, elephants will undermine the very foundations of their existence. Natural regulation of population densities no longer operates when restricted areas come under pressure from overcrowding. If the ecological balance is disturbed in this way, corrective intervention by humans becomes essential to redress the balance.

In South Africa's Kruger National Park biologists and zoologists calculate that the vegetation is capable of supporting a maximum of 7,000–8,000 elephants. When that number is critically exceeded, so-called 'control shoots' are carried out from time to time to reduce stocks of elephants to a sustainable level.

In such culling operations, whole cow units are destroyed in order to prevent helpless calves or lone animals from facing a wretched death in bush and steppe. Otherwise there is elephant overpopulation in only three of Africa's thirty-two elephant

countries: Zimbabwe, Botswana, and Namibia. In Zimbabwe (where rigorous action was taken against poaching and elephant stocks actually increased during the worst years of the slaughter) and Botswana, state-supervised trophy-hunting is permitted. This not only works against elephant overpopulation; it also brings a great deal of cash into the country.

A well-heeled American or European needs to spend between 15,000 dollars and 20,000 dollars on a Jeep safari to bag an elephant trophy. The actual shot is often fired by the accompanying game warden, who supervises the whole expedition. What matters is the trophy to be carried home, the elephant's foot wastebasket for the den. A qualified technician accompanies the hunt from the outset to remove and prepare legal trophies – tusks and feet. The meat is distributed among the local people.

In the countries of East and West Africa ravaged by civil war (Sudan, for example, or large areas of the Congo Basin), elephant hunting is subject to no such controls and international regulations and as a result the population is decimated.

Orphaned young bulls, deprived of a proper upbringing by mothers and 'aunts' in intact cow groups, often demonstrate abnormal behavior in the wild. In South Africa's Pilanesberg Animal Park, lonely young bulls joined up with white rhinos and even tried to mount the females. Also, large numbers of rhino carcasses were found that had clearly been lacerated by the tusks of a 'killer elephant'.

## Repercussions of the bloodbath

The huge carcasses are loaded by crane and taken off to meat factories for processing.

Elephant stocks in Africa's national parks and protected areas have to some extent recovered. But the after-effects of the great elephant slaughter and catastrophic drought are as yet unforseeable and more and more problems are becoming apparent.

The age structure of elephant herds is now badly out of kilter. It was mainly older bulls that were shot because of their bigger tusks. Age-groups of particular importance as regards reproduction and a healthy younger generation have been either greatly reduced or wiped out altogether.

Among cows, too, older animals were shot first as supplying a slightly larger quantity of ivory. Moreover, the first to die during the drought were older cows whose worn tusks could no longer deal with such tough emergency rations as wood and bark. And of course their suckling calves died too. The dearth of older animals interrupted the transmission of long experience to the younger generation; there was no guidance, no leadership. Isolated groups of young animals began wandering aimlessly about the African steppes. Behavioral disturbances became apparent.

In the Pilanesberg Animal Park in South Africa's Transvaal (northwest of Johannesburg), there were abnormal killing frenzies by many young bulls unschooled by mothers and 'aunts.' These were orphans that, having survived culls in the Kruger

National Park, had been taken into captivity and later re-released into the wild in Pilanesberg and so were lacking many natural instincts.

Young bulls that had joined herds of white rhinos were repeatedly observed trying to mount female rhinos. Several rhino carcasses were found ripped to pieces – obviously by elephant tusks. There were even attacks on people. And again torn rhino carcasses were found littering the steppe. When a professional hunter cornered the wildest of the crazed elephants and delivered the 'coup de grâce,' the dying animal still contrived to kill its own killer in desperation.

## Forests continue to die

Once upon a time, primeval forest covered the earth. Now, 80 percent of it has been destroyed. And in a couple of hundred years the rest will be gone too, felled and burnt, if present trends continue. In Asia, at the beginning of the 20th century, vast areas of uninterrupted rain forest were still home to hundreds of thousands of elephants. In Thailand and Cambodia, the proportion of forest to total surface area has dropped from 70 to 20 percent in a short space of time. In Malaysia and on the island of Sumatra, where the last retreat of the remaining 2,000–3,000 elephants is under serious threat from slash and burn on a massive scale, the situation looks even worse.

In the countries lining East Africa's Gulf of Guinea, the only surviving areas of tropical forest are deep inland. The elephant population was once huge here; now, only small groups remain. In Cameroon and in the (still) extensive forest areas of the Congo Basin, European timber companies have pursued a disastrous policy of clear felling.

Recently, attempts have been made to persuade such companies to adopt less harmful practices.

Exploitation of natural resources should be 'sustainable,' according to the latest buzzword. In other words, only as many selected trees should be felled as nature is capable of replenishing.

If that happened, elephants would have the opportunity (further promoting the survival of the species) of contributing their enormous strength to the task of dragging felled trees out of standing forest. Of course, a protective timber policy does not maximize profits in the short term. Permanent damage to the environment does not feature in the company's books. But it is there all the same: erosion of the soil, desertification of entire regions, and far-reaching consequences with regard to unnatural climatic change.

At the species-protection conference in Harare, a motion was put forward to restrict the trade in mahogany. The mahogany tree, capable of growing to a height of 160 feet and living for 800 years, is believed by some experts to be threatened with extinction. The motion was quashed by the lumber industry, acting in alliance with the main producer countries: Brazil, Malaysia, Singapore, Indonesia …

A lone elephant strolls through a ravaged river forest that once presented a green and pleasant landscape.

In the courtyard of the Palace Hotel in Sun City, a gambling paradise built in the desert northwest of Johannesburg, there stands, cast in bronze and set on a marble plinth, this impressive giant of the steppes. It is a monument of rather special provenance. South African sculptor Danie de Jager wanted his colossal work to commemorate 'Shawu,' one of the largest bull elephants ever to have inhabited the country. Shawu died a natural death in the Kruger National Park in 1982. He stood more than 11 feet at the shoulder; his overall height, from the tips of his ears to the soles of his feet, was nearly 15 feet. His tusks, which are displayed in the park's splendid 'Oliphants Camp,' measured nearly 10 feet in length and weighed over 100 pounds apiece. The plaster model, steel armature, and fibreglass covering took more than a year to manufacture. This meticulously accurate work of art was cast in Pisa, Italy. Cynics spoke of an anticipatory death mask for the last of the breed, copies of which might be sold to governments and commercial organizations with particularly bad consciences so far as the environment is concerned.

Selective logging in rain forests is more economic in the long term than destructive clear felling. Besides preserving vital resources, it gives the elephant a chance to demonstrate his usefulness, dragging felled trees out of healthy standing forest.

## The rising tide of humanity

A convoy of safari trucks pauses for tourists to admire a primordial giant. The elephant could be a key player on the side of the peoples of Africa in the major enterprise that is species protection.

The greatest threat to elephants, whether of the African or Asian variety, comes from the alarming shrinkage of their living-space as a result of the human population explosion. The number of people living in the countries of Southeast Asia and Africa increases by about 3 percent per annum. In other words, it doubles every thirty to forty years! The threat to elephants is obvious.

Back at the end of the 18th century, long before there could be any question of over-population, British economist and demographer Thomas Robert Malthus (1766–1834) drew attention to the problem of population increase and its inherent tendency to outgrow the available food supply. In 1968, the population of the world having since quadrupled in the wake of the Industrial

Revolution, the Club of Rome calculated in hard figures the life-threatening crisis in which the whole human race would find itself if population increase and severe environmental destruction continued unabated. We have been warned.

In Southeast Asia, of the enormous territory over which elephants once roamed, only scattered pockets remain. Wild habitat in untouched forests survives only in remote and inaccessible mountain regions within Burma (now called Myanmar), Thailand, and eastern India. National parks, in which elephants have a chance to prove their usefulness for the tourist industry, tend to be surrounded by farmers whose cattle herds invade reserved areas and cause destruction.

Once upon a time there were millions of elephants. Now there are perhaps between 30,000 and 40,000 of them left. A further 10,000 or so live in captivity, the majority as laborers in remote mountain regions where teak is harvested and tractors and heavy trucks have no access as yet. In many places, after years of service such animals share the unemployed fate of their human colleagues and are simply 'put out to grass' as the machinery takes over.

Everywhere, human settlements encroach on the elephant's already restricted areas of retreat. Conflict between human and animal becomes inevitable. Under pressure, elephants always return to their old haunts, where they may cause appalling damage to crops that have meanwhile been planted there. Cordoning-off has been largely unsuccessful. Even electric fences help only to a limited extent; bulls soon learn to disarm these menacing barriers by pushing over the posts that carry the current and rendering the system useless.

# Hope in Africa

In Africa there is still abundant living-space for wild animals: inaccessible swamps and jungles, remote mountain regions, vast expanses of semi-barren steppe ill-suited to agricultural exploitation. Links can be created between such areas and the continent's already extensive national parks. International conservation organizations are working in conjunction with African governments to put in place sound, long-term solutions that will also take account of genetic requirements – that is to say, permit gene exchange between populations. If the mighty elephant is guaranteed sufficient habitat, other large mammals under threat will also survive in its shadow and be preserved for the human race. So too will countless smaller forms of life, both fauna and flora.

African villagers have little sympathy with efforts to protect wild animals in special reserves. Where poverty and want prevail, the demands of personal life take precedence. A family's own fields may actually be in danger from elephants. Individuals have no stake in the benefits of Africa's greatest capital asset, its unique animal population. The revenues from safari tourism and controlled trophy-hunting flow into remote state coffers or seep away through sometimes obscure channels.

Whether international efforts to save the elephant succeed or fail will depend on how far it is possible to involve broader sections of the population in the activities of this great enterprise of species protection. Substantial aid from the world's wealthier countries will also be required. Protection of endangered species is an international responsibility, not just a local concern.

Vast areas of Africa are useless for agricultural purposes, comprising rugged mountain regions, swamps, and arid wasteland. Such niches could provide the elephant as well as many other endangered animal species with a saving refuge and a last chance of survival.

## Survival in the care of humanity

Previous double page:
This dreamlike scene is present reality, not distant memory. Elephants graze peacefully at the foot of Africa's Kilimanjaro massif, a picture of hope.

For the elephant, the days of roaming at liberty in the wild are nearly at an end. Animals will be offered sanctuary in reserves and national parks, where human supervision and stock controls can guarantee them a more or less normal life in intact social groups – always provided that the human species will concede that it is not the measure of all things, no matter how powerful it is, and that the planet does not belong to it alone.

The anthropocentric world-view was corrected long ago by the natural sciences. The human race is itself a product of the animal kingdom, and we depend on animals for our existence. It would be an act of self-destruction to gauge the right of other life-forms to exist purely by whether they benefit us. How we deal with animals is also a question of ethics. Philosopher Arthur Schopenhauer, while meditating on the subject of compassion for living creatures, wrote: "The presumption that animals have no rights, the delusion that our conduct towards them is without moral significance ... that there are no obligations toward animals, is nothing short of the grossest barbarity ... Compassion for animals is so intimately bound up with goodness of character that it may confidently be asserted that a person who is cruel to animals cannot be a good person ..." Psychiatrists have gone further still.

Living-space on our planet is finite. The resources we are so busy squandering are not inexhaustible. Yet increasingly we humans place greater and greater demands on an ever-diminishing amount of room. According to a German encyclopedia ('Meyers Konversations-lexikon') of 1895, a hundred years ago the earth's population stood at 1,480 million. In 1964 it was 3,220 million, in 1991 an astonishing 5,384 million. And that figure is expected to double in roughly forty to fifty years. Further extrapolation is surely superfluous!

In an essay on the plight of animals, critical Catholic theologian Eugen Drewermann wrote: "What we are engaged in now is tantamount to paralyzing the entire driving force of evolution; it consists in favoring a single species on this earth and regarding all other forms of life purely in terms of how they promote the survival interests of Homo sapiens ... The question we face today is whether we wish to give continued approval to the exponential growth of the human species or whether we take fewer people as our goal."

There is a place for the elephant in the restricted living conditions available on our planet. For thousands of years this animal has shown proof of exceptional adaptability, overcoming the most difficult of circumstances. It will even cope with saying farewell to the unlimited freedom of life in the wild, provided that protected niches are left for it in the care of humanity.

As their predecessors did millions of years ago, two gray giants move slowly through the countryside accompanied by a flock of cattle egrets, whose foraging offers some relief from irritating parasites. Today, the elephant's future lies totally in human hands.

458

Retreat into the reserve

# Appendix

## Elephants in Africa

NUMBERS OF AFRICAN ELEPHANTS AND SIZES OF THEIR
DISPERSAL AREAS IN INDIVIDUAL COUNTRIES

| Country | Official elephant stocks | Probable elephant stocks | Dispersal area in sq. miles |
|---|---|---|---|
| Botswana | 62,998 | 8,500 | 31,533 |
| Burkina Faso | 1,469 | 580 | 8,231 |
| Cameroon | 1,100 | 6,600 | 90,835 |
| Central African Republic | 1,750 | – | 121,396 |
| Ethiopia | 847 | – | 39,762 |
| Gabon | – | 61,700 | 101,892 |
| Ghana | 245 | 420 | 12,065 |
| Ivory Coast | 551 | 250 | 14,165 |
| Kenya | 13,834 | 5,200 | 52,125 |
| Malawi | 1,111 | 540 | 3,238 |
| Mali | – | 610 | 13,135 |
| Mozambique | 825 | 180 | 180,738 |
| Namibia | 5,843 | 3,000 | 56,117 |
| Rwanda | 39 | – | 487 |
| South Africa | 9,990 | 20 | 8,762 |
| Swaziland | 20 | – | 108 |
| Tanzania | 73,459 | 12,400 | 164,240 |
| Uganda | 1,318 | – | 5,209 |
| Zaire | 4,470 | 13,100 | 571,390 |
| Zambia | 19,701 | 6,500 | 81,831 |
| Zimbabwe | 56,297 | 11,600 | 41,110 |
| Total | 255,867 | 131,200 | 1,598,369 |

Source: African Elephant Database of UCN/SSC/AfESG in collaboration with UNEP/GRID, 1995

## SELECTED NATIONAL PARKS AND WILDLIFE RESERVES

| Country | No. | National park | Area in sq.m. |
|---|---|---|---|
| Botswana | 1. | Chobe National Park | 4,199 |
| Botswana | 2. | Moremi Protected Area | 3,088 |
| Burkina Faso | 3. | Po National Park | 600 |
| Cameroon | 4. | Faro National Park | 1,274 |
| Central African Republic | 5. | Bamingui Bangoran National Park | 4,463 |
| Central African Republic | 6. | Manovo Gouanda St. Floris | 6,718 |
| Chad | 7. | Zakouma National Park | 1,158 |
| Ethiopia | 8. | Omo National Park | 469 |
| Gabon | 9. | Wanga Wongue National Park | 1,486 |
| Ghana | 10. | Mole National Park | 1,891 |
| Guinea | 11. | Mount Nimba Biosphere | 656 |
| Ivory Coast | 12. | Comoé National Park | 4,440 |
| Ivory Coast | 13. | Tai National Park | 1,274 |
| Kenya | 14. | Amboseli National Park | 57 |
| Kenya | 15. | Marsabit National Park | 783 |
| Kenya | 16. | Masai Mara National Park | 617 |
| Kenya | 17. | Tsavo National Park | 8,057 |
| Kenya | 18. | Mount Elgon National Park | 65 |
| Liberia | 19. | Loffa Mano National Park | 888 |
| Mali | 20. | Boucle-du-Baoule National Park | 2,096 |
| Mozambique | 21. | Gorongoza National Park | 1,455 |
| Namibia | 22. | Etoscha National Park | 8,213 |
| Nigeria | 23. | Kainji National Park | 2,061 |
| Senegal | 24. | Niokolo Koba National Park | 3,525 |
| South Africa | 25. | Addo Elephant National Park | 29 |
| South Africa | 26. | Kruger National Park | 7,528 |
| Sudan | 27. | Boma National Park | 8,803 |
| Tanzania | 28. | Katavi National Park | 762 |
| Tanzania | 29. | Kilimanjaro National Park | 291 |
| Tanzania | 30. | Mikumi National Park | 1,247 |
| Tanzania | 31. | Selous National Park | 21,235 |
| Togo | 32. | Keran National Park | 3,861 |
| Uganda | 33. | Kabalega National Park | 1,482 |
| Zaire | 34. | Garamba National Park | 1,930 |
| Zaire | 35. | Kahuzi Biega National Park | 2,316 |
| Zaire | 36. | Maiko National Park | 4,169 |
| Zaire | 37. | Salonga National Park | 14,092 |
| Zaire | 38. | Upemba National Park | 4,528 |
| Zambia | 39. | Kafue National Park | 8,648 |
| Zambia | 40. | Lukuzusi National Park | 1,042 |
| Zambia | 41. | Mweru Wantipa National Park | 1,210 |
| Zimbabwe | 42. | Gona Re Khou National Park | 1,950 |
| Zimbabwe | 43. | Hwenge National Park | 5,659 |

Mediterranean Sea

Benghazi

Alexandria
Suez
Cairo

EGYPT

NUBIA

Aswan

SAUDI
ARABIA

Port Sudan

CHAD

El Fasher

Khartoum

Nile

ERITREA

YEMEN

DJIBOUTI

SUDAN

SOMALI
REPUBLIC

Addis Ababa

CENTRAL
AFRICAN
REPUBLIC

ETHIOPIA

Congo

ZAIRE

UGANDA

RWANDA

BURUNDI

Lake Victoria

Udji

KENYA

Nairobi

Mogadishu

Tabora

Kilimanjaro

Mombasa

Lake
Tanganyika

Kananga

TANZANIA

ZANZIBAR
Dar-es-Salaam

KATANGA

Lake Nyasa

Indian
Ocean

ZAMBIA

Lusaka

Zambesi

MALAWI

MADAGASCAR

Mozambique

ZIMBABWE

MOZAMBIQUE

Bulawayo

Sofala

BOTSWANA

Limpopo

TRANSVAAL

Pretoria

SWAZILAND

NATAL

Durban

SOUTH AFRICA

LESOTHO

pe Town

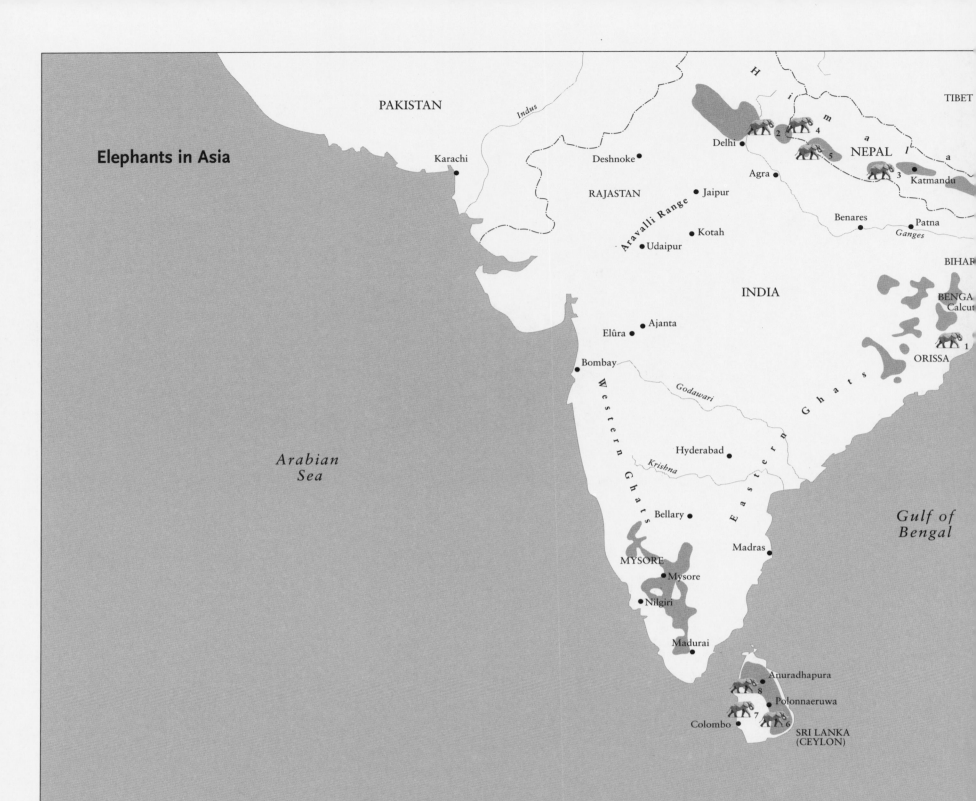

# Elephants in Asia

PAKISTAN

*Indus*

Karachi

Deshnoke

Delhi

Agra

Katmandu
NEPAL

RAJASTAN
Jaipur

Benares
Patna
*Ganges*

Kotah

Udaipur

BIHAR

INDIA

Ajanta
Elûra

BENGA
Calcut

Bombay

*Godawari*

ORISSA

*Arabian
Sea*

Hyderabad

*Krishna*

*Gulf of
Bengal*

Bellary

Madras

MYSORE
Mysore

Nilgiri

Madurai

Anuradhapura

Polonnaeruwa
Colombo
SRI LANKA
(CEYLON)

## ESTIMATED STOCKS OF ASIAN ELEPHANTS

| Country | Minimum | Maximum |
|---|---|---|
| Bangladesh | 280 | 350 |
| Bhutan | 60 | 150 |
| Burma (Myanmar) | 5,000 | 6,000 |
| Cambodia | 2,000 | 2,000 |
| China | 250 | 350 |
| India | 20,000 | 24,000 |
| Indonesia (Sumatra) | 2,500 | 4,500 |
| Laos | 2,000 | 4,000 |
| Malaysia | 800 | 1,000 |
| Borneo (Sabah & Kalimantan) | 500 | 2,000 |
| Nepal | 50 | 85 |
| Sri Lanka | 2,500 | 3,000 |
| Thailand | 1,500 | 3,000 |
| Vietnam | 300 | 400 |

Source: IUCN's Species Survival Commission's Asian Elephant
Specialist Group, WWF Offices in Bhutan, Nepal, Vietnam and
India, 1995

All numbers based on estimates.

## SELECTED NATIONAL PARKS

| Country | No. | National Park |
|---|---|---|
| India | 1. | Simlipal Reserve |
| India | 2. | Rajani Corbett National Park |
| Nepal | 3. | Royal Chitwan National Park |
| Nepal | 4. | Shukla Phanta Reserve |
| Nepal | 5. | Royal Bardia |
| Sri Lanka | 6. | Yala National Park |
| Sri Lanka | 7. | Pinnawella Elephant Orphanage |
| Sri Lanka | 8. | Wilpattu National Park |
| Sumatra | 9. | Kerinci Soblat National Park |
| Sumatra | 10. | Way Kambas National Park |
| Sumatra | 11. | Leuser Reserve |
| Thailand | 12. | Khao Yai National Park |
| Thailand | 13. | Petchabum Range |
| Thailand | 14. | Thung Yai/Naresuan Huai/Kha Khaeng Wildlife Sanctuary |

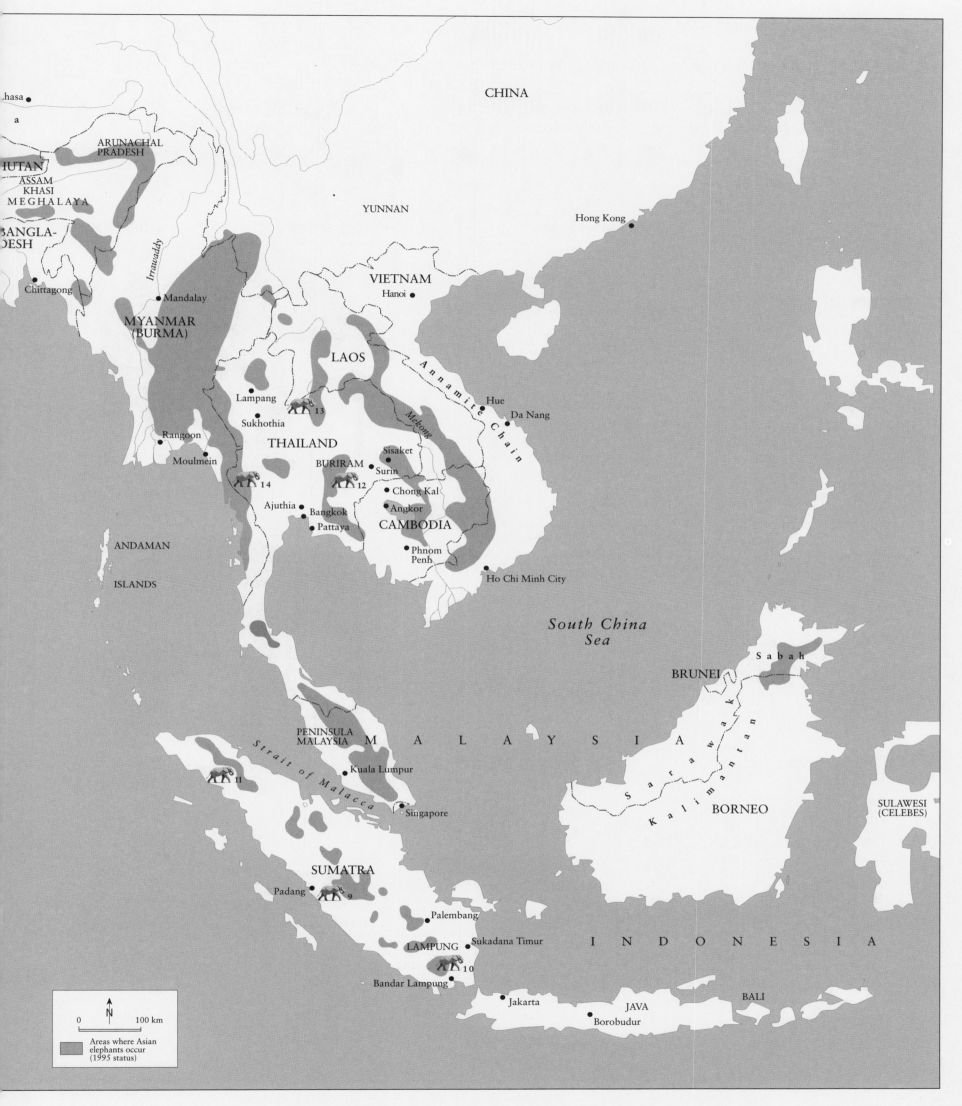

CHINA

Lhasa

ARUNACHAL
PRADESH

BHUTAN

ASSAM
KHASI
MEGHALAYA

BANGLA-
DESH

Chittagong

YUNNAN

Hong Kong

Irrawaddy

Mandalay

MYANMAR
(BURMA)

VIETNAM

Hanoi

LAOS

Lampang

Sukhothia

Hue

Da Nang

Rangoon

THAILAND

Moulmein

Sisaket

BURIRAM

Surin

Ajuthia

Bangkok

Chong Kal

Angkor

Pattaya

CAMBODIA

Phnom
Penh

Ho Chi Minh City

ANDAMAN

ISLANDS

South China
Sea

BRUNEI

Sabah

PENINSULA
MALAYSIA

M A L A Y S I A

Sarawak

Strait of Malacca

Kuala Lumpur

Kalimantan

BORNEO

SULAWESI
(CELEBES)

Singapore

SUMATRA

Padang

Palembang

Sukadana Timur

I N D O N E S I A

LAMPUNG

Bandar Lampung

Jakarta

JAVA

BALI

Borobudur

0        N        100 km

Areas where Asian
elephants occur
(1995 status)

# African and Asian elephants

## DIFFERENCES BETWEEN AFRICAN AND ASIAN ELEPHANTS

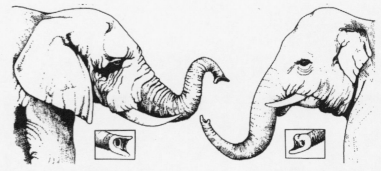

**AFRICAN ELEPHANT**　　　　**ASIAN ELEPHANT**

| | African elephant (*Loxodonta africana*) | Asian elephant (*Elephas maximus*) |
|---|---|---|
| Weight | 4–7 tons | 3–5 tons |
| Skin | wrinkly | smoother |
| Height at shoulder | 10–13ft | 6–10ft |
| No. of ribs | up to 21 pairs | up to 20 pairs |
| Highest point | on shoulder | on head |
| Line of back | concave | convex or straight |
| Line of belly | slopes down toward hind legs | either almost straight or sagging in middle |
| Shape of head | not foreshortened from front to back, no bumps, no hollow | foreshortened from front to back, with bumps on top of head, hollow forehead |
| Size of ears | larger; extend beyond neck | smaller; do not extend beyond neck |
| Top edge of ear muscle in adults | folded in middle | folded outward |
| Teeth | diamond-shaped lamella section of molars | very foreshortened lamella section |
| Tusks | present in both sexes, larger in the male | mostly in males, rudimentary or absent in females |
| Trunk | more rings, less rigid | little ringing, more rigid |
| Tip of trunk | two 'fingers' | only one 'finger' |
| No. of nail-like structures | 4 or 5 on front foot 3, 4, or 5 on hind foot | 5 on front foot 4 or 5 on hind foot |
| Food | mainly leaves | mainly grass |

**AFRICAN ELEPHANT**

**ASIAN ELEPHANT**

## DEVELOPMENT OF AFRICAN ELEPHANT

| | calf | calf | young animal | (half-grown) | (sexually mature) |
|---|---|---|---|---|---|
| Age in years | 1 | 2–3 | 3–8 | 5–15 | 10–25 |
| Characteristic | toothless | weaning | calf with visible tusks | not yet sexually mature | cows often with calf already |
| Shoulder height (male) | 3ft | 3–4ft | 4–7ft | 8ft | 10ft |
| Shoulder height (female) | 3ft | 3–4ft | 4–6ft | 6ft | 7ft |
| Weight (male) | 275lb | 275–650lb | 0.5–1 ton | 1–1.5 tons | 1.5–3 tons |
| Weight (female) | 275lb | 275–650lb | 0.5–1 ton | 1–1.5 tons | 1.5–3 tons |
| Tusk weight | has no tusks | | | 5–22lb | 11–45lb |

## GLACIAL AND INTERGLACIAL STAGES OF THE EUROPEAN ICE AGE

| Central Europe | Northwest Europe | Years ago |
|---|---|---|
| Holocene | Holocene | 10,000 |
| Würm Glacial | Weichsel Glacial | 75,000 |
| Eemian Interglacial | Eemian Glacial | 125,000 |
| Riss Glacial | Saale Glacial | 250,000 |
| Holstein Interglacial | Holstein Interglacial | 385,000 |
| Mindel Glacial | Elsterian Glacial | 480,000 |
| Cromerian Interglacial | Cromerian Interglacial | 800,000 |
| Günz Glacial | Menapian Glacial | 900,000 |
| | Waal Interglacial | 1,300 000 |
| Donau Glacial | Eburon Glacial | 1,600 000 |
| | Tegelen Interglacial | 2,000 000 |
| Biber Glacials | Pre-Tegelen Glacial | 2,300 000 |

| Era | | Millions of years ago | System | |
|---|---|---|---|---|
| Cenozoic | Cenophytic | | Quaternary | Holocene / Pleistocene |
| | | 1.8 | Tertiary | Pliocene / Miocene / Oligocene / Eocene / Paleocene |
| Mesozoic | Mesophytic | 65 | Cretaceous | Upper / Lower |
| | | 140 | Jurassic | Malm / Dogger / Lias |
| | | 210 | Triassic | Keuper / Muschelkalk / New Red Sandstone |
| Paleozoic | Paleophytic | 250 | Permian | Upper / Lower |
| | | 285 | Carboniferous | Upper / Lower |
| | | 360 | Devonian | Upper / Middle / Lower |
| | | 410 | Silurian | Upper / Middle / Lower |
| | | 440 | Ordovician | Upper / Lower |
| | | 505 | Cambrian | Upper / Middle / Lower |
| Pre-Cambrian | Eophytic | 570 | Proterozoic | |
| | | 2,500 | Archean | |
| | | 4,500 | Formation of the earth's crust | |

| | young adult | mature adult | old animal | senile animal |
|---|---|---|---|---|
| Age in years | 20–35 | 30–45 | 40–55 | over 55 |
| Characteristic | still growing | | still in leading role | often solitary |
| Shoulder height (male) | 11ft | 11–12ft | 12–12.5ft | |
| Shoulder height (female) | 8ft | 8–10ft | over 10ft | |
| Weight (male) | 3.5 tons | 4.5 tons | 5–6 tons | 5 tons |
| Weight (female) | 2.5 tons | 2.5 tons | 3 tons | |
| Tusk weight | 22–90lb | 45–130lb | 65–175lb | 90–220lb |

# Elephants in veterinary medicine

Elephant-breeding in the care of humans and in the particular conditions of zoos and animal reserves calls for constant attendance by veterinary surgeons with professional training in wild-animal medicine and a great deal of practical experience. Until quite recently, teaching at veterinary colleges was confined to the diseases and handling of agricultural working farm animals and household pets. Nowadays the zoo-animal branch of veterinary science is able to draw on an extensive literature and a large number of treatment protocols; however, much research work remains to be done.

A fruitful network of international exchanges, covering both practical experiences and theoretical research findings, has since developed between the Berlin Institute for Zoo and Wild Animal Research, the Hamburg's Hagenbeck Animal Park, the National Zoological Park of the Smithsonian Institution in Washington, D.C., the zoos of Zurich and Rotterdam, the Kruger National Park in South Africa, and the Working Elephant Breeding Project in Burma (Myanmar).

# The pill for elephants

The management of South Africa's Kruger National Park is looking for ways of achieving birth control in elephants in order to avoid the need for culling (the method normally used to correct excessive population growth but severely criticized by international societies for the prevention of cruelty to animals).

In 1986, scientists from the Berlin Institute and a group of American scientists sponsored by various societies for the prevention of cruelty to animals and headed by Montana Zoo's Jay Kirkpatrick were given a chance to conduct practical trials of contraceptive procedures on wild elephants. Working closely together, the two groups experimented with various ideas. The Germans tried hormone treatments while the Americans tested a method of immunological contraception.

A total of fifty-two animals were selected: twenty-one for the US project, ten for the German group, while a further twenty-one animals were fitted with radio collars and promptly re-released into the wild. Before the study began, all the fifty-two animals were examined with the aid of a newly invented ultrasound diagnostic appliance.

The Berlin scientists implanted five tiny capsules containing the hormone preparation oestradiol behind the ears of each animal. These gradually released the drug into the bloodstream. According to Professor R.R. Hofmann, director of the Berlin Institute, over the next eight months none of the cows treated became pregnant.

The American experiment was designed to induce total sterility. The animals were injected with a vaccine obtained from hogs. The proteins this contains, which are taken from a thin layer surrounding the egg cells (the 'zona pellucida') trigger violent immune reactions. In earlier trials conducted on horses and zoo elephants, the immune reaction had been so powerful that parts of the genital tract were even affected. In the Kruger National Park experiment, some of this contraceptive effect was lost. Eighteen of the twenty-one animals vaccinated were then recaptured, and eight of them were pregnant! Of the untreated cows that had been fitted with radio collars, just under 90 percent of them conceived again.

Following its successful trials, the Berlin Institute is continuing its research program. The ideal hormone dosage for the elephant 'pill' still needs to be determined. It is hoped to extend the contraceptive effect of capsule implantation from the present period of around eight months to two years. Also, the oestradiol dose is to be reduced through combinations with other drugs.

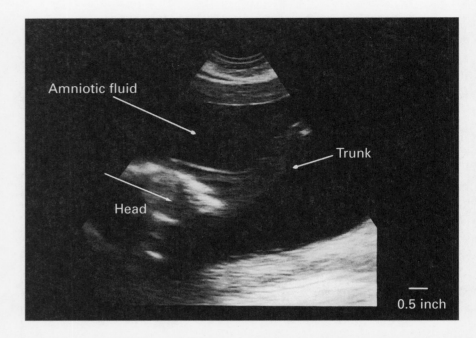

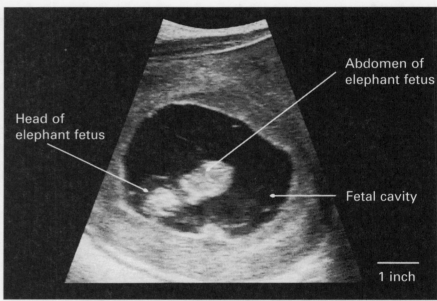

A pregnancy test being carried out on an elephant cow, using the ultrasound scanner developed at the Berlin Institute for Zoo and Wild Animal Research (see also illustration below left).

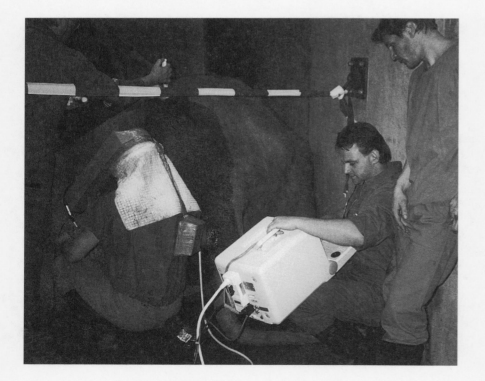

# Ultrasound scanning in elephants

At the Hagenbeck Animal Park a specially adapted ultrasound scanner has now been successfully tested on elephants. The usual equipment normally fails to achieve sufficient penetration of elephant tissue. In 1994, veterinary surgeons Hildebrand and Göritz notched up a world first, showing an elephant fetus on an ultrasound screen and supplying definitive evidence of pregnancy. Earlier tests using blood and urine samples had often proved unreliable and led to serious treatment errors. The new equipment, which permits a detailed examination of an animal's genital tract to be carried out from the intestine, can for the most part be used without anesthesia.

The new ultrasound scanner also makes it possible to say at an early stage whether an elephant cow was capable of taking when mated with a bull. Elephant keepers have often wondered why, despite repeated matings, particular cows have not conceived. The Berlin scientists have now shown that benign growths in the wombs of certain cows, notably older animals, formerly blocked the flow of semen. Such disorders can now be treated with drugs. The new findings are of enormous importance as regards making up the breeding groups that are so urgently required to replenish zoo stocks through captive breeding, rather than by taking animals from the wild.

# The occurrence of 'arcus scleralis' in elephants

## by Henning Wiesner, Munich

The special fascination of zoo life is undoubtedly, for the animal keeper, having direct contact on a daily basis with the animals entrusted to his or her care. The sheer numbers of different species and shapes represented make the zoo as workplace one of almost unique liveliness and variety. It is this close, intense relationship between humans and animals that zoo biology as a modern branch of the natural sciences has to thank for a wealth of discoveries in many fields (anatomy, pathology, physiology, ethology, etc.).

Some of those discoveries are based partly on chance observations, which are all the more surprising for the fact that, despite being around an animal all day and every day and hence thoroughly familiar with it, one has not noticed anything earlier. This is the story of one such observation.

## Arcus scleralis

During an eye examination being carried out on a 19-year-old African elephant bull who was going blind because of an infection (namely iridocyclitis, hypopyon, bilateral panophthalmia), a small opalescent ring was seen encircling the iris (see photos). The reason why this really rather striking colored formation in the eye of the African elephant had escaped our notice before may have been because the lashes cast such a long shadow, making observation difficult, and also because, with the eyelids in constant movement, part of the eyeball is always covered. Consequently, the ring is only clearly visible in its entirety when the animal has been immobilized. A similar formation in old people is known as arcus lipoides or arcus senilis and consists of fat and cholesterol deposits. Eye function is not impaired by it.

When human ophthalmologist Dr. Merck of Munich was called in to conduct a clinical examination, he actually referred to the bright ring in the elephant's eye by analogy as the formation arcus lipoides.

Little is known about its occurrence in animals. In certain canine species (German shepherd, beagle, husky, Airedale, and collie) it may appear in adult animals. An eye modification in rabbits described as primary lipid keratopathia can be induced by artificial hypercholesterinamia. Then, however, such modifications occur for the most part centrally in the superficial corneal stroma rather than in the form of a peripheral ring, which means that they are only partly comparable with arcus lipoides. In fox terriers, arcus lipoides is usually regarded as pathognostic for a lipid accumulative disorder, not unlike Wolman syndrome in humans (Schäfer 1988).

In 1992 a histological examination of a complete eyeball of an African elephant cow was carried out by Dr. E. Schäfer of the Pathology Institute of Munich's Radiation and Environmental Research Company. This showed that the eye ring impressing clinically as arcus lipoides in fact consists of pale, tough sclera anterior joining the peripheral cornea. This gives us, as the morphological equivalent

of arcus lipoides in humans, what in the African elephant we must call arcus scleralis, as we also know it in the bird's eye. Clinically, these different ring formations are deceptively similar, if not indistinguishable.

How far the occurrence of arcus scleralis in mammals depends on species, sub-species, age, or individual is not known and will require further research. It was absent, for example, in the marsupials, bears, wolves, maned wolves, hippos, alpacas, and ruminants that we examined on a stochastic basis. In cats, we managed to detect it in a very narrow form only in the Sumatran tiger and in lions. In one species of tapir it is fragmentarily present, while in Indian and white rhinos and in Przewalski's horse and the kiang it occurs in an extremely narrow, unobtrusive form. Among primates, it is clearly visible in guerezas of all ages as well as in adult mandrills, siamangs, and silver gibbons, though not in juveniles of those species (arcus lipoides?). Visibility of the ring usually depends on the angle of incidence of light, but nowhere is it as strikingly evident as in the eye of the African elephant.

Since this arcus scleralis was absent in all six of our Asian elephants, we looked both in person and with the aid of a questionnaire at a total of forty-three places where Asian elephants are kept. Our investigations showed that arcus scleralis occurred in only about 20 percent of animals studied and even then in a markedly fainter and more blurred and fragmentary form than in African elephants.

Interestingly, in none of the places polled, including those in India and beyond, had this arcus scleralis come to anybody's attention before this time.

## Sacred elephants

However, a glance at the history of Indian elephant husbandry shows that earlier generations were very well aware of arcus scleralis and that animals with this (for the species) relatively rare characteristic enjoyed particular esteem. For example, the Mogul emperors in the 16th century preferred elephants 'with bright eyes' (Zimmer 1979). In most illustrations of the period the white eye ring of the ruler's riding elephant is very distinctly portrayed (Kurt 1992).

This is undoubtedly no accident but evidence, instead, of the detailed powers of observation that characterized a time when elephant husbandry in the Indian cultural sphere was in its heyday. The sacred elephant 'Airavata' and other elephant deities were shown as white, and the white portrayal of the eye ring should be seen in this context. After all, the divine white elephant is seen as the incarnation of Indra. This is also why, in ritual processions in India, temple elephants are whitened with rice flour.

The idea of the 'sacred elephant' is still very much alive in India today, as is impressively demonstrated by two stone elephants in Changu Narayan, near Kathmandu in Nepal, which guard a temple complex dating from 1634. In both statues, the concentric ring around the iris

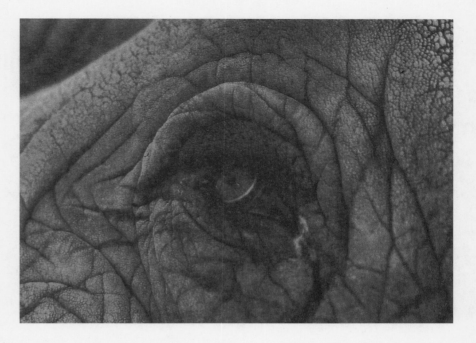

was deliberately highlighted by the original sculptor and was quite recently given additional emphasis with a fresh application of white paint to regain the original look.

Another noticeable feature of these elephants idealized as temple guardians is that they have five toes on their front and also on their hind feet. In other words, they display an atavistic relic, since as a rule Asian elephants have only four toenails on their hind feet. Such atavism is extremely rare, and again it indicates the special status of the sacred elephant, which the artist sought to stress in this way. In the ancient Trivandrum Sanskrit no. X, 1910, the 'Lucky Signs' chapter contains the following pertinent comment: 'The elephant has twenty toes on its feet' (Zimmer 1979).

That great connoisseur of the Asian elephant, Fred Kurt, informed me personally in 1991 that, in Indian elephant markets, when an elephant is for sale its value is sometimes fraudulently enhanced by the seller's naively pretending that

*The opalescent white ring around the iris does not, contrary to earlier assumptions, impair the elephant's vision. Indians even see it as enhancing the animal's beauty (see also illustration below).*

it has five hind toes by gluing shells to its hind legs to look like a fifth toenail.

## Black ring and 'evil eye'

In many places in Europe where elephants are kept it is customary to apply oil in a ring around the animals' eyes. Depending on the skill of the keeper, this produces a black ring that has the effect of making the eye look much larger. A survey of our staff as well as of the staffs of other zoos and circuses has failed to come up with an adequate explanation for this action. It is often said that elephants' eyes are particularly sensitive to wind.

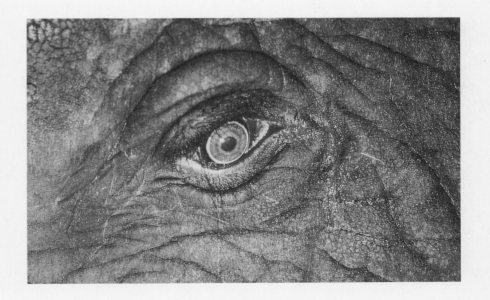

# Elephants in zoos

## The middle class established the zoological garden

The 1789 French Revolution, which secured certain liberties for the French bourgeoisie, also benefited the animals of the Versailles menagerie. Some animals were actually set free, though most (as a stopgap measure) were transferred to Paris's Botanical Gardens, the 'Jardin des Plantes.' It was the birth of the oldest urban zoological garden still in existence today.

That honor had almost fallen to the Swiss more than two centuries earlier. The idea of establishing a botanical garden in conjunction with live animals and opening it as a public park had been conceived by the greatest naturalist of his day, Dr. Conrad Gesner (1516–65) of Zurich. However, the city fathers turned his thoroughly tempting offer down, and it was not until 1929 that Zurich received its 'bourgeois' zoo.

The founding of Paris's 'Jardin des Plantes' zoo is of great importance in the history of zoological gardens. Director de Saint-Pierre drew the attention of the National Assembly not only to the animals present at Versailles but also to the possibility of using his garden to educate the public in natural history. Until then, people had seen animals only in traveling menageries, where they were exhibited as curiosities and freaks. Following the foundation of the 'Jardin des Plantes' the mayors of Paris enacted an ordinance banning traveling menageries. This was the first guarantee that a zoo could survive as the steady flow of visitors was assured.

## The middle class

The 19th century saw a series of zoos founded liked beads on a necklace:

| | |
|---|---|
| 1828 London | 1831 Dublin |
| 1835 Bristol | 1836 Manchester |
| 1838 Amsterdam | 1843 Antwerp |
| 1844 Berlin | 1857 Rotterdam |
| 1858 Frankfurt | 1859 Copenhagen |
| 1859 Philadelphia | 1860 Cologne |
| 1861 Dresden | 1862 Melbourne |
| 1864 Moscow | 1864 New York (Central P) |
| 1865 St. Petersburg | 1865 Hanover |
| 1865 Karlsruhe | 1865 Breslau (Wroclaw) |
| 1868 Mulhouse | 1869 Kharkov |
| 1870 Buffalo | 1874 Basel |
| 1874 Poznan | 1874 Chicago |
| 1874 St. Louis | 1875 Münster |
| 1875 Cincinatti | 1875 Calcutta |
| 1878 Leipzig | !881 Wuppertal |
| 1882 Cleveland | 1882 Tokyo (Ueno) |
| 1882 Adelaide | 1899 New York (Bronx) |

The late 19th century saw the expansion in Europe of the ideas and theories of Charles Darwin, which became the basis of modern biology. The knowledge that man too was a product of the evolution of life on earth decisively influenced the foundations of zoos during that period.

## Zoos today

The Second World War inflicted heavy damage on many zoological gardens in Europe; in fact, some disappeared altogether. The post-war years produced many people who in adverse and sometimes adventurous circumstances made sure that 'their' zoo and 'their' animals pulled through. Most zoos at the time were scenes of devastation, but for careworn visitors they represented oases of green amid the deserts of ruined cities.

### The period after the First World War

| | |
|---|---|
| 1922 Djakarta | 1926 Chicago |
| 1928 Bremerhaven | 1928 Detroit |
| 1930 Chester | 1931 Prague |
| 1932 Saarbrücken | 1933 Bochum |
| 1933 Belfast | 1934 Duisburg |
| 1934 Heidelberg | 1936 Glasgow |
| 1936 Osnabrück | 1937 Augsburg |
| 1937 Straubing | 1937 Emmen |
| 1938 Krefeld | 1939 Lodz |

### The period after the Second World War

| | |
|---|---|
| 1949 Gelsenkirchen | 1949 Caracas |
| 1950 Magdeburg | 1950 Eskilstuna |
| 1953 Dortmund | 1954 Tokyo (Tama) |
| 1954 Cottbus | 1955 Tierpark Berlin |
| 1956 Rostock | 1957 São Paolo |
| 1957 Delhi | 1957 Katowice |
| 1958 Portland | 1958 Erfurt |
| 1959 Jersey | 1961 Salzburg |
| 1961 Darmstadt | 1962 Innsbruck |
| 1962 Louisville | |

A new, proud era began for zoological gardens. The findings of animal psychology and behavioral research, some obtained in zoos (by Oskar Heinroth, for one example), were now incorporated into all areas of zoo-keeping. Even before the middle of the 20th century Heini Hediger, who successively directed the zoos in Bern, Basel, and Zurich, postulated the four main functions of a zoological garden:

1. The first and noblest function of a zoological garden consists in providing a broad spectrum of the urban public with a recreational space.
2. Visitors must be given an optimum amount of accessible information about natural history, the principal objective being to convey an understanding of the disastrous effect that the human race is having on nature and the environment.
3. Zoological gardens must serve to protect nature in the broadest sense, not just by explaining and teaching natural history. This function also involves promoting the idea of an intact living-space for animals and providing zoo-bred specimens to recolonize abandoned habitats and boost threatened populations.
4. Natural conservation and species protection call for detailed knowledge. Zoos must actively devote themselves to research, whereby zoology, ecology, psychology, physiology, parasitology, all of veterinary medicine, and various other disciplines all form branches of zoo biology.

## Elephant stocks in North America: Summary and prospects

The relatively large number of elephants in North America (600) would appear adequate for a self-sustaining population. However, as we have seen, there are problems associated with the overall composition of that elephant population as regards age structure, number and distribution of bulls, and availability of the young cows coming into maturity that form so essential a component of any successful breeding program.

The 322 animals living in zoos, wild-animal, and safari parks are divided between a total of 92 institutions. However, 52 of those belong to only five sites (Jackson GAP, San Diego WAP, Tampa Bush Gardens, Vallejo Marine World, and Rockton), which means that 270 elephants are divided among 87 institutions. This gives an average of something like three animals per institution, yet eleven sites have only a single animal and thirty-one sites have only two. In other words, nearly half of the zoos, wild-animal parks, and safari parks covered (i.e. forty-two out of ninety-two) have only one or two elephants!

As regards the elephant population in private establishments and circuses and the category of 'performing elephants' (which includes those involved in circus acts, those used by film studios, and those that give rides in zoos and parks as well as for all manner of events), more than half (149 animals) are owned by eight companies (Riddle, Beatty-Cole, Carden, Carson & Barnes, King Royal, Ringling, Cuneo, and Steele). The remaining 129 animals are divided among a total of 58 owners, making the average a little over two, except that 19 owners have no more than one animal each.

Unless over the next few years successful efforts are made through rational breeding management to obtain a substantially higher breeding quota, it will not be possible to maintain North America's elephant stocks without introducing animals from outside. Artificial insemination, though widely advocated and occasionally practiced, has not so far proved successful in elephants. Even if it did, the immense outlay of technical, financial, and personnel resources would inhibit its large-scale use, at least for the present.

In as little as ten years, the elephant population of both species (the Asian in particular) will have dropped appreciably; in twenty years, there will be a drastic decline in stocks of both African and Asian elephants. There are still enough suitable animals available to halt this unfortunate process. However, intensive communication and collaboration on the part of all concerned will be essential in order to help this endangered species survive the 21st century – or as Heidi Riddle, the Director of Operations at Riddle's Elephant Farm in Arkansas, put it quite succinctly at that organization's conference in Jacksonville, Florida, in January 1971:

'Opening up the lines of communication between facilities and interested individuals is the best way to help all elephants worldwide.'

# Index

# Select bibliography

## General

Adams, Jack: Wild Elephants in Captivity, Carson 1981

Blond, G.: Schicksal der Elefanten, Memmingen 1960

Buffon: Naturgeschichte des Elephanten nach Büffon von A., Nuremburg 1799

Carrington, R.: Elephants, London 1958

Edwards, D. L.: All about Elephants, New York 1941

Eisenberg, John F., et al.: Asian Elephants, Washington 1990

Fenner, P. R.: Elephants, Elephants, Elephants. Stories of Rogues and Workers, Tuskers and Trekkers, Jungle Trails and Circus Tanbark, New York 1952

Fragment einer Schrift über den Elefanten, vornehmlich nach Aristoteles, Plinius, Varro, Aelian und Pausanias, bei Gelegenheit der Ankunft des Elefanten Maximilians I. (Innsbruck 1552, Universitäts-bibliothek, Fragm. 81)

Freeman, D.: Elephants. The Vanishing Giants, London 1980

Freeman, M.: Elephants and Whales, Amsterdam 1994

Herbert, A.: The Elephant, London 1916

Holder, C. F.: The Ivory King. A Popular History of the Elephant and its Allies, New York 1888

Lockhart, G. and Bosworth, W. G.: Grey Titan. The Book of Elephants, London 1938

Murray, N.: Elefanten, Munich 1975

Murray, N.: The Love of Elephants, London 1976

Museum für Völkerkunde (Ed.), Munich: Mensch und Elefant, Frankfurt a. M. 1994

Petri von Hartenfelss, G. C.: Elephantographia curiosa, Erfurt 1715

Robinson, W. W.: Elephants, New York 1935

Sanderson, I. T.: The Dynasty of Abu. A History and Natural History of the Elephants and their Relatives Past and Present, London 1963

Schlegel, A. W. von: Zur Geschichte des Elephanten, in: Indische Bibliothek, 1, 1820, pp. 129–229

Sukumar, Raman: The Asian Elephant. Ecology and Management, Cambridge (UK) 1992

Sunamoto, E.: The Elephant, Osaka 1931–1932

Tennant, T. O.: The Natural History of the Elephant, with a Minute Description of that Animal, London 1771

Time-Life, Elephants and Other Land Giants, Amsterdam 1977

Tournier, G.: Les éléphants, Paris 1909

Williams, H.: Elefanten, Frankfurt a. M. 1889

## Africa

Allen, G. M.: Zoological Results of the George Vanderbilt African Expedition of 1934. Pt. 2, The Forest Elephant of Africa, in: Proc. Acad. nat. Sci. Phila., 1937, Vol. 88, pp. 15–44

Aubreville, A.: À la recherche de la forêt en Côte d'Ivoire, in: Bois Fôret Trop. 57, 1958, pp. 12–27

Caldwell, K.: Elephant Domestication in the Belgian Congo. Reprinted from Report of Game Warden, Kenya, to the Uganda Government, 1925, in: J. Soc. Pres. Fauna Emp., N. S., Part 7, pp. 71–82, London 1927

Davidson, B.: African Kingdoms, Time-Life-International (Nederland) N.V., 1967

Douglas-Hamilton, I. and O.: Among the Elephants, London 1975

Dröscher, V. B. (Ed.): Rettet die Elefanten Afrikas, Hamburg 1990

Eisenberg, J. F., McKay, G. M. and Jainudeen, M. R.: Reproductive Behavior of the Asiatic Elephant (Elephas maximus maximus L.), in: Behaviour 37, 1971, pp. 193–225

Fischer, R.: Die schwarzen Pharaonen, Herrsching 1986

Gavron, J.: Dämmerung im Reich der Elefanten, Munich 1994

Hanks, J.: A Struggle for Survival – The Elephant Problem, Johannesburg 1979

Hendrichs, H. and Hendrichs, U.: Dikdik und Elefanten, Ökologie und Soziologie zweier afrikanischer Huftiere, Munich 1971

Jeannin, A.: L'éléphant d'Afrique: zoologie, histoire, folklore, chasse, protection, Paris 1947

Künkel, R.: Elefanten. Afrikas freundliche Riesen, Hamburg 1981

Laws, R. M.: Aspects of Reproduction in the African Elephant, Loxodonta africana, in: E. Afr. Wildl., 5, 1969, pp. 46–52

Martin, C.: Die Regenwälder Westafrikas, Basel, Berlin 1989

Melland, F. H.: Elephants in Africa, London, New York 1938

Moss, C. and Colbeck, M.: Das Jahr der Elefanten, Munich 1997

Oberjohann, H.: Meine Tschadsee-Elefanten, Grenchen 1950

Payne, K. B., Poole, J. H. and Langbauer, W. R.: Infrasonic Calls in Free-ranging African Elephants, in: Elephant Memories, Ed. Moss, C., 1989

Poole, J. H. and Moss, C. J.: Musth in the African Desert (Loxodonta africana), in: Nature 292 (5826), 1981, pp. 830–831

Poole, J. H.: Kenya's Elephants – A Very Different Story to Tell, in: Swara,

Jan.–Feb. 15, 1992, No. 1, pp. 29–31

Ricciardi, M.: Vanishing Africa, London 1971

Ross, D. H.: Elephant. The Animal and its Ivory in African Culture, Los Angeles 1992

Rushby, G. G.: The Elephant in Tanganyika, London 1953

Shoshani, J., Hillmann, J. C. and Walcek, J. M.: 'Ahmed,' the Logo of the Elephant Interest Group: Encounters in Marsabit and Notes on his Model and Skeleton, in: Elephant 2, 1987, No. 3, pp. 7–32

Sikes, S. K.: The Natural History of the African Elephant, London 1971

Smith, J. A., Hanks, J. and Short, R. V.: Biochemical Observations on the Corpora Lutea of the African Elephant, Loxodonta africana, in: J. Reprod. Fert. 20, 1969, pp. 111–117

Smuts, G. C.: Reproduction and Population Characteristics of Elephants in the Kruger National Park, in: J. South African Wildlife Management Ass. 5, 1975, No. 1, pp. 1–10

Stockley, C. H.: The Elephant in Kenya, London 1953

Ward, R.: The Elephant in East Central Africa, London undated

## Antiquity – Greece – Rome

de Beer, G. R.: Alps and Elephants. Hannibal's march, London 1955

Curtius, Q.: The History of the Wars of Alexander the Great, London 1747

Friedlaender, L.: Darstellungen der Sittengeschichte Roms, Leipzig 1910

Grimal, P.: Römische Kulturgeschichte, Munich, Zurich 1961

Huß, W. (Ed.): Karthago, Darmstadt 1992

Suetonius: The Lives of the Caesars, Harvard, 1998

Vardiman, E. E.: Die grosse Zeitwende zwischen Hellenismus und Urchristentum, Vienna 1978

Whitaker, J.: The Course of Hannibal over the Alps Ascertained, London 1794

## Art

Abbott, G. H.: The Elephant on Coins, Sydney 1919

Arnold, B.: Kamerun: Die höfische Kunst des Graslandes, (Die Schatzkammer 33), Dresden 1980

Barret, D. and Gray, B.: Die Indische Malerei, Geneva 1980

Ben-Amos, P.: Men and Animals in Benin Art, in: Man 2, 1976, No. 2, pp. 243–252

Ben-Amos, P.: The Art of Benin, New York 1980

Coomaraswamy, A. K.: History of Indian

and Indonesian art, New York 1927

Coppin, G. (Ed.): Der Elefant, Munich 1989

Dark, P.: Benin Art. London 1960

Dark, P.: The Art of Benin. Chicago, Chicago Natural History Museum 1962.

Deneck, M.-M.: Indische Kunst, Wiesbaden undated

Druce, G. C.: The Elephant in Medieval Art and Legend, in: Archaeological Journal, 76, 1919, pp. 1–73

Ehnbom, D. J.: Indische Minaturen, Die Sammlung Ehrenfeld, Stuttgart 1988

Ettinghausen, R.: Die arabische Malerei, Lausanne 1969

Filippi, G. G.: India, Miniature e Dipinti Dal XVI al XIX secolo. La collezione di Howard Hodgkin, Milan 1997

Fischer, E. and Himmelheber, H.: Das Gold in der Kunst Westafrikas, Zurich, Museum Rietberg 1975

Fischer, E. and Himmelheber, H.: The Arts of the Dan in West Africa, Zurich, Museum Rietberg 1984

Fischer, E. and Himmelheber, H.: Die Kunst der Guro, Zurich, Museum Rietberg 1985

Fischer, E. and Homberger, L.: Masks in Guro Culture, Ivory Coast, New York, Center for African Art 1986

Frobenius, L.: Der Kameruner Schiffs-schnabel und seine Motive, in: Abhand-lungen der Kaiserlichen Leopoldinisch-Carolinischen Deutschen Akademie der Naturforscher, 1897, No. 1, Vol. 70

Garrad, T. F.: Akan Weights and the Gold Trade, London 1980

Germann, P.: Das plastisch – figurliche Kunstgewerbe im Grasland von Kamerun, in: Jahrbuch des Städtischen Museums für Völkerkunde zu Leipzig, 1910, No. 4, pp. 1–35

Heckscher, W.: Bernini's Elephant and Obelisk, in: Art Bulletin, 1949, 29, pp. 155–182

Kecskési, M.: African Masterpieces and Selected Works from Munich – Staatliches Museum für Völkerkunde, New York, Center for African Art 1987.

Knoerzer, H.: Jumbos Passion. Elefanten in Kunst und Kommerz, Lübeck 1996

Kunz, G. F.: Ivory, and the Elephant in Art, in Archaeology and in Science, Garden City, New York 1916

Lévêque, J.-J. and Ménant, N.: La peinture islamique et indienne, Lausanne 1968

Luz, Chr.: Das exotische Tier in der Kunst, Stuttgart 1987

Meyer, E.: Mittelalterliche Elefantenleuchter, in: Weltkunst, 19, 1949, No. 1

Niangoran-Bouah, G.: The Akan World

of Gold Weights. The Weights and Society, Paris 1987

Pal, P.: Elephants and Ivories in South Asia, Los Angeles 1981

Seckel, D.: Kunst des Buddhismus, 1980

Slatkes, L. J.: Rembrandt's Elephant, in: Simiolus, 11, 1980, No. 1, pp. 7–13

Snead, S.: Animals in four Worlds, Sculptures from India, Chicago 1989

Thibout, M.: L'éléphant dans la sculpture romane franáaise, in: Bulletin Monumental, 1947, Vol. 105, pp. 183–195

Topsfield, A.: Indian Paintings and Drawings from the Collection of Howard Hodgin, London 1991

Welch, C.: Gods, Kings and Tigers. The Art of Kotah, Munich 1997

**Capture – Domestication**

Brown, G. C.: Elephant Catching in Mysore, London 1890

Macphail, J. G. S.: The Bandala Method of Hunting Elephant on Foot, in: Sudan Notes, 1930, Vol. 13, pp. 279–283

Mayer, C.: Trapping Wild Animals in Malay Jungles, New York 1921

Roocroft, Alan, and Zoll, Daniel Atwell: Managing Elephants, Ramona 1994

Ruhe, H.: Wilde Tiere frei Haus, Munich 1960

Ryhner, P. R.: Auf Tierfang durch die Welt, Herrenalb 1961

Schmidt, M. J.: Breeding Strategies for Domesticated Elephants, in: Proceedings of the Asian Elephant Specialist Group Meeting, Ed. Santiapillai, C., Chiangmai 1980

Schulz, Chr.: Auf Großtierfang für Hagenbeck, Leipzig 1926

Tennent, Sir J. E.: The Wild Elephant, and the Method of Capturing and Taming it in Ceylon, London 1867

**China – Japan**

Beurdeley, M.: China-Chinesische Sammler durch die Jahrhunderte, Munich 1964

Bishop, C. W.: The Elephant and its Ivory in Ancient China, in: JAOS, 1935, No. 41, pp. 290–306

Chang, H. T.: On the Question of the Existence of Elephants and Rhinoceros in North China in Historical Times, in: Bull. Geol. Soc. China, 1926, Vol. 5, pp. 99–105

Christie, A.: Chinesische Mythologie, Wiesbaden 1968

Gascoigne, B.: Das kaiserliche China und seine Kunstschätze, Vienna, Munich, Zurich 1980

Mody, N. H. N.: A Collection of Nagasaki Colour Prints and Paintings, Tokyo 1969

**Circus**

Bannerman, J.: The Tragic Death of the Great Jumbo, in: Maclean's Mag., Montreal, 12. Nov. 1955

Barnum, P.T.: The Life of P.T. Barnum, Written by Himself, 1855

Büsing, E.: Mit 20 Zirkuselefanten um die Welt, Munich 1938

Erni, F. X.: Rolf Knie, Elefanten und Artisten, Bern undated

Fox, C. P.: Old Time Circus Cuts, New York 1979

Fox, C. P. and Parkinson, T.: The Circus in America, Waukesha 1969

Hagenbeck, C.: Von Tieren und Menschen, Berlin 1907

Halperson, J.: Das Buch vom Zirkus, Düsseldorf 1926

Haufellner, A.; Kurt, F.; Schilfarth, J. and Schweiger, G.: Elefanten in Zoo und Zirkus, Munich 1993

Jennison, G.: Animals for Show and Pleasure in Ancient Rome, Manchester 1937

Kurt, F. and Knie, L.: Elefanten und Tiger im Circus Knie, Zurich, Munich 1980

Lewis, G.: Elephant Tramp, Boston 1955

Malhotra, R.: Manege frei, Artisten und Zirkusplakate von Adolph Friedländer, Dortmund 1979

Manning-Sanders, R.: The English Circus, London 1952

Murray, M.: Circus! From Rome to Ringling, New York 1956

Rankin, J.: Historical Researches on the Wars and Sports of the Mongols and Romans in which Elephants and Wild Beasts were Employed or Slain, London 1826

Renevey, M. I.: Le Grand Livre du Cirque, Geneva 1977

Richards, R.: Life with Alice. 40 years of Elephant Adventures, New York 1944

Sembach-Krone, F.: Circus Krone, Munich 1969

Tyrwhitt-Drake, G.: Beasts and Circuses, Bristol 1936

Tyrwhitt-Drake, Sir G.: The English Circus and Fair Ground, London 1946

Zapff, G.: Jumbo auf dem Drahtseil, Berlin 1987

**Hunting**

Akeley, C. E.: Elephant Hunting in Equatorial Africa with Rifle and Camera, in: Nat. Geogr. Mag., 1912, Vol. 23, pp. 779–810

Bell, W. D. M.: The Wanderings of an Elephant Hunter, London 1958

Blunt, D. E.: Elephant, London 1933

Cooper, R. D.: Hunting and Hunted in the Belgian Congo, London 1914

Craig, G.C.: Records of Elephant Hunting Trophies Exported from Zimbabwe 1987–1993, Harare 1993

Cumming, R. G.: Five Years of a Hunter's Life in the Interior of South Africa, London 1850

Daniell, W.: Elephant Hunting. A Panoramic View of the Capture and Taming of Wild Elephants on the Islands of Ceylon, London 1835

Finaughty, W.: The Recollections of William Finaughty, Elephant Hunter, 1864–1875, Philadelphia 1916

Hardwick, A. A.: An Ivory Hunter in North Kenya. The record of an Expedition through Kikuyu to Galla-land in East Equatorial Africa with an Account of the Rendili and Burkeneji Tribes, London 1903

Harland, David: Killing Game. International Law and the African Elephant, Westport 1994

Hubback, T. R.: Elephant Hunting in the Federated Malay States, London 1905

Hunter, J. A.: African Hunter, New York 1954

Lake, J. A.: Killers in Africa, New York 1953

Langsdorff, Baron de: Une chasse à l'éléphant en Ouganda, in: Tour du Monde, N.S., 15, 1909, pp. 517–28

Ligers, Z.: La chasse à l'éléphant chez les Bozo, in: Journal de la Société des Africanistes 30, 1960, pp. 95–99

Lyell, D. D.: The African Elephant and its Hunters, London 1924

Moffett, C.: Hunting on Elephant, in: McClure's Mag., 1898, Vol. 12, pp. 136–146

Muirhead, J. T.: Ivory Poaching and Cannibals in Africa, London 1933

Neumann, A. H.: Elephant-hunting in East Equatorial Africa, being an Account of three Years Ivory-Hunting under Mount Kenya and among the Ndorobo Savages of the Lorogi Mountains, including a Trip to the North End of Lake Rudolph, London 1898

Selous, F. C.: A Hunter's Wanderings in Africa. A Narrative of nine Years spent amongst the Game of the Far Interior of South Africa, Containing Accounts of Explorations Beyond the Zambesi, London 1890

Stanley, W. B. and Hodgson, C.: Elephant Hunting, London 1929

Stigand, C. H.: Hunting the Elephant in Africa, and other Recollections of thirteen Years' Wanderings, New York 1913

Swann, A. J.: Fighting the Slave-Hunters in Central Africa, London 1969

Taylor, J.: Pondoro. Last of the Ivory Hunters, New York 1955

**India–Himalayas–Ceylon (Sri Lanka)**

Allen, Ch. and Dwivedi, S.: Livre of the Indian Princes, London 1984

Behr, H.-G.: Die Moguln, Basel 1990

Byrne, Peter: Tula Hatti, the Last Great Elephant, Boston 1991

Chaturvedi, M. D.: The Elephant and I, in: Nat. Geogr. Mag., 1957, No. 4, Vol. CXII, pp. 489–506

Daniel, J.C. (ed.): A Week with Elephants, Bombay 1995

Frembgen, J. W.: Rosenduft and Säbelglanz, Munich 1996

Gascoigne, B.: Die Grossmoguln, Munich 1973

Gupta, S. K.: Elephant in Indian Art and Mythology, New Delhi 1983

Ions, V.: Indische Mythologie, Wiesbaden 1968

Kurt, F.: Remarks on the Social Structure and Ecology of the Ceylon Elephant in the Yala Nationalpark, in: IUCN: The Behaviour of Ungulates and its Relation to Management, Calgary 1974, pp. 618–634

Kurt, F.: Zoologische Exkursionen in den Kanha-Nationalpark, Zurich 1973

Kurt, F.: Indiens Tierwelt in Gefahr, in: Freunde des Kölner Zoos, 13, 1970, No. 2, pp. 43–46

Miall, L. C.: Anatomy of the Indian Elephant, London 1878

Mode, H.: Das frühe Indien, Essen 1984

Naravane, V. S.: The Elephant and the Lotus, London 1965

Nawrath, A.: Unsterbliches Indien, Vienna, Munich 1956

Nila-kantha, of Raja-mangalam. The Elephant Lore of the Hindus. The Elephant Sport (Matanga-lila) of Nila-kantha, London 1931

Praetorius, J.: Horti Indiae Orientalis sive Physiologiae de Elephante, Hamburg 1607

Rensch, B. and Altevogt, R.: Visuelles Lernvermögen eines Indischen Elefanten, in: Zeitschrift für Tierpsychologie, 10, 1953, No. 1, pp. 119–134

Sanderson, G. P.: Thirteen Years among the Wild Beasts of India, Edinburgh 1907

Shahi, S. P.: Elephants in Central India, in: WWF Monthly Report, Jan. 1986

Singh, M.: Himalayan Art, (UNESCO Art Books), Madanjeet und UNESCO, 1968

Tennent, Sir. J. E.: Sketches of the Natural History of Ceylon. Narratives and Anecdotes, Illustrations of the Habits and Instincts of the Mammalia, Birds, Reptiles, Fishes, Insects, etc. including a Monograph of the Elephant, London 1868

Ward, G. C.: Die Maharadschas,
(Schatzkammern und Herrscherhäuser
der Welt), Munich 1984

Watson, M.: Anatomy of the Indian
elephant, in: J. Anat., Land., Second
Ser. V, 1871, Vol. 6, pp. 82–94

Zimmer, H.: Spiel um den Elefanten.
Ein Buch von indischer Natur,
Cologne, Düsseldorf, Munich 1976

**Ivory**

Alpers, E. A.: Ivory and Slaves. Changing
Pattern of International Trade in East
Central Africa to the Later Nineteenth
Century, Berkeley, Los Angeles 1975

Hahner-Herzog, I.: Tippu Tip und der
Elfenbeinhandel in Ost- und
Zentralafrika im 19. Jahrhundert,
Munich 1990

Hegemann, H. W.: Elfenbein in Plastik,
Schmuck und Gerät, Hanau undated

Kühnel, E.: Die Islamischen
Elfenbeinskulpturen, Berlin 1971

Kunz, G. F.: Ivory and the Elephant in
Art, Archaeology, and in Science, New
York 1916

'Les Ivoires.' Évolution décorative du Ier
siècle à nos jours, Paris 1972

Natanson, J.: Early Christian Ivories,
London 1953

Natanson, J.: Ivory. A History and
Collector's Guide, London 1987

Philippowich, E. von: Elfenbein, Munich
1982

Randall, R. H., Jr., (Ed.): Masterpieces of
Ivory, New York 1985

Reichard, P.: Das afrikanische Elfenbein
und sein Handel, in: Deutsche
Geographische Blätter, 12, 1889,
pp. 132–168

Spinage, C. A.: A Review of Ivory
Exploitation and Elephant Population
Trends in Africa, in: East African
Wildlife Journal 11, 1973, pp. 281–289

Thornton, Allan, and Currey, Dave: To
Save an Elephant. The Undercover
Investigation into the Illegal Ivory
Trade, Toronto 1992

Williamson, G. C.: The Book of Ivory,
London 1938

Wilson, D. and Ayerst, P.: White Gold. The
Story of African Ivory, London 1976

**Middle East and Egypt**

Esin, E.: Mekka und Medina, Frankfurt
a. M. 1964

Gerster, G.: Nubien – Goldland am Nil,
Zurich 1964

Henning, H.: Die Welt der Perser, Essen
1984

Schmökel, H.: Ur, Assur und Babylon,
Essen 1984

Shinnie, P. L.: Meroe: A Civilization of
the Sudan, New York 1967

Vacquié, P.: Les éléphants du cercle de
Nioro (Soudan), in: Notes Africaines
47, 1950, pp. 98–99

**Prehistory**

Carrington, R.: A Guide to Earth History,
London 1956

Carrington, R.: Mermaids and
Mastodons, London 1957

Cohen, C.: Le destin du mammouth,
Paris 1994

Cuvier, Baron G. L. C. F. D.: Sur les
éléphants vivants et fossiles, in:
Annales du musée d'Histoire Naturelle,
1806, Vol. 8, pp. 1–58, 93-155,
249–269

Cuvier, Baron G. L. C. F. D.: Sur le
Grand Mastodonte, in: Annales du
musée d'Histoire Naturelle, 1806,
Vol. 8, pp. 270–310

Cuvier, Baron G. L. C. F. D.: Le Règne
Animal, Paris 1817

Cuvier, Baron G. L. C. F. D.: Recherches
sur les Ossements Fossiles,
Paris 1834

Darwin, Ch.: The Descent of Man and
Selection in Relation to Sex, 1871

Engesser, B.: Fejtar, O. and Major, P.:
Das Mammut und seine
ausgestorbenen Verwandten, Basel
1996

Garutt, W. E.: Das Mammut, Wittenberg
1964

Gayrard-Valy, Y.: Zeugen der Eiszeit,
Ravensburg undated

Goodwin, G. G.: The First Living
Elephant in America, in: J. Mammal.,
1925, Vol. 6, pp. 256-263

Haynes, G.: Mammoths, Mastodonts,
and Elephants, New York 1991

Kahlke, H.-D.: Die Eiszeit, Leipzig, Jena,
Berlin, undated

Maglio, V. J.: Origin and Evolution of the
Elephantidae, in: Transactions of the
American Philosophical Society, New
Series, Vol. 68, Part 3, 1973

Osborn, H. F.: The Angulation of the
Limbs of Proboscidia, Dinocerata, and
other Quadrupeds in Adaption of
Weight, Boston 1900

Osborn, H. F.: A Mounted Skeleton of
the Columbian Mammoth (Elephas
columbi), New York 1907

Osborn, H. F.: Hunting the Ancestral
Elephant in the Fayum Desert, in:
Century Mag., 1907, Vol. 74, pp.
815–835

Osborn, H. F.: The Elephants and
Mastodonts Arrive in America, in: Nat.
Hist. N. Y., 1925, Vol. 25, pp. 3–23

Osborn, H. F.: The Romance of the
Woolly Mammoth, in: Nat. Hist. N. Y.,
1930, Vol. 30, pp. 227–241

Osborn, H. F.: Evolution and Geographic
Distribution of the Proboscidea, in:
J. Mammal., 1934, Vol. 15, pp.
177–184

Osborn, H. F.: Proboscidea, New York
1936–1942

Pfizenmayer, E. W.: Mammutleichen und
Urwaldmenschen in Nordost-Sibirien,

Leipzig 1926

Smith, G. E.: Pre-Columbian
Representations of the Elephant in
America, in: Nature Lond., Nov. 1915,
Vol. 15, pp. 340–341

Smith, G. E.: Pre-Columbian
Representations of the Elephant in
America, in: Nature Lond., Dec. 1915,
Vol. 16, pp. 425

Sutcliffe, A. J.: On the Track of Ice Age
Mammals, London 1985

Tobien, H.: Die paläontologische Geschichte der Proboscidier (Mammalia)
im Mainzer Becken (BRD), in: Mainzer
Naturwissenschaftliches Archiv, 1986,
Vol. 24, pp. 155–261

**Southeast Asia**

Bock, C.: Temples and Elephants. Travels
in Siam in 1881–1882, Reprint
Singapore 1986

Evans, G. H.: Notes on Elephants in
Burma, Simla 1894

Gale, U. T.: Burmese Timber Elephants,
Rangoon 1974

Gallot, J.: The Elephant of Siam,
Philadelphia 1931

Gee, E. P.: Wild Elephants in Assam, in:
Ceylon Game and Fauna Protection
Society, Vol. 5, Colombo 1949,
pp. 98–104

Gee, E. P.: How Clever is an Elephant?,
in: Ceylon Game and Fauna Protection
Society, Vol. 5, Colombo 1950,
pp. 150–154

Gee, E. P.: Wild Elephants Dying in
Assam, in: Ceylon Game and Fauna
Protection Society, Vol. 5, Colombo
1950, pp. 170

Giles, F. H.: Adversaria of Elephant
Hunting (Phya Indramontri
Srichandrakumara), in: Journal of
the Siam Society, 23, 1930, No. 2,
pp. 61–70

Giles, F. H.: Elephant Hunting in the
Korat Table-land, in: Journal of the
Siam Society, 23, 1930, No. 2,
pp. 71–95

Hagenbeck, J.: Im Reich des weissen
Elefanten: Macht und Reichtum Siams
verstricken in gefährliche Abenteuer,
Frankfurt a. M. 1954

Hallett, H. S.: A Thousand Miles on an
Elephant in the Shan States, London
1890, Reprint Bangkok 1988

Heurn, F. C. van: De olifanten van
Sumatra, Den Haag 1929

Kurt, F.: Das Elefantenbuch. Wie Asiens
letzte Riesen leben, Hamburg 1992

Lair, Richard C.: Gone Astray. The care
and Management of the Asian Elephant
in Domesticity, Bangkok 1997

Mazzeo, D. and Antonini Ch. S.: Angkor-
Monumente grosser Kulturen,
Luxembourg 1979

McKay, G.M.: Behaviour and Ecology of
the Asiatic Elephant in Southeastern

Ceylon, in: Smithsonian Contribution
to Zoology, 1973, No. 125

Mury, F.: Les éléphants au Siam et au
Cambodge, in: Nature, 28, 1900,
No. 1, pp. 159–162

Oliver, R. C. D.: On the Ecology of the
Asian Elephant, Diss, Oxford 1978

Oliver, R. C. D.: Asian Elephant, in:
Evolution of Domesticated Animals,
Ed. Mason, I. L., London, New York
1984, pp. 185–193

Payne, K. B. et al.: Infrasonic Calls of the
Asian Elephant (Elephas maximus),
in: Behavioral Ecology and
Sociobiology, 1986, No. 18,
pp. 297–301

Santiapillai, C. and Jackson, P.: The
Asian Elephant. An Action Plan for its
Conservation, Gland 1990

Santiapillai, C. and Suprahman, H.:
Elephants in Indonesia (Sumatra), in:
WWF Monthly Report, Dec. 1985

Scheuermann, E. and Jainudeen, M. R.:
'Musth' beim Asiatischen Elefanten
(Elephas maximus), in: Der
Zoologische Garten (NF), 1972, No.
42, pp. 131–142

Smith, A. W.: Working Teak in the Burma
Forests, in: Nat. Geogr. Mag., Aug.
1930

Sukumar, R.: The Asian Elephant.
Ecology and Management, Cambridge
1992

Sukumar, R.: Ecology of the Asian
Elephant in Southern India. II. Feeding
Habits and Crop Raiding Pattern, in:
Journ. Trop. Ecology, 1990, No. 6,
pp. 33–53

Temple, Sir R. C.: The Thirty-seven Nats.
A Phase of Spirit-Worship prevailing in
Burma, London 1906–1991

Toke, G. U.: Burmese Timber Elephant,
Rangoon 1974

Western, D. and Lindsay, W. K.: Seasonal
Herd Dynamics of a Savanna Elephant
Population, in: Afr. J. Ecology, 1984,
No. 22, pp. 229-244

Williams, J. H.: Elephant Bill, London
1950, Vienna 1953

**Stone Age drawings – Saharan rock
paintings**

Brodrick, A. H.: Prehistoric Painting,
London 1948

Butzer, K. W.: Landschaftswandel der
Sahara im Klimageschehen der Erde,
in: Sahara – 10 000 Jahre zwischen
Weide und Wüste, Cologne 1978,
pp. 170–172

Frobenius, L.: Ekade Ektab. Die
Felsbilder Fezzans, Leipzig 1978

Garlake, P.: The Hunter's Vision. The
Prehistoric Art of Zimbabwe,
London 1995

Jelinek, J.: Mathrndush, In Galgien. Two
Important Fezzanese Rock Art Sites, in:
Anthropologie, 22, 1984, No. 2,

pp. 117–170

Jelinek, J.: Mathrndush, In Galgien. Two Important Fezzanese Rock Art Sites, in: Anthropologie, 22, 1984, No. 3, pp. 237–275

Jelinek, J.: Tilizahren, the Key Site of Fezzanese Rock Art, in: Anthropologie, 23, 1985, No. 2, pp. 125–165

Jelinek, J.: Tilizahren, the Key Site of Fezzanese Rock Art, in: Anthropologie 23, 1985, No. 3, pp. 223–275

Le Quellec, J. L.: Chronologies, Symbolisme et art rupestre au Sahara, Paris 1993, pp. 28–44

Lewis-Williams, J. D.: The World of Man and the World of Spirit: An Interpretation of the Linton Rock Paintings, in: Margaret Shaw Lecture 2, Cape Town 1988, The South African Museum

Lhote, H.: Die Felsbilder der Sahara, in: Sahara – 10 000 Jahre zwischen Weide und Wüste, Cologne 1978, pp. 70–80

Lhote, H.: Les gravures rupestres de l'oued Djerat, Tassili-n-Ajjer. Mémoires du centre de recherches anthropologiques préhistoriques et éthnographiques, Algiers 1975

Lhote, H.: The Search for the Tassili Frescoes, London 1973

Lutz, R. and G.: Rock Engravings in the SW-Fezzan, Libya, in: Memorie della Società Italiana di Scienze Naturali e del Museo Civico di Storia Naturale di Milano, Vol. XXVI-Fasc. II. L'arte e l'ambiente del Sahara preistorico, dati e interpretazioni, Milan 1993, pp. 333–358

Mori, F.: Zur Chronologie der Sahara-Felsbilder, in: Sahara – 10 000 Jahre zwischen Weide und Wüste, Cologne 1978, pp. 253–260

Mori, F.: L'arte preistorica Sahariana. Arte culture del Sahara preistorico, Rome 1992, pp. 21–30

Mori, F.: La cronologia assoluta, in: Tadrart Acacus, Turin 1964, pp. 223–240

Muzzolini, A.: L'évolution des Climats au Sahara, in: L'art rupestre préhistorique des massifs centraux sahariens, (International Series 318), 1986, pp. 47–52

Muzzolini, A.: Chronologie raisonnée des diverses écoles d'art rupestre du Sahara central 1993. Memorie della Società Italiana di Scienze Naturali e del Museo Civico di Storia Naturale di Milano Vol. XXVI-Fasc. II. L'arte e l'ambiente del Sahara preistorico, dati e interpretazioni, Milan 1993

Striedter, K. H.: Felsbilder der Sahara, Munich 1984

**War**

Armandi, P.: Histoire militaire des éléphants, depuis les temps les plus reculés jusqu'à l'introduction des armes à feu, Paris, London, Frankfurt 1843

Breloer, B.: Alexanders Kampf gegen Poros. Ein Beitrag zur indischen Geschichte, in: Bonner orientalistische Studien, 1933, 3

Digby, S.: War-horse and Elephant in the Delhi Sultanate. A Study of Military Supplies, Oxford 1971

Gaidoz, H.: Les éléphants à la Guerre, in: Revue des deux Mondes, 1874, pp. 481–513

Krebs, W.: Elefanten in den Heeren der Antike, in: Wissenschaftliche Zeitschrift der Universität Rostock, (ges. sprachwiss. Reihe 2/3), 13, 1964, pp. 205–220

Pilkington, C.: Elephant over the Alps, London, New York 1961

Scullard, H. H.: The Elephant in the Greek and Roman World, Cambridge 1974

**Zoo**

Althaus, T.: Knie Zoo, Rapperswil 1991

Dittrich, L.: Beitrag zur Fortpflanzung und Jugendentwicklung des Indischen Elefanten, Elephas maximus, in Gefangenschaft mit einer Übersicht über die Elefantengeburten in europäischen Zoos und Zirkussen, in: Zoologischer Garten (NF) 34, 1967, No. 1–3, pp. 56–93

Dittrich, L.: Säugetiere im Zoo, in: Grzimeks Enzyklopädie – Säugetiere, Ed. Grzimek, B., Vol. 5, Munich, 1988, pp. 602–639

Dittrich L.: Über die Nachzucht des Asiatischen Elefanten (Elephas maximus) in europäischen Tiergärten, in: Zoologischer Garten (NF), 47, 1977, No. 3–4, pp. 296–302

Dittrich, L.: Lebensraum Zoo, Freiburg 1977

Edwards, J.: London Zoo from Old Photographs 1852–1914, London 1996

Frädrich, H. and Klös, H.: Bongo, in: Sitzungsberichte der Tagung über Elefanten in Zoo und Zirkus im Institut für Zoo- und Wildtier-forschung (Sonderband), Berlin, 2.–4. Juli 1993

Hagenbeck, C.: Von Tieren und Menschen, Leipzig 1928

Haufellner, A.: Notizen zu der gefährlichen Elefantenbullenhaltung in Zoo und Zirkus und die Geschichte von 'Shenka,' dem friedlichen Riesen im Circus Alberti, Baldham 1990

Haufellner, A.: European Elephant Group, Elefanten in Zoo und Zirkus, Dokumentation Part I, undated.

Heoliger, H.: Skizzen zu einer Tierpsychologie in Zoo und Zirkus, Zurich 1954

Heoliger, H.: Gefährliche Väter. Elefantenbullen verursachen in Europa fast regelmäßig tödliche Unfälle, in: Das Tier, 3, 1963, No. 8, pp. 32–34

Howard, A. L.: 'Motty' – Birth of an African/Asian Elephant at Chester Zoo, in: Elephant, 1, 1979, No.3, pp. 36–41

Keller, R. und Schmidt, C. R. (Ed.): Das Buch vom Zoo, Luzern, Frankfurt a. M. 1978

Klös, H.-G.: Die Arche Noah an der Spree, Berlin 1994

Kock, K.: Elefanten – Mein Leben, Hamburg 1994

Niemeyer, G. H.: Hagenbeck, Hamburg 1972

Poley, D. (Ed.): 'Berichte aus der Arche.' Natur und Artenschutz im Zoo, Stuttgart 1993

Schlawe, L.: Die für die Zeit vom 1. August 1844 bis 31. Mai 1968 nachweisbaren Tiere im zoologischen Garten zu Berlin, Berlin 1969

Schlawe, L.: Zur Geschichte der Zoologischen Gärten, in: Das Buch vom Zoo, Ed. Keller R. und Schmidt C. R., Luzern, Frankfurt a. M. 1978, pp. 17–33

Shoshani, S. L., Shoshani, J. and Dalinger, F., Jr.: Jumbo. Origin of the World and History of the Elephant, in: Elephant, 2, 1986, No. 2, pp. 86–122

# Picture credits

Author and publisher both made intensive efforts, right up until going to press, to locate all owners of rights to illustrations and text. Any persons and institutions who may not have been reached and who assert rights to illustrations or text used in this publication are asked to contact the publisher immediately.
(a = above, t = top, b = bottom, r = right, l = left, c = center)

A.B.P.L., Sandton (Republic of South Africa), 68, b, © Beverly Joubert, 92, t, photo: Tim Liverbedge, 92, b, photo: Peter Chadwick, 95, photo: Daryl Balfour, 339, photo: Gavin Thompson, 2/3, © Peter Lille, 10, © Lorna Stanton
Agence Rapho, Paris, 365, ©Lennart Nilsson
Agentur Anne Hamann, Munich, 395, r, b, r, t, photo: Thomas Höpker
Alain Anthony, 375, t
©Archaeological Receipts Fund, Athens, 376, b
Archiv Carl Hagenbeck, Hamburg, 234, t, 270, b, 270, r, t, 270, l, t, 271, t, 271, r, b, 271, l, b, 271, c, b, 279, r, b, 281, t, 292, r, b
Archiv European Elephant Group, 262, l, t, 275, r, 275, l, 426, t, c, b, from: 'Das Tier und wir,' 1940, Tierpark Hellabrunn AG, Munich, 433, b
Archiv für Kunst und Geschichte, Berlin, 26, 33, 37, t, 38, r, t, 39, l, b, 115, t, 119, l, 178, b, 203, 217, 218, l, photo: Erich Lessing, 219, 222, 223, 224, b, 237, 239, b, 243, b, photo: Erich Lessing, 254/255, 257, r, t, 269, b, 269, t, 332, b, 349, t, 400, r, t, 404, l, b
Archiv John Edwards, 263, European Elephant Group
Archiv Karl Gröning, Hamburg, 6 (Inhalt), 9 (Inhalt), from: Peter Garlake 'The Hunters Vision. The Prehistoric Art of Zimbabwe,' Zimbabwe, undated, 18, b, 21, l, 23, t, from: Richard Carrington 'Elefanten,' Diana Verlag Zurich, 1962, 28, l, photo: Michael A. Vaccard, 29, r, b, 30, photo: Michael A. Vaccard, 32, 35, b, from: Andrew Leith Adams 'Notes of a Naturalist in the Nile Valley and Malta,' 1870, 38, l, b, Illustration after: Klippstein and Kaup 1836, 39, r, t, 43, l, b, 44, r, 54, l, b, 54, l, t, after einem photo von J. Vertut, 60/61, 66/67, 69, r, b, 77, l, b, 110, r, t, photo: Gisela Floto, 116, t, 116, l, b, 116, r, b, after a photo by Werner Forman, 117, b, from: 'Schatzkammern and Herrscherhäuser der Welt. Die Kaiser von China.' Verlag Manfred Pawlack, Herrsching, undated, 118, 125, b (and back of jacket, 2nd from l), 128, r, photo: François Bertin Grandvaux, 128, l, b, from: Kuypert 'De elephantis in nummis obviis' Hagae Comitum, 1719, 130, photo: Department of Archeology, Hyderabad, 132, t, 137, r, 137, l, t, from: Ghulam Yazdani 'Ajanta,' Oxford University, London, undated, 137, l, b, 138, r, t, 138, l, t, 148, l, b, photo: Federico Patellani, 158, r, 158, l, after: 'Himalayische Kunst,' UNESCO 1968, 159, l, after: Heinz Mode 'Fabeltiere and Dämonen,' Edition Leipzig, 1973, 166, b, 177, t, photo: Dirk Bakker, 180/181, (and back of jacket, far r) © Nihonhoso Shuppank Yokai Tokyo-to, Tokyo, 184, b, photo: Gisela Köstler, 185, t, 186, 188, l, b, ©The Chinese University of Hong Kong/Simon Kwan Collection, 190, t, 191, l, 193, l, after: John Ranking 1826, 198, r, t, 199, r, 205, 211, r, t, photo: Henry B. Beville, Washington, 230, r, 231, r, b, 238, t, 240, l, t, 240, r, t, 256, l, 257, l, t, 258, l, b, 258, r, b, 258, t, 259, b, 260, 261, b, 262, r, t, 265, 266, r, t, from: Charles Philip Fox/Tom Parkinson, 'The Circus in America,' Wisconsin, undated, 266, l, t, from: Charles Philip Fox/Tom Parkinson, 'The Circus in America,' Wisconsin, undated, 266, b, from: Charles Philip Fox/Tom Parkinson, 'The Circus in America,' Wisconsin, undated, 267, t, from: Charles Philip Fox/Tom Parkinson, 'The Circus in America,' Wisconsin, undated, 267, b, from: Charles Philip Fox/Tom Parkinson, 'The Circus in America,' Wisconsin, undated, 276, r, b, 276, l, t, 278, r, Archiv Zirkus Knie, Rapperswill, 279, l, photo: Anthony Barboza, 279, r, t, photo: Anthony Barboza, 280, 282, l, t, photo: Fred Lindinger, 284, t, from: Charles Philip Fox/Tom Parkinson, 'The Circus in America,' Wisconsin, undated, 285, b, from: Charles Philip Fox/Tom Parkinson, 'The Circus in America,' Wisconsin, undated, 286, b, 288, r, b, 288, l, b, 289, b, 293, r, b, 293, l, b, 294, l, b, 294/295, 298, r, t, 308, r, from: Hugo Adolf Bernatzik 'Der dunkle Erdteil Afrika,' 1930, 316, 318, 325, b, 327, 330/331, 331, t, from: Peter Garlake 'The Hunter's Vision. The Prehistoric Art of Zimbabwe,' Zimbabwe, undated, 333, b, 334, t, 350, r, from: Peter Garlake 'The Hunter's Vision. The Prehistoric Art of Zimbabwe,' Zimbabwe, undated, 350, l, b, from: Peter Garlake 'The Hunter's Vision. The Prehistoric Art of Zimbabwe,' Zimbabwe, undated, 351, t, from: Peter Garlake 'The Hunter's Vision. The Prehistoric Art of Zimbabwe,' Zimbabwe, undated, 351, r, b, from: Peter Garlake 'The Hunter's Vision. The Prehistoric Art of Zimbabwe,' Zimbabwe, undated, 351, r, c, from: Peter Garlake 'The Hunter's Vision. The Prehistoric Art of Zimbabwe,' Zimbabwe, undated, 352, r, t, photo: Dirk Bakker, 366/367, 371, r, 376, t, 376, r, c, 377, c, © Sacro Convento Di San Francesco, Assisi, photo: Gerhard Ruf, 377, l, © Victoria & Albert Museum, London, 380, l, b, 385, r, t, 395, l, b, 395, l, t, 400, l, t, 403, r, b, photo: Ernst Gasser, 403, l, t, 404, c, b, 404, c, 404, r, t, 404, r, b, 408, t, 408, b, 409, t, 409, b, 412, t, 412, b, 413, r, 414, r, c, from: Fritz Rumpf/Oswald A. Erick 'Spielzeug der Völker,' Berlin 1922, 414, r, b, 414, r, t, 417, c, 418, l, b, from: 'Punch,' 418, r, b, 418, r, t, from: 'Punch,' 420/421, from: 'Heinrich Kley,' Verlag Albert Langen, Munich 1925, 438, l, b, from: 'De Telegraaf' 18.12.1929, 447, t, all following © The Illustrated London News Picture Library, 139, b, 167, b, 232, r, b, 232, l, b, 232, r, t, 233, b, 234, b, 262, b, 296, t, 296, b, 296/297, 297, t, 299, r, b, 299, l, b, 314, 320/321, 321, r, t, 368, l, b, 438, l, t
Ardea London Ltd., 49, r, photo: P. Morris
Astrid Fischer-Leitl, Munich, 17, r, 21, r, 51, b, 53, b, after: DER SPIEGEL 5/1979, 54, r, 110, r, b, 192, b, 198, b, 201, 208, 218, r, 220, r, t, 429, l; and maps and tables in Appendix
from: 'Tiere der Welt. Enzyklopädie in Farbe.' Gondrom Verlag, Bayreuth 1977, 466, t, Drawings: Andrzej Bielich
from: Peter Lasko: 'Ivory. A History and Collector's Guide' , Words & Vision Ltd./Phoebe Philips Editions, London 1987, 378/379, t, 193, r, 195, r, t
from: 'Die Tiere der Welt.' Mosaik-Verlag, Gütersloh 1987, 466, b, Drawings: ©Priscilla Barrett 1986
AV- Bilderbank, Munich, photo: Lothar Schiffler, 374, t, 374, c, 374, b, 393, l, t, 393, l, b, 404, l, b, 414, l, t
Wilfried Bauer, Hamburg, 396, t and b, 425, 427, 434/435
Bayrisches Nationalmuseum, Munich, 410, t, 410/411, b
Peter Hill Beard, 332, l, t
Raffaello Bencini, Florenz, 390, l
Bildarchiv photo-Marburg, Marburg, 242, t,
Bildarchiv Preußischer Kulturbesitz, Berlin, 159, r, 233, t, 249, photo: Jörg P. Anders, 379, c, photo: Bartsch, 401, photo: Bartsch
Bilderberg, Hamburg, 136, r, photo: Klaus D. Francke
Bodleian Library, Oxford, 210, t
Daniel Boschung, Zurich, 422
©Brinkhoff/Mögenburg, Phantom der Oper, Hamburg 416, b
Bulloz, Paris, 242, l
Wilhelm M. Busch-Archiv e.V., Hamburg, 276, l, b, 282, r, t,
Camera Press/Picture Press Life, Hamburg, 235, photo: François Chalais
Christie's Images, London, 399, r, b, 399, r, t, 399, l, t
Cinetext, Frankfurt, 28/29, t, 417, b
Cinetext, Frankfurt © The Walt Disney Company, 417, l, t, 417, r, t,
Cliché Bibliothèque Nationale de France, Paris, 166, r, t, 192, t, 196, 202, b, 206, l, 207
Collection Maurice Bonnefoy, 355, l, b, photo: John Meek, 355, r, b, photo: John Meek
Collection of Ernst Winizki, 356, l, t,
Collection of Howard Hodgkin, London, 134, 135, 144, 152, b, 314/315, 319, t
County Museum of Art, Los Angeles,124, 152, l, c, 169, r, t, 1997 Museum Associates
Courtesy of the Dipartimento di Scienze Antropologiche, Archeologiche e Storico-territoriali of the University of Turin, 367, r, t, photo: Riccardo Gonella
Courtesy Ronald Feldman Fine Arts, New York, © The Andy Warhol Foundation for the Visual Arts/VG Bild-Kunst, Bonn 1998, 386, photo: D. James Dee
©G. Dagli Orti, Paris, 37, b, 255, t
Glyn Daniel, Cambridge, 213, b
Dembinski Photo Associates, 60, photo: Stan Osolinski
Deutsches Elfenbeinmuseum, Erbach, 364,
Deutsches Textilmuseum, Krefeld, 226, b, Katholische Pfarrgemeinde St. Servatius, Siegburg
Ulrich Döring, Tansania, 61, front cover
Domkapitel, Aachen, 246, r, t, photo: Jeitner
Doris Wiener Gallery, New York, 176, r, t
Field Museum of Natural History, Chicago, 360, l, b
Eberhard Fischer, Zurich, 325, t
©Paul Flora, Innsbruck, 250, l
FOCUS, Hamburg, 344/345, photo: Michael Nichols, 53, t, photo: Peter Menzel
Fratelli Alinari, Florenz, 257, l, b
Mitchell Funk, New York, 64
Gamma, Paris, 182, photo: Olivier Blaise, 183, b, photo: Olivier Blaise, 334, b, photo: Louise Gubb, 336/337, photo: Mae Cam
Georg Gerster, Zurich, 177, l, b, 191, r, 212, b
Giraudon, Paris, 220, l, t
Graphische Sammlung der Eidgenössischen Technischen Hochschule, Zurich, 385, b
Graphische Sammlung der Staatsgalerie Stuttgart, 385, l, t
Dörte Gröning, Munich, 78, 79, back cover, 173, t, 226, t, 368, t, 415, b, 436, t, 436, b, 437, 448
©Hachette, Paris, 415, r, t, 415, l, t, from: Jean de Brunhoff 'Histoire de Babar,' Paris, 1939
Halliday Photographs, Sonia Primrose, Weston Turville, 230, l
Claus Hansmann, Munich, 108, 109, 113, 126, 127, t, 127, b, 131, 140, 149, 151, 153, b, 162, (and front of jacket far r), 178, t, 179, b, 215, 236, 238, b, 251, 253, 256, r, 259, t, 264, 31 9, b, 383, 397, 398, 399, l, b, 402, 404, l, t, 413, l, 442, 384, b, Liselotte Hansmann
Franz Hartmann, 105, b
Georg Helmes, Aachen, 110, l, t
Kurt Henseler, Tübingen-Bühl, 375, b
Herbert M. Cole, Santa Barbara, 354,b
Herzog- Anton-Ulrich-Museum, Braunschweig, 378, r, b, Museumphoto: B.P.Keiser
Karin Heßmann photo-Design, Dortmund, 394
Hoa Qui/Bildagentur Schuster, Oberursel, 358, l, t, photo: C. Pavard, 358, l, b, photo: C. Pavard
©Jiri Hochman and Martin Hochmann, 16, 17, l, photo: Moravské Zemské Muzeum, Brno, 22, l, 22, r, photo: Moravské Zemské Muzeum, Brno, 24, photo: Moravské Zemské Muzeum, Brno, 25, 34, 40, photo: Moravské Zemské Muzeum, Brno, 44, photo: Moravské Zemské Muzeum, Brno, 49, l, 48, 50, t
Illinois State Museum, Springfield, 23, b, Illustration and photo: Robert Larson
Institut für Zoo- und Wildtierforschung, Berlin, 62, t, photo: IZW/Göritz, 468, t and c, photo: Hildebrandt/Göritz
James A. Mounger Collection, New Orleans, 353, r, t
Keystone Pressedienst, Hamburg, 225, b, 70, l, b, 285, t, 284, b, 287, b, 432, t
Hans-Günther Kiesel, Norderstedt, 433, t, 438, r, b, 438, r, c, 439, t, 439, b
©Kiscadale Publications,174/175, from: Paul Strachan 'The thirty-seven Nats.' A Phase of Spirit Worship Prevailing in Burma, (facsimile) London, 1991
©Könemann Verlagsgesellschaft mbH, Cologne, 115, b, photo: Andrea Jemolo, 391, photo: Achim Bednorz, 288, t, photo: Robert Polidori, 289, t, photo: Robert Polidori, 376, l, c, photo: Andrea Jemolo
König Postkarten Verlag, Cologne, 389, b, © Boyd Webb
Hansjörg Künzi, Neuhausen, 132, b
Fred Kurt, Aichach, 298, l
Kunsthalle der Hypo-Kulturstiftung, Munich, 212, r, t, photo: Jürgen Liepe
Kunstverlag Hofstetter, Ried , 250/251
Lane Picture Agency Frank, Stowmarket (Suffolk), 308, l, photo: Frank Lane, 309, t, photo: Frank Lane
Lincoln State Museum, 51,t, photo: Peter Menzel, 1992
Linden Museum, Stuttgart, 360, r, b
Magnum, London, 119, r, photo: Brian Brake
Mary Evans Picture Library, London, 46/47
MhB Menschen helfen Behinderten e.V., Tübingen, 387, c, photo: Hermann Schwartz
Wolfgang Müller, Oberried, 146, r, t, 160, 161, 163, 170, t, 170, 171, t, 172, 173, l, b, 173, r, c, 173, r, b, 189, r, t, 190, r, b, 228, 229
Horst Munzig, Mindelheim, 449, t, 450, 106, 107
Musée de l´horlogerie, Geneva, 403, r, t, photo: Yves Siza
©Musée Nationale d´Histoire Naturelle, 36, photo: D. Serrette
Musées Royaux des Beaux-Arts de Belgique, Brussels © Salvador Dalí, Fundación Gala Salvador Dalí/ VG Bild-Kunst, Bonn 1998, 389, t
Museum für Kunst und Gewerbe, Hamburg, 188, t, Sammlung Reemtsma, 268, 278, l
Museum für Kunsthandwerk, Frankfurt a.M., 400, l, b
Museum Rietberg , Zurich, 152/153, 133, b, 145, 189, b, 357, t
National Geographic Image Collection, Washington, 20, Karel Havlicek, National Geographic Society, Washington, 41, photo: Jonathan Blair, 50, b, photo: Dave Arnold, 199, l, Tom Lovell, 247, André Durenceau, 300, photo: James P. Blair, National Geographic Society Image Collection, Washington, 346/347, photo: Des & Jen Bartlett, 449, b, photo: Maria Stenzel
Nationalmuseum, Copenhagen, 240, b
Natural Science Photos, Watford, 458/459, photo: R. Kemp
Natur-Museum Senckenberg, Frankfurt a. M., 35, t
©Newton, Tokyo, 44/45 (and front of jacket, far l,) photo: Takumi Yamamoto
Okapia, Frankfurt a. M., 29, l, b, photo: F. Pölking, 68, t, photo: OSF/Martyn Colbeck, 76, photo: OSF/Steve Turner, 77, t, photo: OSF/Martyn Colbeck, 80, t, photo: OSF/Martyn Colbeck, 82/83, photo: Martyn Colbeck, 89, b (and back of jacket, far l,) photo: Berndt Fischer, 90, t, photo: OSF/Martyn Colbeck, 93 (and front of jacket, 2nd from r,) photo: OSF/Martyn Colbeck, 96, photo: OSF/Martyn Colbeck, 96–97, photo: OSF/Martyn Colbeck, 97, photo: OSF/Martyn Colbeck, 98, photo: OSF/Martyn Colbeck, 99, t, b, photo: OSF/Martyn Colbeck, 102–103 (and back of jacket 2nd from r,) photo: OSF/Martyn Colbeck, 104, t, photo: OSF/Martyn Colbeck, 105, t, photo: Joan Root, 299, t, photo: OSF/Dieter and Mary Plage, 301, photo: OSF/Dieter and Mary Plage, 302–303, l, r, photo: OSF/Dieter and Mary Plage, 309, b, © Prof.B.Grzimek, 337, r, photo: OSF/ Safari, 446, photo: OSF/Steve Turner, 447, b, © NAS/S.O. Lindblad, 455, photo: OSF/Martyn Colbeck
Jim Olive, Houston, 43, l, t
Luciano Pedicini/Archivio dell' Arte, Naples, 242, r, b

©Ann & Bury Peerless Picture Library, Birchington-on Sea, 184, t
Gisela Pferdmenges, Hamburg, 54, r, b, 179, t, 405, l, t, 405, r, b, 405, l, b
Photoarchiv Emil Schultheß Erben, Zurich, 148, r, b, 348, r, 362–363
R.E.A. e.V./Barbara Voigt, Hamburg, 56, 88, r, b, 101, l, b
Rapho/FOCUS, Hamburg, 129, photo: Emile Luider
Dirk Reinartz, Buxtehude, 273, 74, t
Rex Features Ltd., London, 328/329
Yves Rivière, Paris, 387, t
©RMN, Paris,15, b, photo: Gérard Blot, 197, photo: R.G. Ojeda, 200/201, photo: R.G. Ojeda, 227, photo: Hervé Lewandowski, 312
Robert Estall Photo Library, Boxford Sudbury, 359, photo: Angela Fisher, 358, r, b, photo: Angela Fisher
Roger Viollet, Paris, 168, t, 168, b, 169, l, t, 169, b, 176, l, b, 177, r, b, 190, l, b, 245, 244, 246, l, b, 248, t, 255, r, b, 276, r, t, 277, b, 287, c, 292, l, 323, b, 326, 356, l, b, 390, r, 424, t, 424, 432, b
Rosenwald Collection, © 1998, Board of Trustees, National Gallery of Art, Washington, 198, l, t
Doran H. Ross, Los Angeles, 355, t
Royal Geographical Society, London, 373, t
Jens Rüchel, Hamburg, 58, t, 209, 286, t, 424, b, 429, r, t, 430/431, l, r, 438, r, t, 440, r, l, 441
Barbara Saller, Hamburg, 66, l, b, 69, l, b, 70, l, t, 70, r, b, 77, r, b, 194, b, c, 194, r, b, 211, b, 377, r, 381, r, t, 381, l, t, 381, b, 381, r, c, 380, l, t, 414, l, b, 423, 428, t, 429, r, b, 428, b
Save Bild /Auscape, Augsburg, 13, photo: Frans Lanting, 18, t, photo: Ferrero/Labat, 19, t, photo: D.Parer & E.Parer, 19, b, photo: Maywald, 30–31, photo: Frans Lanting, 57, photo: Frans Lanting, 58, b, photo: C. Frederiksson, 59, photo: Frans Lanting, 63, photo: P.Arnold, © Nicole Duplaix, 66, t, photo: J.S. Flannery, Save Bild /Minden Pictures, Augsburg, 67, photo: Ferrero-Labat, Save Bild /Minden Pictures, Augsburg, 69, t, photo: Frans Lanting, 71, photo: F. Krahmer, 72–73, photo: Frans Lanting, 74, photo: Frans Lanting, 75, photo: Frans Lanting, 81, photo: J.P.Ferrero, 84–85, photo: Dianne Blell, 86–87, photo: Frans Lanting, 88, l, t, photo: F. Krahmer, 89, t, photo: Gavriel Jecan, 90, b, photo: Frans Lanting, 91, t, photo: J.P.Ferrero, 91, b, photo: Jim Brandenburg, Save Bild, Augsburg, 94–95, photo: Frans Lanting, 100, photo: Ferrero-Labat, 101, t, photo: Frans Lanting, 101, r, b, photo: Ferrero-Labat, Save Bild/Coleman Inc., Augsburg, 104, b, photo: A. Sycholt, 183, t, photo: Frans Lanting, 311, photo: Frans Lanting, 335, photo: Jim Brandenburg, 340/341, photo: P. Weimann, 342/343, photo: P. Weimann, 343, t, photo: C.Kaiser, 443, photo: Frans Lanting, 444/445, photo: Frans Lanting, 451, t, photo: A. Sycholt, 452, photo: Frans Lanting, 454, photo: Frans Lanting, 456/457, photo: Ferrero/Labat, Save Bild/Auscape, Augsburg, 460, photo: Frans Lanting, Save Bild/P.Arnold, Augsburg
Scala S.p.A., Antella (Florence), 14, 15, t, 111, 210, l, b, 211, l, t, 210, r, b, 220, r, b, 221, 224/225, 231, l, t, 294/295
Walter Schollmayer, Hamburg, 128, t (and front of jacket 2nd from l) 146, l, t, 146, b, 147, 148, t, 150, 156, l, t, 157
Balthasar Schrott, Bressanone, 214
P.L. Shinnie, Calgary, 213, l, c, from: 'Meroe,' 1967, fig. 27
Sipa Press, Paris, 419, r, b, photo: Sobol, 419, l, b, photo: Sams, 419, t, photo: Sobol
Sotheby´s London, 381, l, c, 195, l, 387, b
Staatliche Antikensammlung, Munich, 204, t
Staatliche Porzellanmanufaktur, Meissen, 400, r, b, 382, photo: J.Kaendler and P. Reinicke
Staatliche Schlösser und Gärten Baden-Württemberg /Staatliches Vermögens- und Hochbauamt Heilbronn, 396, t
Staatliches Museum für Völkerkunde, Munich,121, photo: p. Autrum-Mulzer, 138,

b, 139, t, 164, Archiv, 188, r, b, photo: S. Autrum-Mulzer, 189, l, t, photo: p. Autrum-Mulzer, 194, l, b, photo: p. Autrum-Mulzer, 338, 406, r, b, photo: p. Autrum-Mulzer, 407, l, t, photo: p. Autrum-Mulzer
Stadtmuseum, Berlin, 416, r, t, photo: Ludwig Binder
Stephen P. Huyler, Camden, 156, r, 156, b
Stonehenge Press Inc., London, 128, l, c, photo: Seth Joel, 378, l, b, photo: Seth Joel, 380, r, b, photo: Seth Joel, 380, r, t, photo: Seth Joel
St. Petersburg Zoological Museum, 43, l, r, t, ©Nikolai Ignatiev/Network 'Mammoths'
Karl-Heinz Striedter, Frankfurt a.M., 348, l, Drawing: Gisela Wittner, 349, l, b, Drawing: Gisela Wittner
S.S. Sukhy, Nairobi, Kenia, 451, b
SWT Bild/Das Fotoarchiv, Essen, 252, 185, b, 283, t, 323, t, 414, l, c, 436, c
SYGMA/Pandis Media, Munich, 55, © Jean Clottes/Ministère de la Culture, 416, l, t, photo: G.Abegg
Tambaran Gallery, New York, 361, l, t, photo: M.Zarember
Tate Gallery Publications, London © VG Bild-Kunst, Bonn 1998, 388, photo: John Webb
©1998, The Art Institute of Chicago, 4 (Frontispiece)
The British Library, London,166, l, t, 216, 241, t
The British Museum, London,112, 371, l, 133, l, 202, t, 352, l, b, 354, t, 384, t
The Faletti Family Collection, Phoenix, 361, r, photo: Denis J. Nervig
The Field Museum of Natural History, Chicago, 361, l, b, photo: Denis J. Nervig
The Fowler Museum of Cultural History, Los Angeles, 62, b, Drawing: Jill Ball, 114, r, b, Drawing: Sylvia Kennedy, after Sillar and Meylar (1968), 70, r, t, photo: Denis J. Nervig, 353, b, photo: Denis J. Nervig, 353, l, t, photo: Denis J. Nervig, 356, r, b, photo: Denis J. Nervig, 357, b, photo: Denis J. Nervig, 356, r, t, photo: Denis J. Nervig, 360, l, t, photo: Denis J. Nervig
The Israel Museum, Jerusalem, 366, b, Collection of Israel Antiquities Authority
The Master And Fellows Of Corpus Christi College, Cambridge, 248, b
© The Metropolitan Museum of Art, New York, 117, t, 154
The Palace of Lost City, Sun City, South Africa, 453, t
The Pierport Morgan Library/Art Resource, New York, 241, b
The Royal Scottish Museum, Edinburgh, 379, b
The Walters Art Gallery, Baltimore, 257, r, b
Julian Thomann, Hamburg, 392, 393, r, b, 393, r, t
Thomas Stephan , Munderkingen, 52, t, © Eberhard-Karls-Universität Tübingen, Institut für Ur- and Frühgeschichte und Archäologie des Mittelalters, 165, 167, t, 187, l, b, 187, r, b, 282, b, 291, 304/305, 306, t, 307, r, t, 307, b, 453, b
Peter Thomann, Hamburg, 65, Fotografische Sammlung Peter Thomann, 187, t, 405, r, t, 407, b, ©Lothar Schmid, 407, c, ©Sammlung Dr. Jaeger, Neu-Ulm
Time-Life, Washington, 12, 322, t, 322, b
Tom Stack & Associates, Key Largo, 27
Tony Stone Images, Munich/Hulton Getty, 317, t, 317, b, 332, r, t
Topkapi Museum, Istanbul, 231, r, c, 231, r, t
Trustees of the Chester Beatty Library, Dublin, 140, reproduced by kind permission
Wilhelm Turda, Bad Schönborn, 406, l, 406, r, t
Ullstein Bilderdienst, Berlin, 274, r, b, 274, c, 277, t, 283, b, 287,t
Uni-Dia, Großhesselohe, 114, l
Victoria & Albert Museum, London, 120, 125, r, t, 125, l, b, 139, c, 143, 155, 206, r, 239, t, 293, t, 313, 324
Visum, Hamburg, 290, photo: Jörg Modrow, 306, b, photo: Jörg Modrow, 307, l, t, photo: Jörg Modrow, 336, l, b, photo: Georg Fischer
C.H.Walker, Bedfordview (Republic of South Africa), 310
Warshaw Collection of Business Americana,

Archives Center, NMAH, Smithsonian Institution, Washington, 369
©Ernst Wasmuth Verlag GmbH & Co., Tübingen, 194, t
Henning Wiesner, Munich, 469, t and b
Yalla, Paris, 272
Ylla/Rapho, Paris, 136, l
Xavier Zimbardo, Gonesse, 122/123
Zodiaque, St.Leger-Vauban, 243, t
Zoological Society of London, London, 261, t
Zoological Institute/Academy of Science, St. Petersburg, 42, t, b

## Text credits

p. 14: Die Bibel oder die ganze heilige Schrift des Alten und des Neuen Testaments nach der deutschen Übersetzung d. Martin Luther. Privileg. Württ. Bibelanstalt, Stuttgart 1947.

p. 30: Das Gilgamesch-Epos, Reclam Verlag, Stuttgart 1958, lines 36, 83, 85, 160

p. 36: Wendt, H.: Im Tiefkühlschrank der Natur, in: Grzimeks Tierleben. Entwicklungsgeschichte der Lebewesen (Ergänzungsband), ed. von Herberer, G. and Wendt, H., Kindler Verlag, Zurich 1972, p. 486f.

p. 96: Moss, C. and Colbeck, M.: Das Jahr der Elefanten. Frederking & Thaler, Munich 1997, p. 180

p. 112: Schmöckel, H.: Ur, Assur und Babylon, Gustav Kilpper Verlag, Stuttgart 1955, p. 117

p. 118: Zimmer, H.: Spiel um den Elefanten. Eugen Diederichs Verlag, Cologne, Düsseldorf, Munich 1976, p. 44–48, 87, 23

p. 122: Die Bibel nach der Übersetzung Martin Luthers. Deutsche Bibelgesellschaft, Stuttgart 1985

p. 142–144: Blochmann, H.: The Ain I Akibari by Abul Fazl ´Allami, Kalkutta 1873, p. 117, 131.

p. 166: Leonowens, A. H.: The English Governess at the Siamese Court. Being Recollections of six years in the Royal Palace at Bangkok, Boston 1873, p.116–120.

p. 188; p 192–193: Marco Polo: Von Venedig nach China. Die größte Reise des 13. Jahrhunderts, ed. von Kunst, Th. A. Edition Erdmann im K., Thienemanns Verlag, Stuttgart, Vienna, Bern 1984, p. 156, 202–205, 132

p. 201: Quintus Curtius Rufus: Geschichte Alexanders des Großen, Verlag Heimeran, Munich 1954, p. 581f.

p. 209: Fischer, R.: Die schwarzen Pharaonen. Tausend Jahre Geschichte und Kunst der ersten innerafrikanischen Hochkultur, Gustav Lübbe Verlag, Bergisch Gladbach 1980, p. 130

p. 210: Polybios: Geschichte. Gesamtausgabe in zwei Bänden. Bibliothek der Alten Welt, Artemis & Winkler Verlag, Düsseldorf, Zurich 1961, Vol. 1, p. 497f.

p. 214: Makkabäer 6, lines 28–40, 42–48, in: Die Apokryphen, nach der deutschen Übersetzung Martin Luthers, Cansteinsche Bibelanstalt, Württembergische Bibelanstalt, Stuttgart 1971, p. 251f.

p. 226: Ammianus Marcellinus: Res gestae, Rolfe, J. C., Heinemann, London 1963, Vol. 1 (Books XIV – XIX), Buch XIX, ch. 1, p. 471, lines 2, 3a; Vol. 2 (Books XX – XXVI), Buch XXIV, ch. 6, p. 461, line 8. p. 230: Koran, 105. Sure, Übertragen von Max Henning, Reclam Verlag, Stuttgart 1991

p. 240: Physiologus. Frühchristliche Tiersymbolik, ed. Treu, U., Verlag Werner Dausien, Hanau 1981, pp. 80–84

p. 248: Matthaeus Parisiensis: Chronica Majora, ed. von Luard, H. R., London 1880, Vol. 5, p. 489

p. 250: König Johann III: Brief zu dem Geschenk an Maximilian (III) (Mitte 16. Jhd.), in: Damals, 1996, No. 12

p. 288: Rilke, R. M.: Die Gedichte, Insel Verlag, Frankfurt a. M. 1992, p. 476

p. 300–301: Kurt, F.: Das Elefantenbuch, Rasch

und Röhring Verlag, Hamburg 1992, p. 59, 60, 62, 63, 65

p. 316: LIFE Magazine, 1967, 62, 18.

p. 326: Zur Erinnerung an die Reise des Prinzen Waldemar von Preussen nach Indien 1844–1846, Berlin 1853, Vol. 1, p. 16

p. 327: Orwell, G.: Einen Elefanten erschießen, in: Im Innern des Wals. Erzählungen und Essays, übers. von Gasbarra, F., Copyright - 1975 by Diogenes Verlag AG, Zurich 1975

p. 426, 430, 435: Kock, K.: Elefanten – mein Leben, Rasch und Röhring Verlag, Hamburg 1994, p. 211, 157

p. 436: Das Hagenbeck-Buch, ed. von Mordiek, Weidlich, Wiese, Hamburg 1995, p.112

p. 435: Sanderson, I. T.: Dynastie der Abu, Verlag Hallweg, Bern, Stuttgart 1966, p. 195

p. 458: Schopenhauer, A.: Preisschrift über die Grundlage der Moral, ed. von Ebeling, H., Felix Meiner Verlag, Hamburg 1979, p. 136, 139

p. 458: Drewermann, E.: Denn es fühlt wie Du den Schmerz, in: Spiegel special 1, 1997, p. 122–124

Appendix:
Berichte aus der Arche. Nachzucht statt Wildfang. Natur- und Artenschutz im Zoo. Menschen und Tiere. Die Zukunft der Zoos, ed. Poley, D., Georg Thieme Verlag, Stuttgart 1993

Wiesner, H.: Zum Vorkommen des Arcus scleralis beim Elefanten, in: Der Zoologische Garten, Stuttgart 1992, pp. 287–293

Differences Between African and Asian Elephants, in: Elefanten. Enzyklopädie der Tierwelt, Jahr Verlag, Hamburg 1992, p. 39 (by kind permission of Weldon Owen Publishing Pty. Ltd., Sydney)

# Acknowledgements

The period between a book's conception and its eventual publication is a lengthy one and often merits a history of its own. In this case there were many people along the way who believed in the project. My thanks to Dr. Ruth Liepman of Zurich, J. Fischer of H. Roger-Viollet, Paris, and finally Dr. Andreas Pöllinger, Munich.

My friend Martin Saller worked with inexhaustible patience on the various versions of the text, because the glued-up maquette went through many changes on its long journey. Many thanks, therefore, to publisher Ludwig Könemann, who brought the odyssey to an end by including the book in his publishing program.

Many authors have tackled the subject of elephants over the last couple of centuries. I would particularly mention Briton Richard Carrington and American Ivan T. Sanderson.

Two animal keepers gave me enormous assistance: Robert Müller of Hellabrunn Zoo in Munich and Jens Rüchel of Hamburg's Hagenbeck Animal Park.

The managers of both institutions, Henning Wiesner of Hellabrunn and Dr. Claus of Hagenbeck, also helped frequently.

Alexander Haufellner of the European Elephant Group, with his records of zoo and circus elephants in Europe and North America offered much advice and made his documentation available.

And the following members of the staffs of museums and collections provided encouragement and support:

Dr. Ursula Göhlich of the Paläontologisches Museum, Munich;

Dr. Stefan Bursche of the Museum für Kunst und Gewerbe, Berlin;

Dr. Regina Hickmann and Dr. Lore Sander of the Museum für Indische Kunst, Berlin;

Dr. Dorothea Schäfer and Dr. Wolfgang Stein of the Museum für Völkerkunde, Munich;

Dr. Doran H. Ross of the H. Fowler Museum of Cultural History, University of California, Los Angeles.

By way of thanking all the many agencies and institutions that supplied photographs, may I express my particular gratitude to :

Heidrun Klein of Bildarchiv Preussischer Kulturbesitz, Berlin;

Silke Opitz of Bildarchiv Foto Marburg;

Dieter Weber of Save-Bildagentur, Augsburg.

Many thanks are also due to the photographers who supplied work for the book and particularly to those great animal photographers Martyn Colbeck and Frans Lanting. I am grateful to them all.

Claus Hansmann and Matthias Holzapfel helped enormously with images from the Kunstgeschichtliches Bildarchiv Claus Hansmann, Munich.

Karl Gröning

The Publishers wish to express their gratitude for tireless support in the extensive research required for this publication: to Dr. Heike Patzschke for translations from the Japanese; to Astrid Roth for tracking down source material; to Claudia Hammer for obtaining reproduction permissions; to Ms. Hahn of the Worldwide Fund for Nature, Frankfurt, for furnishing statistics; to Kirsten Skacel and Thomas Ristow for proof-reading; to Daniel Spanke M.A. for art-historical research; to Dr. Matthias Seidel of the Pelizaeus Museum, Hildesheim, for valuable information from the realm of Egyptology.

Copyright © 1998 Könemann Verlagsgesellschaft mbH,
Bonner Straße 126, D-50968 Cologne

Art Director and Design: Peter Feierabend
Project Coordinator: Kirsten E. Lehmann and Franziska Sörgel
Picture Research: Barbara Linz
Assistants: Fenja Wittneven and Barbara Köthe-Löhausen
Layout: Birgit Beyer
Cartography: Astrid Fischer-Leitl
Production Manager: Detlev Schaper
Production: Mark Voges
Reproduction: CDN Pressing Verona, Italy

Original title: Der Elefant in Natur- und Kulturgeschichte

Copyright © 1999 for the English edition
Translation: Patricia Cooke, Elaine Richards, Janet Richmond, and J. A. Underwood
in association with First Edition Translations Ltd., Cambridge
Realization of the English edition: First Edition Translations Ltd., Cambridge
Printing and binding: Mohn Media - Mohndruck GmbH, Gütersloh
Printed in Germany

ISBN 3-8290-1752-9
10 9 8 7 6 5 4 3 2

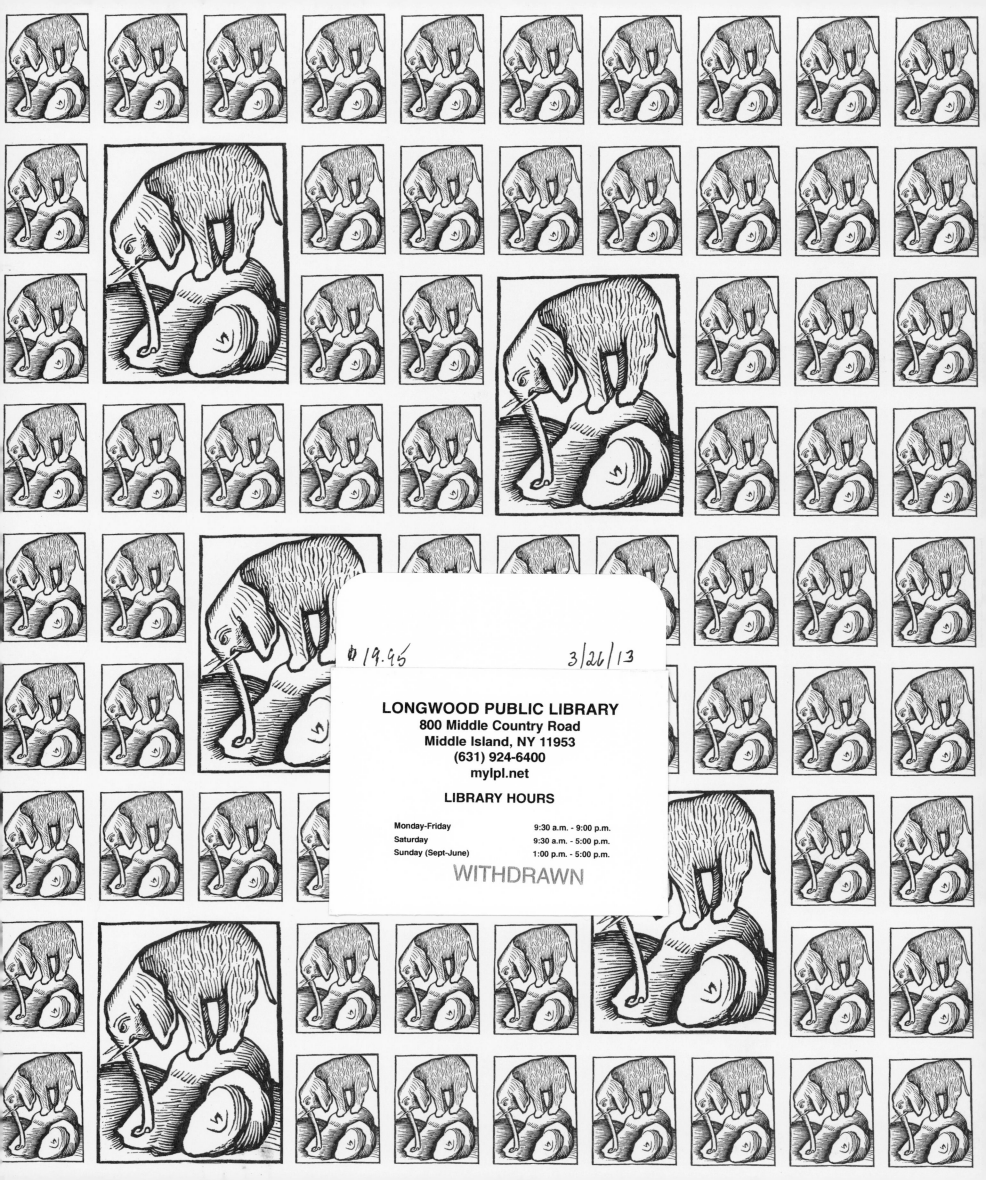